UP FROM EDEN

KEN WILBER

UP FROM EDEN

A TRANSPERSONAL VIEW
OF HUMAN EVOLUTION

SHAMBHALA
BOULDER 1983

SHAMBHALA PUBLICATIONS, INC.
1920 13th Street
Boulder, Colorado 80302

Grateful acknowledgment is made to the following for permission to use copyrighted material:

Houghton Mifflin Company and Dr. Julian Jaynes for excerpts from *The Origin of Consciousness in the Breakdown of the Bicameral Mind* by Julian Jaynes, copyright © 1976 by Julian Jaynes.

Macmillan Publishing Co., Inc. for excerpts from *Escape from Evil* by Ernest Becker, copyright © 1975 by Marie Becker.

Main Currents for excerpts from "Foundations of the Aperspective World" by Jean Gebser, first published in English in *Main Currents,* vol. 29, no. 2, 1972. Copyright © 1972 by *Main Currents.*

Mentor/New American Library for excerpts from *The Next Development in Man* by L. L. Whyte (New York: Mentor, 1950).

Princeton University Press for excerpts from *The Origins and History of Consciousness* by Erich Neumann, trans. R. F. C. Hull, Bollingen Series XLII. Copyright © 1954 by Princeton University Press.

Random House, Inc. for excerpts from *The Gnostic Gospels* by Elaine Pagels, copyright © 1979 by Elaine Pagels.

Viking Penguin Inc. for excerpts from *The Masks of God: Primitive Mythology* by Joseph Campbell, copyright © 1959, 1969 by Joseph Campbell; from *The Masks of God: Oriental Mythology* by Joseph Campbell, copyright © 1962 by Joseph Campbell; from *The Masks of God: Occidental Mythology* by Joseph Campbell, copyright © 1964 by Joseph Campbell. Reprinted by permission of Viking Penguin Inc.

Wesleyan University Press for excerpts from *Life Against Death* by Norman O. Brown, copyright © 1959 by Wesleyan University.

Library of Congress Cataloging in Publication Data
Wilber, Ken.
    Up from Eden.
    Reprint. Originally published: 1st : Garden City,
N.Y. : Anchor Press/Doubleday, 1981.
    Bibliography: p.
    Includes index.
    1. Human evolution—Miscellanea.   I. Title.
BF1999.W558   1983   128   82-42678
ISBN 0-87773-228-0 (pbk.)
ISBN 0-394-71424-5 (Random House)

For my mother, my father, and my wife, Amy

CONTENTS

PREFACE

"Mankind," said Plotinus, "is poised midway between the gods and the beasts," and the task of this volume is to trace the curve of history and prehistory that brought mankind to that delicate position. We will pick up the story, as it were, right about the point that man or manlike creatures appeared on the earth, several millions of years ago, during the times now fabled as dim Eden and prehistoric paradise. We will follow the story up and through our present era, and then, straining to see into tomorrow, continue with a picture of our possible future evolution. For if men and women have come up from the beasts, then they will likely end up with the gods. The distance between man and the gods is not all that much greater than the distance between beasts and man. We have already closed the latter gap, and there is no reason to suppose that we shall not eventually close the former. As Aurobindo and Teilhard de Chardin knew, the future of humankind is God-consciousness, and we will want to examine this future in the entire context of human history.

But if men and women are up from the beasts and on their way to the gods, they are in the meantime rather tragic figures. Poised between the two extremes, they are subjected to the most violent of conflicts. No longer beast, not yet god—or worse, half beast, half god: there is the soul of mankind. Put another way, humankind is an essentially tragic figure with a beautifully optimistic future—if they can survive the transition. I have, therefore, told the story of mankind's growth and evolution from a tragic angle—we tend anyway to be much too glib about our rise up from the apes, imagining each new evolutionary step as a wonderful leap forward that brought new potentials, new intelligence, and new abilities. That is in one sense quite true, but it is equally true that each new evolutionary step forward brought new responsibilities, new terrors, new anxieties, and new guilts. The beasts are mortal, but they do not know or fully understand that fact; the gods are immortal, and they know it—but poor man, up from beasts and not yet a god, was that unhappy mixture: he was mortal, and he knew it. And the more he evolved, the more conscious he became of himself and his world, the more he grew in awareness and intelligence—the more he became conscious of his fate, his mortal and death-stained fate.

In short, there is a price to be paid for every increase in consciousness, and only that perspective, I believe, can place mankind's evolutionary history in the proper context. Most of the accounts of man's evolution err to one side or the other of that equation. They either overemphasize the growth aspect, seeing man's evolution as nothing but a series of great advances and great leaps forward, thereby ignoring the fact that evolution is not a happy-go-lucky series of sweetness-and-light promotions, but a painful process of growth. Or they tend to the opposite direction and, seeing the agony and despair of mankind, look back nostalgically to that lost Eden of innocence, prior to self-consciousness, wherein man slumbered with the beasts in blissful ignorance. This view tends to see every evolutionary step out of Eden as being a crime. With very persuasive evidence, they show that war, hunger, exploitation, slavery, oppression, guilt, and poverty *all* came into existence with the rise of civilization and culture and man's increasing "evolution." Primal man, on the whole, suffered none of those problems—thus, if modern, civilized man is a product of evolution, then please give us less of it.

What I am saying is that, in the main, both views are correct. Each step in the evolutionary process *was* an advance, a growth experience, but it was bought at a high price—it demanded new responsibilities, and responsibilities that mankind did not always live up to, with such tragic results as we will chronicle in the following pages.

I have chosen to tell the story of mankind's "painful growth" in terms of several major "eras." I have done this mostly as a matter of convenience, and do not hold to the "rigid era" school of history (although I do hold to a structural/developmental view of individual consciousness, and thus the "eras" I will present are based on the average structure of consciousness dominant at each period). Further, to introduce a thread of continuity to what is, after all, a quite complex story, I have tried to hold the number of cited authorities to a minimum. In each major field (mythology, anthropology, psychology, etc.), I have selected one or two "guides," and have used their quotations to the exclusion of all others.

Thus, in mythology, I selected Joseph Campbell—when I came to a point in the narrative that demanded a supporting quote, I would try to find one from Campbell first, even though for "academic reasons" I could have given any of a dozen quotes from other authorities. In the same way, for existential anthropology, I selected Becker and Brown; for "eras," Jean Gebser; for biological evolution, L. L. Whyte; for psychological evolution, Erich Neumann. In restricting my quotations to a few authorities, I hope I have enabled the reader to find the following chapters to be four or five voices speaking to him in harmony, telling the story of mankind's growth, and not just a jumble of massive quotations from innumerable sources (most of the sources are simply listed in the Bibliography).

Obviously, then, this book is not presented as a definitive sociological thesis backed by precise and massive documentation. It is a deliberately simplified and generalized account. It is meant to serve both as a simple introduction to, and explanation of, the overall "big picture" of the historical development and evolution of consciousness, and as a prolegomenon to future studies of a more precise and detailed nature. For the same reason, the reader will find in this book precious little detailed anthropological and archaeological data. For one thing, the data from which I have drawn my conclusions have been already presented by others in all the standard texts, and I saw no reason (and had no room) to merely repeat these conventional observations. For another, I am dealing, essentially, with the *meaning* of these data in the overall evolution of consciousness, and so the discussion concentrates on just that.

Finally, this book contains, as its central theoretical platform, not just the perennial philosophy, and not just a developmental-logic, but a sociological theory based upon both. The perennial philosophy and the developmental-logic are presented in the first few chapters, but the sociological theory—because it is somewhat more complex—is introduced gradually, and is only fully suggested in the second half of the book. Those who find the book's first half somewhat lame sociologically will find more substance in the second half.

Here, then, is the story of the soul poised midway between the beasts and the gods; the soul that has come up from the animals on its way to the heavens; the soul caught up in an evolutionary arc that has destined it for immortality; and the soul that, in just recent times, has discovered that fact.

K.W.
Lincoln, Nebraska
Winter 1980

He whose vision cannot cover
History's three thousand years,
Must in outer darkness hover,
Live within the day's frontiers.

GOETHE,
Westöstlicher Diwan

Man may be excused for feeling some pride at having risen, though not through his own exertions, to the very summit of the organic scale; and the fact of his having thus risen, instead of having been aboriginally placed there, may give him hopes for a still higher destiny in the distant future.

CHARLES DARWIN,
The Descent of Man

INTRODUCTION

Nothing can stay long removed from God, nor long divorced from that Ground of Being outside of which nothing exists, and history—not as a chronicle of individual or national feats, but as a movement of human consciousness—is the story of men and women's love affair with the Divine. On again, off again; loving and loathing; moving toward and recoiling from—history as the sport and play of Brahman.

Traditionally, the great problem with viewing history in theological terms has been not a confusion as to what history is, but a confusion as to what God might be. If we assume that history has some sort of *meaning*, then we must also assume that it points to something *other* than itself, which is to say, it points to something other than individual men and women.[422] This great Other, in its grandest sense, has often been assumed to be God, or Spirit, or the Ultimate.[4] Since God is assumed to be other than, apart from, and altogether beyond human beings, history has thus been viewed as a playing out of a pact, a covenant, or a pledge between God and his peoples.

We cannot forget that, in the West, God and history are profoundly inseparable—Jesus is absolutely significant to the Christian not just because he is the Son of God, but because he was a *historical* event, a token of God's intervention in the *historical* process, a pact between man and God. Moses brought not merely ethical commandments, but a *covenant* between God and his peoples, a covenant to be played out in the course of history. For the Judaeo-Christian world—i.e., the Western mind—history is the unfolding of a pact between God and man, a movement ultimately to bring man and God together.

No matter how amusing this view of history strikes the sober, scientific, and empirical mind, it is a view that weighs heavily in the background of our Western psyche—none of us, I believe, escapes its influence. At one time we saw history as a movement from paganism to Christ Jesus, culminating in the Day of Judgment, that one, far-off, divine event toward which all creation moves. Today, we see history as a process of scientific evolution, moving from the amoeba to the reptile to the ape to man. These two views are not all that different: both see a movement from lower to higher, from worse to better; both are believed in religiously; both promise a tomorrow that is better (or more "evolved") than today; both see a hierarchical movement from sin (less evolved) to salvation (more evolved). While the content is certainly quite different, the form is basically identical. And the form is *historical*. "Biology," says Carl Sagan, "is more like history than it is like physics."[360] More to the point, a point scientists seem rarely to grasp, is Whitehead's demonstration that scientific laws are "an unconscious derivative from medieval theology."[424] In essence, both see history not merely as a going, but a going *somewhere*.

But the scientific view—history as mere evolution—suffers one great defect, or rather, limitation: it cannot explain or even suggest the *meaning* of this going-somewhere.[375] Why evolution? For what purpose history? What is the meaning of this going-somewhere? There is no scientific meaning of the word "meaning"; there is no empirical test for value.[433] Thus, the positivists, who are scientists disguised as philosophers, would not even allow us to ask these questions—since they cannot be answered scientifically, they should not be asked to begin with. The answer to "What is the meaning of history?" is "Don't ask." And while there are some immensely good things to be said for logical positivism, that type of mere linguistic analysis is not strong enough to cure the soul of wonder.

Science *cannot* pronounce on the meaning or purpose of any phenomenon it encounters.[177] That is not its job, that is not what it is engineered to do, and we certainly should not hold that against science, as many romantics do. The tragedy is that science moves into scientism by saying, "Therefore meaning does not exist, since science can't measure it." There is, however, no scientific proof that scientific proof alone is real. Thus, we needn't prematurely cut ourselves off from such important concerns as "meaning" simply because a microscope does not detect them. A physician can describe the intricate biochemical processes that constitute your living being; he can to some extent repair them, cure them of disease, and operate tc remove malfunctions. But he cannot then tell you the *meaning* of that life whose every working mechanism he understands. I doubt, however, that he would then conclude, "Your life therefore is meaningless."

It's just that, as *scientist,* he *cannot* pronounce on life's meaning, cultural meaning, history's meaning.

If, then, we are to ask the question "What is the meaning of history?" we are brought back to the only major answer yet offered: the theological—history is the unfolding of a pact between humanity and God. Even if one disagrees with the view itself, it is generally agreed that it *can* explain the why, the whence, and the *meaning* of that going-somewhere which we call history: its movement is divine and its meaning transcendent.

Theology can effectively work with the meaning of history because it is willing to postulate (or, as theologians would prefer, know by revelation) a sublime Other.[213] Since God is *other* than men, women, and history, God can confer meaning upon history—something that history could never do for itself. To give a simple analogy: When someone says, "What is the meaning of the word 'tree'?" the easiest way to answer is simply to *point* to a real tree. The tree itself has no meaning, but the word "tree" does, simply because it *points* to something *other* than itself. If there were no real tree, the word "tree" would have no meaning, because it could point to nothing other than itself. Just so, history without Other is history without meaning.

Unfortunately, the orthodox Western conception of God is not simply as a psychological Other (separated from us by unconsciousness) or a temporal Other (separated from us by time), or an epistemological Other (separated from us by ignorance). Rather, Jehovah—God of Abraham and Father of Jesus—is an ontological Other, separated from us by nature, forever.[71] In this view, there is not just a temporary line between man and God, but an unmovable boundary and barrier. God and man are forever divorced—they are not, as in Hinduism and Buddhism, ultimately one and identical. Thus, the only contact between God and man is by airmail: by covenant, by pact, by promise. God promises to watch out for his chosen people, and they in turn promise to worship no other gods but him. God promises his only begotten Son to his peoples, and they promise to embrace his Word. God's contact is by contract. Across this gaping abyss God and man touch by rumor, not by absolute union (samadhi), and thus history was viewed as the unfolding of this contract, this covenant, through time.

But there is a much more sophisticated view of the relation of humanity and Divinity, a view held by the great majority of the truly gifted theologians, philosophers, sages, and even scientists of various times. Known in general as the "perennial philosophy" (a name coined by Leibniz), it forms the esoteric core of Hinduism, Buddhism, Taoism, Sufism, and Christian mysticism, as well as being embraced, in whole or part, by individual intellects ranging from Spinoza to Albert Einstein, Schopenhauer to Jung, William James to Plato.[210, 375, 420] Further, in its purest form it is not at all anti-science but, in a special sense, trans-science or even ante-science, so that it can happily coexist with, and certainly complement, the hard data of the pure sciences.⁴³³ This is why, I believe, that so many of the truly brilliant scientists have always flirted with, or totally embraced, the perennial philosophy, as witness Einstein, Schrödinger, Eddington, David Bohm, Sir James Jeans, even Isaac Newton. Albert Einstein put it thus:

> The most beautiful emotion we can experience is the mystical. It is the sower of all true art and science. He to whom this emotion is a stranger . . . is as good as dead. To know that what is impenetrable to us really exists, manifesting itself as the highest wisdom and the most radiant beauty, which our dull faculties can comprehend only in their most primitive forms—this knowledge, this feeling, is at the center to true religiousness. In this sense, and in this sense only I belong to the ranks of devoutly religious men. (Quoted in 168.)

Or the world's first great microbiologist: "Happy is he who bears a god within, and who obeys it. The ideals of art, of science, are lighted by reflection from the infinite." That was Louis Pasteur.

The essence of the perennial philosophy can be put simply: it is true that there is some sort of Infinite, some type of Absolute Godhead, but it cannot properly be conceived as a colossal Being, a great Daddy, or a big Creator set apart from its creations, from things and events and human beings themselves. Rather, it is best conceived (metaphorically) as the ground or suchness or condition of all things and events. It is not a Big Thing set apart from finite things, but rather the reality or suchness or ground of all things.

A scientist who guffaws at the existence of any sort of "Infinite" but unashamedly marvels aloud at the "laws of Nature (with a capital N)" is unwittingly expressing religious or numinous sentiments. According to the perennial philosophy, it would be acceptable to speak symbolically of the absolute as the Nature of all natures, the Condition of all conditions (did not St. Thomas say that God is *natura naturans*?). But notice, in this regard, that Nature is not *other* than all life forms: Nature is not something set apart from mountains, eagles, rivers, and people, but something that, as it were, runs through the fibers of each and all. In the same way, the Absolute—as the Nature of all natures—is not something set apart from all things and events. The Absolute is not Other, but, so to speak, is sewn through the fabric of all that is.

In that sense, the perennial philosophy declares that the absolute is One, Whole, and Undivided—very like what Whitehead called "the seamless coat of the universe." But note that "seamless" does not mean "featureless." That is, to say that Reality is One is not to say that separate things and events don't exist. When a scientist says, "All things obey the laws of Nature," he doesn't mean, "Therefore, no things exist." He means that all things subsist in a type of balanced Wholeness, a wholeness he calls Nature and whose laws he attempts to describe. As a first approximation, the perennial philosophy describes the Ultimate as a seamless whole, an integral Oneness, that underlies but includes all multiplicity. The Ultimate is prior to this world, but not other to this world, as the ocean is prior to its waves but not set apart from them.

This concept is not, as the logical positivist would have it, a meaningless or nonsensical concept—or rather, it is no more meaningless than the scientific reference to Nature, to the Cosmos, to Energy, or to Matter. Just because the ultimate, the integral Wholeness, does not exist as a separate and perceptible entity, does not mean it doesn't exist. Nobody has ever seen Nature—we see trees and birds and clouds and grass, but not some specific thing we can isolate and call "Nature." Likewise, no scientist has ever seen Matter—he sees what he calls "forms of matter"; but nobody, no scientist, layman, or mathematician, has ever seen a pure bit of just matter. We see wood, or aluminum, or zinc, or plastic, but never matter. Yet I doubt any scientist would say, "Therefore, matter doesn't exist." All sorts of intuitive and non-scientific certainties lead the scientist to state that matter is real—and, in fact, for the great majority of scientists, matter is the *only* real, even though they have never seen it, touched it, or tasted it.

The same thing, of course, holds for Energy, since mass and energy are interconvertible. No scientist has ever seen energy, even though he talks of "forms of energy," such as thermodynamic energy, nuclear binding energy, and so on. Although he has never seen just pure and plain energy, he certainly doesn't say, "Thus energy isn't real." But long ago, the geologist and philosopher Ananda Coomaraswamy saw precisely the crux of this "scientific assumption": "This is the predicament of the positivist or 'nothing-morist,' that in acknowledging the reality only of that which can be grasped, he is attributing 'reality' to things that cannot be grasped because they never stop to be, and is driven, in spite of himself, to postulate the reality of some such abstract entity as 'Energy'—a word that is nothing but one of the names of God."[98]

Keeping in mind that the perennial philosophy defines God not as a Big Person but as the Nature of all that is, then Coomaraswamy is obviously quite right, and it matters not one whit whether we say all things are forms of Nature, forms of Energy, or forms of God. I am not, of course, trying to *prove* the existence of the Absolute—I am simply suggesting it is no more improbable than the existence of matter, energy, nature, or cosmos.

Now, when a person believes that the ultimate is some sort of Big Parent who watches after all his offspring as a shepherd over sheep, then that person's notion of religion is petitionary. That is, the aim of his religion is simply to receive protection and benediction from that god, and in turn to worship and give thanks. He lives in accord with what he believes to be that god's laws, and generally hopes, as a reward, to be able to live forever in some sort of heaven. The aim of this type of religion, quite simply, is *to be saved*. Saved from pain, saved from suffering, saved from evil, saved ultimately from death.

I have no quarrel with all that—it simply forms no part of the perennial philosophy whatsoever, and thus is not a view I am here advancing. For the "religion" of the perennial philosophy is quite different from salvation. Since the Ultimate is here pictured as an integral Wholeness, the aim of this type of religion is not to be saved but to *discover that wholeness*. And thus, to find oneself whole as well. Albert Einstein called it the removal of the optical delusion that we are separate individuals set off from the Whole:

> A human being is a part of the whole, called by us "Universe"; a part limited in time and space. He experiences himself, his thoughts and feelings as something separated from the rest—a kind of optical delusion of his consciousness. This delusion is a kind of prison for us, restricting us to our personal desires and to affection for a few persons nearest us. Our task must be to free ourselves from this prison. (Quoted in 168.)

According to the perennial philosophy, this "discovery of Wholeness," the removal of the optical delusion of separateness, is not merely a belief—it is not a dogma one accepts on mere faith. For if the Ultimate is indeed a real integral Wholeness, if it is equally part and parcel of all that is, then it is also completely present in men and women.[208] And, unlike rocks, plants, or animals, human beings—because they are *conscious*—can potentially discover this Wholeness. They can, as it were, awaken to the Ultimate. Not believe in it, but discover it. It would be as if a wave became conscious of itself and thus discovered that it is one with the entire ocean—and thus one with all waves as well, since all are made of water. This is the phenomenon of transcendence—or enlightenment, or liberation, or moksha, or wu, or satori. This is what Plato meant by stepping out of the cave of shadows and finding the Light of Being; or Einstein's "escaping the delusion of separateness." This is the aim of Buddhist meditation, of Hindu yoga, and of Christian mystical contemplation. That is very straightforward; there is nothing spooky, occult, or strange in any of this—and this is the perennial philosophy.

But we now return to the concept of history, and we can approach the meaning of history from our new perennial perspective on "religion." If only the notion of God can explain history, and if God is not a Big Person, but the Suchness and Wholeness of all that is, then history is not the story of the unfolding of a pact between man and God, but the story of the unfolding of the relationship between man and the ultimate Whole. Since this Wholeness is contiguous with consciousness itself, we can also say that *his-*

tory is the unfolding of human consciousness (or various structures of human consciousness, as I will try to demonstrate in this book).

This view has no more "hidden metaphysics"—no more "unprovable assumptions"—than has the standard scientific theory of evolution, since both rest, as we have seen, on the same type of "unseeable" postulates. But for the same amount of hidden metaphysics, we can with this view purchase much, much more meaning, coherence, and balance. We can set history in a context that is at once scientific and spiritual, immanent and transcendent, empirical and meaningful. For this view tells us that history is indeed going somewhere—it is going, not toward a final judgment, but toward that ultimate Wholeness. And further, this Wholeness is not only the Nature of all natures, but also the consummate and ultimate potential of human consciousness itself. History, in this sense, is a slow and tortuous path to transcendence.

THE GREAT CHAIN

According to the perennial philosophy, this path of transcendence follows what is called the "Great Chain of Being," which is said to be a universal sequence of hierarchic levels of increasing consciousness.[198, 224, 367, 375, 429, 436] The Great Chain of Being moves, to use Western terms, from matter to body to mind to soul to spirit. Thus history, from this viewpoint, is basically the unfolding of those successively higher-order structures, starting with the lowest (matter and body) and ending with the highest (spirit and ultimate wholeness).

Thus evolution/history—that path of and to transcendence—begins, so to speak, at the bottom, at the lowest rung of the Great Chain, and works itself up from there. And, in a very special sense, the same is true of the human arc of evolution/history. Just as ontogeny recapitulates phylogeny, man's evolutionary history began at the lower rungs of the Great Chain of Being, and it did so *because* it had to recapitulate, in human form, all of the earlier and prehuman stages of evolution. Mankind's appearance was indeed an extraordinary advance, but one that had to assimilate, include, and *then* transcend its predecessors.

Thus, the earliest stages of mankind's evolution were *dominated* by, although not defined by, subhuman and subconscious impulses. And it was out of this subconscious state—dominated by physical nature and animal body—that men and women eventually evolved a self-reflexive and uniquely human mode of consciousness that we know today as the mental-ego.

This historical emergence of the ego from subconsciousness is one of the phenomena we will be following in the subsequent chapters, but as a brief introductory example, take the following summary by Barfield of Ernst Cassirer's studies: "Ernst Cassirer . . . showed how the history of human consciousness was . . . the gradual extrication of a small, but a growing and an increasingly clear and self-determined focus of inner human experience from a dreamlike state of virtual identity with the life of the body and of its [physical] environment [the subconscious realm]."[21] In other words, out of a primitive embeddedness in physical nature and animal body, through a process of extrication and differentiation, came the self-reflexive ego. This was at once the awakening of highly individual awareness and a "loss" of primitive slumber, the almost "paradisical" state of dreamy immersion in the lower rungs of the Great Chain. To continue Cassirer's view, "It is this fact which underlies the world-wide tradition of a fall from paradise; and it is this which still reverberates on in the nature-linked consciousness that we find expressed in myths, in older forms of language and in the totemic thinking and ritual participation of primitive tribes. It is from some such origins as these [i.e., from the subconscious sphere] . . . that we have evolved the individual, sharpened, spatially determined consciousness of today." We will, in the subsequent pages, follow just this loss of primitive embeddedness, the emergence of the ego, and the "fall" of mankind.

But our approach is not one of romantic sentimentalism. That is, I do not lament the emergence of the ego and the loss of archaic innocence, although we may all shudder at some of the horrendous consequences. For, according to the perennial philosophy, the mental-ego, apart from all its shortcomings, is nonetheless something of a halfway mark on the path of transcendence. That is, egoic self-consciousness is halfway between the subconsciousness of nature and the superconsciousness of spirit. The subconsciousness of matter and body gives way to the self-consciousness of mind and ego, which in turn gives way to the superconsciousness of soul and spirit—such is the "big picture" of evolution and history, and such is the context of man's history as well. The whole cycle, this Great Chain of Being, can be displayed as in Fig. 1.

Fig. 1 is presented as a circle, mostly because of its compact nature, but like any diagram it has its flaws. In particular, I warn the reader that this circular figure is not meant to imply that the lowest stage (1) and the highest (8) run directly into each other; they do not. We will explain these points carefully in the last chapters; for the moment, the levels 1 through 8 can best be thought of as progressing successively higher (around the circle), so that each stage stands to its predecessor more as rungs on a ladder than spokes on a wheel. The levels themselves are "vertically" hierarchical, and, although ultimately they all issue from the Absolute, in the meantime they are intermediate stages of return to that Absolute.[64] The ways in

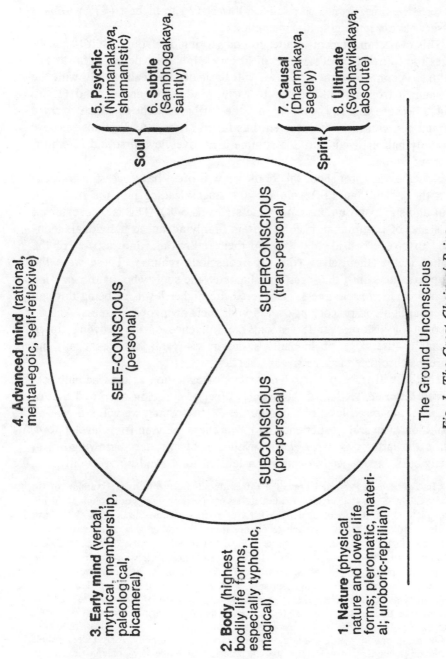

4. Advanced mind (rational, mental-egoic, self-reflexive)

3. Early mind (verbal, mythical, membership, paleological, bicameral)

2. Body (highest bodily life forms, especially typhonic, magical)

1. Nature (physical nature and lower life forms; pleromatic, material; uroboric-reptilian)

5. Psychic (Nirmanakaya, shamanistic)

6. Subtle (Sambhogakaya, saintly)

7. Causal (Dharmakaya, sagely)

8. Ultimate (Svabhavikakaya, absolute)

Soul

Spirit

SELF-CONSCIOUS (personal)

SUPERCONSCIOUS (trans-personal)

SUBCONSCIOUS (pre-personal)

The Ground Unconscious

Fig. 1. The Great Chain of Being

which these levels *are* circular will have to be saved until the last chapters; in the meantime, "rungs on a ladder, lowest (1) to highest (8)" will have to serve as our guiding spatial metaphor.*

This overall movement—matter to body to mind to soul to spirit—constitutes the entire abstract skeleton of history, alpha to omega. As far as this volume is concerned, however, we will basically be dealing only with the movement from nature to body to early mind to advanced mind (levels 1–4), because this is, on the whole, the furthest extent to which *average* human consciousness has evolved thus far in history. As Plotinus said, we are only half evolved—and this volume is an overview, first and foremost, of that first half.

Nonetheless, throughout this book we will often have occasion to mention the higher stages of evolution—the stages leading into the realms of soul and spirit and ultimate Wholeness (levels 5–8). This is so because at all stages of past human history, certain highly advanced individuals managed to evolve considerably beyond their fellows and into aspects of the higher realms themselves (the superconscious realms). These were the prophets, the saints, the sages, the shamans, the souls who, as the *growing tip* of human consciousness, discovered the higher levels of being through an expansion and precocious evolution of their own consciousness. And an account of history that leaves out the influence of the growing tip of humanity—the edge of humanity's greatness—is no history at all, but merely a chronicle of successive mediocrity.

Thus, I will trace *two* parallel strands of evolution as they actually occurred *historically:* that of the *average level* of consciousness, and that of the *most advanced* level of consciousness. The former, we will see, was an evolution of average experience and awareness, moving from level 1 to 4, while the latter was a *correlative* evolution of advanced, growing-tip, or "religious" experience, moving from level 5 to 8. And our account ends,

---

* In *The Atman Project,* I present a rather detailed, seventeen-level version of the Great Chain. Since that precision is not necessary (and probably not possible) in this "big picture" of historical evolution, I have in this volume used only eight basic levels. Needless to say, these eight levels are therefore rather general structures (but precise enough for our present purposes). Further, since I have used the same general terminology in both texts, there is obviously a semantic overlap in certain cases, because some names are forced into extra duty. For example, the "uroboros" in *The Atman Project* refers to a single, precise, and discrete lower level of development, whereas I have chosen to use it here in a more general sense, as the structure most ideally representing *all* lower levels. The correlations of the various terms, as used here and in *The Atman Project,* are, respectively: uroboros—pleroma, uroboros, prototaxic mode, axial, pranic, and image-body; typhon—pranic, image-body, early paleosymbols, parataxic, beginning membership; low membership—membership, paleologic, autistic language, early ego; high membership—early and middle ego; low ego—middle and late ego; middle and high ego—middle and late/mature ego; psychic—low subtle; subtle—high subtle; causal—low and high causal; Spirit/Atman—Ultimate.

more or less, right at the present-day period where the former begins to run into the latter (level 4 in Fig. 1), as we will carefully explain later.

We will also be mentioning the higher stages of evolution toward integral Wholeness and Spirit, because not only is Spirit itself the ultimate stage of evolution, it is the ever-present ground of evolution as well. As we said, this ultimate wholeness is the Nature of all natures, the Condition of all conditions. That is, not only are we moving toward that Wholeness, we also emerged from it, and, paradoxically, *in its embrace we always remain.* The ultimate spiritual Wholeness *is* the ultimate Wholeness of human consciousness as such, and at no point in history or evolution has that Wholeness been lacking.

As the ground, source, and suchness of all manifestation, that ultimate Spirit is the ultimate referent of all history, human or otherwise, and for that reason no account of evolution—even one which deals basically with just its "first half"—can succeed in an explanatory fashion without reference to what Hegel called the "Phenomenology of Spirit."[193] For, as we said, history is the story of the unfolding of Consciousness (Spirit), an unfolding that proceeds from, and back to, the ultimate Wholeness itself. History is the narrative of man's relationship to his own deepest Nature, played out in time, but grounded in eternity.

At the very base of men and women's consciousness, then, lies the ultimate Wholeness. But—and here is the rub—it is *not,* in the vast majority, consciously realized. Thus, the ultimate whole is, for most souls, an *Other.* It is not, like Jehovah, an ontological Other—it is not set apart, divorced, or separated from men and women. Rather, it is a psychological Other—it is ever-present, but unrealized; it is given, but rarely discovered; it is the Nature of human beings, but lies, as it were, asleep in the depths of the soul.

Because the ultimate Wholeness is, for all practical purposes, an Other, *it satisfies our criteria for conferring meaning upon history.* As we have seen, the great theologians have correctly insisted that if history is to have meaning, it must point to something Other than itself. And if it is to have great meaning, it must point to a Great Other, namely God.

But for the perennial philosophy, the Great Other is not an outside God but the Nature and Suchness of one's own being, and thus history points to, and is the unfolding of, one's own true Nature. History, emerging from the Whole, drives to that Whole, the conscious resurrection, in all men and women, of the superconscious All. History has meaning because it points to that All. And history can be consummated because that All can be fully rediscovered.

THE ATMAN PROJECT

The basic Nature of human beings, then, is an ultimate Wholeness (level 7/8). This is eternally and timelessly so—that is, true from the beginning, true to the end, and most importantly, true right now, moment to moment to moment. This ever-present and ultimate Wholeness, as it appears in men and women, we call Atman (after the Hindus), or Buddha Nature (after Buddhists), or Tao, or Spirit, or Consciousness (superconsciousness), or less frequently (because of its loaded connotations) God.

Because Atman is an integral Whole, outside of which nothing exists, it embraces all space and time, and is itself therefore spaceless and timeless, infinite and eternal.[411, 429] Infinity does not, for the perennial philosophy, mean Extremely Big—it means that *spaceless* ground which underlies and includes all space, much as a mirror underlies but embraces all its reflected objects. Likewise, eternity does not mean a Very Long Time—it means that *timeless* ground which underlies and includes all time.

According to the perennial philosophy, then, one's real self or Buddha Nature is *not* everlasting and death-defying; it is rather *timeless* and transcendent. Liberation does not mean going on forever and forever and forever in some sort of a gold-embossed heaven. It means a direct and immediate apprehension of the spaceless and timeless Ground of Being.[367] This apprehension does not show a person that he is immortal—which he plainly is not. Rather, it shows him that where his psyche touches and intersects the timeless Source, he ultimately is all of a piece with the universe —so intimately, in fact, that at that level he *is* the universe.[387] When a person rediscovers that his deepest Nature is one with the All, he is relieved of the burdens of time, of anxiety, of worry; he is released from the chains of alienation and separate-self existence.[193] Seeing that self and other are one, he is released from the fear of life; seeing that being and non-being are one, he is delivered from the fear of death.

Thus, when one rediscovers the ultimate Wholeness, one transcends—but does not obliterate—every imaginable sort of boundary, and therefore transcends all types of battles. It is a conflict-free awareness, whole, blissful. But this does not mean that one loses all egoic consciousness, all temporal awareness, that one goes into blank trance, suspends all critical faculties and wallows in oceanic mush. It simply means that one rediscovers the *background* of egoic consciousness. One is aware of the integral Wholeness *and* of the explicit ego. Wholeness is not the opposite of egoic individuality, it is simply its Ground, and the discovery of the ground does not annihilate the figure of the ego. On the contrary, it simply reconnects it with the rest of nature, cosmos, and divinity. This is not an everlasting state, but a timeless state. With this realization, one does not gain everlasting life in time, but discovers that which is prior to time.

Now according to the perennial philosophy, the rediscovery of this infinite and eternal Wholeness is man's single greatest need and want.[44] For not only is Atman the basic nature of all souls, *each person knows or intuits that this is so.*[29] For every individual constantly intuits that his prior Nature is infinite and eternal, All and Whole—he is possessed, that is, with a true Atman intuition. But, at the same time, he is terrified of real transcendence, because transcendence entails the "death" of his isolated and separate-self sense.[239] Because he won't let go of and die to his separate self, he cannot find true and real transcendence, he cannot find that larger fulfillment in integral Wholeness. Holding on to himself, he shuts out Atman; grasping only his own ego, he denies the rest of the All.

Yet notice immediately that men and women are faced with a truly fundamental dilemma: above all else, each person wants true transcendence, Atman consciousness, and the ultimate Whole; but, above all else, each person fears the loss of the separate self, the "death" of the isolated ego. All a person wants is Wholeness, but all he does is fear and resist it (since that would entail the "death" of his separate self). And there is the dilemma, the double bind in the face of eternity.

Because man wants real transcendence above all else, but because he will not accept the necessary death of his separate-self sense, he goes about seeking transcendence in ways that *actually prevent* it and force symbolic substitutes.[436] And these substitutes come in all varieties: sex, food, money, fame, knowledge, power—all are ultimately substitute gratifications, simple substitutes for true release in Wholeness.[29] This is why human desire is insatiable, why all joys yearn for infinity—all a person wants is Atman; all he finds are symbolic substitutes for it.

Even an individual's feeling of being a separate, isolated, and individual self is a mere substitute for one's true Nature, a substitute for the transcendent Self of the ultimate Whole. Every individual *correctly* intuits that he is of one nature with Atman, but he distorts that intuition by applying it to his separate self. He feels his separate self is immortal, central to the cosmos, all-significant. That is, he *substitutes* his ego for Atman. Then, instead of finding timeless wholeness, he merely substitutes the wish to live forever; instead of being one with the cosmos, he substitutes the desire to possess the cosmos; instead of being one with God, he tries himself to play God.

This attempt to regain Atman consciousness in ways that prevent it and force symbolic substitutes—this I call the Atman project.[436] It is the *impossible* desire that the individual self be immortal, cosmocentric, and all-important, but based on the *correct* intuition that one's real Nature is in-

deed infinite and eternal. Not that his deepest nature is *already* God, timeless and eternal, but that his ego *should* be God, immortal, cosmocentric,
death-defying, and all-powerful—that is the Atman project. And there is either Atman, or there is the Atman project.

The Atman project, then, is *both* a compensation for the *apparent* (i.e.,
ultimately illusory) lack of Atman and a drive to recapture it (consciously). We need only remember those two points: the Atman project is
a substitute for Atman, but it also contains a drive to recapture Atman.
And, as I will try to show, it is ultimately the Atman project which moves
history, moves evolution, and moves the individual psyche. And only when
the Atman project comes to an end does true Atman consciousness stand
forth. That is also the end of history, the end of alienation, and the resurrection of the superconscious All.

THE NATURE OF CULTURE AND THE
DENIAL OF DEATH

We saw that every person's true Nature is Atman (Spirit, level 7/8); and
further, every person intuits, however dimly, just this Atman nature. However, as long as he will not or cannot accept death (Thanatos), he cannot
find literal unity consciousness or Atman consciousness—for that would
entail the surrender and "death" of the isolated self sense. And since he
cannot (yet) accept death and thus find his true Self or his ultimate
Wholeness, he is forced to create a series of *symbolic substitutes* for that
Self (Atman). Lacking a realization of his true Self, which is neither subjective nor objective but merely Whole, he compensates with a symbolic,
subjective, and inward self, and this self then pretends to be cosmocentric,
independent, and immortal. And this is part, the *subjective* part, of the
Atman project.

Until the final resurrection of the true Self in superconsciousness, then,
the false, individual, and separate-self sense *is faced with two major drives:*
the perpetuation of its own existence (Eros) and the avoidance of all that
threatens its dissolution (Thanatos). This inward, isolated, pseudo-self is
fiercely defended against death, dissolution, and transcendence (Thanatos), on the one hand, while aspiring and pretending to cosmocentricity,
omnipotence, and immortality on the other (Eros). These, as we will be
explaining in more detail, are the positive and negative sides of the Atman
project—Eros and Thanatos, Life and Death, Vishnu and Shiva. And the
battle of Life versus Death, Eros versus Thanatos, is the arch-battle and

the basic anxiety *inherent* in all separate selves—a primal mood of fear removed only by true transcendence into Wholeness.

But this brings us to the last major aspect of the Atman project: the separate self—although it pretends and aspires to immortality and cosmocentricity—necessarily fails its purpose to some degree or another. It cannot altogether pull off the charade that it is stable, permanent, enduring, and immortal. As James put it, the fearful background of death is still there to be thought of, and the skull will grin in at the banquet.[213] Until the separate self rediscovers its ultimate Wholeness, the foggy atmosphere of death remains its constant consort. No amount of compensations or defenses or repressions is enough to finally and totally screen out this background dread. That is, nothing the inward self can do will finally choke out this horrifying vision, and so "external" or "objective" props are brought in to help support the Atman project, to help alleviate the terror of death and present the self as immortal. An individual will create or latch on to a host of external or objective wants, desires, properties and possessions, goods and materials—he searches for wealth, fame, power, and knowledge, all of which he tends to imbue with either infinite worth or infinite desirability. But since it is *precisely* infinity that men and women truly want, all of these external, objective, and finite objects are, again, merely substitute gratifications. They are *substitute objects,* just as the separate self is a *substitute subject.* These, as we will see, are the outward and inward branches of the Atman project: objective and subjective, out there and in here.

My point, then, is just this: the world of objective substitute gratifications is nothing other than the world of *culture.*† And culture—external substitute objects, material or ideal—serves the same two closely interrelated functions as the inward substitute subject: namely, provides a source and promise and flow of Eros (life, power, stability, pleasure, mana) and avoids or resists or defends against Thanatos (death, diminution, taboo). This is why, even in archaic societies, "anthropology discovered that the basic categories of . . . thought are the ideas of mana and taboo. . . . The more mana [Eros] you could find to tap, the more taboo [Thanatos] you could avoid, the better," for the whole cultural project is "two-sided: it aims toward . . . an absolute 'beyond' in a burst of life affirmation, but it carries with it the rotten core of death denial. . . ."[26]

Death denial, the frantic pace away from Thanatos—this is the very crux of the "negative" side of the Atman project, and its role in culture formation has been absolutely extensive and pandemic. Culture, truly, is what a separate self does with death—the self that is doomed only to die, and knows it, and spends its entire life (consciously or unconsciously) trying

† Culture is not the *sole* objective substitute gratification (*any* objective realm is ultimately a substitute gratification); but culture is the *major* human realm of objective compensatory activity.

to deny it, both by constructing and manipulating a subjective life and by erecting "permanent" and "timeless" cultural objects as outward and visible signs of a hoped-for immortality. Hence could Rank classify all societies on the simple basis of their "immortality symbols." Hence could Becker point out that "societies are standardized systems of death denial," for every "culture is a lie about the possibilities of victory over death."

> Man wants what all organisms want: continuing experience, self-perpetuation as a living being [Eros]. But we also saw that man had a consciousness that his life came to an end . . . ; and so he had to devise another way to continue his self-perpetuation, a way of [pretending to transcend] the world of flesh and blood, which was a perishable one. This he did by fixing on a world which was not perishable, by devising an "invisible-project" that would assure his immortality. . . .
> This way of looking at the doings of man gives a direct key to the unlocking of history. We can see that what people want in any epoch is a way of transcending their physical fate, they want to guarantee some kind of indefinite duration, and culture provides them with the necessary immortality symbols or ideologies; societies can be seen as structures of immortality power.[26]

"Wanting nothing less than eternal prosperity," concludes Becker, "man from the very beginning could not live with the prospect of death. . . . Man erected cultural symbols which do not age or decay to quiet his fear of his ultimate end."[26] In short, culture is the major outward antidote to the terror generated in the face of death; the promise, the wish, the fervent hope that the skull will not in fact grin in at the banquet.

THREE QUESTIONS

We will be looking, then, at the evolution of various structures of consciousness or modes of self out of the subconscious immersion which characterized the dawn state of humanity. We will follow the emergence of the self out of its primitive embeddedness in nature and body (levels 1 and 2), up to the modern era of a highly individualized and "independent" ego which is differentiated from nature and body (level 4). Further, I will suggest that a given mode of self sense supports a particular type or style of culture (which in turn inculcates that mode of self), since in the main these two projects are correlative. Mode of self and style of culture lean upon each other as the two major strands of the Atman project.

Consider some of the fundamental points we will encounter: As men and women emerged from the subconscious sphere and lost the protection of ignorance, as they became more aware of their separation, vulnerability, and mortality, what defenses did they have to construct? What were the costs of those defenses on their fellow human beings? More importantly, at each stage of evolution out of the subconscious, did men and women have any sort of access to the superconscious realms? Could they see into any of the higher stages of evolution and spiritual release?

These are some of the main themes we will be discussing, and they can be summarized with three simple questions. In each given society and at each stage of evolution:

1. What are the major forms of real transcendence available to men and women? That is, are true paths to Atman, to the superconscious, available?

2. Failing that, what *substitutes* for transcendence are created? That is, what are the forms of the Atman project, both subjective as self and objective as culture?

3. What are the costs of these substitutes on one's fellow men and women? What price the Atman project?

For what we will find is that history is the saga of men and women working out their Atman projects on one another, in both negative (Thanatos) and positive (Eros) sides, creating thereby kings and gods and heroes on the one hand, and strewing recklessly the corpses of Auschwitz and Gulag and Wounded Knee on the other.

And we will find that history does indeed have meaning, both on a large scale—as the movement from subconsciousness to superconsciousness—and on an individual scale—for any soul who, at any time, opens himself to immediate transcendence to the superconscious All in his own case. This is both the "death" and the transcendence of his separate self, and—for him—the end of history, the end of the exclusive tyranny of time, the end of the optical delusion of separateness, the resurrection of the All and the return to Wholeness. Of course, the number of individuals of any given time who have actually awakened to the All has always been quite small; and it will probably be thousands, maybe millions, of years before mankind as a whole evolves into superconsciousness. Except for those few, then, who individually choose the path of transcendence, it is quite true that history is, and will remain, the chronicle of men and women born too soon.

I

TALES OF DIM EDEN

1 The Mysterious Serpent

By the time the earliest hominids appeared on the face of the earth—in their protohuman form, perhaps as early as six million years ago—evolution had already succeeded in bringing forth a remarkable series of increasingly complex, sensitive, and responsive structures of being. Beginning approximately fifteen billion years ago, with the so-called Big Bang, evolution had succeeded in moving, *in hierarchic order,* from simple insentient and lifeless atoms to vegetal life, and beyond vegetation to simple animal forms (protozoan, amphibian, reptilian), and then to higher animal forms (mammalian, with simple mental images and paleosymbols). All of that, i.e., all of those lowest substages of the Great Chain of Being, were, so to speak, waiting for the first hominids. And all of that composed the substructure upon which, and beyond which, human consciousness would be built.

It seems to be a general fact that each stage of evolution goes beyond its predecessors but must nevertheless include and integrate them into its own higher order. As Hegel would put it, "To supersede is at once to negate and to preserve."[193] That is, each stage of evolution *transcends* but *includes* its predecessors. Thus, early life forms (plants) went beyond but included lifeless matter and minerals in their makeup; and animals went beyond plant forms (simple life) but included life in their makeup. Just so, humans go beyond but include animal characteristics, and, by implication, humans include but transcend *all* prior evolutionary stages.[224, 360]

As the first hominids or protohuman creatures emerged in evolution, they emerged upon and around a basic core of natural and animal structures that were *already* defined by previous evolution. And while man would eventually transcend that core, he had from the start to include it, to assimilate it, to grow through it before he could grow out of it. His earliest human ontogeny was a recapitulation of cosmic phylogeny. The earliest human species was at once a faltering step forward in evolution and an encapsulation of *all* previous evolution.

Dawn Man, in other words, began his career *immersed* in the subconscious realms of nature and body, of vegetable and animal, and initially "experienced" himself as indistinguishable from the world that had already evolved to that point. Man's *world*—nature, matter, vegetable life and animal (mammalian) body—and man's *self*—the newly evolving center of his experience—were basically *undifferentiated,* embedded, fused and confused. His self was his naturic world; his naturic world was his self; neither was clearly demarcated, and this, basically, in unconscious homage to his past.

With self and other confused, with inner experience and external natural world undifferentiated, with no real capacity for true mental reflection or verbal representation, this whole period must have been an experience of a time before time, a story before history—with no anxieties, no real comprehension of death and thus no existential fears. For these reasons (and others), Neumann has suggested, and rightly I believe, that this original structure of human consciousness, this primitive and archaic identity, is best referred to with the mythological terms "pleroma" and "uroboros."[311] "Pleroma" is an old gnostic (and Jungian) term signifying the potential of *physical* nature (*prakriti* in Hinduism). "Uroboros" is the primordial mythic symbol of the serpent eating its own tail, and signifies self-possessed, all-enclosing but narcissistic, "paradisical" but reptilian (or embedded in lower-life forms). The pleroma-uroboros, then, stands as the archetype and perfect symbol of this primitive awareness: embedded in physical nature (pleroma) and dominated by animal-reptilian impulses (uroboros). And while, as I said, the first protohumans had already moved *beyond* those lowest of stages, they were initially *dominated* by them. Hence, although the pleroma-uroboros *by itself* represents matter and nature, it also represents, as a mythic metaphor, the primal atmosphere of Dawn Man.

Thus, the uroboros, as I use it, is a very general term which refers both to *all* the lowest levels and sublevels of the Great Chain (matter, vegetable, and lower animal-bodily life) *and* to the first protohuman forms of life which were just escaping from those lowest levels. All of this is simply collapsed, for convenience, as "level 1" in Fig. 1, and referred to collectively as the "uroboros," the serpent of nature, the home of Dawn Man.

As we will see, the uroboros especially is the structure lying behind the universal myths of a Garden of Eden, of a time before the "fall" into separation and knowledge and reflection, a time of innocence. "Our dreams are tales told in dim Eden," said Walter de la Mare, and the uroboros, the great and mysterious serpent, slumbers there in paradise. Whatever else we may say, the serpent was there in Eden.

I would like now to turn to some of the evidence that the Dawn State of man was one of dreamy immersion in and oneness with the material and natural world—the state we have also called the subconscious sphere (because it lacks self-conscious reflection). I would like in particular to cite the excellent studies of Jean Gebser. But before I do that, I want briefly to explain Gebser's work as a whole, since I intend to make extensive use of his particular reading of the anthropological record. Gebser's major work is entitled *Ursprung und Gegenwart*.[158] For Gebser, the Ursprung is "our primordial Origin," the timeless and spaceless Whole, "the wholeness which existed at the very beginning, prior to time."[159] Gegenwart is "our living Present, the unity of all that relates to time and the temporal, the Present which, as it actualizes reality, encompasses all phases of time—yesterday, today, and tomorrow, and even the pre-historical and the timeless."[159] These are all very familiar concepts to the perennial philosophy.

In *Ursprung und Gegenwart,* Gebser outlines a "unique human event: the unfolding of consciousness," and he does so in terms of four major "structures of consciousness which have occurred [in man's history]." These four structures he calls the archaic, the magical, the mythical, and the mental/rational. In Gebser's words:

> The structuring which we have uncovered seems to provide a clue to the foundations of consciousness, and to enable us to furnish a contribution to the history of how man became conscious. This structuring rests upon the recognition that clearly distinguishable worlds have come to the fore during the development of Western man (and not him alone), whose unfolding took place in mutations of consciousness. The problem which we face thus rests upon a cultural-humanistic analysis of the different structures of awareness, and the ways in which they emerged.
>
> To accomplish this, we use the method of pointing out the structures of consciousness during the various "epochs," on the basis of their peculiar modes of expression in images as well as in languages, as revealed in valid records.[159]

I will be explaining all these structures later, but for the moment let us simply note (with reference to Fig. 1) that Gebser's "archaic structure" corresponds closely with our "pleromatic-uroboric (level 1)," the "magical" with the "typhonic (2)," the "mythical" with the "membership (3)," and the "mental" with the "egoic (4)." In deference to and respect for Gebser's pioneering work, whenever I refer to the lower levels of the "spectrum of consciousness" (or Great Chain of Being) as they unfolded in anthropological sequence, I will usually prefix the names of the spectrum levels with Gebser's terminology. Thus: the archaic-uroboric, the magical-typhonic, the mythic-membership, and the mental-egoic. These will be the major "epochs"—actually, the major stages in the growth of consciousness—that we will outline in this volume.

We return, then, to the first structure of consciousness and the culture or society that it supported: the archaic-uroboric. In Gebser's view, we "are able to glimpse therein the first glimmer of an age when world and man are just emerging [as differentiated entities]. It is closest to, if not identical with, the biblical paradisiacal primal state. It is an age when the soul still sleeps; thus it is . . . the period in which there is a complete *lack of separation or distinction* between the individual and the whole."[159], *

Gebser is by no means alone in this opinion. It has received a rather widespread acceptance from scientists to philosophers to psychologists. We have already seen the conclusion of Ernst Cassirer's monumental *Philosophy of Symbolic Forms:*[76] ". . . the history of human consciousness was . . . the gradual extrication of a small, but a growing and an increasingly clear and self-determined focus of inner human experience from a dreamlike state of *virtual identity with the . . . body and its environment* [uroboric fusion]. [Man] has had to wrestle his subjectivity out of the world of his experience by polarizing that world gradually into a duality. And this is the duality of objective-subjective, or outer-inner." Barfield concludes that "it is from some such origins as these"—from uroboric-naturic fusion—"and not from an alert, blank stare of incomprehension that we have evolved the individual, sharpened, spatially determined consciousness of today."[21]

E. Neumann, in his classic *Origins and History of Consciousness*[311]—one of the books that will be our constant companion on this odyssey—concurs precisely with Cassirer and Gebser: "The original situation which is represented mythologically as the uroboros corresponds to the psychological stage in man's prehistory when the individual and the group, ego and unconscious, man and the world, were so indissolubly bound up with one another that the law of *participation mystique,* of unconscious identity, prevailed between them." Neumann, of course, is echoing a conclusion also

* Gebser has charged his archaic structure (and to some degree, his magical structure) with the degenerate and romantic fallacies, simply because he fails to differentiate pre-subject/object from trans-subject/object. That is the only basic disagreement I have with his works, and so I have deleted those small romanticisms from his account. I do not mean to misrepresent him in this regard; I have simply used those aspects of his work which I consider most accurate. The interested reader can consult his original works.

accepted by C. G. Jung and by Lévy-Bruhl, and summarized by Gowen thus: "The uroboros represents a primal, undifferentiated, dreamy autistic state in which man did not know himself as separate, and did not have self-conscious life. *Genesis* describes this state as 'Eden' and tells us that when man ate of the tree of knowledge, he lost his innocence, and was cast out (into space, time, and personality)."[168] And Neumann himself concludes:

> If [archaic, primal man's] existence in the uroboros was existence in *participation mystique,* this also means that no ego center had as yet developed to relate the world to itself and itself to the world. Instead, man was all things at once. . . . Not only is the psyche open to the world, it is still identified with and undifferentiated from the world; it knows itself as world.[311]

There is, of course, no decisive way to prove or disprove whether that was the actual condition of Dawn Man. There is, however, one last piece of circumstantial evidence upon which we may draw: if, even in some few ways, ontogeny recapitulates phylogeny—that is, if the infant and the primitive share at least a few general characteristics, even though radically different in context—then our case is a little clearer. For psychologists today are almost universally agreed upon one fact of infant development, a fact stated by Piaget thus: "During the early stages the world and the self are one; neither term is distinguished from the other . . . *the self is material,* so to speak."[329] Pleromatic-uroboric. Notice, however, that the "world" with which the self is identified at this early stage is *not* the mental world, not the world of higher intelligence and symbols and concepts; it is not the world of higher emotions or altruistic love or feeling-attention; it is not an identity with subtle or psychic, linguistic or logical or causal realms—because *none* of those have yet emerged. Rather, this early state is primarily a *material* identity and uroboric fusion (protoplasmic consciousness, Piaget calls it).† And Piaget is not alone. In fact, Freud and the whole psychoanalytic movement, the entire Jungian tradition, the Klein-

---

† Thus, when Piaget says, of the infant, that "the world and the self are one," by "world" he means basically a *material* world (level 1). This has confused a lot of researchers because it sounds like a "mystical" state or supreme unity. But when the mystic says, "In the highest state, the world and the self are one," by "world" he means *all* worlds, levels 1–8. So where the infant is one with the *first* level, pre-subject/object, the mystic is one with *all* levels, 1 through 8, trans-subject/object. Failure to differentiate these states (they sound similar in words) makes the mystic appear to be regressing; or, conversely, it makes the infant—and Dawn Man—appear to be in some sort of mystical, transcendent state of samadhi. So it is important to remember that when Gebser, Piaget, Cassirer, Neumann, Freud, etc., say that in the earliest stages of development self and "world" are one, by "world" they mean the lowest stage of the Great Chain of Being, *not* the entire Chain itself. So do not confuse uroboric-naturic fusion with mystic oneness.

ians, the modern ego psychologists such as Mahler, Loevinger, and Kaplan, and the cognitive psychologists in general—all essentially agree that the infant's first structure of consciousness is this type of material fusion consciousness, *pre*-subject/object (*not* trans-subject/object!), largely ignorant of boundaries and space and time.

And as for the acceptability of applying these facts, in a very general fashion, to the earliest stages of human anthropological development as

Fig. 2A. Brass shield from Africa.

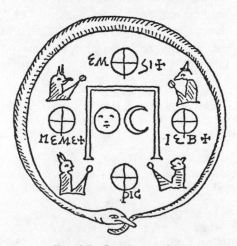

Fig. 2B. Ceptic woodcut.

well? I am not going to make a drawn-out argument for this, but simply take it as highly probable that, as Arieti's classic study (which won the National Book Award for Science) put it: "What is of fundamental importance is that the [two] processes [phylogeny and ontogeny] to a large extent follow similar developmental plans. This does not mean literally that in the psyche . . . ontogeny recapitulates phylogeny, but that there are certain similarities in the [two] fields of development and that we are able to individualize schemes of highest forms of generality which involve all levels of the psyche in its [two] types of development. We also recognize concrete variants of the same overall structural plans in the [two] types of development [a fact we will soon state as: deep structures are invariant, surface structures are culturally conditioned and variant]."[6] The whole point is that it should not surprise us at all if, looking back into those tales of dim Eden, we find the faint traces and misty trails of the ever-circling uroboros, the mysterious serpent of early evolution, standing at the base of human phylogeny just as it does ontogeny.

That archaic-uroboric state, then, comes to mean many different things at once. In terms of growth stages, in terms of the emergence from the subconscious, it is the lowest state of consciousness, the crudest, the least differentiated, the one endowed with least awareness (centered on level 1). Many religious-anthropologists, of course, would like to see this state as angelic, for it was prior to the emergence of reason, logic, personality, division, and subject/object. But their opinion, otherwise well-intended, is supported by a simple failure to distinguish between *pre*-personal and *trans*-personal, pre-mental and trans-mental, pre-egoic and trans-egoic. They understand that Atman is indeed without ego, without subject/object duality, without division, but they then confuse pre and trans and thus imagine that Eden was some sort of trans-personal heaven, whereas it was simply a pre-personal slumber. This archaic-uroboric period does indeed appear angelic in many ways, but it is the bliss of ignorance, not of transcendence. There is no evidence whatsoever that any of the higher realms of the superconscious were understood, lived, or consciously mastered. Quite the contrary, as we have said, it was a time of slumber, pre-personal slumber, in the subconscious sphere, the life of the lilies of the field. And if we must see it as angelic, then let us remember the Sufi master Khan's definition of an angel: "An angel is a soul who has not grown sufficiently."

Thus, the uroboros—even though it was a state of primal naturic unity, or rather, *because* it was a state of primal naturic unity—was dominated by unconscious Nature, by physiology, by instincts, by simple perception, sensations, and emotions. Thus Neumann, who spoke of the uroboros as that time when "the ego germ still dwells in the pleroma, the 'fullness' of the unformed God, and slumbers in the bliss of paradise," could also point out that in the uroboric state, man "swims about in his instincts like an animal. Enfolded and upborne by great Mother Nature, rocked in her arms, he is delivered over to her for good or ill. Nothing is himself; everything is world. The world shelters and nourishes him, while he scarcely wills and acts at all. Doing nothing, lying inert in the unconscious, merely being there in the inexhaustible twilit world, all needs effortlessly supplied by the great nourisher—such is that early, beatific state."[311]

We see, then, precisely why that state *was* beatific—it was pre-personal, not trans-personal, and subconscious, not superconscious. To emphasize that this uroboric state, this state of beatific but archaic consciousness, is ruled by instincts and biological drives, Neumann also calls it the "alimentary uroboros," the world of "visceral psychology." Thus physiologically, the uroboros—as the serpentine center—may be thought of as the reptilian complex (primarily) and the limbic system (secondarily). This obviously does not imply that uroboric men and women had no cerebral cortex—only that it was not predominant. That is, it was not serving all of the functions it serves today, such as abstract logic, language, and conceptualization. There stands anyway the fact that in almost all mythologies the uroboric symbol is a serpentine reptile. The reptile: instinctual and unselfconscious behavior, embedded in mother nature, rooted in the subconscious sphere. And there, I believe, is the actual state of the Garden of Eden universally described by mythology.

Thus, it is not altogether surprising to hear Dr. Sagan suggest that "perhaps the Garden of Eden is not so different from Earth as it appeared to our ancestors of some three or four million years ago, during a legendary golden age when the genus *Homo* was perfectly interwoven with the other beasts and vegetables [the subconscious sphere]. These [Eden myths] all correspond reasonably well to the historical and archaeological evidence."[360]

In this chapter, however, I have devoted very little attention to the precise archaeological evidence presented by such scholars as Gebser, Neumann, Berdyaev, Sagan, etc., dealing with the archaic-uroboric era, with the mythic Eden. The reason is that these scholars themselves have already discussed the evidence rather extensively—they have described the period itself, the archaeological remains, the likely structure of its societies. I see no reason to merely repeat their data.[57, 69, 85, 90, 92, 136, 249, 252]

I should at least mention, however, that the archaic-uroboric period, as I am using it, is a very general term referring to the whole mood of the pre-*sapiens* human: to the times of *Australopithecus africanus, Homo habilis,* and into *Homo erectus.* That covers a period beginning perhaps as early as three to six million years ago and stretching to around 200,000 years ago. This dawn period, the pre-personal Eden, represents in a very global fashion the great transition from mammals in general to man in particular, and stands further as the great subconscious ground out of which the figure of the ego would eventually emerge. But let me emphasize that while I have not detailed the extensive archaeological specifics—from the

Fig. 3. A member of Australopithecines, *perhaps as early as 5 million years ago. This is a perfect example of "humans" in the uroboric period; advanced beyond all prior evolutionary stages (matter, plant, animal) but still embedded in, and dominated by, the lower levels themselves. All of the lower stages and substages of the Great Chain (matter, plant, reptile, and mammal), and protoman embedded in them, we collapse for convenience into one stage/level, and that is the uroboros. Since the lower levels are dominated by food and matter, we also use the uroboros specifically to refer to food exchange.*

invention of stone and bone tools to the use of fire—I mean to imply all of that. It is just that I am trying here to "describe" the dawn period from the "inside"—the subjective side. What might Dawn Man have experienced, before he developed language, higher-order emotions, and self-consciousness? The answer suggested by our authorities is: subconscious Har-

mony, Eden, unreflecting physical fusion and embeddedness—the uroboros. "I do not know where to find in any literature," said Thoreau,
"whether ancient or modern, any adequate account of that nature with
which I am acquainted. Mythology comes nearest to it of any." And the
mythological symbol of the uroboros—in the round, self-contained,
narcissistic, naturic embeddedness—stands as the closest account that I can
find of the "subjective" dawn state of humankind. And not only was this
apparently the dawn state of man, it is most definitely the dawn state of
every human child born ever since. The "dragons of Eden" are with us
still.

But we cannot let the account rest there, because although it is indeed
the substructure through which, and upon which, higher human consciousness was to be built, the uroboros (level 1) was not *in and by itself*
the defining *essence* of mankind. For the essence of a being is determined
not by the lowest to which it can sink—animal, id, ape—but the highest to
which it can aspire—Brahman, Buddha, God. And thus, even in the archaic-uroboric times, during which mankind was undoubtedly attached to
the lowest levels, we have to look elsewhere for the *defining* heart of humanity, for a clue to its real nature, and thus for an indication of what future evolution might unfold from that essence.

To give but one example: according to Vedanta psychology—a psychology of the perennial philosophy—men and women possess three major
states of consciousness: waking, dreaming, and imageless deep sleep (and
a fourth which transcends and integrates them all). For reasons that seem
perfectly legitimate, but almost impossible to explain in a short space, the
waking state is said to correspond to the physical body (levels 1–2),
dreaming to the subtle mind (levels 3–4), deep sleep to the transcendent
realm of the soul (levels 5–7), and the fourth to the Absolute (level 8).
Each of these realms can *potentially* be entered in full *consciousness,* it is
said, so that all the levels of consciousness, including the higher realms of
subtle soul and spirit, are said to be man's given *potential.*[174]

Thus, according to this example, even in the archaic-uroboric state,
humankind already possessed all higher states as *potentials*—gross, subtle,
and God-transcendent—and for the simple reason that they woke, dreamt,
and slept. All the levels of consciousness, in other words, including the
higher realms, were contained in an undifferentiated and potential state in
primal man. In a sense, all the levels of being—the Great Chain of Being—
were *present* but *unconscious.* Let us provisionally agree with this Vedan-
tic view (it is in essential agreement with the perennial philosophy in general), and let us then call the sum total of these unconscious structures the
ground unconscious (the ground unconscious is listed in the lower left portion of Fig. 1, as the point "out of which" the various levels evolve).

Now the ground unconscious is similar to, but not quite the same as, the
ultimate Atman. The easiest way to think of the difference is to imagine
Atman as the total realization or total actualization of the potentials

merely enfolded in the ground unconscious. When all the *enfolded* potentials in the ground unconscious *unfold* as actualities, that is full and prior Atman. Paradoxically, Atman is always fully present, first to last, but, in its unrealized state, it constitutes the ground unconscious. Or we could say that the ground unconscious is, in a sense, "half" of Atman—the sleeping half. But we needn't become overly technical (the interested reader can consult *The Atman Project,* where the developmental-logic behind the concept is fully explained). We need only provisionally adopt the hypothesis that, even in primal man, all the various structures of consciousness were enwrapped and enfolded in the ground unconscious (which is really the way Gebser seems most often to use the term "Ursprung"), and out of this containment the various states of being—the Great Chain of Being—would emerge in consciousness, starting with the *lowest* and ending with the *highest.* Starting, that is, with nature and pleroma and uroboros (level 1), then moving to the higher emotion-body (2), then to the subtler structures of mind and ego (3–4), and then into the transcendent structures of spirit and superconsciousness (5–8). A movement, we have said, from subconsciousness to self-consciousness to superconsciousness. And at this early period, only the lowest structures, represented by the uroboros, had yet *clearly* emerged.

But to state that the ground unconscious contains all the structures of being ready to unfold in a hierarchic fashion, does not mean that history is therefore perfectly determined as to the details of that future unfoldment. For, as I have tried to explain elsewhere, the ground unconscious contains only the "deep structures" of human consciousness, but not their "surface structures."[432] And while the *deep* structures of each level (such as nature-uroboros, typhonic-body, mythic-membership, rational-ego, subtle-soul, etc.), are indeed *determined and bound* by an invariant and cross-cultural developmental-logic, the *surface* structures of each level are molded and conditioned by the force of *cultural* and *historical* contingencies. In short, deep structures are natively given, surface structures are culturally molded.

This is essentially what the great anthropologist George Murdock had in mind when he concluded that "if we compare human behavior to a fabric [composed of warp and woof], the warp [deep structure] remains everywhere much the same, for the student of culture is forced to recognize the essential 'equality and identity of all human races and strains as carriers of civilization' [a quote from A. L. Kroeber]. The woof [surface structures], however, varies with the number and variety of cultural [and historical] influences."[137] Jurgen Habermas, on the even surer basis of developmental-logic, has made a similar point.[292]

To give an example: The deep structure of the human body (level 2) is given and determined by the Ursprung: two legs, two arms, 208 bones, one liver, etc. But what one does with the body—its *surface structures* of social labor, play, and work—are largely conditioned and controlled by the social and historical environments in which these surface structures exist. Furthermore, as successively higher-level deep structures emerge, their surface structures can be repressed, oppressed, and distorted by coercive social forces, a fact that can be understood and reconstructed only in light of *actual historical contingencies,* not merely abstract (but otherwise all-important) deep structures (which was Marx's critique, correct as far as it goes, of Hegel). We will return to this important topic throughout our presentation.

Think of it this way: if you picture an eight-story building, each of its floors is a *deep structure,* and the rooms, furniture, objects, etc., on each floor are its *surface structures.* We will be following the unfolding of successively higher deep structures (levels 1–8) out of the ground unconscious, an unfolding that is perfectly determined as to its sequence and deep form; but we will also see and acknowledge that their *surface structures* are decisively molded and created by the historical moment in which they happen to find themselves. However, since this is an introductory volume, we will be dealing basically only with the unfolding of deep structures; but the practical importance of surface-structure history and conditioning must always be borne in mind, since, in the real day-to-day world of living, it is that surface historical conditioning which is so vitally significant and so demands our conscious understanding, as the discipline of hermeneutics, in whose ranks I count myself, continues to remind us.‡

‡ Hermeneutics is the science of interpretation, or the determination of the *meaning* of mental productions (e.g., what is the meaning of *Macbeth?* of last night's dream? of your life?).[156] As such, it is a trans-empirical discipline, for no amount of analytical-empirical-scientific data, no matter how complete, can totally establish meaning (e.g., give me a scientific proof of the meaning of *War and Peace*). Rather, meaning is established, not by sensory data, but by unrestrained communicative inquiry and interpretation.[177] The truth of the naturic realm (level 1/2) is decided by empirical (sensory) inquiry, but the truth of the mental realm (level 3/4) is established only by intersubjective discussion among a community of concerned interpreters, whose data is not *sensory* but *symbolic.*[433] The point is that even though truths in the mental-symbolic sphere are non-empirical and cannot be determined by empiric-scientific inquiry, nonetheless they *can* be decided. There is a perfectly legitimate way to *ground* mental truths, and that ground is a "community of like-minded interpreters." "Only a community of interpreters can generate the intersubjective basis for a set of criteria that might validate the truth claims forming a coherent interpretation."[316] Thus, while hermeneutics is *not* empirically factual or verifiable, neither is it mere subjective license or ungrounded opinion, because it is forged in the fire of intersubjective discourse and inquiry among a community of concerned scholars whose demands for *good interpretation* are every bit as stringent as those for good empirical facts.

Further, symbolic-mental productions always exist in a particular historical context, and a subjective grasp of that context is necessary to highlight their meaning. Thus, while water is and always will be H_2O, regardless of the historical circumstances, the meaning of, for example, Australian totemic-increase ceremonies can only be understood by a clear comprehension of the historical context in which they were practiced. This is why Habermas draws such a sharp line between analytic-empirical inquiry (level 1/2) and historical-hermeneutic inquiry (level 3/4).[177] I add, however, that

At any rate, to return to the uroboric period: There is one last—but definitely not least—reason that we choose the symbol of the serpent-uroboros to represent the entire Dawn State of mankind. According to the discipline of kundalini yoga (and entirely independently of Western psychological corroboration), mankind does indeed contain all the higher levels of consciousness as a true potential, a potential known in general terms as "kundalini energy," which is said to lie dormant, asleep, in the unconscious (the ground unconscious) of all men and women.[419] And the lowest state of kundalini—the state wherein it *initially* slumbers, waiting to rise upward toward higher levels—is represented always as a *serpent* (and is actually called "the serpent power"), which is said to lie coiled at the *base* of the human spine, the lowest "chakra."[14] This simply means that man's potential for higher consciousness starts out at the lowest base of his being, at the first chakra, the center of material, pleromatic, alimentary, visceral-food impulses (the first chakra is said to represent food and physical matter). From this lowest state (or chakra), the serpent power (consciousness itself) is said to evolve or awaken to successively higher centers of awareness, moving *precisely* through the levels of the Great Chain of Being, from the lowest material or natural state (level 1) toward the brain-mind center (level 4), and then into truly superconscious states (especially level 5, but also beyond).[166] From this viewpoint, the evolution of consciousness *is* the evolution upward of the serpent power, and, according to kundalini texts, this power, in its earliest, lowest, and initial starting point, is precisely represented by the uroboros, the serpent of Eden. Further, the serpent-uroboros is said not to be just an arbitrary symbol, but a *literal* rendition of the actual *form* of the lowest state of the ground unconscious, a form vividly disclosed in kundalini meditative disciplines, and a form universally acknowledged by all similar disciplines[410]—a claim I have found, by and large, to be perfectly supportable.

The point is that by emphasizing the uroboric beginnings of mankind,

---

against hermeneutics, as a "narrative foil," must be brought developmental-logic, as Habermas is struggling to demonstrate.[292] The conclusion is that these two disciplines (hermeneutics and phenomenological developmental-logic), when combined, would cover *both* surface structures (historical-hermeneutics) and deep structures (developmental-logic).

Finally, if you are looking for masses of empirical investigations and conclusions in this book, it should be understood from the start that I, along with Habermas, Gadamer, Taylor, Ogilvy, etc., consider exclusive empiricism to be radically and violently reductionistic, no matter how cleverly concealed; the demand for "empirical proof" is really a demand to strip the higher levels of being of their meaning and value and present them only in their aspects that can be reduced to objective, sensory, value-free, univalent dimensions (i.e., level 1/2). While we will not shun empirical data (that would miss the point), neither will we confine ourselves to empirical data (that would miss the point completely). The basic approach of this book is a hermeneutical or interpretive reading of the text of history (evolution), set in a developmental-logic derived from a phenomenological inquiry into the deep structures of consciousness development (set forth in *The Atman Project*).

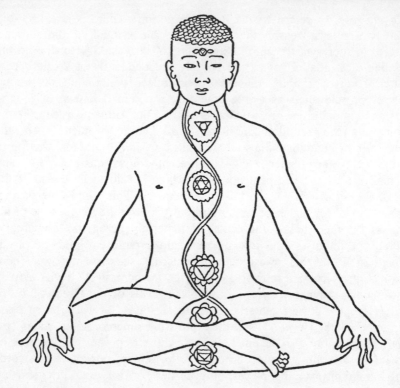

Fig. 4. The Great Chain according to kundalini, showing the seven major chakras (stages/levels) as they appear in the human compound individual. The two curved lines represent, approximately, sympathetic and parasympathetic currents in the body and, in the brain, left and right hemispheric functions. The locations of the chakra centers themselves are not merely symbolic, but actual. The first (i.e., anal) chakra represents matter (as in faecal matter), the second, sex (genitals), the third, gut reactions (emotions, power, vitality), the fourth, love and belongingness (heart), the fifth, discursive intellect (voice box), the sixth, higher mental-psychic powers (neocortex), the seventh, at and beyond the brain itself, transcendence. There is precisely nothing "occult" or mysterious about their locations.

and by recognizing the serpent power and its rise through higher structures, we can bring our entire historical account of the evolution of consciousness into full accord with kundalini theory, a fact of no little significance. While I will not always mention the evolution of consciousness as the evolution of kundalini, the reader might bear in mind that I have taken the chakra view into consideration at each stage of development and evolution. We will, however, explicitly mention again the serpent power when we reach the Egyptian period, and thus, if the reader now simply remembers that, during the archaic-uroboric period, the kun-

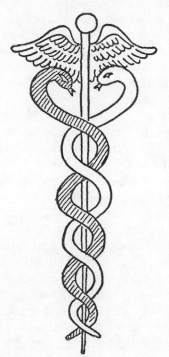

Fig. 5. Caduceus. There is no mistaking what this common symbol represents; it even has seven stages.

dalini potential lay at its earliest and lowest state, coiled at the base of the spine (in the region of the anus and genitals, representing graphically the material, instinctual, and animal functions from which, and beyond which, kundalini evolves), then its progress by the time of the Egyptian period—the higher stages kundalini had managed to reach via evolution—will become very apparent, and stand as auxiliary but powerful supporting proof of our overall thesis.*

Finally, we might note that the archaic-uroboric estate involved the least developed form of the Atman project. The uroboric self was indeed driven by the Atman project—as *all* manifest things are—but it was most primitive in its operation. The uroboric Atman project, the uroboric drive to unity, was centered on alimentary impulses, simple instinctual forms of unity (such as food), and material unity and embeddedness. Still asleep in the Garden of Eden, mankind did not consciously ponder how to regain paradise.

---

* At the same time, I don't want to appear to say that the actual discipline of kundalini yoga embodies *all* of the higher and highest levels of consciousness. Kundalini per se ends, in its most recognizable form, at level 5 (and the *beginning* of level 6), and belongs basically to the Nirmanakaya class of religious experiences (which I will explain in subsequent chapters).

So it is to the next major stage of unfoldment, that of the magical-typhon, that we will have to look for the first signs of a rudimentary enlightenment and transcendence into superconscious realms, on the one hand, and for aggravated substitutes for Atman, a more developed and intensified Atman project, on the other. This is very like the story of the Prodigal Son/Daughter—which is not so much a story as it is *the* story of mankind and consciousness. As Campbell has demonstrated, all Hero myths show three movements: separation, initiation, and return. With archaic man, slumbering unwittingly in nature, there is as yet no real separation, no Fall, and thus no enlightened Heroes. And this necessary separation and Fall is precisely what is glorified in that most enigmatic of Catholic services, Holy Saturday, the Blessing of the Paschal Candles: *O certe necessarium Adae peccatum* . . . "O necessary sin of Adam—O happy fault that merits a redeemer such as Christ." No sin and separation from earthly Eden, no remembrance and return to heaven.

In the archaic-uroboric state, Adam had not yet sinned and separated from the primal embeddedness of the subconscious. In the following sections, therefore, we will among other things trace out the apparent Fall—or rather, the hierarchical series of mini-falls, because the Fall becomes progressively more apparent with each successive structure of consciousness. We will see that there occurred successive stages of emergence out of the subconscious, a movement that was both a "fall"—in the sense that it entailed separation, anxiety, and guilt—and a necessary growth out of subconsciousness. At the next major stage, the magical-typhon, we see this Fall in its most rudimentary and painless form; at the mythic-membership stage, it takes on a definite and articulated form; and then, at the mental-egoic stage, around the second millennium B.C., an absolutely unprecedented cry of anguish, guilt, and sorrow screams out from the world's myths, narratives, and records, for at that point, mankind had finally emerged from its great sleep in the subconscious, and was faced with the stark awareness of its own mortal and isolated existence. No longer protected by the subconscious, and not yet awakened to the superconscious, mankind—stuck in the middle—cried out to gods that would no longer answer and wailed to a goddess no longer there. The world, quite simply, was never to be the same.

II
TIMES OF THE
TYPHON

2 The Ancient Magicians

As we move out of the dim tales of lost Eden, we come now to the earliest times that can, with a modicum of assurance, be accurately described. And by that statement, I do not mean just descriptions of archaeological or physical remains, since, as I have said, I am trying in this volume especially to describe, or rather suggest, the "subjective flavor" or "subjective mood" of consciousness which defined each of its various stages of evolution, and not confine myself to the standard, empirical descriptions of physical and material archaeological remains. I am especially, but not solely, looking at archaeological remnants for a clue as to the mood of consciousness that reciprocally produced and supported those artifacts. From that *mood* of consciousness (which gives us a first approximation), we attempt more precisely to suggest the *mode* of consciousness behind it, and we then check this proposed mode or structure of consciousness with the actual *structure* of the archaeological, anthropological, and cultural remains of the corresponding period. Of the period we are about to enter, and with that "subjective mood" in mind, I suggest quite simply: the first men and women to appear on the earth during these times (about 200,000 years ago) were not just simple hunters and gatherers—they were magicians.

Let me begin to explain that statement by first describing some of the characteristics (reconstructed by the "mood/mode" approach, and supplemented by limited but appropriate ontogenetic/phylogenetic parallels) of this early stage of consciousness, a stage we call the bodyself or "typhon." As individual humans began to emerge from archaic and protoplasmic consciousness, as they first started to climb out of the uroboric realm, consider what they faced: For one, they were beginning to awaken to their own *separate* existence, with all the potentials and all the perils therein. For another, they simultaneously had lost that primal and archaic innocence of the uroboric Eden. In Eden, men and women "lacked" Atman or Spirit—only in the sense that they were at the lowest stage on the Return to Spirit—but they did not know or realize that "lack," and hence did not consciously suffer its absence.[30] The uroboric self was indeed driven by the Atman project (as all manifest things are), but in an instinctual and purely unconscious fashion. As men and women moved out of Eden, however, not only did they still "lack" Spirit, they began to vaguely intuit that lack, and consciously suffer for it. And thus the Atman project naturally intensified. In the simplest terms, the *drive* to superconscious unity and the integral Whole was increasing its pressure on consciousness.

Thus, as man finally succeeded in dispersing the old uroboric fusion, he was no longer protected (by that subconscious ignorance) from both the vision of his mortality and the pain of his Atman-lack. As he emerged from the subconscious uroboros, he thus began to awaken to his vulnerability, his finiteness, and his incompleteness. To be able to live with this increasingly precarious situation, he had to (1) start *defending* his increasingly separate self (against death and Thanatos), while (2) trying to make it *appear* stable, permanent, enduring, immortal, and cosmocentric (life and more life—Eros). The Atman project, which was present but slumbering in the uroboric self, begins to intensify in the typhonic self.

In the old uroboric Eden, the "self" appeared cosmocentric because it was unconsciously embedded in and as the material cosmos and the naturic environment at large. *There* was its primitive unity, its archaic Atman project or Unity project.[436] But when that primitive state of affairs no longer obtained, the now increasingly *separate* self had to devise other and more refined means of cosmocentricity. A *higher form* of the Atman project had to be devised. And this the typhonic self accomplished by focusing and centering consciousness *from* the naturic world *onto* the individual organism. The self was now separate from the natural world, but seemed *central* to it—and there was its new cosmocentric vision: to be the focal point of the natural world, and to defend this focal self against all odds. The individual created a new and higher substitute self "in here" and a new and higher world "out there"—"higher" because both were, for the first time, differentiated from each other and thus no longer totally fused and confused. Thus there arose, sometime in the dim past of prehistory, the awakening of a defended self-in-here versus the world-out-there.[6, 21, 38, 76, 311]

Now although man at this early stage had succeeded in the difficult and necessary task of transcending his previous fusion state, the resultant differentiation between the new and higher self and its new and higher world was not absolute. On the contrary, from all we know the boundary between the two was utterly fluid. Although the individual was no longer fused to the naturic world, he was nevertheless magically interconnected with it. That is, uroboric elements were still present and still exerting their tendency toward merger and embeddedness. Again, we see something *similar* to this in the development of the infant today. As Piaget so clearly explains: "During the early stages [of uroboric consciousness] the world and the self are one; neither term is distinguished from the other. But when they become distinct, these two terms begin by remaining very close to each other: the world is still conscious and full of intentions, the self is . . . only slightly interiorized. At [this] stage there remain in the conception of nature what we might call 'adherences,' fragments of internal experience which still cling to the external world,"[329] and, we might add, fragments of the external world which still cling to the self—since, in fact, the two were once one.

At this early stage, then, although the self is distinguished from the naturic environment, it remains magically intermingled with it. The cognitive processes at this stage thus confuse not only subject and object, but whole and part. That is, just as the subject is "in" the object and the object is "in" the subject ("adherences"), so the whole is in the part and vice versa.* Freud called this cognition the primary process and he saw it operating most vividly in dreams.[140] For dreams are dominated by condensation and displacement—images transform easily and readily in a type of magical plasticity, and one image can symbolize several different things at the same time. Sullivan[384] called this the "parataxic mode," where the "undifferentiated wholeness of experience [uroboros] is broken down into parts, which are still not connected in any logical way."[51] And although they are not connected in any logical way, the parts of experience *are* connected by a type of magical association and contamination. And that is the magical primary process, the mode of knowing and experiencing which dominates this early, typhonic stage.

Arieti draws the obvious conclusion: "A hominid . . . at the phantasmic [primary process fantasy] level would have great difficulty in distinguishing images, dreams, and paleo-symbols from external reality. He would have no language [language begins at level 3] and could not tell

---

* To those mystically inclined, this might sound like some sort of very advanced cognition, like a type of holographic or Dharmadhatu interpenetration, but it is nothing of the sort. The mystic doctrine of mutual interpenetration—"all in one and one in all"—means that each part is *both* perfectly itself and perfectly one with the whole. The primary process simply can't tell the difference between the part and the whole to begin with.

himself or others, 'This is an image, a dream, a fantasy; it does not correspond to external reality.' He would tend to confuse psychic with external reality, almost as a normal man does when he dreams. Whatever was experienced would become true for him by virtue of its being experienced. Not only is consensual validation from other people impossible at this level, but intrapsychic or reflexive validation cannot even be achieved. This [level] is characterized by *adualism:* lack of the ability to distinguish between the two realities, that of the mind and that of the external world."[6] Because the subject and object, and because various objects themselves, are not yet totally differentiated, they all remain magically interconnected or "adual."

Finally, before we begin to examine the archaeological record itself, let me comment upon the term "typhon." In a general sense, the term was chosen to suggest a stage of development wherein self and body are not yet clearly differentiated. At this early stage (level 2), the logical, verbal, and conceptual mind is not yet developed (level 3/4). The mental capacities, such as they are, are simple and crude by any standards, consisting basically of primary process or magico-imagery, paleosymbols, and proto-linguistic structures. Since the mind is not yet developed, it does not have the capacity to differentiate itself from the body, and thus the self likewise is embedded in and undifferentiated from the body. As we will eventually see, man did not learn to clearly distinguish self from body until quite late in his evolutionary career—in fact, he would eventually develop a severe lesion between self and body, ego and flesh, reason and instinct. But prior to that time, self and body were more or less fused and confused—they were totally undifferentiated. The angel and the animal, the man and the serpent, were one.

This state of affairs, crude but fascinating, is marvelously represented by

Fig. 6. The typhon. The typhon refers generally to the period of earliest Homo sapiens (*Neanderthal and Cro-Magnon*) *and is itself a structure of consciousness dominated by body-bound mentality and instincts. In the typhon, the mind is only crudely developed, and what mind there is (images, paleosymbols) is completely undifferentiated from the body. For this reason, the typhon is also used to refer specifically to emotional-sexual energies, prana, the second and third chakras.*

the mythical being of the Titan, offspring of the Earth Goddess Gaea. I have chosen the Titan known as Typhon, who, according to legend, was the youngest child of Gaea, to represent this psychological structure. "Typhon," says Campbell, "the youngest child of Gaea, the goddess Earth. . . . The Titan's form, half man, half snake, we are told, was enormous. He was so large that his head often knocked against the stars and his arms could extend from sunrise to sunset."[71] Half man, half serpent—man and animal, man and uroboros, still intertwined. . . . There is the typhonic self, the self that has differentiated its body from the environment but not yet differentiated its own mind from its body.

Freud seemed to penetrate to the heart of this early condition: the ego, he said, was "first and foremost a body-ego."[145] That is, in the early stages of development, the self is centered on the body, and not so much on the mind—it is basically a body-ego, not a mental-ego. Thus, the previous stage—where the body and the environment are fused and confused—we called the archaic-uroboric. And the next stage—where the body (level 2) is differentiated from the environment (level 1), *but before* the mental-ego (level 3 or 4) emerges and differentiates from the body—just that is the typhon, the body-ego or bodyself.

To show just how archaic—yet magical and awe-inspiring—the primitive typhon or bodyself being was, I have included a portrait of man-as-typhon, in Fig. 7. Actually, this is the now famous "Sorcerer of Trois Frères," an etching found in the Paleolithic cave site of Trois Frères, France. "The pricked ears are those of a stag; the round eyes suggest an owl; the full beard descending to the deep animal chest is that of a man, as are likewise the dancing legs; the apparition has the bushy tail of a wolf or wild horse, and the position of the prominent sexual organ, placed beneath the tail, is that of the feline species—perhaps a lion. The hands are the paws of a bear."[69] But notice: the figure represents an entity distinct from its surroundings—it is not a pleromatic or uroboric self. But it is magically composed of all sorts of different and "confused" parts—it is a "man," but one still interconnected not only with its body but with the bodies of nature, from owl to bear to lion. In other words, it is typhonic.

But what else is it? Who drew it, and what did it mean? "The Count Bégonën and the Abbé Breuil first supposed it to represent a 'sorcerer,' but the Abbé now believes it to be the presiding 'god' or 'spirit' [a nature god, not transcendent God] controlling the hunting expeditions and the multiplication of game. Professor Kuhn suggests the artist-magician himself."[69] One thing we are sure of: "The whole cave," says Campbell, "was an important center of hunting magic; these pictures served a magical purpose; the people in charge here must have been high-ranking highly skilled magicians (powerful by repute, at least, if not in actual fact)."[69] And further, "if the vivid, unforgettable lord of the animals in the hunters' sanctuary of Trois Frères is a god, then he is certainly a god of sorcerers, and if a

Fig. 7. The Sorcerer of Trois Frères

sorcerer, he is one who has donned the costume of a [nature] god."[69] For my own part, based on the whole typhonic mood, I think he is probably all three or four interpretations magically rolled into one: a nature god, magic sorcerer, hunting spirit, and artist himself. So there it is: the (self) portrait of a nature god or sorcerer as magical-typhon. And further, I suggest, this sorcerer-magician *experienced* himself and his world much as he (accurately) painted it.

As far as we know, this is the oldest (self) portrait of a human ever found.

We say, then, that as men and women emerged from their uroboric slumber in Eden, they emerged as magical-typhons. And it is to that time we now look.

WHEN THE DREAM WAS REAL

We may begin with Jean Gebser's excellent summary of the magical-typhon. First, he notes (and explicitly in connection with direct archaeological evidence) that the magical (typhonic) structure displays the "first 'centering' in man which will later lead to his [fully individual] self."[159]

Figs. 8 and 8A. Typhonic figures. The classic typhon is half serpent, half man; but any figure that is structurally half animal and half man is a typhonic figure.

The notion of the new and higher self being constructed by the centering and focusing of awareness is one we just explained, and it further tallies with Sullivan's conclusion that "out of this focusing of alertness the self is evolved."[51] Uroboric consciousness—that dim and diffuse awareness described by Cassirer—is focused and heightened into brighter areas of awareness, a process that eventually leads to a more centered self.

And, Gebser continues, precisely because of this initial, but as yet rudimentary, focusing and centering of the bodily typhon, "man first becomes dissociated [rather, differentiated] from the [subconscious] 'harmony,' from his identity with the [naturic] whole. Here is the first state of becoming aware. . . . The more pronouncedly he detaches himself from his identity with the [naturic] whole, the more he begins to become a *particular* being."[159]

However, Gebser points out, although man is beginning to detach himself from the whole (of subconscious nature), he still retains a strong type of "interconnectedness with nature, and [therefore displays a] magical response to being thus interwoven—which gives him power and makes him a creator." There is, however, as yet no real mental-ego; that is, the egomind (level 3 or 4) has not yet truly emerged from the ground unconscious and differentiated from the body. The self is only a bodyself, for "responsibility is lodged in the external world and its objects, a sure sign of egolessness."[159]

And as for the primary process—that magical cognition of whole/part equivalency that, I have suggested, dominates this level? Gebser is very definite:

> Every point, be it real or unreal, whether it be bound causally or only symbolically into the whole, not only may be connected to every other point but *identified* with it. . . . One point may with full validity and effectiveness take the place of another. . . . The magical world is, hence, also a world of the *pars pro toto,* in that the part can and does stand for the whole.[159]

Thus, we are not surprised to find that, as Professor Mickunas recently described this magical-typhonic structure as it appears anthropologically, "the world with its objects and events is charged with vital and magical powers; man too is charged by these powers. . . . Each point (or person or thing) is interchangeable with any other . . . within the magical continuum [so that] these effects are experienced, and constitute the basis for magic."[298]

Not only does this magical, primary process cognition best account for totemistic identification, it is—according to Gebser and Mickunas—easily seen in primitive art and action: "A man [in primitive hunting rites] draws the animal in the sand before dawn, and when the first sun-ray touches the drawing, he shoots an arrow into the drawing, thus killing the animal; 'later' he slays the animal, and performs a ritual dance at evening. All these actions and events are *one*—identical, not symbolical."[298] Thus, as Neumann has it, "between the hunted animal and the will of the hunter there existed a magical . . . rapport."[311]

We moderns are most familiar with this type of magical atmosphere in the form of voodoo, where the practitioner, by sticking pins in a doll effigy, tries to effect a change in the actual person—and usually for the worse. This "works" because, to the magical mentality, the doll and the person are *one,* not symbolical. And for the primitive typhonic man—may I remind the reader of the eerie Sorcerer of Trois Frères?—this type of cog-

Fig. 9. The totem. A perfect example of magic-typhonicism—man still structurally linked to animal ancestors. This reflects the lower levels of the Great Chain through which human beings evolved, but in which they were initially embedded, and by which they were initially controlled.

nition was an entire and primal *mood* of consciousness, and it was electrically charged and shot through with magic: "Man's original fusion with the world [level 1], with its landscape and its fauna, has its best-known anthropological expression in totemism, which regards a certain animal as an ancestor, a friend, or some kind of powerful and providential being. The sense of kinship felt by a human member of the totem for the totem animal and ancestor, and for all animals of that species, is carried to the point of identity. There is abundant evidence that such kinships are not just matters of belief, but matters of fact, i.e., psychological realities which sometimes result in telepathic hunting-magic, etc. There is no doubt that early man's view of the world rests on identity relationships of this kind."[311] Frazer:

> Belief in the sympathetic influence exerted on each other by persons or things at a distance is of the essence of magic. Whatever doubt science may entertain as to the possibility of action at a distance, magic has none; faith in telepathy is one of its first principles. A modern advocate of the influence of mind upon mind at a distance would have no difficulty in convincing a savage; the savage believed in it long ago, and what is more, he acted on his belief with a logical consistency such as his civilised brother in the faith has not yet, so far as I am aware, exhibited in his conduct.[136]

No wonder that even the earliest modern anthropologists, when first investigating this typhonic period, were universally struck by what they would eventually see as its defining characteristic: magic! Thus, as E. B. Tylor, the "first giant" of modern anthropology, put it, "An attempt is made [in my works] to refer a great part of the beliefs and practices included under the general name of magic, to one very simple mental law, as resulting from a condition of mind which we of the more advanced races [or rather, cultures] have almost outgrown, and in doing so have undergone one of the most notable changes which we can trace as having happened to mankind."[137] And what was this "one very simple mental law"? It was, according to Tylor, just this: "Man, in a low stage of culture, very commonly believes that between the object and the image of it there is a real connexion . . . and that it is accordingly possible to communicate an impression to the original [object] through the copy [image]."[137] This is, as Opler summarized it, "the tendency of man in early stages of mental evolution to confuse an object with the image of it, the word with what is represented, dream with reality."[137]

And that "simple mental law" occurred for a simple but precise reason: because the subject and object, psyche and world, were not yet fully differentiated, then likewise the (mental) image of the object was not yet fully differentiated from the (physical) object itself—and *that* was the simple most distinguishing characteristic of magical (primary process) cognition: between the object and the symbol of the object "existed a magical rapport." To manipulate the symbol was to affect the object symbolized.

Frazer, the "second giant" of modern anthropology, would subdivide this "basic mental law" into two "fundamental principles of magic."[136, 190] As I would preface it, *because* the object and its symbol are confused, this gives rise to two immediate effects. According to Frazer, they are:

1. *The law of similarity,* wherein "like produces like," or, as we would now say, similarity is confused with identity, so that, among other things, all subjects with similar predicates appear identical and thus can be perfectly interchanged (Freud's "displacement"). This means, specifically (as Von Domarus would clearly explain), that the members of a class are equated, or wholes with similar parts are confused, or subjects with similar predicates are identified. For example, if one red-haired person causes trouble, another red-haired person will also cause trouble; if one black object is evil, all black objects are evil; and so on. Each member of the class can be magically interchanged with each other, to equal effect. The reader will have no difficulty identifying modern holdovers from this primitive magical confusion—it is part of everything from superstition to prejudice.

2. *The law of contagion,* wherein, we would now say, proximity is confused with identity, so that entities once in contact remain forever associated or "cross-contaminated." This also means that any *part* of an entity "contains" the entire essence of the entity. The part, since it was once in contact with the whole, now "carries" the essence of the whole: the whole is thus collapsed in each of its parts (Freud's "condensation"). This means, specifically, that a member of a class and the class itself are equated, the subject and predicate are undifferentiated, the whole and part are confused. For example, if a particular man carries power, so does a lock of his hair; if a rabbit is good luck, so is its foot; etc.

The point is that, when subject and object are undifferentiated, then image and entity are confused, symbol and object are conflated, and thus subject and predicate, whole and part, class and member, are all "magically one." And there, in a phrase, was the atmosphere, the *mood,* of the typhonic self.

Small wonder, then, that as for "art" in the typhonic times, Campbell points out that "in most of the [Paleolithic] caves the animals are inscribed one on top of the other, with no regard for aesthetic effect. Obviously the aim was not art, as we understand it, but magic." Furthermore:

No less than fifty-five figures of practitioners of magic have been identified among the teeming herds and grazing beasts of the various

Fig. 10. Paleolithic cave drawings at Trois Frères, St.-Giroud, France. Notice the overlapping figures: "not art, as we understand it, but magic."

[Paleolithic] caves. These make it practically certain that in that remote period of our species the arts of the wizard . . . or magician were already well developed.[69]

"In fact," Campbell concludes, "the paintings themselves were an adjunct of those arts, perhaps even the central sacrament; for it is certain that they were associated with the magic of the hunt, and that, in the spirit of that dreamlike principle of mystic participation . . . their appearance on the walls amounted to a conjuration of the timeless principle, essence, noumenal image, or idea of the herd into the sanctuary, where it might be acted upon by a rite."[69]

But, having said all that, we now reach a crucial point in the discussion of "primitive magic." *Without in any way* denying the essential characteristics of the magical primary process, which we have just defined, we now *add* a crucial point, a point overlooked by most of our already-quoted authorities. It is not so much that magic is a hallucinatory or primitive misperception of an otherwise clear and distinct reality, but rather that magic is a more or less *correct perception* of a primitive and *lower level* of reality. It is not a distorted perception of a higher reality, but a correct perception of a lower reality. In fact, primitive magic is the more or less accurate "reflection" of the pranic level (level 2), the level of emotional-sexual energies, the level of pre-differentiated reality which does indeed operate by associations and contagions. Magic reflects this *vital* nexus, not a logical nexus, and, as far as it goes (which, of course, is not very far), it is largely accurate. Thus, the magical primary process is not so much wrong as partial, not so much inaccurate as incomplete.

Freud himself seemed often to realize this fact. However, since it is a subtle distinction, he did not always abide by it. On the one hand, Freud clearly recognized that the earliest forms of cognition were "magical," and thus, because these magical forms "came first" in psychological development, he called them "the primary process." He also recognized that these primitive and partial forms were superseded in development by more advanced forms of awareness, forms of logic and rationality, which Freud called "the secondary process." So far, so good. However, in comparison with the secondary process, the primary process seemed to be, not a true reflection of a lower and partial reality, but a pure and simple distortion of the "only" reality (secondary process). And thus Freud usually called the primary process a simple "distortion" or "incorrect version" of reality, a distortion that is effectively inhibited by the "real" secondary process. But on occasion Freud notoriously wavered, and a much more complete view comes through: "The processes described as 'incorrect' [the magical primary processes] are not really falsifications of our normal procedure, or defective thinking, but the modes of operation of the [early] psychic apparatus when freed from inhibition [by higher levels]."[140] There is the important distinction, precisely the distinction I have in mind: the primary process is primitive but accurate as far as it goes.

Most of us moderns, of course, are directly immersed in the magical primary process and the level of the Great Chain it so accurately discloses (level 2) only during sleep with dreams. The world of the dream is the world of magic, a true reflection of the typhonic sphere (level 2): the world is plastic and shaped at whim, condensation and displacement rule, wholes and parts become each other.† But that magical world, primitive but real enough, which in us moderns has been relegated to the state of dreaming, was apparently *conscious* in our remote ancestors. As Freud put it, "What once dominated waking life, while the mind was still young and incompetent, seems now to have been banished into the night."[140]

"In this primitive magical state," concludes Neumann, "there was no clear dividing line between man and the animals, man and man, man and the [naturic] world. Everything participated in everything else, lived the same undivided and overlapping state in the world of the unconscious as in the world of dreams. Indeed, in the fabric of images and symbolic presences woven by dreams, *a reflection of this early situation still lives on in us,* pointing to the original promiscuity of human life."[311]

> The ability of all contents to change shape and place, in accordance with the laws of similarity and symbolic affinity [our two laws of magic], the symbolic character of the world, and the symbolic meaning of all spatial dimensions—high and low, left and right, etc.—the significance of colors, and so forth, all this the world of dreams

† In my opinion, a complete theory of dreams would include two basic premises and one distinguishing characteristic. The distinguishing characteristic is pretty much accepted by all dream researchers, and it is that the dream (REM) state is largely non-verbal and non-egoic: in the dream, your normal ego "dissolves," so to speak—it is a "non-egoic" state. But the two premises follow from the generally unrecognized fact that there are actually two quite different modes of non-verbal and non-egoic awareness: one is pre-verbal and pre-egoic, the other is trans-verbal and trans-egoic. Thus the dream, in my opinion, is the royal road to pre-verbal reality, especially level 2 (and, of course, to aspects of experience *repressed* during the verbal-Oedipal period). But it can *also* disclose and represent trans-verbal and trans-egoic realities (especially level 5, sometimes 6, but not beyond). A failure to appreciate these two different non-egoic dimensions has, on the whole, tarnished the dream theories of most psychological researchers, East and West alike. The West tends to see the dream as *only* pre-verbal, the East tends to see it as *only* trans-verbal. Both are, in my opinion, partially true. This is why the dream state often discloses *infantile* memories (via images) and/or *present-day* pranic impulses clothed in imagery—*and* why it can also disclose psychic and clairvoyant capacities (level 5). At the same time, this is not to deny that the dream, or aspects of it, can also serve problem-solving functions (à la Adler), although I think this a rather secondary role. Needless to say, all my comments in this chapter apply to the pre-verbal dream—the magical primary process. We will discuss psychic capacities, not in connection with the dream state per se, but rather as a direct and waking-state potential.

shares with the dawn period of mankind. . . . Dreams can only be understood in terms of the psychology of the dawn period, which, as our dreams show, is still very much alive in us today.[311]

It is, as we will see, a general fact that the conscious elements of one stage tend to become the unconscious elements of the next, continually, stage by stratified stage.‡ Thus, the primitive typhonic men and women apparently experienced even while "awake" a magical level that is retained in us moderns pre-eminently in dreams.* So it is that each night, as we sink back into the sphere of the dream, we each and all are converted into sorcerers, soaring above the ground in magical flight and transforming the world at whim. And each night, in the dream, we meet face to face with our ancestors, and even converse occasionally, I daresay, with the Sorcerer of Trois Frères.

‡ More specifically: Each *stage* of development embodies a *mode* of self, and further, what is the *whole* of the self at one stage forms merely a *part* of the whole of the next. But not all of the old self is consciously carried by the new self. Once a stage is superseded by its successor, that *stage* itself becomes a *level* of the individual, or a *conscious component* of the higher self. However, the old *mode* of self does *not* become a conscious component of the next mode of self, but is relegated to the submergent unconscious. For example, at the typhonic stage, the mode of self is bodily-pranic. When that stage is superseded by the mind, the body becomes a *level* in the compound individual and a conscious component of the higher self, but the mode or sense of being an exclusively bodyself is not retained in consciousness. The individual consciously retains access to his body, but *not* the experience of being just a bodyself. *That* is relegated to the submergent unconscious. Likewise, the child will consciously retain language, but not the experiential self that learned language, and so on. But notice that *all* past structures are retained: the stages are retained as conscious components, the modes as subconscious memory.

* Both Freud and Adler tended to the view that dreaming is precipitated by a buildup of unresolved tensions, so that the less the tensions, the less the urgency or necessity for dreaming activity. I believe that is a very secondary issue. The dream state is a simple, natural, necessary activity of the typhonic-pranic level, and it will occur, with or without tension buildup, simply as an expression of this lower level which is now compounded in our own makeup. At the same time, if aspects of this level are *repressed*, then those aspects do cause a tension buildup that expresses itself most insistently in dream activity, but not there alone. This is the difference between the archaic unconscious and the repressed-submergent unconscious (see *The Atman Project*). The dream, at any rate, is pre-eminently a display of a past *mode* of self, and secondarily an outlet for what is now a lower level of self (in reference to the previous footnote).

THE MAGICAL BODYSELF VS.
ACTUAL PSYCHIC ABILITY

Now as magical—and in that sense marvelous—as this state might have
been, it obviously was a very weak structure of consciousness. The self
was indeed magically interconnected with the environment, but for that
very reason it was also unprotected from invasion by unconscious elements
within and extra-somatic factors without. It was definitely *not* trans-sub-
ject/object, but still somewhat pre-subject/object. It was therefore a time
of danger, a time of taboo, a time of superstition. The self system had not
fully separated itself from the subconscious sphere, but remained magically embedded in it, and every time consciousness tried to rise up and disengage itself from its entrapment, the magical world merely sucked it back
in. The magical structure itself must have been, in many ways, quite terrifying.

That said, is it possible that the *most advanced* individuals of this period
might—just might—have been awakened enough to actually "plug in" to
true *psychic* capacities, capacities said by the perennial philosophy to exist
at level 5?[64, 436] In the midst of all that emotional magic, were any *actual*
psychic feats performed?

There is, of course, no way of knowing. ESP, for example, does not
leave fossil remains for all to see. But before we dismiss this possibility altogether, let us at least listen to one of the most rational and sober-minded
psychologists of the West—Sigmund Freud. It is not generally realized that
Freud had a profound interest in such "psychic" events as telepathy. In
fact, he stated quite plainly in a letter to Carrington that if he had his life
to live over, he would devote it to psychic research.[401]

Basically, Freud stated his position on psychic telepathy very simply:
"By inserting the unconscious between the physical and what has been
regarded as the mental, psychoanalysis has prepared the way for the acceptance of such processes as telepathy."[62] This has led some of Freud's
followers to suggest that in some levels of the "unconscious we find not
fantasies, but telepathy."[62] Freud himself devoted several papers to the
possible relationships between psychoanalysis, dreams, telepathy, and psychic readings. "He suggested," as Ullman summarizes it, "that information
is picked up via thought transference [telepathy] from the unconscious of
the person seeking the reading."[401] The unconscious for Freud, of course,
was most readily displayed in pre-verbal dreams—in the primary process,

that is. And right there his thoughts start to go wrong, because he wants to explain psychic in terms of magic.

Beyond those simple suggestions, therefore, Freud's thoughts on the matter are not of much theoretical use, despite the wringing they have been given by Eisenbud, Ehrenwald, Fodor, et al.,[104, 401] and simply because he confused magic (level 2) and psychic (level 5). Thus, he had no firm theoretical foundation to differentiate the true from the hallucinatory, the advanced from the primitive, the real from the hopeless (and neither do his psychic followers, who have been completely sidetracked by Freud's initial confusion). All I want to emphasize here is that even Freud—that archetypal rationalist, ultraconservative and sober in the matters of "transcendence"—was honest and open-minded enough to acknowledge that not all psychic phenomena were mere rubbish, which was a truly heroic act of intellectual fortitude, rather like John Locke acknowledging that not all mental knowledge is first sensory.

Naturally, anthropologists have been rather reluctant to approach the primitive psyche with the view that the psychic level (5) actually, though *rarely,* exists. Nonetheless, those few who have done so seem rather impressed. That great psychoanalytic anthropologist Weston La Barre "has attributed the ability to handle snakes among members of Appalachian cults as being some form of PK [psychokinesis] and has also hypothesized that psi may play a role in the religious ceremonies of American Indians."[403] Dr. Van de Castle, professor of clinical psychology at Virginia Medical School, states, "Perhaps indicative of a new stance among anthropologists is the position taken by Ralph Linton, who took some considerable care to distinguish between psi [5] and delusional phenomena [2]. In a similar vein, Long . . . cautioned that it is important for the anthropologist to distinguish between the effects of suggestion . . . and psychic energy when attempting to understand 'faith-healing.' "[403]

All the evidence on psi is not yet in; experiments in general have been positive but not absolutely conclusive. Nonetheless, lack of evidence is not evidence of lack; and in these cases one simply has to weigh the data gathered to date and consider the arguments of both sides. I personally find it most persuasive that the greatest psychologists—of whom, by their very profession, we would expect a special sobriety—have quite explicitly come down in favor of the existence of some form of paranormal phenomenon. From Freud to Jung to William James, the word has been that "the authenticity of this phenomenon can no longer be disputed today" (Jung).

Finally, then, I believe we must bow to the work of M. Eliade, who—with the possible exception of Lévi-Strauss—is the greatest living authority on primitive mentality and culture: "We now touch upon a problem of the greatest importance . . . that is, the question of the *reality* of the extrasensory capacities and paranormal powers ascribed to the shamans and medicine men. Although research into this question is still in its beginning, a fairly large number of ethnographic documents has already put the authenticity of such phenomena beyond doubt."[117]

Thus, we can reach a few tentative conclusions: (1) During this period, consciousness *on the average* had fully reached level 2: that of the magical-typhon, with self and proto-mind undifferentiated from the body, and the body-typhon itself magically intertwined with the naturic world. (2) On the other hand, a few—a very few—of the truly advanced shamans and medicine men had personally evolved far enough to have access to true psychic capacities, or level 5 (a point to which we will return in Chapter 4). Thus, already, we see the importance of differentiating between *average-mode* consciousness and *most advanced* consciousness, for, as early as typhonic times, certain exceptionally evolved individuals had already moved quite beyond the average mode. Confusing these two modes— in this case, confusing magic and psychic—has had the most regrettable consequences for the science of man at large.

But to return to the average-mode consciousness of the typhonic level: It is quite fascinating to look at the corresponding stage in today's infant development, the similar stage where the self is more or less differentiated from the environment, but remains a body-ego. Brown, in a poetic but otherwise accurate summary of the psychological data of this stage, puts it thus:

> The "postural model" of the body consists of "lines of energy," "Psychic streams," Freud's "libidinal cathexes," which are, like electricity, action at a distance; flux, influx, reflux; connecting . . . one body with other bodies. "The space in and around the postural model is not the space of physics. The body-image incorporates objects or spreads itself in space." "In an individual's own postural image many postural images of others are melted together." "We could describe the relation between the body-images of different persons under the metaphor of a magnetic field with stream-lines going in all directions." A Magnetic field, of action at a distance; or a magical field; "magic action is an action which influences the body-image irrespective of the actual distance in space."[62]

Brown is summarizing the thoughts not only of Schilder, the authority on body-image, but also the relevant thoughts of Freud, Isaacs, Klein, and Fenichel. Somehow, it all points to this structure as being "a proto-mental system in which physical and mental activity is undifferentiated," or "a kind of body-thinking."[62]

The body (level 2) differentiated from the naturic environment (level 1), but the mind (level 3/4) not yet developed or differentiated from the body—there is the bodyself, the typhon. The magical-typhon. When men and women emerged from the uroboros, they emerged as magicians.

3 The Twilight Dawn of Death

We have seen that the magical-typhonic beings lived in a dreamlike world of animistic connections—interfused with body, cosmos, and nature. The dawn world of mankind was the world of the dream. . . .

But dreams are not always peaceful, blissful, or even enjoyable—for there are also nightmares. Because even while dreaming, or while "awake" under the same magical primary process, there is still a definite boundary between self and not-self, between subject and object, in here vs. out there. And wherever there is boundary, there is fear.

What has been so very difficult for Western psychology to grasp is that there are at least two major but quite different forms of fear and anxiety. One form is pathological or neurotic terror: any type of anxiety that can legitimately be traced to "mental illness," pathological defense mechanisms, or neurotic guilt. But the other form of terror is not due to a mental aberration or a neurotic illness—it is a basic, unavoidable, inescapable terror inherent in the separate-self sense. Man's prior Nature is Spirit, the ultimate Whole, but until he discovers that Wholeness, he remains an alienated fragment, a separate self, and that separate self necessarily is faced with an awareness of death and the terror of death. It is not a circumstantial terror. It is *existential,* given, inherent, and it remains so until Spirit is resurrected and the self is *one* with *all* possible others.

The Upanishads put this fact beautifully: "Wherever there is other, there is fear."[208] That has been perfectly obvious to the East for at least three thousand years. But fortunately, the existential psychologists in the West have finally—after decades of orthodox psychiatry's trying to reduce existential fear to neurotic guilt—exposed and explained this essential point with such clarity that it can no longer be overlooked. "The essential, basic arch-anxiety (primal anxiety)," wrote the great existential psychologist Médard Boss, is *"innate to all isolated, individual forms of human existence. In the basic anxiety human existence is afraid of as well as anxious about* its 'being-in-the-world.' "[54] And, Boss adds, only if we understand that can we "conceive of the seemingly paradoxical phenomenon that people who are afraid of living are also especially frightened of death." The point is that the apprehension of this existential terror is not illusion but reality, and suffering its impact is not neurotic but accurate. In fact, the *failure* to apprehend this terror is only achieved by a strenuous denial of reality, an illusory and magical façade thrown over the innermost terror of simply existing.[340] Most of us, of course, are not directly aware of this primal fear underlying our workaday egos, and Zilboorg knows why:

> If this fear were as constantly conscious, we should not be able to function normally. It must be properly repressed to keep us living with any modicum of comfort. . . . We may take it for granted that the fear of death is always present in our mental functioning. . . . No one is free of the fear of death.[443]

Once the typhon emerged from its archaic-uroboric slumber, it was faced, necessarily, with existential dread. To be sure, the uroboric self undoubtedly experienced some low-grade forms of death terror, for it *was* something of a "self," at least on an instinctual and apelike level.[6] But the situation was immensely compounded in the case of the typhon, for the increasing keenness of consciousness brought an increasing awareness of vulnerability. Thus, once the typhon began to emerge from its embeddedness in nature, it was increasingly faced with existential fear, with dread, with death. Historically, there seems to be little doubt about this, for "the Neanderthal [early typhonic] graves and bear sanctuaries, our earliest certain evidences of religious ritual, point to an attempt to cope with the imprint of death."[69] And thus our defining formula for this period: when the typhon emerged from the uroboros, he emerged with the imprint of death.

Now once this death imprint awakens, there are two, and only two, major things that can be done with it. Men and women, that is, have two choices in the face of Death and Thanatos: they can deny and repress it, or they can transcend it in the superconscious All. As long as one holds on to the separate self sense, one must repress death and its terror. In order to transcend the death terror, one must transcend the self. That is, there is *nothing* the separate self can *do* to *actually* get rid of death terror, since the separate self *is* that death terror—they come into existence together and they only disappear together.[240] The only thing the separate self can do with death is deny it, repress it, dilute it.[25] Only in the superconscious All, in actual transcendence, is the death terror uprooted, because the separate self is uprooted as well. But until that time, "*consciousness of death* is the primary repression, not sexuality."[25]

Now the denial of death is part of the Atman project—it is, as we said, the negative side of the attempt to regain Atman consciousness. Once *any* mode of self emerges out of the ground unconscious, it is faced with two major drives: the perpetuation of the particular form of its own illusory existence (Eros) and the avoidance of all that threatens its own particular dissolution (Thanatos). This is true from the uroboros to the typhon to the ego to the soul (although, of course, the specifics vary drastically). On the positive side (and that doesn't mean "on the good side"; it simply means the Eros side), it searches out all sorts of substitute gratifications that *pretend* to fulfill its desire for Unity, for Wholeness, for infinity and eternity and cosmocentricity. On the negative side (the Thanatos side), it screens out or represses anything that threatens death, dissolution, transcendence, extinction. And we say that both of these are forms of the Atman project because they are both driven by a *correct* intuition that one's deepest Nature is indeed infinite and eternal, but an intuition that is corrupted by its application to the separate self, which is absolutely finite and mortal.

Thus Eros—the desire to have more life, the desire to have everything, to be cosmocentric—is driven by the correct intuition that in reality one *is* the All. But, when applied to the separate self, the intuition that one *is* the All is perverted into the desire to individually *possess* the All. In place of being everything, one merely desires to have everything. That is the basis of all substitute gratifications, and that is the insatiable thirst lying in the heart of all separate selves. That is the positive side of the Atman project, and it is quenched only by Atman.

In the same way, the denial of death is based upon the correct intuition that one's prior Nature *is* indeed timeless, eternal, immortal beyond history. But when that intuition of timelessness is applied to the separate self, it is perverted into the desire to simply live forever, to go on going on, to avoid death everlastingly. Instead of being timeless in transcendence, one merely substitutes the desire to live forever. In place of eternity one substitutes death denial and immortality strivings. And that is the negative side of the Atman project—the rancid immortality of death denial.

"The great scientific simplification of psychoanalysis," wrote Becker, "is the concept that the whole of early experience is an attempt by the child to deny the anxiety of his emergence."[25] And in just the same way, the great anthropological simplification is the concept that the whole of mankind's history, early and late, is an attempt to deny the anxiety of its emergence out of the archaic-uroboric slumber in Eden—an absolutely necessary and desirable emergence, but one fraught with fear and trembling, and shadowed by the skull of death.

TIME AS DEATH DENIAL

Now there are many different ways to deny and repress death, and many different results of such efforts—most of which we will encounter in this volume. But one of the most significant involves *time* (another involves *culture,* as we will soon see). For a moment, then, I would like to linger on this connection between death and time.

Sensitive philosophers have always been intrigued by the covenant between death and time. Hegel said that history is what man does with death.[381] Brown said time was created by the repression of death.[61] These are rather difficult notions, but I think the matter can be put simply. The ultimate Whole, or Atman-Spirit, is timeless—there is no past, no future, no time. Or, if one prefers, all time is now, in the eternal Present spoken of by the mystics (e.g., Gebser's Gegenwart).

In ultimate reality, then, there is no time, no past, and no future. In particular, note that eternity, we might say, is a condition of no-future. But death is also a condition of no-future. Obviously, something which dies, which ceases to exist, has no future. Thus, when man *denies death,* he refuses to live without a future, and therefore he refuses to live timelessly. In denying death he denies the condition of no-future, and thus he denies eternity.[434] In short, to deny death is to demand a future—in order to avoid death, man pictures his separate self going forward in time. He wants to meet himself tomorrow. In fact, he projects himself through tomorrow's time in order to repress death, and thus, as Brown put it, "the war against death [the repression of death] takes the form of a preoccupation with the past and future. . . . Life not repressed is not in historical time . . . only repressed life is in time, and unrepressed life would be timeless or in eternity."[61]

But time is not merely a denial of eternity—man would never adopt it were it only that. Time is a substitute for eternity, for it allows one the illusion of continuing and continuing and continuing. . . . It is a form of the Atman project, of substituting a pretend everlastingness for the reality of the timeless Present. And as long as there is a separate self, it *needs* time—and needs it as a promise that the skull will not grin in today.

But, as we will see in this volume, there are different structures, or different types, of time that exfoliate from the Timeless. In ascending, expanding, and evolving order, corresponding with the levels of the Great Chain, we have: (1) the pre-temporal ignorance of the pleroma-uroboros; (2) the simple, passing present of the typhon (the uroboros lives in the simple present, just as the typhon does, but the uroboros is largely ignorant of itself as a separate individual *living in* the discrete present, and thus, in that sense, the uroboros is pre-temporal); (3) the cyclic, seasonal time of mythic-membership; (4) the linear and historical time of the mental-ego; (5-6) the archetypal, aeonic, or transcendent time of the soul; (7-8) the perfectly Timeless eternity of Spirit-Atman.

These different forms of time seem, in the main, to arise with correlative modes of self or structures of consciousness.[436] Each successively higher mode of self represents an expansion and extension of consciousness, and thus each higher mode of self can grasp increasingly extended temporal modes, from the simple present to historical time to archetypal, aeonic time, until time itself vanishes back into its Source, and disappears as a necessary but intermediate ladder of transcendence.

At the same time, however, as new forms of separate self are created, they are necessarily exposed to new forms of death and death terror. And as new forms of death terror emerge, new forms of death denial are necessary, and the projection of the self sense through the new and correlative temporal sequence is a major form of that death repression. To put it less accurately but more succinctly: the more death threatens, the more extended a time series is needed to deny it. Time becomes a ticket to immortality.

On the simplest uroboric level, this death denial is so primitive it hardly deserves the name—nonetheless, it does show up as the simple drive for food, or material exchange to perpetuate the organism. At this level, death denial (like its parent, the Atman project) is largely instinctual and subconscious, and although this alimentary drive does indeed exist *in* the simple present, it is not fully aware *of* the simple present—its subjective mood, as we said, was not clear and evident, and so it was, in that sense, a pre-temporal mood, a "pre-temporal time," the time of the Dawn. But the point is that even in this simple biological impulse to preservation via food, or the eating and assimilation of nature (level 1), we find the subconscious impact of non-being. As Becker put it, there is thus "the ever-present fear of death in the *normal biological functioning of our instinct of self-preservation.*"[25] That is fairly straightforward and obvious.

But that lowest level of pre-temporal and subconscious instinct does not particularly interest us, because it is "strong enough" to drive only food assimilation, not psyche and culture. Time exists to deny death; the uro-

boros denies death via food—no-food is its death, and so no-food energizes
its time. Thus, once the uroboros obtains food, time ceases to exist for it.
A full stomach does not recognize tomorrow. To the uroboros, a full stomach is immortality—there is the lowest, or one of the lowest, forms of the
Atman project. This simple biological self-preservation of food exchange
can serve no higher function, demand no higher time, create no existential
terror. Death at that level is not really consciously apprehended—and so
neither is time. The whole sphere is subconscious, "pre-temporal time,"
"pre-mortal death."

Put it this way: animals do indeed instinctively drive toward self-preservation if immediately threatened or presently hungry, but man made that
whole "instinct," and his self, *conscious* and *precarious,* and there is the
great difference! But it is even more than that—it wasn't just that man became conscious of the lower instincts, but that man contained entirely
different and higher instincts, and this changed altogether the meaning of
"self-preservation." For what one means by "self-preservation" depends
first of all on what one means by "self," and since there are different levels
of self, there are different levels and different types of self-preservation
and death denial. And it is to these higher forms, beyond food and biological self-preservation, that we must look for real existential death and thus
real existential time.

So, while fully acknowledging that the uroboros has its alimentary death
denial or Atman project, its material self-preservation via food, we also realize this was carried out largely instinctively and subconsciously, in that
world of "pre-mortal death" and "pre-temporal time" that governs lower
life and matter.

By the time of the typhon, however, the new and higher individualized
self faced a new and higher apprehension of death, and thus needed new
and higher death denials—one of which was the conscious engagement and
promise of *time.* The mode of time at this level was still the basic passing
present, but it was no longer lived subconsciously. It was no longer
sufficient to flow with whatever the present brought, ignorantly rejoicing in
the immortality of food and swaying naïvely with the lilies of the field. The
new self had to *preserve* the present, to consciously *carry it* forward to the
next present, and the next, and the next, as a promise that death would not
touch it now. This was self-preservation, indeed, but it was no longer
merely of food but of a self sense, an image-self, an individual body-being.
Death denial no longer involved the need to feel food, but the need to feel
the self sense, now and now and now again.

Thus, the *constant effort* to preserve the typhonic self sense showed up
in a *constant time demand,* a demand that the present move perpetually to
its successor, not randomly and subconsciously as before, but carried and
coddled by the new self sense. The typhon was not just living *in* the simple
present, like his ancestors, he was now aware *of* the simple present and its

needs. Thus, no longer simple eating, but the Great Hunt! No longer the lilies of the field, but the labor of temporal preservation! And why else but a denial of death? "Such constant expenditure of psychological energy on the business of preserving life would be impossible," Zilboorg points out, "if the fear of death were not as constant. The very term 'self-preservation' implies an effort against some form of disintegration [Thanatos]; the affective aspect of this is fear, fear of death." Also, says Zilboorg, the greater portion of this fear of death "must be properly repressed," and this "means also to maintain a constant psychological effort to keep the lid on and inwardly never relax our watchfulness."[443] I am simply adding (as a way to bring together the important philosophical ideas on death, death denial, and time) that this *constant effort* of death denial, at each level of the Great Chain, shows up as the *constant time* of that level (whatever form it may take)—and this occurs until self, death, and time all vanish into the Radiant Source of the entire Chain itself.

During this early and still rather primitive typhonic period, the simple moment-to-moment preservation of the self sense was sufficient to repress death: time, although now consciously engaged, was still merely the passing present. And by and large, the primitive hunters and gatherers of typhonic prehistory, who constituted the earliest societies of small groups of twenty or thirty people, lived pretty much moment to moment, or at most, day to day.[426] That is, of course, a great simplification, but the point is that the new self-sense preservation involved a time preservation still centered more on the immediate present and its immediate future, not on extended historical sequences.[215] The typhon was worried about the future of the present, not the future of the future. Thus there was no real ability or need to farm, to harvest, to extensively plan, to cultivate for next year, because for all practical purposes next year didn't exist. Death for the typhonic hunter was in the present, not in some future destiny, and thus a consciously *continuing* present sufficed to avoid death. No more time was needed at this stage; no more time was understood. For a typhonic hunter, immortality consisted in living until tomorrow.

This is why, for primitive typhonic beings, "all death is a consequence of [present] violence and is generally ascribed not to the natural destiny of temporal beings but to magic."[69] That is, death is an abrupt, present, and magical occurrence, which might or might not happen *now*—it is not something that occurs in a distant future. Extended time does not yet pervasively enter the picture.

To summarize: With the typhonic emergence of the first "focused" self, there arose as well the first true imprint of death. And thus the first actual or conscious mode of time was likewise engaged, and engaged (in part) as a way to deny the imprint of death by promising that the present would not end, promising immortality by promising another present, moment to moment to moment. Without any doubt whatsoever, men and women were well on their way through the gates of Eden and into the world of mortality, and they took time with them as a first defense.

THE PROP OF CULTURE

We have suggested that typhonic men and women were already too awakened as separate selves to secure their immortality by merely eating or biologically surviving, as was the case in uroboric times (or, that is, in all lower life forms). On the one hand, consciousness was simply growing and expanding—the Atman project does, after all, drive toward Atman and superconsciousness. On the other hand, more substitutes for the increasing intuition of Atman-lack, and more defenses against the increasing comprehension of vulnerability and mortality, had to be fashioned. This "complexification of consciousness," to use Teilhard de Chardin's phrase, eventually led, in a way never quite possible for the uroboros, to *cultural activities*. And the simple aim of culture was to serve the two arms of the Atman project: the manufacture of more *mana* (Eros) and less taboo (Thanatos). The same two-armed structure was, of course, also true for the creation of time, and so we might say that once time was created *by* an expansion of consciousness and *as* a new death denial, culture was what was done with that new time. They are perfectly interrelated (which is precisely why "culture is what man does with death"); but we now look more specifically to the details of culture itself, especially in its drive to manufacture mana and avoid taboo.

We haven't far to look, because magic was the means to both. Magic rites, magic rituals, magic dances, magic hunting, magic death denials. During that early period society was, beyond biological needs, a cultural activity of magical compensations—a magical Atman project writ large.

Especially magical death denials, the negative side of the Atman project. "Among the Australian Aranda," Campbell tells us, "the village where a death has occurred is burned to the ground, the person's name is never mentioned . . . and a dance and wild commotion of shouting, ground-beating, and mutual mayhem is enacted by the relatives on the grave itself."[69] All of this, of course, is designed to magically ward off both the death of those still living and the return of the deceased spirit, which was usually feared as a death dealer and mischief maker itself.

For the day-to-day world of the all-necessary hunt, which was the central form of the new immortality project, it has been suggested that "the daily task and serious concern of dealing death, spilling blood, in order to live, created a situation of anxiety that had to be resolved, on the one hand

Fig. 11. Cro-Magnon man. This is what we call "high typhonic," to differentiate it from its cruder predecessor, the Neanderthal or low typhonic. Neanderthal lived around 50,000 to 200,000 years ago; Cro-Magnon, around 10,000 to 50,000 years ago. For simplicity's sake, we refer to this whole period as typhonic, but most of our comments in this volume refer to the high-typhonic man. The low-typhonic man was almost entirely pre-verbal, possessing only images (primary process) and the crudest of paleo-symbols. High-typhonic man was still largely pre-verbal, but in addition to images he probably possessed more complex paleosymbols, modifiers, commands, and some nouns. But because both were predominantly pre-verbal and body-based, we refer to the whole structure as typhonic.

by a system of defenses against revenge, and on the other by a diminish-
ment of the mystique of death."[69] For, as Frobenius points out, "it takes a
powerful magic to spill blood and not be overtaken by the blood-
revenge."[153] Thus we come to the single and simple formula of the negative side of the Atman project for primitive typhonic humans: in Campbell's words, *Where there is magic there is no death.*"[69] And power, in
primitive typhons, simply went to the man with the most magic, the most
ability to both ward off death and deal out death. He held the strings of
the Atman project—and thus the key to both individual psyches and the
cultural project at large.

> Skilled hunters and warriors could actually display these special
> powers in the form of trophies and ornamental badges of merit. The
> scalps of the slain enemies and the teeth, feathers, and other orna-
> ments were often loaded with magical power and served as protec-
> tion. If a man wore a large number of trophies and badges showing
> how much power he had and how great were his exploits, he became
> a great mana figure who literally struck terror into the hearts of his en-
> emies.[26]

In short, "magic is employed both to defend against [death] and to deliver
it to others."[69]

That for the "negative" or Thanatos side of the Atman project. On the
Eros (or "positive") side, we expect to find the search for surplus life,
extra Eros, more self-survival and enrichment. Take, for instance, the following summary of the works of the great anthropologist Hocart, who
"saw the universal ambition as the achievement of prosperity—the good
life [which is simply *more* Eros]. To satisfy this craving, only man could
create that most powerful concept which has both made him heroic and
brought him utter tragedy—the invention and practice of ritual, which is
first and foremost a technique for promoting the good life and averting
evil. Let us not rush over these words: ritual is *a technique for giving
life.*"[26] I don't know how our point could be put any plainer!

Even at this early stage in prehistory, men and women were consciously
driven to generate Eros, to help or guarantee the perpetuation of the separate self. Ritual was a booster shot to a newly emerging self which was
aware that other selves die; a technique to go on going on in the finite
realm while attempting to increase the powers of that realm. As but one
example: "In the famous totemic increase ceremonies of the Australian
aborigines, primitive men imagined that by going through the motions of
imitating animal births they could increase the number of kangaroos,
emus, grubs in the world. The technique was so precise that the aborigine
could even prescribe the color of the kangaroos—brown, say, rather than
gray."[26]

The point appears to be quite straightforward: "By means of the techniques of ritual men imagined that they took firm control of the material world, and at the same time transcended that world by fashioning their own invisible [Atman] projects which made them [appear to be] supernatural, raised them over and above material decay and death." In fact, says Becker, primitive man "set up the whole cosmos in a way that allowed him to expand symbolically and to enjoy the highest . . . pleasure: he could blow the self-feeling of a mere organismic creature all the way up to the stars."[26] And there is a perfect, but perfect, description of the positive side of the Atman project, the attempt to be cosmocentric, central to existence, omnipotent. With ritual, as the first technique for the Atman project, man succeeded in "blowing himself up as the center of concern of the universe."[26] In his prior Nature he *is* the universe, but in his separate self he merely desires and pretends to be cosmocentric, and ritual was one of the first techniques for just that project—that immortal Atman project.

Gazing back into that dim prehistory—seeing perhaps to the very edge of our vision, beyond which all goes blurry—we see that at the very emergence of men and women out of uroboric Eden, *cultural* activities were necessary to take up the slack in the ever-increasing Atman project. Food no longer constituted immortality; simple biology no longer sufficed. *Time* was needed; *culture* was needed. The new and higher self expressed new and higher needs, faced new and higher forms of death, and thus demanded new and higher death denials and self-preservations. Individuals gathered together in increasingly larger groups to share these expanding Atman projects and extend consciousness through inter-subjective cultural activities, very rudimentary to be sure, but trans-biological nonetheless. The new time, self, and culture were all simultaneously the products of a higher and expanding consciousness, a system of elaborate substitute gratifications, an expression of higher life, and a fetishistic denial of higher death. Magical rites and ritual, magical death denials and time preservation, cultural possessions and charms and paraphernalia: these new substitute objects, like the new substitute subject they supported, were both compensations for Atman-lack *and* a faltering drive toward that Atman. Mankind had taken a decisive step up the ladder of the Great Chain of Being—with all the new potentials, and all the new perils, therein.

Not yet, however, were men and women forced into working out their Atman projects *on each other*—not, at least, to any great extent. For one of the horrifying things we will soon discover is that as people became substitute objects, those people became *victims*. This was not yet the case in typhonic times. It is fairly agreed that in typhonic hunting societies, there existed neither large-scale inequality, rank, war, exploitation, nor privately hoarded property. "Labor is divided on the basis of age and sex. Rights to the band's territory are collective. Society is based on kinship ties and is egalitarian. Trade consists of reciprocity in goods, favors, and labor. There is no warfare as we know it."[253] Even Becker, intent on disclosing man's dastardliness from day one, found that "in the most egalitarian primitive societies . . . there is no distinction of rank, little or no authority of one individual over another. Possessions are simple and there is no real difference in wealth; property is distributed equally."[26] These things are, of course, always relative, but this period of mankind's prehistory was probably the closest thing to a free and non-oppressive society that has ever existed—or might ever exist.* For the more men and women emerged on that *necessary* climb from the subconscious, the more *difficult* their substitute gratifications became to achieve and sustain, so that they were soon forced into playing out their Atman projects on their fellow human beings. And as people became substitute objects, those people became victims of one sort of cruelty or another. The rage at being only a finite creature was soon turned into rage at other finite creatures, so that today the world is split into several large and heavily armed camps of finite creatures, glutted in overkill, bent upon mutual destruction.

There is only one solution to this tangled mess of inter-clobbering Atman projects, and that is to open the soul to that which it ultimately desires—Atman consciousness itself. I am not, however, so naïve as to believe that this will ever happen on any sort of large scale (not for thousands of years, if ever). Thus, as we will see, the next-best thing is to arrange individual Atman projects so that they overlap in mutually supportive ways—what Ruth Benedict called synergy. At the same time, there have been *individuals* who have trodden the path to Atman; individuals who, tiring of their substitute gratifications and substitute worlds, relinquished their grasping in time and stood open to the ultimate Whole. These were, and are, the great Heroes of mankind, the men and women who saw more than can be grasped by the hands, who fell out of the cave of shadows and were drenched in the light of Being. Rare as those souls have been, they represent nothing less than the destiny of consciousness, the resurrection of the superconscious All.

The question, then, is whether or not, in the dim past of the magical-typhons, men and women had evolved far enough out of the subconscious so that some of them could return to the superconscious. Had they moved out of earth's Eden enough to consciously desire a discovery of spirit's Heaven? If so, did they make it? If so, what did they see?

---

* I do not mean to idealize these societies per se; they were relatively benign, not because they were consciously virtuous or highly developed morally, but rather because they were relatively simple and unsophisticated, in *both* good and evil.

4 Voyage into the Superconscious

We are now on the trail of the earliest societies of which we have any substantial records, and peering back into that early state, there is one aspect that stands out quite above all the others. It was not a cultural activity, or a particular ritual, or a peculiar type of societal organization. It was an individual, a very extraordinary individual. It was the shaman.

Now the shaman traditionally has been viewed, by orthodox psychiatry and anthropology, not as a super-man but as a super-psychotic. "The shaman," explains Dr. Van de Castle, "is currently perceived as psychotic, because he keeps insisting that he is able to demonstrate phenomena that the anthropologist 'knows' are nonexistent. The shaman must therefore be delusional, for there is no correspondence possible between his perceptions and beliefs and the way the 'real world' of the anthropologist operates."[403] None of this is to say, however, that *all* shamans are awakened to the Transcendent and that no shamans are psychotic or at least superb quacks. Many (I would say most) shamans, clearly, were quite delusional or at least fraudulent, and in their pitiful attempts to exploit others into believing that they were quite exceptional and heroic souls, we see the saddest side of the Atman project at work—what we might call the "tall tales" side.

But the pressing question is, were *any* shamans truly awakened to some of the higher states of consciousness? And as we search among the black crows for one white crow to support our point, we actually run into a respectable flock of them. In fact, it can now be said with absolute assurance that the shaman—the true shaman—was the first great voyager into realms of the superconscious. And we must realize how truly extraordinary that was—for hundreds of thousands of years ago, this soul saw, he *saw,* not only the depths of his own being but also the destiny and fate of consciousness. And we can only stand in deepest awe and admiration for those isolated souls, perched on the mountaintops far away from their fellows, who were quiet enough in their own hearts to hear the call of the Beyond. The Eskimo shaman Najagneq told the anthropologist Rasmussen that there was a supreme Self which is "the inhabitant or soul (*inua*) of the universe. All we know is that it has a gentle voice like a woman, a voice 'so fine and gentle that even children cannot become afraid.' What it says is: *sila ersinarsinivdluge,* 'be not afraid of the universe.' "

No wonder the classic symbol of the shaman was a bird: to fly beyond the confines of earthbound mortality and death terror and soar the skies of the All.

In the great paleolithic cavern of Lascaux, in southern France, there is the picture of a shaman dressed in bird costume, lying prostrate in a trance and with the figure of a bird perched on his shaman staff beside him. The shamans of Siberia wear bird costumes to this day, and many are believed to have been conceived by their mothers from the descent of a bird. In India, a term of honor addressed to the master yogi is Paramahamsa: paramount or supreme (*parama*) wild gander (*hamsa*). In China the so-called "mountain men" or "immortals" (*hsien*) are pictured as feathered, like birds, or as floating through the air on soaring beasts. The German legend of Lohengrin, the swan knight, and the tales, told wherever shamanism has flourished, of the swan maiden, are likewise evidence of the force of the image of the bird as an adequate sign of spiritual power. And shall we not think, also, of the dove that descended upon Mary, and the swan that begot Helen of Troy? In many lands the soul has been pictured as a bird, and birds commonly are spiritual messengers. Angels are but modified birds.[69]

"But," Campbell reminds us, "the bird of the shaman is one of particular character and power, endowing him with an ability to fly in trance beyond the bounds of life, and yet return."

It is the nature of this shamanistic trance that has so confused, or at least puzzled, orthodox psychologists and anthropologists. But Mircea Eliade, whose *Shamanism* is the definitive study of the subject, gives us a

painless introduction to the nature of the shamanistic trance: "The shaman remains the dominating figure; for through this whole region in which
ecstatic experience is considered the religious experience par excellence,
the shaman, and he alone, is the great master of ecstasy. A first definition
of this complex phenomenon, and perhaps the least hazardous, will be:
shamanism = technique of ecstasy." Campbell explains it thus:

> As Eliade has pointed out, the shaman's power rests in his ability
> to throw himself into a trance at will. Nor is he the victim of his
> trance: he commands it, as a bird the air in its flight. The magic of his
> drum carries him away on the wings of its rhythm, the wings of spirit-
> ual transport. . . . And it is while he is in his trance of rapture that
> he performs his miraculous deeds [which involve] that background
> . . . reality which for most others is crusted over.[69]

It is in just these "trances of ecstasy" that the vision—the vision which lifts
the shaman out of the ordinary and marks him or her as extraordinary—is
given. And it is the nature of just this ecstatic vision that concerns us.

EXISTENTIAL CRISIS AND THE LION'S ROAR

There is a difference between *translation* and *transformation:*

Once an individual *transforms* to a particular level of consciousness,
then he continues to *translate* both his self and his world according to the
basic structures of that level.[436] Once mankind had transformed out of the
uroboric to the typhonic, it then translated its world, internal and external,
according to the major cognitive structures characteristic of that level.
Transformation, in other words, is a type of vertical shift or even mutation
in consciousness structures, while translation is a simple horizontal movement within a given structure.

It comes to the same thing to say that translation is a change in surface
structures, and transformation is a change in deep structures. Recall our
simple analogy of an eight-story building: each of its floors is a deep structure, while all the particular objects (rooms, furniture, offices, etc.) on
each floor are its surface structures. Translation, then, is moving around
on one floor; transformation is moving to a different floor altogether.*

---

* Transformation is, precisely, what Gebser means by "mutation in consciousness"
and what Hegel means by *aufheben* and, approximately, what Piaget means by ac-
commodation and Polanyi by emergence.

Translation has one major, basic, and fundamental purpose: to maintain the given level (or "floor") of the self system, to hold it stable, equilibrated, constant. That can be put in several ways: translation acts to secure the specific substitute gratifications of that level,[29] to reduce uncertainty,[24] reduce tension,[147] maintain constancy amid flux and change,[128] support and extend Eros.[25] Translation, in short, aims at fortifying a particular floor in the building of consciousness, not in changing floors altogether.

One of the best ways of describing translation, therefore, is to say that it seeks to preserve the life of the separate-self sense and hold it against those forces, internal or external, sacred or profane, higher or lower, which threaten its present form of existence. That is, *the aim of translation is to ensure that Eros outweighs Thanatos,* that Life wins out over Death, that the boundaries of the self do not collapse in the face of the Void. Translation succeeds, so to speak, as long as the death of its present level or floor is not imminent, and its job is precisely to deny the death of that given level.

However, should Thanatos exceed Eros, then the present form of translation tends to fail and even break down. One of the many forms of this process is the so-called nervous breakdown. Certain pressures, stresses, and disintegrating strains—Thanatos, in general—accumulate to the point that they outweigh the strength, the vitality, and the life—Eros, in general—of the self system. At that point, translation tends to fail miserably—thought processes become disoriented, affective elements over- or underfire, and "breakdown" or regression to a lower floor occurs. As moving around on one floor becomes impossible, changing floors altogether becomes imminent. But I must emphasize that the "breakdown" or surrender of a mode of translation and the subsequent transformation is not necessarily, not even usually, a bad thing. Growth and evolution, for instance, require transformation—the replacement of old translations by newer ones, the moving to a *higher* floor of awareness.

But in any case, the point is that *when Thanatos exceeds Eros, translation fails and transformation ensues.* As one floor "dies" (in its exclusive domination of consciousness), a different floor emerges. But transformation can go in any number of different directions. There can be *regressive* transformation back into archaic structures, the pre-personal uroboros, the subconscious sphere—a move down the Great Chain. There can be *progressive* transformations to higher and more organized structures of consciousness—as we will see later. There also can be truly transcendent transformations into realms of the superconscious—a giant leap upward to the fifth, sixth, or seventh floors (since they presently exist as potential in the ground unconscious of all beings). I have written about these transformations elsewhere;[436] all we need to remember here is that when translation fails, transformation ensues, and the transformation itself can—depending on numerous variables—be toward higher structures or lower structures, progressive or regressive.

I mention all this because it will help us understand not only the nature of the shamanistic experience, but also the nature of the evolutionary changes in history itself. For what we are actually following in our survey of human evolution is the successive failures of certain modes of translation, followed by a *transformation* to new modes of translation, and so on to the present (and, I presume, into the future). In other words, evolution is a successive shift and unfolding, via transformation, of higher-order deep structures, within which operate, via translation, higher-order surface structures.

We return to the individual in the primitive typhonic state: once he had matured, which is to say, once he had transformed out of infantile and uroboric structures and embraced the translations of the magical-typhon, then he more or less stabilized at that point. He would, that is, continue to translate his world according to the structures of the typhon (magic images, primary processes, etc.) and according to the cultural sentiments and units of meaning of the group. As long as Eros outweighed Thanatos, as long as the self sense was relatively secure in its grasping, then translation continued and equilibration reigned.

However, if Thanatos persistently and consistently outweighed Eros, due to internal or external causes, then translation failed its soothing and consoling function, crises ensued, and *transformation* resulted. And, depending upon circumstances, it could be a transformation either to a lower or to a higher structure of consciousness.

It is fascinating, then, that as early as the shamanistic hunting period, according to Joseph Campbell, two entirely different forms of major *psychological transformations* (not mere translations) were recognized: one, what we would call psychotic, but two, that known as shamanistic. Campbell is both explicit and decisive on this point:

> It has been remarked by sensitive observers that, in contrast to the life-maiming psychology of a neurosis (which is recognized in primitive societies as well as in our own, but not confused there with shamanism), the shamanistic crisis, when properly fostered, yields an adult not only of superior intelligence and refinement, but also of greater physical stamina and vitality of spirit than is normal to the members of his group.[69]

The true shamanistic experience, in other words, produces *not* a breakdown to lower states, but an actual breakthrough to higher modes of being, resulting in "greater physical stamina and vitality of spirit." As Silverman points out, "In primitive cultures in which such a unique life crisis resolution is tolerated, the abnormal experience (shamanism) is typically beneficial to the individual, cognitively and affectively; he is regarded as one with expanded consciousness." And if we return to our expert on shamanism, Mircea Eliade, the case is quite definitely clinched: The shaman "has succeeded in integrating into consciousness a considerable number of experiences that, for the profane world, are reserved for dreams, madness, and post-mortem states. The shamans and mystics of primitive societies are considered—and rightly so—to be superior beings; their magico-religious powers also find expression in an extension of their mental capacities. The shaman is the man who *knows* and *remembers,* that is, who understands the mysteries of life and death."[117]

But notice immediately that the psychotic break and the shamanistic voyage *both* involve a severe crisis, "for the overpowering mental crisis here described [in the case of a tundra shaman] is a generally recognized feature" of shamanism, and it is certainly a feature of psychotic breakdown. I am suggesting that the crisis, in both cases, is precisely a crisis in translation, engendered whenever Thanatos outweighs Eros consistently; and the severe and prolonged disruption or failure of translation *necessitates* a transformation to a different structure or level of consciousness.

However, the psychotic break is a transformation to lower, infantile, and archaic structures—it is regressive, at least in some significant ways, and therefore *the individual tends to lose access to the upper* and normal levels of consciousness. That is, in regressing from the typhonic level back into archaic levels, he loses access to the typhonic mode, and thus is socially invalidated by other typhons. But the shaman's transformation is not regressive—or, at any rate, it does not result in permanent regression. It is rather a transformation to higher modes of consciousness—as far above normal typhonic consciousness as the psychotic was beneath it. The shaman, because he *transcends* the typhon without obliterating it, *retains access* to normal typhonic awareness—he can still communicate with "normals" and could, if he wanted, pass himself off as perfectly typical, something that truly regressed psychotics cannot do. "And though the temporary unbalance precipitated by such a crisis [shamanistic] may resemble a nervous breakdown, it cannot be dismissed as such. For it is a phenomenon *sui generis;* not a pathological but a normal event for the gifted mind in these societies, when struck by and absorbing the force of what for lack of a better term we may call a hierophantic realization: the realization of 'something far more deeply interfused,' inhabiting both the round earth and one's own interior. . . . The crisis, consequently, cannot be analyzed as a rupture with society and the world. It is, on the contrary, an overpowering realization of their depth, and the rupture is rather with the comparatively trivial attitude toward both the human spirit and the world that appears to satisfy the great majority."[69]

The shaman was *transformed*—a true transformation into realms of the superconscious. "Among the Buriat, the animal or bird that protects the shaman is called *khubilgan,* meaning 'metamorphosis,' from the verb *khubilku,* 'to change oneself, to take another form.' "[69] To transform. And the transformation was quite dramatic—it entailed nothing less than the death and transcendence of the separate-self sense. Death, Thanatos, Shiva, and Sunyata—the very thing all separate selves are dedicated to resist, the very thing that translation is geared to avoid, the very thing that freezes cold the heart of mortal beings—just that is what the shaman accepts and passes through. "The same thing happens to every . . . shaman," said the Tungus shaman Semyon. "Only after his shaman ancestors have cut up his body and separated his bones can he begin to practice."[69] The acceptance and transcendence of death, an act that is also the transcendence of the separate self and the resurrection of superconsciousness—there is the shamanistic voyage, and it announced a theme that would, in later centuries and millennia, still be reverberating through the hearts of all mystics and sages. Said the shaman Nikitin, "I am to lie there like a dead man for three days and shall be cut to pieces. On the third day I shall rise again."[69]

The true shamanistic experience was nothing less than the death and transcendence of the separate self—the separate self that had just emerged out of archaic-uroboric times is here, for the first time in the history of the world, transcended. And the transcendence of that self tended to disclose—at its peak—nothing less than the original source and suchness of all souls and all worlds: the ultimate Whole, the superconscious All. "The total crisis of the future shaman," our expert tells us, "can be valuated not only as an initiatory death, but also a symbolic return to the precosmogonic chaos, to the amorphous and indescribable state that precedes any cosmogony."[117] The Source, the Suchness, the Spirit.

Thus, the basic form of the shamanistic experience is straightforward: Thanatos (death) exceeds Eros, crisis ensues (which involves the acceptance of death and Thanatos), mere translation ceases, and transformation to higher orders of consciousness results, orders that by their very nature transcend self, space, time, life, and death. "The shaman is the man . . . who understands the mysteries of life and death."

There is, however, no doubt that even true shamanistic religion is extremely crude, very unrefined, and not highly evolved (as we will see in the next section). Mankind, just emerging from its slumber in the subconscious, was yet a long way from the superconscious, and those few mighty heroes who individually braved death and transcendence saw the All as yet through a glass very darkly. But saw they did—and in that brief vision they glimpsed the destiny and fate of all souls and all history, so that "there have been depths of insight reached by the [shamanistic] mind in the solitude of the tundras that are hardly to be matched. . . ." For at its peak, at the very summit of its vision, the shamanistic experience disclosed nothing less than "that sense of an immortal inhabitant within the individual which is announced in every mystical tradition . . . which [itself] neither dies nor is born, but simply passes back and forth, as it were through a veil, appearing in bodies and departing."[69, 70]

Announced, that is, Atman.

THE END OF THE ATMAN PROJECT

We come now to the final chapter in the story of primitive, shamanistic transcendence. We have seen that all man ever basically wants is Unity or Atman consciousness, but all he ever does as a separate self is resist it (because it entails the acceptance of death and Thanatos). This desire for, yet defense against, Atman consciousness is the Atman project. Since man both wants and intuits his real and timeless Nature, but acts so as to prevent its realization, he needs and creates various *substitutes* for transcendence. These substitutes, created by the Atman project, are both subjective and objective, as well as positive (Eros) and negative (Thanatos).

This is precisely why the true shaman, who actually achieved something of a real transcendence, was released from the substitute gratifications of his non-transcending fellow hunters. We know, of course, that he was at least temporarily released from that subjective substitute called self, but he also was released from many of the objective or cultural substitutes. Finding Atman, the Atman project died down.

For instance, one of the apparently common rituals of primitive man involved literally chopping off his finger joints in sacrifice. "I give you this joint [of my finger]," ran the words of the Crow Indian ritual of prayer to the Morning Star, "give me something good in exchange." And they meant it. "During the period of my visits to the Crow," reported Professor Lowie, "I saw few old men with left hands intact."[69] What are these token sacrifices engineered to secure? Is it not now obvious?

It is obvious to Joseph Campbell, and in a few exquisite sentences, he precisely exposes the heart of this matter: "These are the maimed hands, then, of the 'honest hunters,' not the shamans; for the shamans' bodies are indestructible [transcendent] and their great offerings are of the spirit, not the flesh."[69] That is, *the shaman sacrifices his self in transcendence, not his fingers in substitute*. There precisely is the difference between Atman and Atman project; or the difference between real and substitute sacrifice; or again, the difference between esoteric and exoteric religion. But this difference goes right back to the beginning of the separate-self sense, as we imagine it should, for here—with such practices as finger-joint sacrifices and other exoteric rituals—"we are on the trail of the popular rites and myths of the earliest periods of human society of which we have record—

myths and rites of an age far greater, apparently, than that of the sacrifice of the maiden [which we will examine later], and no less great, surely, in their reach across the barriers of space."[69]

Campbell then speaks of the "deep psychological cleavage separating the tough-minded 'honest hunters' from their . . . tender-minded shamans." As we would put it, the former are dedicated to *translating* in search of substitute gratifications, whereas the latter, the tender-minded shamans, are given to actual *transformation* into the superconscious itself. Thus this transformation discloses "an intuition of depth, absolutely inaccessible to the 'tough-minded' honest hunters (whether it be dollars, guanaco pelts, or working hypotheses they are after)."[69]

The dollars, the guanaco pelts, the working hypotheses—and on to fame, fortune, power—these are the fallout from the Atman project, the positive and objective substitute gratifications which seek to present as fulfilled one's wish to be God. And on the negative or Thanatos side: since the separate self will not accept transcendence—for that involves death and *real* sacrifice—it substitutes token sacrifices, sacrifices to buy more life for the self and avoid its ultimate dissolution. And what is so fascinating is that the very earliest examples of this, apparently, are the finger-joint sacrifices —*substitute sacrifices,* bribes for the gods, "give me something good in exchange." "One's little offerings of finger-joints, pigs, sons and daughters . . . seem to have meaning in a sort of mystical barter system; and one's peccadillos, missed by the police, can be counted on to eat from within, like rats, doing the work of the law."[69]

To avoid the instantaneous death of transcendence, people kill themselves slowly and by degrees, dismembering their own Natures in order to preserve their own selves. The individual of today, just as yesterday, will dismember, alienate, and project out of his self system any aspect which either threatens death or can be used in barter against it. Professor Lowie with the primitive Crow "saw few old men with left hands intact." Today, a psychotherapist sees few people of any age "with egos intact." No difference.

Men and women cannot be whole until they rediscover that ultimate Whole—until death-and-transcendence is accepted, until the total sacrificial surrender of the separate self. Until that time, token and substitute sacrifices prevail, the little offerings of barter sacrifices, wherein ritual, whether of the hunt or of the modern office, remains, as Becker knew, "a play of life against death." And more remarkable is that this is a truth we have been able to perceive all the way back to the dawn of primitive man. . . .

"But then, perhaps, on occasion, in the precincts of the temple, dancing ground, or some sacred site, the fleeting wisp of a sense of some mystery beyond, in the face of which all of this is trivial nonsense, may be experienced and therein . . . [an] amplification of the individual's horizon of experience and depth of realization through his spiritual death and resurrection, even on the level of these primitive explorations."[69]

SHAMANISTIC TRANCE

We come now to the precise nature and content of the shamanistic trance. We said that the shamanistic voyage was indeed one of transcendence, but one that remained very low-grade, even crude, or adolescent. We said that the shamanistic vision saw into realms of the superconscious, but did so darkly. We are now in a position to be more precise.

In *The Atman Project,* I presented evidence (based on Vajrayana, Zen, Bubba Free John, etc.) strongly suggesting that "religious experience" actually consists of three broad but rather different classes, each with its own techniques, its own path, and its own characteristic visions and experiences. The lowest class is that of the Nirmanakaya (see Fig. 1), commonly known as kundalini yoga, which deals with bodily-sexual energies and their sublimation upward toward the crown-brain center, known as the sahasrara. Kundalini yoga basically covers the ascent of consciousness from its lowest point of descent (the root pleromatic chakra) up to the sixth chakra (and the beginning of the seventh or crown chakra).[439] The next class—that of the Sambhogakaya—goes further, and follows the ascent of consciousness *at* and *beyond* the sahasrara into seven (some say ten) higher realms of extremely subtle consciousness.[373] The third and highest class—the Dharmakaya—follows consciousness to its ultimate root, where man and God are transformed into each other, where the subject/object dualism is permanently dismantled, where ultimate Atman is resurrected as the perfect Life, Destiny, and Condition of every form that rises upon it.[387]†

In the first class, the emphasis is on the body and on bodily energies.[362] In the second class, the emphasis is on the subtle realm of light and audible illuminations and subtle sounds (nada).[345] In the third class, the em-

---

† Technical points: The Nirmanakaya *realm* refers specifically and technically to levels 1 through 4; but because the Nirmanakaya *path* leads through those levels *to* level 5 (and the beginning of level 6), I have, in shorthand, simply called level 5 the Nirmanakaya level, since this is its epitome and summit. Likewise, the Sambhogakaya *realm* technically refers to levels 5 and 6, but since the Sambhogakaya *path* leads from 5 *to* 6, I have called level 6 the Sambhogakaya level. This is a purely semantic choice; unfortunately, it is a choice necessitated by certain ambiguities in Eastern texts. Finally, in *The Atman Project,* level 5 was termed "low subtle" and "astral-psychic"; level 6 was termed "high subtle." Here, I simply call level 5 "psychic" and level 6 "subtle." Again, semantic only.

phasis is upon transcending all of the foregoing by uprooting the separate-self sense altogether.[337] The first class talks of trance, of bodily ecstasy, of swooning in release, and is usually accompanied by psychosomatic changes of a dramatic and overt variety (kriyas)—all of which results, at its peak, in certain psychic intuitions and powers (level 5).[419] The second class speaks of subtle light and bliss, beyond the gross sensations of the physical body, and is usually accompanied by a drastic quieting of the gross psychosomatic body and a release into the subtle realm at and beyond the sahasrara—all of which results, at its peak, in a revelation of One God, One Light, and One Life (level 6), which underlies and gives birth to all lower and manifest realms.[361] The third class speaks of no particular experiences whatsoever, but rather aims for the dissolution of the experiencer itself, the radical undercutting of the subject/object duality in any form—all of which results, at its peak, in the Supreme Identity of the soul and the One God-Light, so that both God and soul are united, and vanish into, the ultimate unity of Atman (level 7/8).[46, 63, 386]

These three classes are not three different yet equal "experiences" of the Ultimate Source, but rather successively closer approximations of that Source (the Svabhavikakaya, or Atman-Spirit).[64] They represent successively hierarchic structures of superconsciousness, levels 5 through 7, leading finally to the Origin and Condition of all three realms and classes (level 8).‡

The rest of this volume will explore and explain these three different classes and the three realms they address. The above is simply a short introduction; all I want to emphasize here is that failure to differentiate these quite different forms of religious experience and practice has led otherwise well-intentioned spiritual anthropologists to a series of garbled conclusions. Thus, it is common today to speak of the true shaman as if he represented a totally enlightened sage (level 7/8), whereas in fact he was merely the first explorer of the Nirmanakaya class of religious experience— the lowest and crudest form of valid religious experience, reflecting a conscious understanding only of the lowest levels of the superconscious realms (level 5). The shaman was not the first great mystic-sage (or Dharmakaya explorer); he did not even understand the saintly realms of the Sambhogakaya; he was simply the first master of kundalini/hatha yoga.* At the very

‡ Although levels 7 and 8 are different, the difference is a subtle one, generally beyond the scope of this volume. Thus, I will sometimes refer to them as being different levels, but more often will treat them as "one" level (level 7/8). I do this only because, in the context of this volume—devoted to general overviews—it is a truly minor point. Nonetheless, I present a brief technical explanation of these differences in Chapter 14; otherwise, see *The Atman Project*.

* And then only in a rudimentary form. I said that kundalini yoga *can* lead up to the *beginning* of level 6 (the sahasrara), but the shaman reached, on the whole, not much past level 5 (the ajna chakra).

peak of this Nirmanakaya path, one can indeed intuit Atman consciousness, although it is rare. Nonetheless, the evidence is that some shamans did surpass their own path and intuit clearly Atman consciousness (such, anyway, was Campbell's conclusion). For the rest, however, their simple trances of ecstasy served only as glimpses into the lower and psychic realms of superconsciousness.

One of the reasons that the previous chapter dwelled on the subject of telepathy is that psychic phenomena in general (psi) are traditionally said to exist only on the lowest levels of the superconscious realms—in the Nirmanakaya region (level 5), epitomized by the sixth or ajna chakra (the spot between and behind the eyebrows, the "third eye" of the psychics).[436] That the shaman, the most highly evolved individual of typhonic times, could master certain psychic feats, as well as throw himself at will into kundalini trance, all more or less hang together as Nirmanakaya events.

We can summarize all of this as follows (and in reference to Fig. 1): During typhonic times, the *average mode* of self sense was that of the magical body (level 2), which itself was not a truly psychic or telepathic body, but rather represented the simple "magical" cognition of the pranic level. This was the "primary process," which confuses whole and part as well as subject and predicate, and thus follows the simple outlines of emotional and vital (pranic) associations and contagions (and is, as far as it goes, an "accurate reflection" of that crude level). The average self sense worked out its Atman project through this magical atmosphere, using magico-ritual and fetishistic thinking to ward off death and increase mana, to present itself as immortal and to see itself as cosmocentric. This was the period of animism, pure and simple.

Certain *most advanced* individuals, however, despairing of the ordinary typhonic translations, developed and implemented the earliest-known techniques of significant *transformation* into realms of the superconscious. They represented, not average-mode consciousness, but advanced-tip consciousness. These were the true shamans. However—and to speak rather poetically—since consciousness *on the whole* had advanced no further than the typhonic level, then when the typical shaman "jumped" into the superconscious realms, the *farthest* he got was into the Nirmanakaya class—the class of ecstatic body trance, of actual psychic capacity, of ajna chakra opening, and so on (level 5). But for all of these true shamans, there was, to some degree or another, a release from the typhonic Atman project, a release from gross mortality, and a glimpse, however initial, into realms of the superconscious soul. These shamans, high and low, were the true Heroes of the typhonic times, and their individual and daring explorations in transcendence could only have had a truly evolutionary impact on consciousness at large.

THE PASSING OF MAGIC

We of today have all come up from the times of the magical-typhon. But we have not escaped them, for the conscious elements of one stage of development become the unconscious elements of the next.† Roheim, that perky psychoanalyst and anthropologist, put it just right: "What we fail to recognize is that all symptoms and defense mechanisms *are a form of magic*. . . . Primitives have magic in conscious form, whereas with us it can function only . . . if it is unconscious." Only if it is unconscious—only in dreams, only at night, only away from the light of reason and logic.

Magic—the cognitive pledge of allegiance to emotional-sexual realms—still exerts a modern influence in the form of paleological thinking and neurotic symptoms, for these are first and foremost nothing but sabotage efforts from past and lower evolutionary stages, stages not outgrown and integrated but disowned and dissociated. Magic not outgrown erupts today as neurotic symptoms and emotional obsessions: conflict-ridden obsessions which conceal a hidden wish for emotional-sexual impulses and gratifications. Those bodily or typhonic impulses, when not outgrown, transformed, and integrated, remain lodged in the recesses of an otherwise higher-order self, and there disguise themselves as painful neurotic symptoms, compulsions, obsessions.

In other words, a neurotic symptom (in the classic sense) is the result of a person on level 3 or 4 subconsciously trying to recapture the pleasures of level 2, but doing so in a way that hides or muddles what would otherwise be a conscious shock at their true regressive and primitive nature. A neurotic symptom is a subconscious allegiance to, and re-enactment of, Eden—in a properly disguised form, of course. But, as even Freud realized from the start, neurotic symptoms—such as hysteria, obsessions, compulsions, and depressions—follow precisely the logic of the magical primary process, and thus represent at heart nothing but undigested holdovers from that lower stage of evolution.

To give a very brief example of how this occurs—and to remind the reader of Freud's general discoveries—say that an adult and otherwise rational individual is suffering from a terrifying phobia of all red-haired women. In analysis, he might discover that, when three years old, he suffered violent and repeated trauma at the hands of a particular red-haired aunt. Under the spell of the magical primary process, which domi-

† As explained in the footnote on page 53.

nates that early stage, he forevermore confused the class of *all* red-haired women with *one* member of that class (his aunt), and thus he unrealistically panicked in the presence of *any* red-haired woman, which resulted in neurotic phobia, anxiety, obsession, and so on. He never outgrew this primitive magical cognition, which, as we saw, confuses and equates all subjects with similar predicates (e.g., all women with red hair), and thus he never outgrew his neurotic phobia, a classic example of magical displacement and condensation.‡

Thus, as Freud found, the years of infancy are so important today in the formation of neurotic symptoms simply because infancy today should be the period of evolving and developing *beyond* magic, beyond bodyself and primary process. A failure to do so—through fixation and repression—leaves one with an unconscious allegiance to infantile magic which is then expressed in neurotic conflict (which *is* a *conflict* because the mature aspects of the personality are fighting this allegiance). In this sense, neurosis is a subconscious belief in magic, a refusal to surrender gracefully that primitive bodily and emotional-sexual stage with its primitive wishes and ideas. When Freud found sexual impulses underlying so many neurotic conflicts, he was simply discovering the whole atmosphere of this pranic-magical level, with its emotional-sexual energies, its bodily impulses, and its magical primary process cognition. It was really nothing much more spectacular than that.

In typhonic times, magic was not a neurotic symptom because it was a collective and, as far as it went, appropriate way and stage of life. *Today,* however, when average and collective consciousness extends far beyond that primitive level, magic is a neurotic symptom because it represents the failure to *outgrow, transform,* and *integrate* that old way of life, a way that, when thus disowned and dissociated and repressed, erupts vengefully in neurotic symptoms, in obsessions of reason, in compulsions of behavior.

In short: *magic not transformed and integrated becomes magic disguised in disease. There* is *the* central and essential discovery of Freud, and as far as it goes in that limited arena, his logic is still proving infinitely superior to that of his critics. State it in terms of learning theory, state it in terms of linguistics, state it in terms of sociobiology—but Freud absolutely nailed shut the essential and general features of these earliest and lowest levels of the Great Chain. Beyond these lower levels I am no fan of Freud —within them, however, I have searched in vain for a greater genius.

To return to our historical point: we are fast approaching the time when

‡ I am not denying other causes of phobic anxiety, e.g., conditioned responses, projections, biochemical triggers, etc.; nor am I suggesting psychoanalysis is the best cure for phobia (it isn't; desensitization, apparently, is). I am simply using Freud's discoveries about the structural logic of symptoms to show that certain symptoms result from a failure to integrate past evolutionary stages, and the structures of those symptoms match the structures of those stages.

magic in general was transformed and assimilated in a higher mode of consciousness. The magical-typhon was indeed the first major step out of the subconscious—it was both a necessary growth and a mini-fall out of uroboric Eden. But as we now rush out of the Paleolithic and toward the Mesolithic, mankind was poised for the second major step.

III
MYTHIC-MEMBERSHIP

5 Future Shock

Such, apparently, was the magical-typhonic structure of consciousness, something similar to which probably served mankind from 200,000 years ago forward. Prior to that time, consciousness shades back into the archaic-uroboric darkness, pre-differentiated, pre-personal.

But we are now rapidly approaching the tenth millennium B.C., where "a stage of social organization matured that was almost completely antithetical to that of the hunting peoples."[69] But more than the simple maturation of a new social organization, this stage of evolution was actually "a new, and certainly magnificent, though somewhat horrifying, crisis of spiritual growth." For at this date we are "on the brink of a prodigious transformation, certainly the most important in the history of the world."[69]

Mankind was starting to wake up, and wake up very quickly, from its prehistoric slumber in subconscious Eden. But what specifically occurred at this date, some 12,000 years ago, that was the most important transformation "in the history of the world"?

In a word, humankind discovered farming. Simple farming—it seems too minor or even too insignificant an event to have actually been responsible for one of the single greatest transformations in the history of our species. Yet the anthropological evidence is clear and unequivocal: when man became a farmer, he sustained the most prodigious mutation in consciousness that had yet appeared. So complicated and numerous were the changes in mankind's life and consciousness brought about through farming, they will have to be sorted out carefully and their significance chronicled.

I am not, however, going to suggest that farming per se *caused* this prodigious transformation, but rather that farming was the most obvious *effect,* or perhaps vehicle, of a deeper transformation in structures of consciousness: it was the earliest expression, that is, of a shift from magical-typhonic to what we will call mythic-membership consciousness (level 3).

Consider that for literally millions of years men and women wandered the face of the earth, gathering and hunting as the present need arose, without the ability, understanding, or desire to farm and cultivate.[426] That is, still close to the lilies of the field, mankind took no extended thought of the morrow, and therefore neither toiled nor tilled the earth. Even into typhonic times individuals' needs were met in the simple moment-to-moment self-preservation of the hunt and the basic magical rites that expressed their simple desires in the present. In group ritual, or in shamanistic trance, they had access to a rudimentary but valid transcendence; otherwise the simple substitute gratifications related to moment-to-moment survival and magico-ritual were adequate to satisfy Eros and avoid Thanatos. Immortality for a hunter was to live until tomorrow. The world of the typhon, although no longer "pre-temporal" (uroboric), was primarily centered on the simple world of the passing present.

But the world of farming is the world of *extended time,* of making present preparations for a *future* harvest, of being able to gear the actions of the present toward significant future goals, aims, and rewards. The farmer works not only in and for the present, as does the hunter, but also in and for tomorrow, which demands an expansion of his thoughts and deeds and awareness *beyond* the simple present, and a replacement of immediate impulsive discharges of the body with directed and channeled mental goals. In short, with the advent of farming, men and women entered an extended world of tense, time, and temporal duration, expanding their life and consciousness to include the future. This, to say the very least, is no small achievement.

Impulse delay and control, the ability to postpone, channel, sublimate, and offset otherwise instinctive body-bound activities and typhonic magic—this is the expanded world of the farmer. "Thus, the pyramid builder is a farmer, and so is today's salaried bread-winner . . . with his profit sharing and health insurance and retirement benefits. The penitent fingering rosary beads, the hymn singer, the doer of good works are, without exception, farming."[253] Even the writer of those good words, when writing them, was farming. The point is that they all "share the farming mode, the farming consciousness, which has altered us all."[253]

The ability and necessity to delay and control impulsive animal gratifications, emotional-sexual impulses, and typhonic magic, in favor of temporal and mental goals, was also heightened in the early farming communities by simple virtue of the larger number of people living in close proximity. "In the paleolithic hunter's world, where the groups were comparatively small—hardly more than forty or fifty individuals—the social pressures were far less severe than in the later, larger, differentiated and systematically coordinated long-established villages and cities. . . . In such a society, there is little room for individual play. There is a rigid relationship not only of the individual to his fellows, but also of village life to the calendric cycle; for the planters are intensely aware of their dependency upon the gods of the elements."[69] Thus, in farming cultures, "adulthood consists in acquiring, first, a certain special art or skill, and then the ability to support or sustain the resultant tension—a psychological as well as sociological tension—between oneself (as merely a fraction of a larger whole) and others of totally different training, powers, and ideals, who constitute the other necessary organs of the body social."[69] This is why Skinner, for instance, "sees farming as the beginning of delayed reinforcement, with all that implies. While the consequences of the hunter's acts are reasonably clear and immediate [because low and primitive], the farmer has to take strenuous action in the spring (plowing and planting), and then wait several months for the rewarding consequences. More powerful [and sophisticated] means of control are thus necessary to bridge the gap."[253] And this is compounded, to return to our original point, with the massive increase in communal population, the differentiation of physical skills, and the proliferation of mental ideals—all of which were necessary but highly complex aspects of the new body politic, and all of which demanded an equally sophisticated psychology.

Yet why? and how? Why in the first place would individuals voluntarily agree to surrender impulsive and typhonic gratifications for future mental goals? Why, as Keynes wryly put it, is it a case of jam tomorrow and not jam today? What could have *allowed,* as well as *compelled,* whole communities to give up impulsive gratifications for higher and future goals?

Our suggested answer: what *allowed* it was the full-fledged emergence of language; what *compelled* it was a new and heightened death seizure.

THE SKULL GRINS IN

I think, to begin with, that a basic and profound expansion of consciousness *allowed* man to picture the future more clearly, and thus plan and farm for it. At the same time, and for the same reason, he also apprehended his own mortality more vividly, and this *forced* him to project his existence through the future so as to meet himself tomorrow. As an

expression of both his growing consciousness and his new death seizure/
death denial, he projected and created the world-as-farmed. Besides being
able to picture the future through an expanded mentality, he *needed* to
picture that future actually lying ahead of him as a promise that death
would not touch him now. Thus, farming was a growth experience; *and* it
was a forced insurance policy, a preventative measure, not against instinctual hunger but against the death of the new and higher self sense. If hunting supported the bodyself, farming supported the newly emerging
mental-self. And there is the easiest way to account for the mixture of new
potential and new terror that constituted farming consciousness.

That this general period was marked by a new and heightened death seizure seems almost certain, for, as Jaynes's meticulous survey concluded,
"while there had been earlier graves of a sort, occasionally somewhat elaborate [which marked the twilight dawn of death in the typhonic period],
this is the first age [c. 10,000 B.C.] in which we find ceremonial graves as
a common practice."[215] And graves, as Campbell put it, "point to an attempt to cope with the imprint of death." Commonplace graves meant
commonplace death seizure. The skull, indeed, was grinning in at the
banquet—and mankind knew it.

Men and women were simply becoming more and more conscious, on
the one hand, and thus more and more conscious of their existential vulnerability, on the other. Simple typhonic survival, moment to moment, was
therefore no longer enough to contain consciousness, nor could it promise
immortality and avoid death, and thus a longer and more extended temporal world had to be created through which the separate self could imaginatively project its own continuing (but still illusory) existence. That invariably means that the substitute gratifications of the typhonic level were no
longer adequate for the Atman project, were no longer adequate to satisfy
Eros and avoid Thanatos. Thus, translation was starting to fail, and transformation was starting to occur. No longer the simple world of the present,
but the complex world of *tense*—and it was just this tensed-membership
self that recognized and invented farming. Mankind voluntarily surren-
dered present gratifications in order to farm a belief in tomorrow and thus
"buy time" to avoid death and *continue* (on a higher level) the *sensation*
of being a separate self. And, in part, men and women joined their separate selves together in farming communities *in order to buy time.* . . .

LANGUAGE, TIME, AND MEMBERSHIP

Yet the very fact that men and women *could* join together in farming consciousness demonstrated the evolutionary transcendence embodied in this

level. For one thing, farming consciousness was *membership* consciousness —that is, community consciousness or comm-*unity* consciousness: a higher form of unity on the way to ultimate Unity, a joining together and sharing of otherwise individual and isolated beings. For another, the fact that consciousness at this stage *was* a farming consciousness meant that it was no longer committed to spontaneous food, but could submit food, the physical realm, to conscious discipline. That is just another way of saying (and repeating) that farming consciousness was *temporal* consciousness. a consciousness that *transcended* the simple present and therefore could *farm* the world of the future.

Now, if the major psychological dynamic of this temporal consciousness was the repression of death, the major psychological *vehicle* of this temporal consciousness was *language*. For, as researchers from Piaget to Arieti have pointed out, language is *the* great vehicle of time and temporal representation.[6, 126, 329] With language, a sequence or series of events can be represented symbolically and projected beyond the immediate present. Thus, as Robert Hall put it, "language is the means of dealing with the non-present world,"[181] and, conversely, anyone dealing with the non-present is dealing with language.

Further, as I have elsewhere suggested, the key feature of the membership structure is language itself.[436] Thus the membership level of consciousness is well suited—indeed, it is the first structure really suited at all—to support a temporal farming culture. The typhon possessed no truly developed language; it was still largely a bodyself and proto-mind, with magic imagery and paleosymbols, but no extensive linguistic repertoire,[215, 426] and thus it was structurally incapable of extensive temporal consciousness.

The membership self, in short, was simply a *verbal* self. *Because* language transcends the present, the new self could transcend the body. Because language transcends the given, the new self could see into tomorrow. Because language embodies mental goals and futures, the new self could delay and channel its bodily desires. And finally, because language could transcend the physical, it could *represent* physical goods with mental symbols (as we will see). All of this was part of the reproduction of human nature on a new and higher level—the verbal, the communicative, the cultural.

As I have also tried to suggest elsewhere,[436] the predominant mode of language in the membership structure is what Sullivan termed "autistic language," or the *verbal* manifestation of the magical primary process or parataxic-image cognition;[384] or what Arieti called "paleologic thinking."[6] And it is paleologic (level 3), in any of its several forms or stages, that gives the mythic-membership cultures their distinctive stamp: much more refined and articulate than the magical-typhon, more abstract, more detailed and penetrating (as we shall see), yet still contaminated by numerous whole/part and subject/predicate identities (holdovers, rem-

nants, of the magical animism that preceded it). Cognition does not simply
jump from magical/emotional/pranic imagery to logical/rational/con-
ceptual mentality, but rather traverses an intermediate ground of *mythical*
cognition, which one may think of as a "mixture" of magic and logic, and
which informs and structures early language itself. The first language, the
first mind, is a mind of mythic or paleological form. That is precisely why
Gebser termed the whole period "mythical"—such, exactly, was its *structure*. This, then, is the age of the world's greatest and most enduring classical mythologies and classical civilizations: of Egypt and Babylon and
Sumer, of Aztec-Mayan Mexico, and Shang China, and Indus Valley
India, of Mycenaean Crete and earliest Greece.

But we return to language itself, especially in its earliest mythic-membership form. There is today occurring something of a heated debate over
when a fully developed grammatical language first appeared in mankind's
prehistory. Many linguists maintain that language must have been here
from the very beginning of the genus *Homo*—that is, for two million years
or more. Recently, other authorities have been writing drastically different
accounts, the most publicized being that of Julian Jaynes,[215] who insists
that "because language *must* make dramatic changes in man's attention to
things and persons, because it allows a transfer of information of enormous scope, it must have developed over a period that shows archae-
ologically that such changes occurred. Such a one is the late Pleistocene,
roughly from 70,000 B.C. to 8000 B.C." The stages of language evolution,
as Jaynes sees it, are: intentional calls (during the Third Glaciation Period), age of modifiers (up to 40,000 B.C.), age of commands (40,000 to
25,000 B.C.), age of nouns (25,000 to 15,000 B.C.), and finally the age of
names (10,000 to 8,000 B.C.). The essential point is that a rather full-
fledged language emerged fairly recently—probably not much before
50,000 B.C., "a date," says Brewster Smith, "that [fits] the sudden efflores-
cence and diversification of Late Paleolithic culture beginning about
then."[376] And it probably peaked—or reached its developmental zenith of
influence—as late as 10,000 B.C. In our terms, a fairly full-scale language
emerged during the late magical-typhonic and peaked right about at the
beginning of the mythic-membership (in general terms, around the start of
farming cultures).

Beyond those generalizations—which I by and large accept—I am not
sure that we can ever deduce the precise dates for the evolution of language, but this much seems certain: the Mesolithic and Neolithic farming
consciousness could *only* have been supported by a linguistically tensed
consciousness, and very probably was the first to have been so in any
extensive fashion. Earlier stages of language, such as paleosymbols,
modifiers, and intentional calls, certainly entered into magical-typhonic
awareness. But I am fairly convinced that it was only at this Mesolithic-
Neolithic stage that full-fledged language became the *predominant vehicle*

of the separate self (and thus of culture at large). That time seems the very first when developed language became a dominant element in the prevailing structure of consciousness—the structure that we are calling mythic-membership.

Not surprisingly, then, Jaynes speaks often of the role of language in supporting a temporally oriented culture: "It is only language, I think, that can keep him at this time-consuming all-afternoon work [such as farming or planting]. A Middle Pleistocene [typhonic] man would forget what he was doing. But lingual man would have language to remind him. . . . Behavior more closely based on aptic structures (or, in an older terminology, more 'instinctive' [or again, more 'typhonic' or body-based]) needs no temporal priming [by language]."[215] And when he says that "it is, I think, this [newly] added linguistic mentality . . . that resulted in agriculture," we could not agree more—that is precisely the point we earlier argued. Somebody had to be thinking about tomorrow, and thus had to be utilizing tensed language, in order to recognize the agricultural solution to the problem of death and transcendence.

We can see, then, just how tremendously important the emergence of full-fledged language—or at least its extensive use—was in the evolution of consciousness. With language, *the verbal mind could differentiate itself out of the previous bodyself,* it could *rise above* the prison of the immediate and conceive and sustain long-range goals and tasks. "A Middle Pleistocene man would forget what he was doing. But lingual man . . ."

Just as at the previous stage of evolution the bodyself crystallized out of the natural environment, so at this stage the mind is starting to crystallize out of the body. Or we could say, just as the body (level 2) differentiated from the environment (1), so now the mind (3) is starting to differentiate from the body (2). As we said, the lower structures emerge first from the potentiality of the ground unconscious: the environment fell out first, then the body (the typhon), and now the lower mind (the verbal membership mind). We are following the progression of the Great Chain of Being, from matter to body to mind to soul to spirit, and we are at the point where mind is *tentatively* starting to emerge.

THE SYMBOLATE WORLD

From this point on, humanity would be able to reproduce itself not just physically (food) and biologically (sex) but also culturally (mind). For the reproduction of the human mind, generation to generation, is an act of *verbal communication.* This communication is *not* biology on a higher plane, as reductionists and empiricists would like to suppose, because "there can be only one kind of organicness: the organic on another plane would no longer be organic." It is rather trans-organic, trans-biological, trans-body—a higher leap in transcendent evolution. "The dawn of the social [cultural-membership] thus is not a link in any [biological] chain, not a step in a path, but a leap to another plane." The author of those words, A. L. Kroeber, in what is now recognized as a classic paper, called this higher plane the *superorganic*.[137] And the verbal-membership self was just that: superorganic.

One of the most immediate correlates of this superorganic transcendence—besides bodily control, farming mentality, and temporal awareness—was the capacity to create extensive verbal symbolism. Since the membership-self transcended the natural (or simply present) world, it could *represent* that natural world with mental symbols and concepts. Thus it could *operate* on those mental symbols directly without having to perform the cumbersome activities or point to the actual entities represented by the symbols themselves. Verbal thinking can work, for example, with the simple word "tree" without having to physically drag around an actual tree. Linguistic thought is a major transcendence of the limitations and structures of the physical. This is what Piaget would call concrete operational thinking—operating on the world, farming the world, transcending the world, via representational thinking.*

This is not to say, however, as empiricists wish it, that the verbal mind is merely a reflection of the physical world (or that "everything in the mind is first in the senses"), but rather that the mind, because it *transcends* the physical world ("a leap to a higher plane"), possesses the power to represent that world in its symbols. As for the *symbols themselves,* however, they are neither physical nor merely physical-reflecting, but rather constitute a higher level of reality per se—the verbal-mental level, the level Leslie White so accurately called "symbolate," or *"created* by symbolizing." "Symbolizing is trafficking in nonsensory [non-empirical] meanings, i.e., meanings which, like the holiness of sacramental water, *cannot be comprehended* with the senses alone."[137] They are trans-sensory, transbodily, trans-empirical, trans-typhonic, and superorganic. In short, symbols are *presentational* or *creative* (constituting a higher level of reality per se), as well as *reflective* or *representational* (capable of conceptually representing or reflecting lower levels of reality).†

* While this can lead to a host of complications (including neurosis as switched metaphor, à la Lacan, and confusing the symbol with the thing symbolized, à la Buddhists), the solution to these difficulties does not lie in a pre-verbal direction but in a trans-verbal one—we have no need whatsoever to lament the rise of symbolization, only its overextended stay.

† Thus, with words like "rock," "chair," and "rose," the verbal mind can point to entities that exist in the empirical, sensory world, but with words like "pride," "envy," "ambition," "love," "guilt," etc., the verbal mind can point to entities that exist only

The new membership world, the verbal world, was the symbolate world —a new and higher world which is neither reducible to nor explainable in terms of merely empirical transactions.[433] Mankind had simply discovered level 3 in the Great Chain of Being, the first level significantly beyond the empirical, discrete, sensory, bodily, and physical entities of the naturic world. Consciousness was operating on a new plane, an *inter-subjective* plane of shared symbolates that literally transcends the boundaries of discrete organisms through a network of inter-subjective membership and communication.‡ This is precisely what George Mead meant when he said that "the field or locus of any given individual mind must extend as far as the social [membership] activity which constitutes it extends; and hence that field cannot be bounded by the skin of the individual organism to which it belongs."[383] Verbal-membership mentality was simply a new, higher, and more extensive form of unity on the way to Unity.

MONEY AND SURPLUS

The capacity to farm the natural world with increasing efficiency soon led to the production of extra or *surplus* food and goods, and it was just this surplus that would soon change the entire face of history. For the more efficient farming became (especially with the invention of the plow), the less consciousness had to concern itself exclusively with food production.

---

in the mental sphere and *cannot* be found in the physical, sensory, empirical world. Entities such as "pride" are *created* by the mental sphere and exist only in that sphere, as a higher order of processes that transcend mere empirical transactions. This is why we say the verbal mind is both representational (reflecting lower levels) and presentational or creative (constituting a higher level of reality per se). Rocks, trees, etc. (level 1/2), exist independent of mind (3/4), but ambition, envy, etc., do not. And this is *not* to say they are "mere thoughts," as a pejorative epithet, but rather that thought per se *is* a higher level on the Great Chain, perfectly aware of the lower levels but containing activities, capacities, entities, and potentials found nowhere else.

‡ By that I mean nothing so esoteric as actual telepathic connections, only that verbal-membership is not a matter of one isolated organism "talking" to another isolated organism, but is rather a communion and partial identity of individual mentalities, so that these mentalities are, to just that extent, actually linked in a superorganic or literally inter-subjective network, and this network, as Mead says, extends as far as the linkages themselves. It is a noetic network that literally extends far beyond food, body, feeling, and skin boundaries, and represents an actual expansion of consciousness beyond the organism. This is not the highest form of transcendence (there are levels 5 through 8), but it is an initial and very major form of transcendence. We will explore this level more in Chapter 9.

That is, for the first time in history, the availability of a surplus of food freed certain individuals (freed consciousness itself) for other and more specialized tasks: the development of mathematics, the calendar, the alphabet, and writing, etc.—a fact unparalleled in importance for the creation and evolution of civilization itself.[252] It is almost universally agreed that, beginning perhaps as early as the sixth millennium B.C., the food surplus allowed the emergence of specialized classes, such as priests, administrators, educators, etc., who—because they no longer had to hunt or farm themselves—were freed for more detailed and specialized tasks. By 3200 B.C.,[70] these specialists had consequently produced the alphabet, mathematics, writing, the calendar, etc.—the first truly and purely mental productions of the human race. In short, because of farming, consciousness was released from merely physical food and given the time for mental contemplation.

Think of it this way: by being able to surplus-satisfy the lower needs of food and safety, consciousness could spring upward in the hierarchy of motivation (à la Maslow) toward the higher levels of belongingness, membership, and community (and then on to self-esteem, as we will see in the mental-egoic period). Maslow's motivational hierarchy[285] is simply another perspective of the Great Chain of Being.[286, 349, 429, 436] But the historical point is that the verbal-membership self was a self capable of farming the physical in order to free the mental. Only this verbal-self *could* have had the power and foresight to produce the farming surplus and free itself for higher pursuits.

Notice, however, that if farming consciousness could only move this surplus physically, through space, it would have to spend almost all its new time manually transferring these goods from one place to another. It would waste its life in physical barter. It needed a *mental* form of *material* transfer, a rapid and superorganic means of transfer, a *symbolic* means of transfer. And this was money.

With money, mankind could *symbolize* a specified amount of material goods, and then instead of having to always drag and transfer these physical goods from point to point, market to market, field to town, it could in many important cases simply transfer the *symbols* of the goods instead. In other words money, as a mental symbolate, was a significant transcendence of the physical realm, a small but incalculably important vehicle of evolutionary transcendence; it was a way to move and transfer and operate on the physical realm without having to deal cumbersomely with the limitations of that realm itself. Instead of carrying five tons of wheat with you, you could carry five gold coins—that simple. Further, since physical labor was (and is) the primary means of the production of physical food and goods, labor was likewise symbolized with *wages,* and wages, like any money, could be used to buy into the surplus food and goods rapidly being produced.*

None of these advances (or their misuses) would be possible without the power of the symbolizing mind, which embodied the first major transcendence of the material and bodily and natural world (levels 1 and 2). This we have seen in *farming,* this we have seen in *time,* this we have seen in *money.* All were transcendent steps in the growth of consciousness.

THE ATMAN PROJECT IN FARMING CONSCIOUSNESS

But they were something else as well. If they were indeed steps toward Atman, they could also become exclusive substitutes for Atman—they represented not just pure moves toward Atman, but new twists on the Atman project as well. For every stage of evolution is not only moving toward God, it is also fighting God. And that strange mixture—which leads to compromises, compensations, substitutes, and defenses—we call the Atman project. And *every* stage of evolution is not just an unfolding of Atman; it is also an unfurling of the Atman project.

We have already seen, in the first part of this chapter, that farming itself was both a growth in consciousness and a new *immortality project.* We

---

* The theme of this book is that every transcendence (except, of course, the ultimate one) is two-sided: it represents a new and higher potential, but also one that *can* be misused, often with horrendous consequences. The same with money: *because* symbolate money could transcend and represent physical goods, it could also *mis*represent them. In a sense, the study of economics is devoted to that topic. Economics is basically the study of the productive forces and relations of the material sphere necessary to reproduce the human physical body, and, beyond that, a study of the diseases of the relations between the mental symbolates and the goods represented by those symbolates. For instance, if a symbolate (e.g., money) is to accurately *represent* lower levels, it must accurately *reflect* the conditions of those lower levels, even as it transcends them in many other aspects. If the amount of symbolate money created by a society is greater than the amount of goods actually produced by society, the result is inflation. That is, in inflation, that aspect of the mental sphere which, as symbolate money, is to represent physical goods, simply expands (for psychodynamic reasons) beyond the capacities of the physical sphere itself, tending to cause eventual devaluation of that aspect of the mental sphere and possible collapse of the physical. Inflation is simply one example of a higher level failing to accurately reflect and acknowledge a lower level; structurally, it is *identical* to a dissociation neurosis leading to manic-depression (inflation/recession). All of these are examples of an extremely general phenomenon that can occur in any developmental hierarchy (i.e., throughout the Great Chain): the dissociation of higher and lower instead of the differentiation and integration of higher and lower. We will be examining all sorts of dissociations throughout the remainder of this volume.

saw precisely the same thing with the creation of *future time*. But—as we
will see below—exactly the same double-edged Atman project lies behind
the production of *surplus goods,* as well as their symbolization with
money.

For instance, we can begin with Becker: "And so all this seemingly useless surplus [the extra foods and goods that farming consciousness produced, which went way beyond simple physical needs], dangerously and
painstakingly wrought, yields the highest usage in terms of *power* [mana,
the Eros wing of the Atman project]. Man, the animal who knows he is
not safe here, who needs continued affirmation of his powers, is the one
animal who is implacably driven to work beyond animal needs precisely
because he is not a secure animal. The origin of human drivenness is
religious because man experiences creatureliness; the amassing of a surplus, then, goes to the very heart of human motivation, the urge to stand
out as a hero, to transcend the limitations of the human condition and
achieve victory over impotence and finitude."[26]

All of which is indeed true, but true for reasons that Becker, the eternal
existentialist, could not admit. And before we go any further, we must very
briefly examine Becker's overall thesis, because it strongly supports *half* of
our position while vehemently denying the other half (as we will explain),
and we must be able to account for both if we are to go beyond Becker
and effectively escape his criticism.

To begin with, man does hunger for the infinite and for utter transcendence, as Becker maintains, but basically because he strongly intuits
that infinite Spirit is his true and prior Nature. He intuits this infinite nature but erroneously applies that intuition to the finite realm and his finite
self, and it is this prior intuition, diverted from its true Source and applied
exclusively to the finite realm, that *drives* and *compels* man to try to make
earth into heaven, finite goods into infinite value, a separate self into God,
and self-preservation into immortality.

Once that occurs, *then* absolutely all the terrors described by Becker
follow just as he says. But his ideas, taken in and by themselves, are, in the
true sense of the phrase, "half baked." Becker's whole existential position
denies *a priori* any form of *true* transcendence or true Atman. This *a priori*
denial therefore demands that he postulate in man a hunger for an infinite
which *doesn't really exist,* and so he has to derive the genesis of this
hunger—the hunger for immortality and transcendence—solely from man's
capacity to delude himself in the face of terror, a position which overlooks
the age-old wisdom that fear produces superstition, not religion.

In other words, Becker sees the Atman project very clearly, but leaves
out Atman. He then is forced to see the Atman project as a fundamental
lie (his term) which aims at a purely fictional Atman, whereas for us the
Atman project is an intermediate *substitute* for a true Atman. That is, for
Becker, man desires God because man is a spineless coward and needs

some such lie to exist; for us, man desires God because his highest potential *is* real God and he won't rest until he actualizes it.†

Becker received the impetus for most of his notions from Otto Rank, and although he quotes the following from Rank, he ought to have taken it more sincerely: "All our human problems, with their intolerable sufferings, arise from man's ceaseless attempts to make this material world into a man-made reality . . . aiming to achieve on earth a 'perfection' which is only to be found in the beyond . . . thereby hopelessly confusing the values of both spheres."[25, 26] There is a perfect definition of the Atman project. But that definition *works,* it has explanatory power, only if the two spheres which are confused (the finite and the infinite) actually exist to begin with. If one of them (the infinite Atman) is *already* a lie, then the human predicament cannot be explained by a real confusion of the two spheres—it must be explained *only* by one sphere's creating lies about a fictional "sphere beyond." This demands not one lie—the confusing of the two spheres—but *two* lies—the fictional creation of the "sphere beyond" and its subsequent confusion with the finite sphere—and this paints a picture of mankind as capable of *nothing but* lies, a view which no mind can adopt without self-contradiction.

Becker says that those quoted words of Rank are no mere metaphor, but "a complete scientific formula about the cause of evil in human affairs." I would not have written this book if I didn't believe that; the problem with Becker is that he doesn't fully believe it. He believes in the Atman project without Atman, in the confusion of two spheres with one sphere not even existing in the first place, in the drive toward transcendence without transcendence itself. In fact, he derives the fictional belief in, or the lie about, a "second sphere beyond" from a confusion of the two spheres themselves; i.e., he assumes the existence of the second sphere even as he uses it to deny it. The second sphere that Becker overtly needs so badly to add weight to his explanation of the evil-producing confusion of two spheres, he proclaims from the start to be meaningless, nonexistent, and nonsensical. Might as well try to explain all of history and psychology by maintaining that mankind confuses the finite realm with tweedle-dee-dum.

What I am saying is that Becker—who has profoundly influenced the general mood of modern psychology—would have had, if anything, a *stronger* case if he admitted the existence of Spirit, and *then* explained mankind's suffering and evil as failures to reach, or as compromises for, or

† We see this even with the highly existential "problem of death." Becker's position is: because man fears death, he responds with death denials, and thus creates the pure illusion/lie of Eternity. Our position is: because man is presently ignorant of Eternity, he fears death, and thus constructs death denials. An immortality project that was *pure* illusion, and did not have, at least ultimately, a real Eternity as its base, could have no more real psychological impact than the existence of a unicorn project.

as substitutes for, that Spirit. That, anyway, is the course I have taken, and in that light I have reconstructed the important insights of Becker (and Rank and Brown), as suggested in these pages. If this approach is wrong, it will condemn not only my own thesis but eventually Becker's as well. If the entire second sphere is from the start just a lie, then we needn't introduce the second and superfluous lie of confusing the two spheres—there is only a lie to begin with, and *all man's cultural activities are therefore nothing but lies about transcendence*—which Becker has in fact said. But if so, then Becker's own cultural productions—that is, his books, his thoughts, and his entire thesis—are also nothing but a lie. In short, if Becker is right, Becker is lying. On the other hand, if we place Becker (and the existentialists) in a Chinese box embraced but surpassed by the larger box of the transcendentalists, we can salvage the correct (but partial) truths of his thesis—and that is our approach.

We return, then, to Becker's essential (and reconstructed) points: "The origin of human drivenness is *religious* because man experiences creatureliness [finiteness]; the amassing of a surplus, then, goes to the very heart of human motivation, the urge to stand out as a hero, to transcend the limitations of the human condition and achieve victory over impotence and finitude."[26] This *is* true, not because man is a spineless liar (in some cases, that is certainly part of the story), but because he always intuits that his prior nature *is* Transcendent and Heroic Atman, the Immortal One in and beyond all forms. *But,* until he fully and consciously resurrects Spirit in his own case, he necessarily applies this Atman intuition to his own finite and mortal self, and most assuredly *that* is the real confusion, the vital lie, that drives him to try to make finite earth into infinite heaven, to substitute earthly wealth for transcendent security, to turn farming into an insurance policy for death denial, to pile up surplus goods as an immortality project, to cling to the future as a promise of death transcendence, to turn money into God's ape and gold into demonic power. If man cannot find true and eternal Life in timeless Spirit, he will farm for it exclusively in time, fussing about in the temporal realm in search of that which is timeless, and piling up tokens and symbols of this correct but misplaced search. Part truth and part lie—and there is the real confusion of the two spheres that is the Atman project.

Returning now to specifics, we can easily see that precisely the same Atman project applies to the creation and use of *money*. Some early and crude forms of money had probably been in existence since typhonic times (in the form of shells, fish bones, etc.), but only in the market town of farming societies does true money come into its own. And it comes, we have suggested, as a two-edged sword. On the one hand, we already saw that it expressed the capacity of a new and higher consciousness to symbolize and represent lower and physical levels of reality, the power to transcend (but not ignore) physical exchange through symbolic (monetary) exchange.

On the other—and here we join up perfectly with Becker—money could therefore become an extremely powerful symbol of immortality and death denial and cosmocentricity. Instead of using money to allow a vertical transcendence to higher (mental) levels, one could make the horizontal accumulation of money an end in itself. After all, money represented the new surplus of food-life, and therefore more money meant more life, and absolute money meant absolute life or *immortality*—there is the Atman project in undisguised form. "Already Luther," says Brown, "had seen in money the essence of the secular, and therefore of the demonic. The money complex is the demonic, and the demonic is God's ape; the money complex is therefore the . . . *substitute for* the religious complex, an attempt to find God in things."[61] Or, in Becker's very true words, *"Gold became the new immortality symbol."*

> And so the pursuit of money was also opened up to the average man; gold became the new immortality symbol. In the temple buildings, palaces, and monuments of the new cities we see a new kind of power being generated. No longer the power of the totemic [typhonic] communion, but the power of the testimonial of piles of stone and gold.[26]

And most significantly, "We might say that money coinage fit beautifully into this scheme, because now the cosmic powers could be the property of everyman, without even the need to visit the temples: you could now traffic for immortality in the marketplace."[26] And there Becker was deadly accurate. Money was *power,* great condensed mana, and if you could not transcend to real Power and Life, then where better to look for substitutes than in the obsessive accumulation of money? Money as the new immortality symbol—this is precisely the insight that energized Norman O. Brown's penetrating analysis of history, an analysis that disclosed the very blood of civilization to be money as death denial (what we would call the negative wing of the Atman project).[61]

In summary: The new self, the verbal-self, the membership-self, the superorganic self, was a true expansion and extension of consciousness, an expansion that evidenced itself in such sophisticated activities as farming, the beginning of true culture, verbal mentality, symbolic money, a capacity for surplus production, and so on.‡ But (among many other things) this new and expanded self faced a new and expanded vision of mortality, and

‡ While culture of a sort existed in typhonic times, as pointed out in Part II, it was extremely rudimentary and skeletal. Extensive culture, decisive culture, first flowered in farming communities and especially in the early city-states, basically by virtue of the verbal-symbolate mind.

therefore had to fashion a new and expanded form of death denial. With its extended grasp of time, it needed to see itself vastly extended into tomorrow, it needed to meet itself securely in a farmed future. It therefore sought its new immortality, and new cosmocentricity, through symbols of its own farmed surplus or extended life. In other words, it sought immortality through future time, excess farmed goods, money, and gold. Beyond being expressions of a true growth in consciousness, those items became perfect symbols of death denial, bartered tickets to immortality, real confusions of the finite realm with the infinite "realm beyond"—in short, new twists in the Atman project, new attempts to gain Spirit in substitutes.

Thus, farming is time, and—as the slogan today has it—time is money. The connecting link is now so easy to see, because all three—farming, time, and money—are simply forms of symbolic surplus-life. They express and represent expanded consciousness on the one hand, and ritual death denial and heroic cosmocentricity on the other; steps in the growth toward Atman, but steps perverted (in the meantime) into new forms of the Atman project: immortality symbols, cosmocentric ploys, dust for deity.

MEMBERSHIP

There is one other major activity that the mythic-membership structure can support: it is a type of social organization and social control which is much more complex than that of simple hunting bands of the magical-typhonic man.

The very *need* itself for some sort of internal, psychological control of social organization must have been immense. Consider: around 9000 B.C. simple agricultural practices appear simultaneously in several places in the Levant and Iraq—no longer simple tribes of 20 people, but *towns* of around 200.[215] That had *never*, at *any* time, happened before! The only analogy I can think of is to imagine dozens of hunting packs of wolves gathering together and settling down in a town of 200 wolves, all striking up social intercourse.

At any rate, for the first time in mankind's two- or three-million-year history, a large number of people were asked to live together in permanent villages. By 7000 B.C. innumerable farming settlements existed throughout the Near East, and by 5000 B.C. agricultural colonization had spread throughout the Tigris-Euphrates and Nile valleys, swelling the population of some cities to 10,000 inhabitants.[215] This period, from roughly 9500–4500 B.C., we call the "low membership" stage, and for simple convenience we contrast it with the "high membership" stage of around

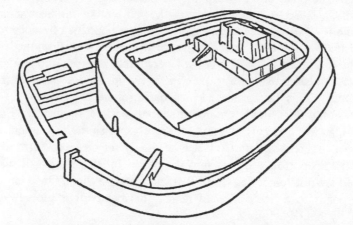

Fig. 12. Temple Oval at Khafajah, Mesopotamia, during the high-membership period. No longer tribes of 20 or 30 people, but cities of 10,000.

4500–1500 B.C., the period dominated by the great classical civilizations of the hieratic city-states, theocracies, and dynasties: Egyptian and Sumerian, for instance, which marked the great flowering of farming consciousness and membership cognition.

But both the low and the high mythic-membership cultures were faced with the great problem of socially controlling a quantity of people that can only be considered *massive* by primitive standards. In what is really a blink in the relative time of man's evolution, he went from groups of 30 to cities approaching 50,000 people. "We might say," points out Joseph Campbell, "that the psychological need to bring the parts of a large and socially differentiated settled community, comprising a number of newly developed social classes (priests, kings, merchants, and peasants), into an orderly relationship to each other . . . , [the need to build] an earthly order of coordinated wills . . . —this profoundly felt psychological as well as sociological requirement must have been fulfilled with . . ."[69] With what?

With, I believe, the mythic-membership structure of consciousness: it is the very nature of this structure that it supports a very basic type of membership cognition and therefore membership culture. And there are two significant features of the tensed-language membership structure that allow it to serve that social function. On the one hand, it is the largely unconscious "repository" of membership cognition, where "membership" is defined precisely as done by Castaneda in his various works (and first explained in detail by others such as Parsons,[324] Leslie White,[421] Whorf,[425] Fromm,[154] and G. H. Mead[293]): "Everyone who comes into contact with a child is a teacher who incessantly describes the world to him, until the moment when the child is capable of perceiving the world as it is described. . . . We have no memory of that portentous moment, simply because none of us could possibly have had any point of reference to compare it to anything else. . . . Reality, or the world we all know, is only a description . . . , an endless flow of perceptual interpretations which we, the individuals who share a specific *membership,* have learned to make in common."[78] This large, unconscious background of membership cognition, basically *linguistic* in nature, of shared sentiments, shared descriptive realities, and shared perceptions, alone can serve as the psychological support of a coherent society. And it is a largely *unconscious* form of social control: the controls are built into the particular description of reality itself, and are not something consciously added onto them. Once an individual responds to a description of reality, his behavior is already circumscribed by that description.

On the other hand, the membership structure, precisely because it is the first to contain large blocs of linguistic elements, can also float specific, internalized, verbal instructions or commands, the earliest of which are usually received from the parents—the so-called proto-superego, which is instrumental in this stage and almost, as it were, embedded in it. The combination of both of these major features of the membership structures —background membership cognition as well as specific, individual information—is, I believe, precisely the psychological structure that supported the early farming communities of the low-membership stage as well as the first great civilizations of the high-membership stage.

THE BICAMERAL MIND

All of this is somewhat similar to Jaynes's theory of the bicameral mind, whose influence I gratefully acknowledge. There is much in his presentation, however, with which I strongly disagree. But let us note specifically the areas where we are in essential agreement: First, Jaynes sees the bicameral mind as a by-product of language. It is "a side effect of language comprehension which evolved by natural selection as a method of behavioral control . . . and operated to keep individuals persisting at the longer tasks of tribal life." Second, if we substitute "mythic-membership structure" for "bicameral mind," the following is perfect: "The bicameral mind is a form of social control and it is that form of social control which allowed mankind to move from small hunter-gatherer groups to large agricultural communities. The bicameral mind . . . was evolved as a final stage of the evolution of language. And in this development lies the origin of civilization."[215]

There are other large areas of agreement. Jaynes speaks of a *collective cognitive imperative* in terms that are very compatible with our description of collective membership cognition. Especially significant is the fact—now almost uncontested—that individual personality (the ego level) rests upon, and indeed grows out of, the membership level, or the "collective cognitive imperatives." In Jaynes's own words:

> [The collective cognitive imperatives] always live at the very heart of a culture or subculture, moving out and filling up the unspoken and the unrationalized. They become indeed the irrational and unquestionable support and structural integrity of the culture. And the culture in turn is the substrate of its individual consciousness, of how the metaphor "me" is "perceived" by the analog "I." . . . The analog "I" and the metaphor "me" are always resting at the confluence of many collective cognitive imperatives.[215]

So that, even today, "as individuals we are at the mercies of our own collective imperatives. We see over our everyday attentions, our gardens and politics, and children, into the forms of our culture, darkly. And our culture is our history. In our attempts to communicate or to persuade or simply interest others, we are using and moving about through cultural models among whose differences we may select, but from whose totality we cannot escape." Indeed, Jaynes's whole point is that egoic self-consciousness (which he simply—and unfortunately—calls "consciousness") historically arose out of the bicameral structure when that structure failed, in and by itself, to support more advanced and complex cultures. In our terminology, as Thanatos exceeded Eros, the translations of the membership level failed, crisis ensued, and transformation upward to the egoic level eventually ensued—a thesis we will later argue for. At any rate, viewing egoic consciousness as arising in large part out of deeper, largely unconscious cultural paradigms places us firmly in league with the researches of E. Fromm, G. H. Mead, Karen Horney, Castaneda, and Whorf.

That, in short, for the background phenomenon of membership cognition. And as for specific information and commands being carried by a proto-superego embedded in the membership structure, Jaynes himself frequently says as much: One aspect of the bicameral mind is an "amalgamation of stored admonitory experience, made up of meldings of whatever commands had been given the individual," usually experienced as a living voice, a "person's inner directing voice, derived perhaps from his parents," and usually assimilated with "the voice or supposed voice of the king [or social leader giving ultimate commands]." In fact, the relationship between a person and his "inner directing voice" was, "by being its progenitor, similar to the referent of the ego-superego relationship of Freud." The "progenitor of the superego" is generally called the proto-superego. And it was this proto-superego, embedded in the membership structure, which carried the specific social commands, arranged in a tight hierarchy of authorities, that allowed the binding together of large numbers of individuals into the first great civilizations.

We come now, however, to the more novel and more hypothetical aspects of Jaynes's thesis. For Jaynes, the "inner directing voice" is experienced as a full-fledged hallucination, which in turn is allowed because of a substantially different brain function. Specifically, he says that in the bicameral mind, Wernicke's area on the right non-dominant hemisphere operated as the source of the hallucinations that were "received" by the left hemisphere. Further, these hallucinations were then often thought to originate from gods—and, in fact, the insights of all higher religions, according to Jaynes, started just that way, as hallucinations of stored admonitory experience.

There seem to be other, less drastic explanations for the same data. For one, modern psychotherapeutic techniques, such as psychosynthesis, Transactional Analysis (TA), and Gestalt therapy, have given us a very detailed view of the psychological nature of "inner voices." Most thinking, in fact, is done in subvocal talking, with a flurry of quiet voices, and frequently as part of a dialogue between Child, Adult, and Parent ego states. Take, for example, the following from Berne:

> There are four dialogues possible between simple ego states: three duologues (P–A, P–C, A–C), and one triologue (P–A–C). If the Parental voice splits up into Father and Mother, as it usually does, and if other Parental figures chime in, the situation is more complicated. Each voice may be accompanied by its own set of "gestures" expressed by a chosen set of muscles or a special part of the body.[36]

He adds that, to a great extent, what people *"do* is decided by voices, the skull-rapping of internal dialogue." In fact, "all your decisions are made by four or five people in your head, whose voices you can overlook if you are too proud to hear them, but they will be there the next time if you care to listen. Script analysts learn how to amplify and identify these voices, and that is an important part of their therapy."

Furthermore, there are, according to TA, four "degrees" of such internal dialogues: "In the first degree, the words run through [a person's] head in a shadowy way, with no muscular movements, or at least none perceptible to the naked eye or ear. In the second degree, he can feel his vocal muscles moving a little so that he whispers to himself inside his mouth. . . . In the third degree, he says the words out loud. . . . There is also a fourth degree, where one or the other of the internal voices is heard as coming from outside the skull. This is usually the voice of the parent (actually the voice of his father or mother) and these are hallucinations."[36]

In TA, the earliest—and also strongest—form of the proto-superego (or Parent in the Child) is called the "electrode" because the individual jumps to its commands, positive and negative, as if an electrode were implanted in his head. The electrode is also frequently found to be present in hallucinations. *But the electrode doesn't have to be hallucinated to be perfectly effective.* That is, just as much social control can be exercised by electrode voices of the first, second, or third degree as by those of the fourth—the voices needn't be hallucinated in order to form the social function assigned to them by Jaynes. Whereas Jaynes would see the electrode as a "vestige of the bicameral mind," it seems just as likely that it's the other way around: the "voices of the bicameral mind" were the expressions of the electrode, or the proto-superego embedded in the membership structure and available in any of its four degrees.

Neither do I agree with Jaynes's thesis that there absolutely was no form of subjective consciousness during the bicameral period (9000–2000 B.C.). It seems more likely that a form of linguistic proto-subjectivity existed during the entire membership period, and especially during the high-membership stage. Whereas I prefer to recognize several major levels of consciousness—with only the "middle" ones being highly self-reflexive, the lower ones being pre-personal and the higher ones trans-personal—Jaynes recognizes only one form of consciousness: egoic, linguistic, subjective, self-consciousness. Consciousness, so narrowly defined, does then appear to leap rather suddenly into existence out of nowhere sometime around the end of the second millennium B.C. (with the end of the bicameral mind), whereas I believe that what Jaynes is describing is merely the shift or transformation upward from the mythic-membership structure of consciousness to the mental-egoic structure of consciousness. Stated thus, we can at least agree with a diluted form of Jaynes's thesis: the ego level, as a dominant, widespread, and largely irreversible mode of separate-self sense, arose only after the breakdown of the bicameral mind (i.e., the breakdown of the mythic-membership structure of consciousness).

Finally, we come to Jaynes's thesis that many of the "voices of the bicameral mind," especially those of the fourth or hallucinated degree, were experienced as voices of the gods, and thus all the ideas of the world's great religions arose from bicameral voices. That some voices were experienced as gods, I do not for one moment doubt; that all gods are *only* voices, I do not for one moment believe. To be fair to Jaynes, he does consistently point out that these voices, even if "hallucinatory," are not "imaginary" or "unreal"—on the contrary, they are organized insights and real information originating in the right hemisphere of the brain and transmitted as voices to the left hemisphere. I suppose that somebody sufficiently attracted to the neo-Helmholtzian view that all consciousness is but physiological fireworks might make fascinating use of Jaynes's thesis in this way: by viewing the right hemisphere as the source of Platonic or "trans-personal" insights (as, e.g., Ornstein does), Jaynes's "voices of the gods" speaking to the individual were in fact voices of the trans-personal realm being broadcast to the personal realm via the newly developed media of language. That would at least account for the spiritual, trans-personal dimensions of many of the voices.

But what even that version would not do is account for the incredibly vast difference in the metaphysical "truth value" of the various types of voices themselves. Let me explain: Jaynes makes it very clear that the great majority of the "voices of the bicameral mind" were concerned with simple day-to-day tasks that were time-consuming and enduring and thus needed temporal or linguistic priming, such as—to use one of his examples—having to obey a command from the chief to set up a fish weir far upstream from a campsite. The command was stored and repeated as needed, usually as an inner voice (of the fourth degree). As a novel situation arose, advice or commands were supplied from the vast store of all the admonitory advice ever given to the individual. Since some of these voices were experienced as, or attributed to, gods, the conclusion for Jaynes is obvious: "The gods, I have said with some presumption, were amalgams of admonitory experience, made of meldings of whatever commands had been given the individual." The corollary of which is: "The function of the gods was chiefly the guiding and planning of action in novel situations. The gods size up problems and organize action according to an ongoing pattern or purpose, resulting in intricate bicameral civilizations, fitting all the disparate parts together, planting times, harvest times, the sorting out of commodities," and so on.

Even *if* all that is true, it in no way accounts for the profusion of brilliant metaphysical and spiritual insights that poured forth from this period of mythic man. Please read carefully the following paragraph, which is from the Pyramid Texts, the "earliest known body of religious writings preserved anywhere in the world, inscribed on the walls of a series of nine tombs (c. 2350–2175 B.C.) in the vast necropolis of Memphis":

Therefore it is said of Ptah: "It is he who made all and brought the gods into being." He is verily the Risen Land that brought forth the gods, for everything came forth from him. . . . He is in all gods, all men, all beasts, all crawling things, and whatever lives. . . . And in this way all the gods and their *kas* are at one with Him, content and united with the Lord of the Two Lands.[70]

That is a perfect intuition and beautiful expression of one Spirit acting in, as, and through *all* beings. And plainly, *that* type of insight or statement or "voice" is quite different from one that says, "Uh, go downstream and build a canoe five cubits by three cubits." Even *if* all the gods were first voices—which cannot be totally correct inasmuch as true god-consciousness is non-verbal—even if they were, there is still in this theory no way whatsoever to account for the difference in metaphysical status of the voices themselves: no way, that is, to *distinguish* the properly *religious* voices from the how-to-make-canoe voices, since both, by this theory, originate in the same way, under the same conditions, and from the same function. In short, I do not see that this theory can offer any way to distinguish religious from non-religious sentiments. And since it cannot account for the specifically religious sentiments, it cannot account for religion at all.

And it is to just this great flourishing of religious sentiments during the mythic-membership period that we now may turn.

6 The Great Mother

There are only two stations at which men and women are perfectly content. One is slumbering in the subconscious, the other is awakened as the superconscious. Everything in between is various degrees of pandemonium. But hundreds of thousands of years ago, mankind took courage and stepped out of the slumber of Eden, renounced its sleep in the subconscious, abandoned its life with the lilies of the field, and began the slow climb back to the superconscious All. It abandoned the life of the sleeping serpent uroboros, abandoned the pre-personal stage shared with the rest of nature, and became, of all the animals, the Prodigal Son lost in the wilderness.

But as men and women first emerged from their pre-personal slumber, some of them were, almost from the start, heroic enough to jump forward into the destiny of mankind and awaken to realms of the superconscious. For the rest, however, there awaited the slow and laborious climb, step by step, out of the subconscious realms, which, tens of thousands of years later, led to their collective awakening as ego—a point which is, as it were, halfway home. For the ego is perched midway between total slumber in the subconscious and total enlightenment in the superconscious, and for this reason alone is the most distressful period of all: the kali yuga (which, incidentally, is said to have begun around 3000 B.C., or about the time of the breakdown of the membership structure and the emergence of the ego).[444]

From the beginning, however, even prior to that first step out of Eden, men and women intuited (to one degree or another) their prior Atman nature, and this acted like a huge unconscious magnet, so to speak, drawing them onward and upward toward that perfect release in the superconscious All. But it also forced them, as a temporary and remedial measure, to fashion all sorts of substitutes for Atman—substitute subjects, substitute objects, substitute sacrifices; immortality projects and cosmocentric designs and tokens of transcendence.

Under this pressure, successive structures of consciousness were created and then abandoned, fashioned and then transcended, constructed and then passed by. *They were created as a substitute for Atman, and abandoned when those substitutes failed.* And evolution proceeded by a series of such abortive attempts to reach Atman consciousness—proceeded that is, via the Atman project, with each step, as it were, getting a bit closer. The same process occurred in the rest of Nature, for as we know evolution is simply a process of greater and greater unfoldings, revealing greater complexities and greater unifications. In man, however—to borrow that phrase of Huxley which so delighted Teilhard de Chardin—evolution became conscious of itself.

In men and women, each successive structure of consciousness was created as a substitute for God, created to present the self as cosmocentric, immortal, and death-defying, created to ensure that Eros win out over Thanatos. But as the translations of each structure finally began to fail their soothing purpose, as their substitute gratifications began to lose their flavor, as Thanatos began to creep past Eros, then translation finally failed, that structure was abandoned and transformation upward to new structures occurred. And into the hands of this new structure was handed the immortal Atman project.

Yet this burdens mankind's awareness with a double weight. Not only do men and women have to contend with the pull of that magnet of the future, that call to superconsciousness; they also have to contend with the vestiges of yesterday. Not only the promise of what they might become, but the burden of what they were. As each new structure of consciousness is laid upon the previous ones, the task becomes one of integrating and conciliating these different structures (as we first suggested in Chapter 4). If not transformed and integrated, the lower almost certainly will contribute to a pathology or general disruption of the higher, simply because what is the *whole* of consciousness at one stage becomes merely a *part* of consciousness at the next, and a part that therefore, upon pain of pathology, must be integrated in the new whole. Thus, as I said, the growing complexity of consciousness brings not only new opportunities but also dreadful responsibilities. And it is just these opportunities—and just these awesome burdens—that we are chronicling.

NEW REALIZATIONS, NEW HORRORS

Our chronological story left off somewhere around the low-membership stage (c. 9500–4500 B.C.), with the discovery and implementation of farming, the creation of a surplus, and the rise of such new immortality symbols as farmed surplus, money, gold, and temporal desires. We saw that farming per se did not originally create the new mythic-membership structure of consciousness, but rather that farming was seized upon by the newly evolving and expanding membership structure as a double solution to a new growth in consciousness and a new form of death seizure. And by the time of the beginning of the high-membership stage, c. 4500 B.C., the farming consciousness of the membership-self had resulted in a literal explosion of cultural activities, cultural products, and cultural monuments, the likes of which, in sheer grandeur and elegance, the world had never seen. For in the short span of a few thousand years, farming consciousness had spectacularly flowered into the magnificent city-states and theocracies of Egypt and Mesopotamia.

Suddenly, very suddenly, civilization had begun.

"What the psychological secret," states Campbell, "of the precipitating moment of an unprecedented culture style may be, we have not yet heard—at least, as far as I know. Spengler wrote of a new sense and experience of mortality—a new death-fear, a new world-fear—as the catalytic. 'In the knowledge of death,' he declared, 'that world outlook is originated which we possess as being men and not beasts.'"[70] A *new* death fear. Indeed, there was a large part of the catalyst (or rather, the negative side of the catalyst, the negative side of the Atman project). We already saw that this membership stage was marked by a new and heightened death fear, requiring new and heightened searches for symbolic or token or pretend immortalities. And there, in a phrase, was the grandeur that was Egypt: the mortuary cults, the Pyramid Age, the mummies, the golden death masks (such as King Tut's, which literally paralyzed and enthralled American citizens during its open display: the immortal fifteen-year-old).

"It is completely obvious," as Campbell points out, "that in the ancient valley of the Nile, in the third millennium B.C., a lived myth—or rather, a myth living itself out in the bodies of men—was turning a neolithic folk culture into one of the most elegant and enduring of the world's high civilizations, literally moving mountains to become pyramids, and filling the

earth with the echoes of its beauty. Yet the individuals in its ban were so
bewitched that, titans though they were in deed, in sentiment they were infantile."[70] And the myth itself? Campbell quotes Eduard Meyer for part of
the extraordinary answer:

> Never on this earth was the task of turning the impossible into the
> possible addressed with so much energy and persistence; the task,
> that is to say, of extending the brief span of a man's years, together
> with all of its delights, into eternity. The Old Empire Egyptians
> believed in this possibility with the deepest fervor; otherwise they
> would never have gone on, generation after generation, squandering
> upon it the whole wealth of the state and civilization. Nevertheless,
> behind the enterprise there lurked the feeling that all of the splendor
> was only illusory; that all the massive means that were being em-
> ployed would even under the most favorable circumstances be able to
> produce only a haunting dreamlike state of existence and not really
> change the facts the least bit. The body, in spite of the magic, still
> would not be alive. . . .[70]

There, in a paragraph, a perfect statement of the "negative" side of the
Atman project: the attempt to deny forever the power of Thanatos, Shiva,
Sunyata. Others have agreed: "In the temple buildings, palaces, and monuments of the new cities we see a new kind of power being generated. No
longer the power of the totemic communion of persons [often found in
magical-typhonic cultures], but the power of the testimonial of piles of
stone and gold. . . . Immortality comes to reside no longer in the invisible world of power, but in the very visible one, and 'death is overcome by
accumulating time-defying monuments.' The pyramid directed its hope of
immortality to the sky which it tried to penetrate, but it displayed itself before men and laid its heavy burden on their backs."[26] Brown puts it thus:

> Every city is an eternal city: civilized money lasts forever. Although
> the ancient Near Eastern city does not yet say, as the Hebrew-Chris-
> tian city says, that its last days shall be greater than its first, yet it has
> already made the decisive step. It endures; time and the city accumu-
> late. But to endure is to conquer death. Civilization is an attempt to
> overcome death. . . . The ambition of civilized man is revealed in
> the pyramid [where reposes] both the hope of immortality and the
> fruit of compound interest [money in time].[61]

That beautifully summarizes the Thanatos or death-denial side of the
new Atman project of membership civilization. As for the positive side,
the Eros side, the attempt to become cosmocentric, omnipotent, and God-
like, we have a decisive commentary from Campbell: "For these [rulers of

dynastic Egypt] supposed that it was in their temporal character that they were god. That is to say, they were mad men. Moreover, they were supported in this belief, taught, flattered, and encouraged, by their clergy, parents, wives, advisers, folk, and all, who also thought they were god. That is to say, the whole society was mad."[70]

"Supposed that it was in their temporal character that they were god"—there is an elegant definition of the positive side of the Atman project. But it was not confined to ancient Egypt: it is rather an essential and universal ingredient in the dynamic of the evolution of the spectrum of consciousness, although it naturally appears in a thousand different forms. That the Egyptians were caught in a blatantly strong form of the Atman project marks them a little different in degree, but not in kind, from the rest of the civilizations of separate selves, from you and from me.

And so, yes, the Egyptians were mad—a conscious madness almost, whereas for us moderns, who also are under sway of the Atman project, that particular form of madness has gone underground, where it slumbers with typhonic magic. For we, too, imagine—even if unconsciously—that in our temporal character we are god, cosmocentric and immortal. If egoic personality, as Roheim put it, is unconscious magic, it is also unconscious madness. Character, said Ferenczi, is a miniature psychosis. And every now and then that madness emerges in blatantly conscious forms as Rasputins, Hitlers, Stalins, and Mussolinis. Make no mistake about it: they *were not weak* characters, but big characters, strong characters, strong egos—which is to say, big psychotics; imagining in their temporal character to be God.

There is an important point about this Egyptian madness, however. As we have said, *every* separate self is mad, in the sense that it necessarily feels itself to be cosmocentric. And as men and women proceeded out of the subconscious, as they extended their capacities and abilities into more expanded realms, they also extended, in many ways, their range of madness. That is, they extended not only the movement toward Atman but also the field through which they could roam with their inflated Atman projects. "In other words, a large part of the subject-matter of our science [of cultural anthropology] must be read as evidence of a psychological crisis of inflation [blowing the self up to god-like proportions] characteristic of the dawn of every one of the great civilizations of the world: the moment of the birth of its particular style."[70] Or we might say with Rank, the moment of the birth of its particular immortality ideology, its own twist on the Atman project, its own peculiar surplus product it tends to farm in its straining toward token transcendence.

Egypt: the single greatest cultural substitute gratification that had yet appeared on mankind's emergence from Eden. However, not all is substitute gratification; not all is substitute subject in here and substitute objects out there. There is the Atman project, but there is also Atman. Both sides must be remembered: the Egyptian madness was madness no doubt, but it was also a monumental growth in consciousness, creativity, and culture. The Egyptians were mad, said Campbell, and "yet out of that madness sprang the great thing that we call Egyptian civilization. Its counterpart in Mesopotamia produced the dynastic states of that area; and we have adequate evidence, besides, of its force in India, the Far East, and Europe as well."[70] Further, with the new growth in consciousness represented by this period of history, we would expect to see a new growth, or a more widespread growth, of transcendence into the superconscious sphere. Mankind as a whole, is, as it were, moving closer to the superconscious realms, and thus individual glimpses into those realms tended to become easier and more widespread. What, then, do the anthropological records show?

"I shall make no further point of this argument," says our mythology guide, "but take it as obvious that the appearance c. 4500–2500 B.C. of an unprecedented constellation of sacra—sacred acts and sacred things—points not to a new theory about how to make the beans grow, but to an actual experience in depth of that *mysterium tremendum* that would break upon us all even now were it not so wonderfully masked."[70] But not just during the high-membership period of classic civilizations but the low-membership period as well, for "when the rites and mythologies even of the most primitive planting villages are compared with those of any tribe of hunters, it is readily seen that they represent a significant deepening . . . of religious feeling. . . . In contrast to the childlike spirit of the mythology of the paleolithic hunt, a new depth of realization is achieved in the horrendous myths and rites of the planting cultures."[69] It could not, I believe, be put much plainer than that.

The mythic-membership structure of consciousness represented a monumental growth over the magical-typhonic, a giant step out of the subconscious sphere. But a step, as we now expect, that also brought new terrors and new horrors. This is absolutely *not* something that I am reading into the anthropological records. We already heard Campbell speak of the "new depth of realization" of this structure, and yet one that was also "*horrendous.*" Horrendous, yes, and shocking—for in the central rite of the great religions of the mythic-membership cultures, we find the secret key not only to the ultimate states of transcendence but also to the terrifying depths of human cruelty. As an archetypal example of the key elements of this central and absolutely significant rite, let us take the following:

> The particular moment of importance to our story occurs at the conclusion of one of the boys' puberty rites, which terminates in a sexual orgy of several days and nights, during which everyone in the village makes free with everybody else, amid the tumult of the mythological chants, drums, and the bull-roarers—until the final night, when a fine young girl, painted, oiled, and ceremonially costumed, is led into the

dancing ground and made to lie beneath a platform of very heavy logs. With her, in open view of the festival, the initiates cohabit, one after another; and while the youth chosen to be last is embracing her the supports of the logs above are jerked away and the platform drops, to a prodigious boom of drums. A hideous howl goes up and the dead girl and boy are dragged from the logs, cut up, roasted, and eaten.[69]

What possibly can be the meaning of such rites? Why would people voluntarily and gleefully participate in such goings-on? Is this nothing but proof positive of an id orgy, replete with destrudo, murderous-sadistic impulses, libido run riot, and capped by a cannibalistic climax? Keep in mind that this rite, or something very similar to it, occurred throughout the civilized farming cultures the world over, as well as in the first high civilizations.

Who is it, then, that is sacrificed? To whom is the sacrifice made? And why?

THE GREAT MOTHER

If there is a dominant figure running throughout the religions of the mythic-membership cultures, it is without doubt that of the Great Mother. "The awesome, wonderfully mysterious Great Mother, whose form and support dominate all the ritual lore of the archaic world, whom we have seen as the cow-goddess Hathor at the four quarters of the festival palette of Narmer, and whose dairyland goddess of the cow, Ninhursag, was the nurse of the early Sumerian Kings, is equally present in the heavens above, in the earth beneath, in the waters under the earth, and in the womb."[70] Professor Moortgat points out that the mother goddess and one of her consorts, the sacred bull, are "the earliest, tangible, significant, spiritual expressions of farming village culture."[70] Thus, "in the neolithic village stage . . . the focal figure of all mythology and worship was the bountiful goddess Earth, as the mother and nourisher of life and receiver of the dead for rebirth."[70]

We will, at the end of the next chapter, be in a position to more precisely comment on all the various meanings of the Mother Goddess, meanings both true and false, real and superstitious, biological and mystical, exoteric and esoteric. This is a very delicate and complicated problem. For instance: Was the Mother Goddess representative of actual transcendence or childish desires for protection? Did she represent actual metaphysical

truth, or was she merely the product of undigested childhood wishes? Was
she representative of Divinity, or just magical crop fertility? Can she be
explained solely in biological and psychoanalytical terms, or are truly mystical and metaphysical interpretations needed?

My own feeling is that *both* naturalistic/biological and metaphysical/
mystical elements are involved, and that both explanations are therefore appropriate and necessary for a rounded theory. Consequently,
I will devote this chapter to a brief study of the biological, natural, and
psychoanalytical explanations of the Mother Goddess, and the next chapter to a study of the transcendent, mystical, and saintly elements of the
Goddess. The Mother Image, in its natural/biological aspects, I will call
the Great Mother, and in its transcendent/mystical aspects, I will call the
Great Goddess. The many similarities—and the vast differences—between
the Great Mother and the Great Goddess will become more and more apparent as we proceed, and I will carefully summarize them at the end of
the next chapter.

We can begin with a decidedly biological example. I have elsewhere
drawn together the evidence that suggests that the Great Mother is, in a
special sense, embedded in both the typhonic and membership structures,
and dominates the psychology of both those stages.[436] This is only true, of
course, in a most general way, but it is a generalization which I intend to
stress heavily, since it seems to explain so much of the material we will be
encountering. To draw on ontogenetic parallels, the basic point, I think, is
fairly straightforward. Louise Kaplan, in *Oneness and Separateness*,[225]
gives the most recent account of what is now a generally accepted tenet of
developmental psychology: the baby at birth does not yet exist as a truly
personal self. Rather, for the first 4–6 months, the baby is literally *one*
with the mother, the environment, and the physical cosmos—what Melanie
Klein called "projective identification."[233] This is the infantile uroboric or
paradisical-Eden state. Starting around 5 or 6 months, that primitive fusion begins to break down, but this is a differentiation that is not completed, more or less, until around 18 months, and is not resolved until
around 36 months. And as the child begins to emerge from that uroboric
fusion, it is faced with the figure—now loving, now terrifying—of the
mother.

And not just the mother, but the Great Mother. As the infant emerges
from its uroboric fusion, the first thing it faces is the mother, and the
mother, for all intents and purposes, is its *entire* world. For this is the
"mother who, in consequence of the biological basis of the family, must
become the whole world of the child."[61] Thus the mother in this regard
can only be thought of as the Great Mother, the Great Environment, or
the Great Surround.[311] And since this separation from the Great Mother
begins at 5 months, is more or less completed at 18 months, but is not
fully resolved until 36 months, the figure of the Great Mother dominates

both the typhonic and membership structures of the child.[436] The Great Mother is embedded in these levels in a way quite unlike any subsequent stages of development. In short, these stages belong to the Great Mother, and pretty much to Her alone—as Kaplan says, "mother is the one partner with whom the baby plays out the separation drama." The father does not significantly enter the picture at all. As we will later see, the father basically enters with the development of the ego level.[311]

Now as the child emerges from the uroboros and develops a rudimentary bodyself set apart from the Great Mother, it also becomes *vulnerable*. Since there is now self, there is now other, and "wherever there is other, there is fear." Fear of extinction, overthrow, dissolution—Thanatos—and all centered on the figure of the Great Mother.[233, 384] The relationship of the bodyself to the Great Mother is thus a relationship of being to non-being, life vs. death—it is existential, not circumstantial.[25] The Great Mother, then, is both the Great Nourisher, the Great Protector, and the Great Destroyer, the Great Devourer—what Sullivan would call the Good Mother and the Bad Mother.[384] But by all accounts, this is an intense relationship, basic, awe-inspiring, fundamental, and consequence-laden.

The Great Mother, then, is initially representative of global, *bodily,* separate, and vulnerable existence in space and time, with consequent desires for a Great Protectress and consequent fears of a Great Destroyer. And it is not hard for me to imagine that something very similar (but not necessarily identical) occurred to mankind on the whole as it emerged from its collective slumber in the uroboric Eden. Just as in the infant, the great "mother is the one partner with whom the baby plays out the separation drama," so also infant mankind, in playing out its early drama of separation from nature ("mother nature") and from fusion with the environment (the Great Surround), had as its constant partner the Great Mother. The Great Mother came thus to represent bodily existence itself, matter and nature, water and earth, and life and death in that naturic realm.[70]

For all these reasons, if your approach to the Great Mother is "good," then She is the Great Protectress, whereas if your approach or actions are "bad," She is the vengeful Destroyer.[126] And here, already, is the psychological dynamic and basis of a *ritual*. Special rites, we will see, are necessary to appease the Great Mother, to keep her as Protectress and prevent her wrathful Vengeance. And as we study those rites, let us keep this basic dynamic in mind, for it is the very key to much that is otherwise puzzling about this period in history and the rituals that defined it.

Now because the Great Mother is embedded in the structures of the typhonic level as well as the membership level, we should look for evidence of some form of Great Mother cult going all the way back to the magical-typhonic period. Obviously, the Mother cults would not, and could not, be as refined, articulate, or well displayed as they are in the lin-

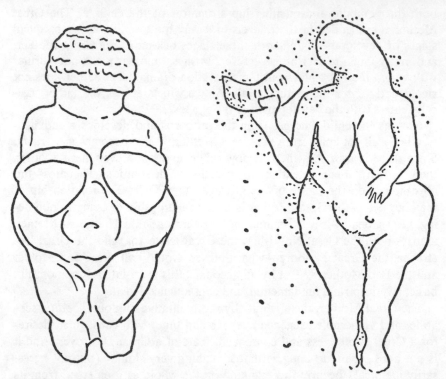

Figs. 13 and 13A. Paleolithic Venus figures, earliest-detected form of the Great Mother.

guistic-membership period, but some evidence should be available. And apparently it is indeed.

As far back as the Paleolithic caves, where the chief objects of mural paintings are the animals of the Great Hunt, the chief object of sculpture is the female figure.[90] Men hardly enter the picture at all, and when they do they are masked or magically modified in form.[92] And more than that, many of the female figurines have been found set up in *shrines,* so that Professor Menghin draws the probable conclusion: these female figurines "represent [an early and initial form of] that same mother-goddess who was to become so conspicuous in the later agricultural civilizations of the Near East and has been everywhere celebrated as the Magna Mater and Mother Earth."[69] As another authority put it, these figures "were, apparently, the first objects of worship of the species Homo sapiens."[69] No wonder that in a single Paleolithic grave site "twenty statuettes of the [Great Mother] goddess were discovered as well as a number of ceremonially buried beasts, [which] speak for the presence of a developed mythology in the late paleolithic, in which the [Great Mother] was already associated with the symbols of the very much later neolithic cult of Ishtar-

Aphrodite: the bird, the fish, the serpent, and the labyrinth."[69] This early form of the Great Mother Campbell nicely calls "Our Lady of the Mammoths"—the crude and initial matriarchy of the Great Hunt.

Thus, all the way back into Paleolithic and typhonic times, we see the Great Mother arise as a correlate of bodily existence itself, an existence epitomized by the biological impact of, and the early dependence on, the mothering one: birth, nursing, weaning, etc. "And from the point of view of the history of thought," concludes Dr. Hancar, "these Late Paleolithic Venus figurines come to us as the earliest detectable expression of that undying ritual idea which sees in Woman the embodiment of the beginning and continuance of life [the Good Mother or Great Protectress], as well as the symbol of . . . earthly matter [mother nature]."[60] In short, says Campbell, the Great Mother "has shown herself at the very dawn of the first day of our own species."*

* Several technical points: As we will later suggest, the Great Mother and the typhonic self simultaneously and correlatively differentiate out of the prior uroboros. The Great Mother then dominates that typhonic stage, and peaks at the mythic-membership stage. We have already followed the emergence and differentiation of the self system from the uroboros to the typhon to the membership; it is fascinating, then, to examine the correlative *emergence and differentiation* of the Great Mother image through those three stages, as it occurred *historically*.

According to Father Schmidt's extraordinary twelve-volume study,[69] archaic societies can be roughly divided into three stages. The very earliest types of human societies (Yahgans, Caribou Eskimo, Pygmies, Kurnai) "do not give rise to either a strong patriarchal or a strong matriarchal emphasis."[60] That is, *the orientation is largely pre-differentiated,* or uroboric. Nonetheless, in some of the mythologies of these simplest of societies, we see, however vaguely, a Great Mother imprint starting, but just starting, to emerge from the uroboros: "The chief personage in the mythology of these little people [the Andamanese] is the northwest monsoon, Bilku, who is sometimes pictured as a spider [a Great Mother archetype, according to Jungians] and whose character . . . is both beneficent and dangerous [Good and Bad Mother]. Bilku is usually said to be a female, and we cannot but recognize in this hardly surprising designation a probable projection of the infantile 'mother imprint.' "[69] But it is a projection still somewhat *fused* to the uroboric and physical sphere. The Great Mother is not yet a differentiated entity.

The next stage of societal development, according to Schmidt, is that of totemistic (magical) hunting groups (typhon). At this stage, as we have seen, there is a cleaner differentiation of self and environment, but it is not complete, so that self and animal nature are magically (totemically) interfused. Society is therefore arranged into clans based upon (1) those totemic identities (holdovers from purely uroboric fusion) and (2) kinship ties (kinship tie means blood tie, which means body-based, or typhonic. Kinship societies are units based on *bodily* interconnections, not *mental* identities; they are the crudest forms of society, based on body-bloodlines and not higher-membership communication).

Naturally, the world of the all-necessary hunt placed a premium on male capacity, and indeed, according to Schmidt, the basic psychology of this stage is masculine. But it is a masculinity that is clearly pre-mental and pre-conceptual, based largely on the physical hunt, the magical totem, and the blood clan. Thus, as Campbell points out, "with the masculine virtues a certain boyish innocence prevails," despite the horren-

Yet even though we recognize that the Great Mother goes all the way back to the earliest typhonic period, we must now concentrate on her more articulate, refined, yet horrendous forms and functions that begin to appear with prominence during the mythic-membership stage. In the earliest typhonic times, the Great Mother was probably not much more than an

---

dous rites of bodily stamina often involved. The point is that this is indeed a type of masculinity, but it is not the *same type* of masculinity that would later define the patriarchy; the former is a body masculinity (called chthonic masculinity by Bachofen and Neumann), the latter is a mental masculinity (called solar patriarchy by Bachofen and Neumann).[16, 311]

Thus, even though these societies were "body masculine" or "adolescent masculine," it was precisely during that period that the Great Mother, like the typhon itself, began clearly to emerge and differentiate from the uroboros. This is why it is not uncommon to find "a paleolithic province where the serpent, labyrinth, and rebirth themes already constitute a symbolic constellation, with the [Great Mother] goddess in her classic role of protectress of the hearth, mother of man's second birth, and lady of the wild things and the food supply. She is here a patroness of the hunt."[69] According to Dr. Hancar, "The psychological background of the idea derives from the feeling and recognition of woman, especially during her periods of pregnancy, as the center and source of an effective magical force."[69] Campbell points out that the various forms of Our Lady of the Mammoths "are the earliest examples of the 'graven image' that we possess, and were, apparently, the first objects of worship of the species Homo sapiens."[69]

The point is that even these body-masculine societies were "ruled," in a sense, by the dawning impact of the Great Mother. This is why Neumann said that hunting societies, even though outwardly masculine, were under sway of the psychology of the Great Mother[311]—a suggestion we will later state as: the Great Mother rules the body realms (body masculinity, therefore, is also under sway of the Great Mother; this is the meaning of chthonic masculinity).

Nonetheless, even though the Great Mother, at this typhonic-hunting stage, is starting to emerge and differentiate from the uroboros, it still remains very close to the uroboros, or, if you will, is "contaminated" by the uroboros. The typhonic self is still given to animal nature, to the sorcerer's Animal Master, to the totem animal ancestor, all of which represent nature *fused,* which is the uroboros, not nature differentiated, which is the Great Mother (or Great Surround). Neumann calls this the maternal uroboros (or, conversely, the uroboric Mother).

It is, then, only at the next major stage—the mythic-membership—that the Great Mother (like the self sense) fully emerges and differentiates from the uroboros. Accordingly, Father Schmidt's next stage—the last of the archaic stages—he calls matriarchal-agricultural. And that is precisely the point we have now reached in our story. At this stage, the Great Mother is fully differentiated from the uroboros; not surprisingly, the Great Mother then encompassed, and even came to represent, *all* the lower levels from which she differentiated: the uroboros became her consort and the typhon her offspring, and she ruled, ultimately, over all nature, biological and material. This also marked the *beginning* of the transition from giving the self over to animal nature with the totem to giving it over to human nature with membership. Nonetheless, in her purest form, the Great Mother represented all nature, matter, instincts, body, crops, earth, fertility, sexuality, emotions, desire, magic, and the beginning of myth. Only at the next stage—the mental-egoic—would the final switch be made from mother nature to human nature, and this marked the beginning of patriarchy, which we will explore in Chapter 13.

impact, a non-verbal shock at separate-self existence, and an expression of simple biological dependence. But by the time of the mythic period, the self sense is more structured, more articulate, and so likewise the Great Mother. Men and women were more conscious of their own tenuous existence, and thus more conscious of the Great Mother—what she was, and what she demanded.

And what she demanded was sacrifice—human sacrifice.

SACRIFICE: THE CORE OF MEMBERSHIP MYTHOLOGY

Let us begin by quickly noticing the most common symbols associated with the Great Mother, symbols that arose, in the main, for simple naturalistic and biological reasons—nothing deeply metaphysical about them (there is, we will see, precious little that is truly metaphysical about the Great Mother or any of her symbols or rites). There is, first and foremost, the natural association of the moon and the womb, for both the lunar and the menstrual cycle run that twenty-eight-day course of watery and oceanic tides. Thus, very early on the Great Mother was associated with lunar and water symbolism. In particular, as the moon is the consort of the Earth, so the moon, or some sort of lunar symbol, was the lover or god-consort of the Earth Goddess. Thus, in mythology we find that the consort of the Great Mother was the lunar-serpent, the lunar-bull, the lunar-pig, and so on.

But notice: at the end of the monthly lunar cycle, the moon "disappears" or "dies"—it goes dark, it goes into the underworld or netherworld. But within three days, behold: the moon is reborn and resurrected! In fact, the moon *must* die if a new cycle is to begin. So the first symbolic equation we must bear in mind is just that: *the consort of the Great Mother is the three-day-dead-and-resurrected god.*

The second important equation is a little more chilling, for it involves the equation of blood with life. Malinowski, Bachofen, Neumann, and others have pointed out that mankind's earliest understanding of sexual reproduction was far from scientifically correct. There was a time, for example, when mankind did not really understand that sexual intercourse led to pregnancy. Consider that intercourse can occur hundreds of times a year, but a pregnancy and birth only once every nine months, at most. Further, in primitive societies children of ages five to twelve are often instructed in intercourse and set to the act, mostly for the howling entertainment of the elders. And no pregnancies. So all this intercourse, and only occasionally a child—to the primitive mind, something else was obviously responsible, and it was something in the woman alone. As a matter of fact, until just recent times, if a marriage could not produce offspring, the woman alone was blamed.

It was not the male semen, then, that caused pregnancy, birth, and new life. And even when it was vaguely understood—as it soon was—that the male was needed as a consort, he was still a very secondary figure. He was merely the bearer of the phallus, and any phallus would do. Hence the predominance in mythology of the phallic Mother, the hermaphroditic Mother, for the "men whom the Mother selects for her lovers may impregnate her, they may even be fertility gods, but the fact remains that they are only phallic consorts of the Great Mother, drones serving the queen bee."[311]

Figs. 14 and 14A. Classic representations of the Great Mother, the serpent Mother. The serpent-uroboros, because it is intimately connected with or to the Mother, shows perfectly her typhonic form. The serpent also represents the phallus of the Great Mother, who is always hermaphroditic (as we will explain in Chapter 13).

This is also why the Great Mother is always portrayed as a virgin—it is not that she is without intercourse, but that she belongs in intercourse to no man whatsoever; she is forever the same, while men are but interchangeable bearers of the consort phallus. As Bachofen put it, "Ever the same Great Mother mates with ever new men." And so, even as virgin, or especially as virgin, she and not the male still reigns over all phallus cults, and all phallus cults are cults of the virgin Great Mother. "Accordingly, the fertility goddess is both mother and virgin, the hetaera who belongs to no man."[311]

Follow this through (and remember we are working with paleologic or mythic thinking): since the Great Mother is both mother and lover as *one,* her consort is both her husband and her son, or her son-lover. Likewise, the son is his own father (as was said of the pharaoh, for instance), although "father" is perhaps too strong a word. For the whole point of these paleological equations is derived from the fact that the father principle per se does not yet, as we said, really enter the picture as an independent force.

This is why the Great Mother is everywhere portrayed as the bride as well as the virgin mother of god. . . . All of this can be understood if we simply remember that at this stage of evolution the father principle is not yet dominant. Mothers and daughters, sons and lovers, wives and brides and consorts—but no real biological fathers. No wonder men in these societies were, as Campbell put it, one jot away from insignificance, and no wonder they banded together in men's clubs and secret societies, which remain to this day as Elks' Lodges, Odd Fellows' Clubs, Shriners' conventions, and so on, in order to escape the dominance of the female principle. And yet, who was the divinity worshipped in these first clubs? The Great Mother, of course.†

At any rate, if in pregnancy the male semen is superfluous, or at best secondary, what constitutes the "substance" of new life? To the primitive it was obvious: the menstrual blood flow of the woman continues periodically throughout her maturity—*except when she is pregnant.* And thus it is this "withheld" menstrual blood that is being converted into the form of a living baby and new life.[311] And therefore the Great Mother *needs blood* in order to bring forth new life. And this equation was supplemented by the otherwise quite accurate perception that *bodily life depends on blood:* take away blood, and you take away life. For either or both of these

† I am aware that such motifs as the virgin birth can be given and were given highly metaphysical meanings in *subsequent* history and evolution. I am denying that they are *only* metaphysical; most were simple paleologic, and can be reproduced today by any child of age five, as the simplest study of Piaget will show. The ways in which some of these motifs *were* taken as *symbols* of transformation and metaphysical truths will be discussed in the next chapter.

reasons, the conclusion was obvious: just as the earth needs rain to bring forth crops, the Great Mother needs blood to bring forth new life.

When we put these two symbolic equations (of the dead and resurrected lunar-god consort and the blood sacrifice for life) together, we straight-forwardly arrive at the perfect logic of the early rites of human sacri-fice: the symbolic consort (human or animal) is sacrificed in blood to the Great Mother, dies, and is resurrected (after three days, according to many myths). In fact, the Great Mother follows the dead god-consort into the dark underworld, and there effects his resurrection, thus ensuring an-other cycle of new life and new fertility and new moon. In the sacrifice it-self, the god-consort is actually uniting (symbolized by sexual inter-course)‡ with the Great Mother, and thus himself is *reborn* or resurrected (becoming, in the process, the father of himself). The Great Mother re-mains throughout as *"the mother-bride of the dead and resurrected god."*[70] Notice that this is precisely the formula of Mary/Jesus—she is both the mother of the dead and resurrected god (Jesus) and the virgin bride of god (the Father). But before Mary and Jesus were Damuzi and Inanna, Tamuz and Ishtar, Osiris and Isis—it is an old, old story.

To put it all in a nutshell: what was the way to appease the Great Mother, to keep her as Protectress and prevent her wrathful Vengeance? Give her what she demands—blood! And likewise, invent a precise way to do it—ritual! Thus, the first great ritual was a ritual of blood sacrifice, offered to the Great Mother—to Mother Nature—in a bartered attempt to quench her desire for blood, blood that, for various reasons, was (not al-together incorrectly) equated with life itself. Blood is indeed bodily life, and if you want to purchase life, you buy it with blood. So goes paleologic; like magic, it works with partial truths; and, like magic, since it is unable to grasp higher perspectives or wider contexts, it arrives at barbaric con-clusions.

Now these early sacrificial rites were carried out in *earnest* and in literal renditions. We have already seen the sacrifice of the maiden-virgin and her young consort in the ritual sex-death, which is one of the earliest and most primitive of ritual sacrifices anywhere. But ritual—and frequently voluntary—sacrifice occurred throughout the periods of the first high civilizations, and indeed, has continued until just recently in parts of Africa and India. The sacrifice itself has taken various forms—initially, it was almost univer-sally of living human beings, but later animals (the goat, bull, boar, horse, lamb) were substituted. When kingship first came into existence, as we shall see, the first kings were sacred, they were viewed as gods and thus as consorts of the Great Mother. And we know what happens to consorts of the Great Mother. There is abundant evidence that the earliest kings vol-

‡ Precisely as in the sex-death ritual described earlier, where various consorts mate with the virgin maiden (Great Mother), the last consort being killed.

untarily submitted themselves to ritual regicide, and frequently at their own hands.

> When his time came, the king had a wooden scaffolding constructed and spread over with hangings of silk. And when he had ritually bathed in a tank . . . he proceeded to the temple, where he paid worship to the divinity. Then he mounted the scaffolding and, before the people, took some very sharp knives and began to cut off parts of his body—nose, ears, lips, and all his members, and as much of his flesh as he was able—throwing them away and round about, until so much of his blood was spilled that he began to faint, whereupon he slit his throat.[69]

In other cases, the king was simply strangled and buried with a living virgin at his side. In yet other cases, just the virgin sacrifice would do, and in latter times, mere animal sacrifice of goats and bulls—the Spanish bullfight being a secularized holdover. But the logic remains the same: the god must die and be reborn of the Great Mother to ensure new life and fertility. Frobenius comments:

> The great god must die; forfeit his life and be shut up in the underworld, within the mountain. The goddess (and let us call her Ishtar, using her later Babylonian title) follows him into the underworld and after the consummation of his self-immolation, releases him. The supreme mystery was celebrated not only in renowned songs, but also in the ancient new-year festivals, where it was presented dramatically: and this dramatic presentation can be said to represent the acme of the manifestation of the grammar and logic of mythology in the history of the world.[153]

We needn't dwell further on the historical details. Let us simply note that a "fury for sacrifice" beset, "at one time or another, every part of the archaic world in the various high periods of its numerous cultures." Most notably, "Sir James G. Frazer, in *The Golden Bough,* has shown that in the early city-states of the nuclear Near East, from which center all the high civilizations of the world have been derived, god-kings were sacrificed [ritually and regularly], and Sir Leonard Woolley's excavation of the Royal Tombs of Ur, in which whole courts had been ceremonially interred alive, revealed that in Sumer such practices continued as late as c. 2350."[70, 136, 438]

In a phrase, what we call civilization, and what we call human sacrifice, came into being together.

THE RITUAL SACRIFICE

We are all probably aware of the stock answer given to the question "why sacrifice?" Which is: it is a magical attempt at fertility, at increasing crops, rain, and so on. And this is certainly true, or certainly partly true, especially when we consider that if the crops failed, all sorts of extra human sacrifices were frequently offered up, usually starting with the king himself. Frazer, for instance, believed the sacrifices were a practical measure, practically conceived, to effect a magical fertilization of the soil. Psychoanalysis has added its own twist: the rites were a technique to expiate guilt for incestuous wishes for the Mother. Others see the ritual as a source of power (mana) generation.

All of which is true. But, in my opinion, what all of those explanations have in common is that the sacrificial ritual was carried out to appease and expiate death guilt (in the form of the Devouring Mother) and thus ensure the fertile future of the separate self, and, beyond that, to increase the separate self's power if at all possible (under the auspices of the Great Protectress). The ritual, in short, was an ingenuous combination of both wings of the Atman project: a way to magically buy off death and a way to make the practitioner of ritual appear "in charge of" the elements of nature, in charge of rain, of fertility, of life itself—in charge of the Great Mother, of Mother Nature—omnipotent, cosmocentric, deified.

That is, the ritual served as a magical substitute for transcendence and immortality, a magical rite to ensure fertility, ensure the future, ensure in fact that death will not grin in at the harvest, while simultaneously presenting the self as central to the cosmos and all-favored among the otherwise vengeful elements of Mother Nature. "Perhaps the most mysterious of all human institutions," says Mumford, "one that has been often described but never adequately explained, is that of human sacrifice: a magical effort either to expiate guilt or promote a more abundant yield of crops."[26] And I am saying it was *both,* playing simultaneously off the desire for absolute life and the desire to expiate the death guilt of the separate self. As Becker has amply demonstrated, the ritual had two sides: Heroism and Repentance, or "the experience of prestige and power [Eros] that constitutes man a hero, and the experience of expiation [of death/Thanatos] that relieves him of the guilt of being human [a separate-self sense]."[26]

There is no need for me to repeat Becker's penetrating analysis; enough to say that I fully agree with it as far as it goes. My point is simply that, when the world is viewed through the eyes of the *mythic structure* of consciousness, ritual offerings and sacrifices are precisely consistent with that structure itself, and they both express and embody the two wings of the Atman project as manifested at that level. In other words, the *form* of the ritual logic (which we have explained throughout this chapter) is precisely what would be expected given only a mythic or paleologically structured world view: appeasement of a naturic Great Mother, pranic associations, Earth worship, emotional-sexual elements, blood rituals, paleological symbolism (moon = god, son = his own father, mother = virgin-bride, etc.). Into those paleological *forms* of consciousness was poured the always prior Atman intuition, and the resultant mixture was an Atman project based on and evidenced in mythic formulas, magical rituals, fetishistic tokens, and sacrificial fury—all representing state-specific grabs at immortality, on the one side, and outlets for cosmocentric drives, on the other. And just there was the heart of the ritual and brutal fury for sacrifice that beset, "at one time or another, every part of the archaic world in the various high periods of its numerous cultures."

However, so significant is the very emergence of human sacrifice itself, so central is it to the motivations of men and women, even to this day, that we will soon return to this topic, and devote an entire chapter to it (Chapter 8). The foregoing thus stands as a simple introduction to the topic itself, a topic soon to be examined in chilling detail.

THE STRUGGLING SELF

There is yet another meaning involved in the ancient sacrifices to the Great Mother—but this meaning is probably not one that could have been known at that time. It serves rather to tell *us,* who can look back in hindsight, something about the structure of the self at that time. That is, the sacrificial priest was probably aware, to some degree, however slight, that he was performing the ritual in order to "ensure" fertility, appease the Great Mother, etc. And the average lay practitioner was probably aware that he had to participate in these rites or else calamity would strike. But what neither could know is that the whole corpus of Great Mother mythology points to the nature of the self sense at that stage in evolution.

For the essence of the Great Mother is that she demanded the dissolution, the sacrifice, of the separate self. Let us note that: the Great Mother demands the dissolution of the self. But the self can dissolve in two entirely different directions: one, it can dissolve in transcendence, it can fall forward into superconsciousness. But two, it can dissolve in regression, in a falling back into the subconscious, in an obliteration of personality and not a transcendence of it. And whereas, for a very few, the Mother was, and still is, the portal to subtle superconsciousness, the way to transcend the personality (as we will see in the next chapter), she was for most that terrible form of inertia which *prevented* the emergence, out of the uroboros and typhon, of a truly strong personality. In this capacity, which for all intents and purposes is actually *the* defining standard of the Great Mother, and the one I will subsequently emphasize, she was the Chthonic Mother, the Mother that sacrificed the newly emerging self by reducing it to one of her mere satellites; she was the Earth Mother, which pulled the newly crystallizing mind back into the body, back into mother nature, back into instincts and will-less subservience to the typhon and the uroboros, back ultimately into that diffuse primal state wherein self and environment cannot be differentiated. As if the Great Mother would not give up her offspring, as if she would not let the self truly differentiate from her and stand on its own—as if all that were happening, the Great Mother sacrificed and dissolved the newly emerging self every time it tried to rise up in independence, so that mankind on the whole remained at this stage nothing but a "momma's boy."

How does one arrive at that type of interpretation? What is the basis for drawing such a conclusion? Actually, the procedure is very simple: one merely takes the whole corpus of what is called "Great Mother mythology" and subjects it to a type of statistical analysis as to the fate of the individuals who come into close contact with the Great Mother, as reported specifically and unequivocally in the myths themselves. What one finds is that the individuals involved with the Mother invariably come to a tragic end, invariably are killed or murdered or commit suicide or are castrated—in general, they are simply devoured by the Mother or one of her deputies. And I am saying that that is symbolic, deeply symbolic, of the nature of the self at that time. For men and women wrote those myths, and it shows that they are having a terrible time summoning the courage to break away from the Great Earth Mother, to clearly differentiate themselves from her and strike out on their own. And every time one of the heroes actually starts to do this, the writer of the myth, as if thinking twice about the terror of "leaving home" and becoming overtaken by guilt at the prospect, finishes off the hero with short dispatch and a quick comment: "Nice try."

All of this is symbolic, as Neumann demonstrated, of the fact that the self at this stage of evolution was not yet strong enough to detach itself from the Great Mother, from mother nature, from the body, the emotions, and the flood of the unconscious. In one exquisite paragraph he saw right to the heart of the matter: "When one knows how the Great Mother wreaks her vengeance in the myths, one can see the story in its proper setting. The self-mutilation and suicide of Attis, Eshmun, and Bata; Narcissus dying of self-attraction; Actaeon, like so many other youths, changed into an animal and torn to pieces; all this hangs together. And whether it be

Aithon burning in the fires of his own passion, or Daphnis languishing in insatiable desire because he does not love the girl Aphrodite sends him; whether we interpret the dragging to death of Hippolytus as madness, love, or retribution—in every case the central fact is the vengeance of the Great Mother, the overpowering of the ego by the subterranean."[311]

The point is that, at this stage of evolution, the newly emerging self was still not entirely independent of the Great Environment and the Great Mother, its existence was somewhat tenuous and faltering, and thus it was frequently sacrificed and dissolved back into typhonic or even uroboric structures—reabsorbed by the Great Mother and returned to infantile embeddedness in nature and body. And this sacrifice—this *prevention* of the emergence of the self—is just what the myths show.*

It is an entire commentary on this whole period that the vast, vast majority of souls were under sway of the Chthonic and Devouring Great Mother, still not strong enough to awaken as self-conscious beings, still struggling to crystallize finally out of subconsciousness, and still succumbing in the attempt.

* I.e., the self system, at this stage in history, was itself nothing but the sacrificed lunar consort of the devouring Great Mother.

7 The Great Goddess

"I am she that is the natural mother of all things, mistress and governess of all the elements, the initial progeny of worlds, chief of the powers divine, queen of all that are in hell, the principal of them that dwell in heaven, manifested alone and under one form of all the gods and goddesses. At my will the planets of the sky, the wholesome winds of the sea, and the lamentable silences of hell are disposed; my name, my divinity is adored throughout the world, in divers manners, in variable customs, and by many names. But the Egyptians, which are excellent in all kind of ancient doctrine, and by their proper ceremonies accustomed to worship me, do call me by my true name, Queen Isis."[71]

"Manifested alone and under one form"—and right there are the words of a Divinity no longer caught in polytheistic fragments, animistic separations, or diverse nature gods and goddesses. Right there, in short, are the initial insights into a truly transcendent Oneness, a Oneness that is not simply the naturic backdrop of the Great Mother or Earth Mother, but rather the One Form and Divine Ground of all space and time, the Great Goddess herself. "Now in the neolithic village stage," says Campbell. "the focal figure of all mythology and worship was the bountiful goddess Earth [the Great Mother, as we saw], the mother and nourisher of life [a simple, natural, biological connection, as we also saw]. In the earliest period of her cult (perhaps c. 7500–3500 B.C. in the Levant) such a mother-goddess may have been thought of only as a local patroness of fertility, as many anthropologists suppose [and rightly so, as far as it goes]. However, in the temples even of the first of the higher civilizations (Sumer, c. 3500–2350 B.C.), the Great Goddess of highest concern was certainly much more than that. She was already, as she is now in the Orient, a metaphysical symbol: the arch personification of the power of Space, Time, and Matter, within whose bound all beings arise and die: the substance of their bodies, configurator of their lives and thoughts, and receiver of their dead. And everything having form or name—including God personified as good or evil, merciful or wrathful—was her child, within her womb."[71]

Already we are starting to see a fundamental difference between the Great Mother—a simple biological nourisher and fertility token, magically blown up to cosmic proportions—and the Great Goddess—a subtle Oneness of actual Transcendence, representative of true Divinity. And by the end of this chapter, I hope to demonstrate not only that these are two entirely different figures, but that they actually subsist in different structures of consciousness: they exist in and at different levels of the Great Chain of Being.

TRUE SACRIFICE

One of the reasons, apparently, that the striking differences between the Great Mother and the Great Goddess have not been often noticed by scholars is that the very same outward symbols, rituals, and ceremonies can be and often were used for both. But this, in fact, is true for every religious sacrament, not just those of the Mother—it can be used *exoterically*, in which case it merely reinforces average-mode mentality, and is motivated by average psychological dynamics; and it can be used *esoterically*, in which case it transcends average-mode mentality and discloses superconscious impulses. But the very same rite, the very same myth, the very same sacrament, can be used for both purposes—and this, apparently, was also the case for Great Mother rites and Great Goddess rites.

Put it a different way: a given rite, ceremony, sacrament, or myth can function as a *symbol,* in which case it evokes higher levels of self and reality, or as a mere *sign,* in which case it simply confirms and strengthens the same mundane level of self and reality.[436] That is, a given rite or sacrament can serve as a symbol of *transformation* or as a sign of *translation.* The first function is properly religious (esoteric), and works to undermine or dissolve the self in God consciousness; whereas the second function is merely substitutive, and serves to perpetuate and strengthen the self sense by securing magical substitutes for God. The same rite, the same myth, the same motifs can and do act in both capacities, depending largely on the psychological state of the individual who confronts them and the understanding he brings to them.* Thus, for example, the Christ figure is, to a mystic, a perfect embodiment and symbol of one's timeless and selfless Essence, whereas to the fortified Christian ego—which, as is the nature of all egos, is in flight from death—the Christ figure is a mere sign of the separate self's hoped-for immortality, a sign of the self's going on forever and forever. Prayer for the former is contemplative; for the latter, petitionary. In the same way, today the Catholic Mass—its physical paraphernalia, its ceremonies, its rites, its dress, its symbols, and its wording—is really meaningful, symbolic, and transformative for only a few individuals. The rest go through the motions as an insurance policy—to cover their bets on immortality.

Precisely the same applies to the *ritual sacrifice,* for there are two forms of sacrifice: literal blood sacrifice and symbolic self-sacrifice. And with the major exception of actually killing someone, the same rites, symbols, paraphernalia, etc., were historically used in both capacities, exoteric and esoteric. I will give a prime example of this in a moment. For now, we simply repeat that the very *notion* of sacrifice was used, by the vast majority of membership individuals, as a purely translative gesture in an attempt to magically ensure fertility and expiate guilt. It was a blood sacrifice of an *other* in order to *save oneself* (as we will carefully explain in Chapter 8). But the simple notion of *sacrifice,* as well as the same rites, ceremonies, and temple gear (sans murder), also served, for an advanced few, as a symbol of transformation and an *aid* to transcendence. And so what did these religious ceremonies mean in their symbolic/transformative function, in their esoteric capacity, as opposed to their literal and exoteric rendition?

Most modern anthropologists fail to ask this question because they fail to distinguish between sign and symbol, exoteric and esoteric, translation and transformation, and so they view *all* religious sacraments as mere fantasy productions with only magical results. I have already agreed that that was indeed true for the vast majority. But those sacraments can also function in an esoteric mode, and those much closer to the heart of the numinous, both as it appears today and has appeared in the past, see more clearly this esoteric meaning. For example, Joseph Campbell: "When the will of the individual to his own immortality has been extinguished—as it is in rites such as these—through an effective realization of the immortality of

---

* This is, I think, precisely what Campbell means when he says that historically and almost universally any given myth has always served two basic purposes: to initiate and engage individuals into normal society so as to bolster typical group mentality, and—in other circumstances—to disengage and detach them from normal society so as to open them to actual transcendence.[69, 70, 71]

being itself and of its play through all things, he is united with that being, in experience, in a stunning crisis of release from the psychology of guilt and mortality."[69]

Notice specifically that what these symbolic ceremonies help to extinguish is "the will of the individual to his own immortality," which is a *precise* definition of the Atman project; and the new Destiny resurrected from the stream of consciousness is the "immortality [or timeless eternity] of being itself," which is a perfect definition of Atman (Brahman). This was a true process of transformation—translation fails as Thanatos exceeds Eros, and transformation ensues—and therefore it effects, as Campbell noted, a *real* and not merely expiatory release from mortality and guilt. The whole point of these esoteric ceremonies, rituals, prayers, etc., was to accept the death of the separate-self sense and thus rise to an identity or communion with the Great Goddess. This was a self-sacrifice, which allowed the individual to transcend his self without obliterating it, murdering it, or regressing to pre-personal stages.

I repeat, however, that for the masses of membership individuals, the sacrificial rites were exoteric, substitutive, magical, fetishistic, serving precisely the purposes explained in the last chapter (and detailed in Chapter 8). They were ritual ramblings to the Great Mother, and represented not trans-personal release but pre-personal dissolution, usually via barbaric murder.

But the sacrificial ceremony, when used in its esoteric form, captured the essence of trans-personal liberation via self-transcendence. These ceremonies and prayers became offerings of one's soul to the Great Goddess, not another person's body in blood to the Great Mother. The Great Mother demands blood; the Great Goddess demands consciousness. The great *outward* difference, therefore, is that offerings to the Great Mother were always sacrifices involving literal body death or blood murder,† whereas the sacrifice of the soul to the Great Goddess was a self-sacrifice which occurred in the heart, and never involved literal body murder. However, with that sole exception of body murder, all the other outward forms of ritual, ceremony, and myth could be, and were often, quite similar.

Take, as the supreme Western example, the great exoteric themes of Christianity: the three-day-dead-and-resurrected god, born of a virgin who is the mother as well as bride of god, the sacrificial lamb who *had* to die in order to ensure new life, whose body we eat and whose blood we drink, whose sacrifice ensures the future. . . .

All of those are exoteric, pagan, Great Mother holdovers—all you have to do to arrive at a perfect Great Mother ritual, as it was actually prac-

---

† Human, animal, or occasionally symbols thereof (when the strength of the body-bound blood ritual was eventually weakened, animals were substituted, and then symbols alone).

ticed, is to really kill someone. And, right at the point in the Catholic Communion, where the wafer and wine are served, simply roast and eat the victim instead (an example of which we earlier quoted). But those same sacraments, without murder, and carried out in a self-sacrificial frame, are perfectly legitimate *symbols* of transformation and *aids* to transcendence. Such, exactly, is the *esoteric* impact of the true Catholic Mass, and such, exactly, is the esoteric meaning of its symbols. Christ is sacrificed (the lamb), he dies to his separate self (the Crucifixion), is reborn to Ascend into Heaven (Actual Transcendence); the eating of his body (bread and wine) is a comm-union that initiates one into that higher Mystical Body or Ultimate Union, which likewise demands the death of one's own separate self so that "not I, but Christ" may reign.‡ All of those symbols, and the rites and ceremonies associated with those symbols, are esoterically meant to function as *supports of contemplation* or symbolic transformers. In that capacity, they are outward and visible forms of inward and spiritual truths. They address a Transcendent Divinity—Great God, Great Goddess—and not a biological, naturic, magic-mythic Great Mother.

Unfortunately, of course, the esoteric underside of Christianity has all but vanished in the West (as we will see in Chapter 14). Thus, most Christians today are exoteric worshippers; that is, most Christians actually practice, in large measure, nothing more than holdovers from pagan Great Mother rituals. The "fundamentalists," especially, are committed to *literal* interpretations of the Bible; i.e., they recognize only signs, not symbols. No wonder that fundamentalist Christianity (along with fundamentalist Islam) has historically been the religion most willing to actually consummate their pagan Great Mother rituals and go ahead and murder, in blood sacrifice, any who disagreed with them. Holy war is nothing but thinly rationalized Great Mother worship, and the exoteric Christians and Muslims, without any doubt whatsoever, have killed more people in the name of a "divinity" than any other peoples in history. The only thing bloodier than a Christian holy war or a Muslim holy war is a Christian holy war on Muslims (or vice versa). And don't say this is a necessary result of religion per se; in Buddhism's 2,500-year history, it has fought not one single religious war.

But aside from that digression; my point is that attempting to judge the meaning and essence of a ritual, ceremony, or sacrament merely by its outward form is a perfectly inadequate approach, because the same outward form can be acting as a sign in translation or as a symbol in trans-

---

‡ "I am crucified with Christ, nevertheless I live; yet not I, but Christ liveth in me" (Galatians 2:20). "Christ died for your sins" means "Christ died to his separate self so as to relieve you of yours." This, surely, is what Christ meant by "No man can be my disciple who hateth not his own soul" (Luke 14:26). As Blake put it, "I will go down to self-annihilation and Eternal Death; Lest the Last Judgement come and find me unannihilate; And I be seiz'd and giv'n into the hands of my own selfhood."

Fig. 15. The Great Goddess. Notice specifically that she is not merely of the earth, but has her head reaching into heaven. Her head itself is halo-encircled. She controls the earth and the underworld, as the chain in her left hand shows, but she herself is transcended and controlled by the ultimate causal Being beyond her, as the chain on her right hand and the cloud

formation. The failure to differentiate these two modes leads, among an extraordinary number of other things, to the inability to tell the difference between the biological Great Mother, which dominated average member-ship mentality, and the transcendent Great Goddess, which represented realms of the superconscious actually discovered by a few transcendent he-roes of that period. And it is to this discovery we now look.

THE SAMBHOGAKAYA VISION: SUBTLE ONENESS

We are now in a position to examine more precisely the nature and con-tent of the true religious experience of the most advanced individuals of the mythic-membership period. That is, we must continue to differentiate, with increasing forcefulness, the transcendent Great Goddess from the merely biological and superstitious Great Mother.

Our essential point can be put simply: from all the available evidence, it seems almost certain that the true priests and saints—the *most highly evolved* souls of this period—saw into the realm of the Sambhogakaya, or the subtle realm of the superconscious (level 6). In typhonic times, the farthest a truly advanced being could see was to the edge of the Nir-manakaya realm (level 5)—and that was just what the shaman did. By the time of the membership period, however, consciousness on the whole had collectively evolved much farther. Thus, the truly advanced heroes of this period could jump much higher, as it were, and start to see into the Sam-bhogakaya realm, the realm that lies beyond the Nirmanakaya (but not as far as the Dharmakaya, to put it all rather crudely). The higher the aver-age mode, the higher the jump-off base for the advanced mode, so to speak. As John White put it, "Each period had its transcendent heroes, but the heroes kept getting taller."

In the Sambhogakaya realm, according to the perennial philosophy, states of intense Oneness begin (but only begin) to disclose themselves (a process that, as we will see, peaks in the Dharmakaya realm). This begin-ning insight into subtle and archetypal oneness leads to the conception of a

above her head show. In the earliest versions of the Great Goddess insight, it was not understood that there was a higher Being beyond the psychic or subtle levels (beyond the Goddess). Only with the coming of the Sun Gods ("the Sun behind the sun") would the subtle level be truly understood and then surpassed. But the Great Goddess was certainly one of the first figures to rise up from chthonic earth and set its head in subtle heaven, and that is just what is depicted in this figure.

One God or One Goddess which underlies and gives birth to all manifest worlds and all lesser god or nature-spirit figures. And it is the *beginning* of just this realization of One God or One Goddess that underlies the *esoteric* religions of this period, a realization *never before expressed* in myth or ritual to any decent degree.

This realization, however, was very crude and approximate at first, so that, historically, there tended to be all sorts of confusion as to just *who* should be the One God/dess in the first place. But the beginning realization was there; we already heard of the earliest-known body of religious writings: "Therefore it is said of Ptah: 'It is he who made all and brought the gods into being.' He is verily the Risen Land that brought forth the gods, for everything came forth from him." *That is a statement which takes as its referent the actual subtle realm* (level 6), the realm of beginning Oneness, the realm of the One God/dess who gives birth to the various lower levels, divine as well as ordinary.

It doesn't ultimately matter whether this archetypal oneness is represented as a God or Goddess; historically, both representations were used for different emphasis. The important fact—and the only fact I want to emphasize—is that historically the transcendent or esoteric Great Goddess myths clearly reflected, and were the first to reflect, this subtle-level oneness or archetypal ground (level 6). This subtle oneness would later (for various reasons) be represented more often by the One God (Jehovah, Aton, etc., as we will see), and then surpassed altogether by the ultimate unity of the Dharmakaya (level 7). But our initial point remains: the first widespread glimpses into subtle oneness occurred under the auspices of the Great Goddess, so that, even to this day, modern saints and sages continue to refer to this *initial* realization as belonging to the Mother Goddess (as even the most cursory study of Hindu and Vajrayana texts will disclose), the Goddess "within whose bound all beings arise and die: the substance of their bodies, configurator of their lives," as Campbell put it.

Our historical point is that, prior to this membership period, it was not understood that there is One Ground or Archetypal Deity which underlies or sub-stands all manifestation. There were all sorts of simple, magical, elemental god figures, animistic nature spirits, etc.; there was a god of fire, a goddess of wind, a god of volcanoes, a goddess of rain (although "god" and "goddess" are perhaps too suggestive terms—they were more like "elemental personifications"). This was the primitive vision that ranged from "animism" to "polytheism," a correlate of the not yet integrated, evolved, and unified psyche. With the rise of the membership structure, however, consciousness on the whole had advanced to the point that, even while the masses still worshipped various gods and goddesses, it was increasingly understood, by an esoteric few, that beyond all of that lay the One and Living God/dess (of the subtle realm), the One Deity that "brought forth the gods, for everything came forth from that [One]." Or, as Isis would herself proclaim: "I am the . . . mother of all things . . . manifested alone and under one form." And while we will eventually see that even this Archetypal Deity gives way to its prior Source in the unmanifest Void (the Dharmakaya), let us have the sense to recognize the greatness of this initial step itself, the first discovery of the subtle or archetypal level.

But precisely as soon as this initial One Form or Archetypal Deity was understood (first in the form of the Great Goddess), it was understood as well that in order *to reach* any sort of oneness (including the cruder form

Fig. 16. Kwannon Bosatu, Japanese Buddhist Goddess of Compassion. An excellent representation of the Great Goddess. Notice her head is surrounded by two halos of light and a ring of fire—all indications of the subtle-level oneness which she is.

of Sambhogakaya oneness now under consideration), it was necessary to *die* to the separate-self sense. The separate self had to be *sacrificed* prior to the Resurrection of Oneness; it had to be crucified prior to the Ascent in Eternity; it had to be burnt in the flames of awareness prior to its ultimate Release.

This central insight, which is really the core of esoteric religion, went all the way back, as we saw, to the shamanistic trance. The shaman accepted the death of his typhonic self, translation ceased, and transformation into superconscious states occurred. How crude it all was, however, resulting only in psychic intuition (level 5). Yet by the time of mythic-membership, we see that the overall growth of consciousness has given this death-demanding transformation a higher and more articulate expression, one which sprang from the subtle heart: accept the death of the membership-self, go beyond farming in time to release in eternity, sacrifice self-immortality and discover the immortality of all Being—in short, let mere translation die and transformation begin.

That simple yet crucial insight—"the sacrifice of self discloses the Eternal"—was the esoteric insight empowering the mythology of self-sacrifice to the Great Goddess, sacrifice carried out in prayer, in contemplation, in meditative ritual and ceremony, in symbolic Mass. Please remember, however, that if "esoteric" means "highest," it also means "least significant," in the sense that this esoteric understanding was possessed by very few, and the masses themselves turned to a fury of sacrifice for other and decidedly less noble reasons, and in literal renditions that could not conceal the underlying barbarism of the Great and Devouring Mother.

THE TWO STRANDS OF EVOLUTION

What we have seen is that, *just as consciousness on the average was evolving, so were the farthest reaches of that consciousness.* Where average (or overall) evolution was producing successively advanced exoteric civilizations and world cultures, the further reaches (or most advanced tip) of consciousness evolution were disclosing successively higher levels of the superconscious sphere. Thus, at the stage when the average mode was magical-typhonic (level 2), the most advanced mode disclosed ecstatic body trance and psychic intuition (5). At the stage when the average mode was membership (3), the most advanced mode was disclosing visions of subtle oneness and transcendent bliss (6). As we will see, when the average mode reached the mental-egoic level (4), the most advanced

*Fig. 17. The Risen Serpent Lord. From a carved vase, inscribed 2025 B.C.
by King Gudea of Lagash. Scholars have often puzzled at how and why the
serpent, of all the animals, has been historically viewed as everything from
the most evil of devils to the highest of all gods. The reason, I believe, is
straightforward, and is determined by noting the* location *of the serpent in
reference to either the human body or the earth. If crawling on the earth,
lying in the ocean, found coiled at the base of any structure, or if located at
or in the lower half of the body, at the feet, genitals, abdomen—and especially if* merged *to the abdomen or trunk (as in the typhon)—the serpent
represents consciousness (kundalini) in its lowest or lower stages of evolution, where it governs food, sex, blood, death, etc.—"evil" in the strict
sense that it drags consciousness down from the higher stages. On the other
hand, if the serpent is shown in an ascendant position, or vertically coiled
in crisscrossed fashion (as in this figure), or elevated on a cross, or if it is
found at or beyond the human head, it represents the higher and highest
stages of the evolution of consciousness (kundalini), stages rightly viewed
as Divine. The same symbol is viewed so differently,* dependent *upon its*
location *vis-à-vis the human body—for that location actually tells at which
level of the Great Chain consciousness is located, and therefore whether it
is devilish or divine. The symbol is* that *of a serpent power because that is
the literal* form *that sudden kundalini manifestation takes (to the mind's
eye). It takes that form, in my opinion, because the serpent-uroboros is the
lowest basic stage to which Consciousness descends in creation, and therefore is the form it often takes in its Ascent and Return to Source, as an example of the lower and lowest being returned to the higher and highest.*

mode began to disclose the ultimate unity of Atman, or the unmanifest Void (7/8). There is, therefore, not just a variety of religious experience, but a true evolution of religious experience, hierarchic in nature, developmental in structure.

Further, this overall evolution of religious experience, culminating in radical Atman consciousness, is simply a prefiguration of the future course of the evolution of average consciousness (or consciousness on the whole), for the former is merely the growing tip of the latter, and where the leaf grows the trunk must follow. (We will return to this topic in our concluding chapters.)

KUNDALINI

I mentioned in Chapter 1 that we would return to the topic of kundalini and see how its progress and ascent was depicted in such advanced civilizations as the Egyptian. Recall that kundalini power—consciousness itself—is said to begin its evolution at the base of the spine, in what is called the first chakra, a chakra that represents earth, matter, and food—in short, the uroboros. From that low estate, it evolves up the spine, through successively higher chakras. The second and third chakras represent emotions, sexuality, and power (the typhon); the fourth represents love and belongingness (membership); the fifth, verbal knowledge and beginning of self-reflexiveness (verbal-membership and start of mental-egoic). At the sixth chakra, consciousness enters the psychic realm (level 5). The sixth chakra is "located" between and behind the eyebrows—the "third eye" of the psychics. The seventh chakra—the crown chakra, located at and beyond the crown of the head*—represents higher transcendence, Light, and Oneness (level 6), which, when fully matured, passes beyond all chakras, high or low, into radical Voidness (level 7/8).

My point can be put both simply and briefly. Fig. 20 is a picture of a standard Pharaonic headdress, with a serpent head located precisely at the sixth chakra. There is no mistaking what such pictures represent. Kundalini —the serpent power—has, at the period in history represented by these pictures, evolved from the base of the spine—the uroboros and typhon—to the higher chakras of psychic and subtle consciousness (definitely as far as the psychic level, and probably, I have argued, into the *beginning*—but only

---

* By which I mean the sahasrara and the seven higher chakras of truly subtle-realm consciousness described by shabd yoga—level 6 in general.

Fig. 18. Subduing the serpent. In regard to the comments on Fig. 17, note this comment by one scholar: "If the 'uraeus' represents the serpent in its creative role, the same reptile is often considered as the incarnation of the spirit of evil, against which one must defend oneself."[39]

Fig. 19. Egyptian initiation—another example of subduing the "evil" serpent so as to release its creative force (kundalini).

Fig. 20. Egyptian headdress. "The positive and negative currents of the Solar Force meet in the forehead where, as it were, their balance registers. The adept kings of Egypt bore upon their foreheads the Uraeus, or Sacred Serpent emblem of this bridle, to signify that they achieved this power." (Le Comte de Gabalis, fifteenth-century text, quoted in Gopi Krishna.[165])

Fig. 21. The universal serpent power. Examples from Judaeo-Christianity and primitive voodoo.

Fig. 21A. "And Yahweh said to Moses, 'Make a fiery serpent, and set it on a pole; and every one who is bitten, when he sees it, shall live."
Fig. 21B. Ancient voodoo symbol

the beginning—of the subtle).† The most highly evolved priests and saints of the period were, all evidence suggests, perfectly aware of psychic and subtle realities, of kundalini or serpent-power transformations, and, like-wise, of the Great Goddess of the subtle realm: "But the Egyptians, which are excellent in all kind of ancient doctrine, and by their proper cere-monies accustomed to worship me, do call me by my true name, Queen Isis."

CONCLUSIONS: GREAT MOTHER VS. GREAT GODDESS

We are now in a position to draw out our final conclusions and quickly summarize.

The basic Mother Image arose as a simple correlate of bodily existence, with such biological impacts as womb birth, breast feeding, separation anxieties, and so on—all of which necessarily center on the *biological mother*. That simple biological dependence, amplified by the notion of the

† Don't let Freud's phallic reductionism confuse you—this is *not* an example of "displacement upward" of sexual energy ("serpent-phallus"). Rather, it is precisely the other way around: sexual energy is one of the lowest displacements downward of kundalini energy. God consciousness is not sublimated sexuality; sexuality is restricted God consciousness.

earth as the mother of farmed crops, accounted for the prevalence of the Mother Image in the basic mythologies of the mythic-membership-self.

Likewise, the average and typical membership-self took recourse in sacrificial rites and beliefs and mythic techniques, largely to appease and assuage the Earth Mother, to magically ensure fertility and crop renewal, to expiate the guilt inherent in the increasingly separate-self sense, to atone for maternal incest, to fetishize seasonal immortality and hide the face of death.

Up to this point, the existence and function of the mother goddess has a more or less naturalistic explanation. We don't need any high metaphysical principles to explain any of that—simple biological science and ordinary psychoanalytical psychology will suffice.

But beyond the average and typical membership-self, struggling as it was with the weight of the Chthonic Mother, certain highly evolved individuals—true priests and saints—had access to actual and redemptive realms of the superconscious. Specifically, through a literal and transformative self-sacrifice, these souls intuited and were actually immersed in the subtle realm of beginning Oneness (level 6), a Oneness that underlies and gives birth to all the lower levels (1 through 5) of space, time, body, mind, and world. All manifestation was seen to be *mother, maya, measure, menses, menstrual, metered*—which are all words stemming from the same Sanskrit root *ma* (or *matr*), which means, essentially, "production." All this manifest world was understood to be a great production, a mahamaya, and seen therefore to be fundamentally *One*. In the next major period, that of the mental-ego, it was understood much more clearly just *what* this world was a production of—an insight that ushered in the patriarchy of the Dharmakaya. But the essential point is that this Oneness was at least initially glimpsed in the mythic-membership period, and it was that actual vision which empowered the supernatural image of the Great Goddess, the One whose body is all manifestation.

That insight, amply expressed in numerous esoteric myths and records of the time (the quotes from Ptah and Isis being perfectly representative), was *not* a simple fluffing up to cosmic proportions of an early memory of the biological mother impact—that accounts, as I just said, for the Great Mother, but not the Great Goddess. The Great Mother reflects the mythic-membership level of reality—still close to the body, to instincts, to nature, and therefore still forming paleological myths and symbols about those lower levels (just as magic was, by and large, a reflection of the even lower typhonic level). The Great Goddess, however, reflects a metaphysical truth —that all is One—and a truly higher level of reality—the *beginning* of the subtle—that can be verified in any number of other ways (from advanced meditation to hermeneutical insight to higher developmental psychology).

Thus, the explanation of the genesis and function of the Great Mother ought not to be confused with that of the Great Goddess. Yet the orthodox anthropologists *reduce* the Great Goddess to the biological Great Mother, and then proceed with thinly disguised glee to explain away all of the true or esoteric religious insights of this period as being merely biological and psychoanalytical in origin. On the other hand, the religious anthropologists usually commit the reverse error: they fail to differentiate the biological Great Mother from the transcendent Goddess, they *elevate* the Great Mother to Great Goddess status, and thus they are forced into trying to read deeply metaphysical insights into every Great Mother ritual imaginable, when, in fact, most were nothing but primitive, crude, magical attempts to coerce the Earth through fetishistic murder.

This overall distinction between the Great Mother and the Great Goddess rests, in part, upon the distinction between the average mode of consciousness and the most advanced mode. Putting all these factors together, we arrive at two general equations for this mythic-membership period:

1. Average mode = mythic-membership (level 3) = farming consciousness = biological Earth Mother or Great Mother = magical sacrifices for fertility and expiation = substitute sacrifices (the Atman project)

2. Most advanced mode = beginning of subtle level (level 6) = insight into one archetypal deity or god/dess = Great Goddess = self-sacrifice in awareness = realization or communion with archetypal oneness = true sacrifice (toward Atman)

I think it is obvious that the average mode and the most advanced mode often interact in their symbolism and tangentially support each other to some degree. For example, take magic and psychic in typhonic times: the feats and acts of a true psychic would immensely (but unintentionally) support the masses in their superstitious belief in the efficacy of simple magic. Likewise, as we will see, Christ's superconscious statements about God the Father supported the much lower-level authority of egoic patriarchy. In the same way, the statements and acts of the true saints who saw into the realms represented by the Great Goddess must have had profound impact on the ordinary mythology of the Great Mother.

At each stage of evolution the reverse influence—the influence of the average on the most advanced—is also frequently evident. To give only one example: the most advanced mode has, for the most part, only the terminology of the average mode through which to express itself. This is one of the reasons (but not the only one) that the initial insight into subtle oneness—a oneness which, as we saw, can be represented as a One God or One Goddess—was most often first stated in maternal terms, as a one Goddess. That subtle oneness historically was first glimpsed, however briefly and crudely, during the matriarchy, or the reign of the Great

Mother. The expression of subtle transcendent oneness was thus more often than not initially expressed in terms of One Goddess. Later, with the rise of the patriarchy, the subtle realm was expressed as a One God—the Father Who art in Heaven.

This is no mere equivocation or wishy-washiness on the part of the saints and sages involved (male and female alike). For, starting with the psychic level, all higher levels are actually trans-verbal and trans-mental, and a change in the mental words and symbols used to best express these otherwise inexpressible and trans-verbal realms reflects not a confusion about the realms themselves, but a real decision about their most expedient metaphors. And the metaphors are, by and large, anchored in the average-mode level of consciousness.

There should be no confusion as to how Great Mother religion and Great Goddess religion could exist side by side, often in the same place, at the same time, and frequently using the same symbols. For this is simply the phenomenon of exoteric and esoteric religion in general. That is, from almost the beginning of mankind's religious expressions, those expressions have been understood exoterically or outwardly, and esoterically or inwardly. Every great world religion, in fact, has *both* exoteric and esoteric aspects, and those aspects usually coexist perfectly with one another, the exoteric rituals serving the masses, the esoteric serving the advanced.[368] All I am doing is applying this perennial distinction to the mythic-membership religions of the Mother Goddess—in each instance, are they exoteric, of the Great Mother, or esoteric, of the Great Goddess?

Just as we were careful to differentiate the magical cognition of the average typhon from the actual psychic insights of the shaman, so now we differentiate the simple mythic-mother image of biological dependence, crop fertility, and sadistic sacrifice—the Great Mother—from the actual Great Goddess of the subtle realm—the Goddess which represented actual transcendence, transformation, and self-sacrifice. And we note that the vast majority of membership-selves were under sway of the Great Mother, an image of bodily dependence and seduction, blown up to mythically cosmic proportions, evidenced in sexual fertility rites, immortality strivings, fetishistic sacrifices, and ambivalent struggle. For that same great majority, the mythic mother acted as the chthonic destroyer of consciousness, the Great and Devouring Earth Mother that pulled the self back into the body, back into instinct, back into the bowels of darkness, and thereby prevented the further evolution from subconscious Earth to superconscious Heaven. And that is just what the majority of myths of this period show (as clearly pointed out by Neumann, Bachofen, Berdyaev, etc.). Only in the next stage of growth, that of the mental-egoic, would consciousness break free from the seduction of the Dark and announce in its myths the coming of the Sun-Light.

Finally, I would like to return to the literal, human, sacrificial rites themselves, the sacrifices to the Great Mother. For the fact that these sacrifices were rendered literally and not symbolically means several things. First and foremost: when a living being was actually sacrificed, especially if against his will, we can assume that this literal rendition was serving the masses in a *substitute function*. That is, it involved not a mystical acceptance and therefore transcendence of death, but a magical attempt to deny death by promising a new and fertile future, a fertile field of blood-soaked crops, a fertile promise of self-survival. It was a magical attempt to secure a future by appeasing death in the present, and in this logic, the more somebody else's blood flows, the less chance yours will.

In other words, we are seeing here the birth of an entirely new form of *substitute sacrifice*—not true self-sacrifice, but brutal victim-sacrifice. That is, murder. Nowhere in history, before this time, do we find murder, calculated cold-blooded murder, on any sort of large scale. It is almost unanimously agreed that in typhonic cultures murder was almost totally nonexistent; war as we know it just did not exist. The most violent substitute sacrifices, as we saw, were of finger joints. But from fingers to whole human beings, and from whole human beings to whole nations—such has been the history of substitute sacrifices, all willingly and bloodily dashed to hell as mankind, driven by its Atman project, began the attempted purchase of an immortal future at somebody else's bloody expense.

8 The Mythology of Murder

HOMICIDE: A NEW FORM OF SUBSTITUTE SACRIFICE

According to Buddhism—actually, to the perennial philosophy in general—the ultimate nature of reality is *sunyata,* which is usually translated as "voidness," "emptiness," or "nothingness."[387] But sunyata does *not* mean blankness or vacant absence. The void does not mean featureless, but seamless[52]—"the seamless coat of the universe," as Whitehead would have it. Sunyata means that, just as the hands and legs and arms are quite different entities but also are parts of one body, so all things and events in the universe are aspects of one ultimate Whole (Atman). This holds, obviously, for men and women as well. The ultimate psychology is a psychology of ultimate Wholeness, or the superconscious All. At any rate, that wholeness, according to Buddhism, is what is real and all that is real. A radically separate and isolated and bounded entity does not exist anywhere.

It follows, then, that to erect a self *boundary* or barrier, and hold a separate-identity feeling *against* the prior Wholeness, requires a constant expenditure of energy, a perpetual *contracting* or restricting activity. This, of course, obscures the prior Wholeness itself, and this—as I have elsewhere suggested—is the primal repression.[429] It is the repression of universal consciousness and its projection as an inside self vs. an outside world, a subject vs. an object.

Arising as a function of this boundary are, as we have seen, two major dynamic factors: Eros and Thanatos. Eros ultimately is the desire to recapture that prior Wholeness which was "lost" when the boundary between self and other was constructed. But to actually gain a true reunion of subject and object, self and other, requires the death and dissolution of the exclusively separate-self sense—and this is precisely what is resisted. Thus Eros cannot find true union, real Wholeness, but is instead driven to find symbolic substitutes for the lost Whole. Eros, then, is the undying power of seeking, grasping, wishing, desiring, perpetuating, loving, living, willing, and so on. And it is *never* satisfied because it finds only substitutes. Eros is ontological hunger.

We come, then, to Thanatos. The boundary between subject and object, self and other, has to be constantly and unceasingly re-created moment to moment—and for the simple reason that it isn't real in the first place. At the same time, the simple force of reality, the "pull" of the ultimate Whole, acts moment to moment to tear down that boundary. *And that "force" is Thanatos.* As the individual, moment to moment, re-creates his illusory boundaries, so reality, moment to moment, conspires to tear them down.

Such is Thanatos, and its real meaning is transcendence. Thanatos is not a force trying to reduce life to inorganic matter, or a repetition compulsion, or a homeostatic principle, or a suicidal wish. Thanatos is the power of sunyata, the power and push to transcend illusory boundaries, but it *appears,* to a self that will not surrender its boundaries, as a threat of literal death and physical mortality.

Thus, everything that is *other* to the self acts as a source of Thanatos: Because whatever is other works for the dissolution of the self boundaries —works for the "death" of the separate-self sense. But *anything* that is other is merely a projection of one's own deepest Nature, the ultimate Whole. So in this sense, and this sense only, Thanatos is a "death wish" because it ultimately issues from one's own Being as the Whole.

Wherever there is boundary, the Thanatos of one's deeper Nature acts, moment to moment, to remove it. As long as there is boundary, there is Thanatos. And one will either submit to Thanatos and transcendence, or one will have to find something else to do with that "death wish." One will have, that is, to find *substitute sacrifices.* For Thanatos arises moment to moment—and it must be handled.

Now on the previous and lower levels of the spectrum of consciousness —such as the uroboric and typhonic—the required substitute sacrifices are both fairly simple and fairly simply executed. The self boundaries themselves are not as rigid, or as complex, or as heavily defended—in fact, they hardly even existed in uroboric times, and were fairly fluid in typhonic. Death and Thanatos could be siphoned off and denied by fairly uncomplicated measures—such as simple self-preservation or, at worst, a few finger-joint sacrifices, as we saw.

But we are here—at the membership level—fast approaching a point where these earlier and simpler forms of substitute sacrifice are no longer sufficient, by themselves, to handle Thanatos. They must be supplemented. The pseudo-self is becoming more complicated, more articulate, and more structured in the world of form. Likewise, the threat of Thanatos is more keenly and complexly apprehended. A new mode of self sense always faces a new form of Thanatos; and to survive in its imaginary world of permanence and perpetuation, it must devise both new forms of substitute seeking (Eros) and new forms of substitute sacrifice (Thanatos).

Now—at least in the ontogenetic cycle of present-day men and women, and probably, as I will argue, to some degree in the phylogenetic cycle as well—this membership level is the first where substitute seeking or Eros begins to take flight in extended or non-present time. For, riding the vehicle of language, seeking begins to switch from instinctual gratifications to temporal, future goals and desires and wants. The self moves into the new world of time, and flings a new set of desires through that higher world.

But this level is also the first major level where Eros can be, in a rudimentary form at least, *retroflected,* or turned back onto the self system (which is similar to the psychoanalytic concept of secondary narcissism). *And just as Eros can be turned in, Thanatos can be turned out.* For at the membership level, we have a self internally complex enough to bind Thanatos and *extrovert* it. And, as Freud well knew, extroverted Thanatos appears as murderous aggression. As Brown says, "It is at this stage, by the transformation of passivity into activity, that the fateful extroversion of the death instinct outward onto the world in the form of aggression takes place."[61]

Let us now translate these psychoanalytic formulations into the context of the spectrum of consciousness. Thanatos is not the "drive to return to the state of inanimate existence," but rather the drive to return the separate self to the most prior state of all, namely that of the ultimate Whole, or Unity consciousness. In one form or another, Thanatos always arises wherever there is boundary and works for the dissolution or transcendence of that boundary, just as the natural flow of water works to undermine any dams or barriers superimposed upon it. But once a barrier *is* placed upon reality, then Thanatos appears, to the self thus bounded, as a terrifying death impact. And it is this death impact that is extroverted, at the membership level, into the peculiarly morbid, vicious, and unmitigated form of aggression known only to mankind.*

But let us note the logical priorities herein involved: under the desire to kill lies the extroverted death impact, and under death impact lies the pull of transcendence. Murder, that is, is a form of substitute sacrifice or substitute transcendence. Homicide is the new form of the Atman project. The deepest wish of all is to sacrifice one's self—"kill" it—so as to find true transcendence and Atman; but, failing that, one arranges the *substitute* sacrifice of actually killing somebody else, thus acting on, and appeasing, the terrifying confrontation with death and Thanatos.

It hardly needs to be said, but it does follow that transcendence, true transcendence, is the only cure for the homicidal animal. If, in killing, all man wants is to kill, then we are all in deep trouble. The kill wish is ultimate and ineradicable. If, on the other hand, in killing, man unconsciously wants transcendence, then there is at least a way out: transcend the self; "kill" the self instead of others.

Let me emphasize, however, that I am not denying the existence of simple, instinctive, biological aggression, in mammals or in humans. The coyote does aggress—but not out of hatred. As Ashley Montagu put it, the coyote doesn't kill the rabbit because it hates the rabbit but because it loves the rabbit—it loves the rabbit the way I love ice cream. Man—and only man—regularly kills out of *hatred,* and for that we will have to look elsewhere than the genes.

I am denying, in other words, that human hatred and overblown murderous impulses are innately biological. Rather, violent hatred is, as Arieti demonstrated,[6] almost entirely a *cognitive* and *conceptual* elaboration, extending quite beyond mere biological aggression, which, by and large, is always in the service of evolutionary trends, whereas the same can hardly be said of human murder and war. I am suggesting that, in the cognitive elaboration between simple biological aggression and wanton human murder,

---

* Although I have used Freud's thoughts to help explain my thesis, I do not mean to imply that he always used the term "Thanatos" as I do; he did not. Interestingly, however, he did use that term to mean almost precisely the same "drive" that the perennial philosophy calls "involution": the drive of the higher toward the lower, ultimately toward inert matter and lifeless being, which is a type of "death wish" (lifeless "matter wish") whose existence I fully acknowledge; I have based much of my overall thesis on the notion of involution itself (which I briefly explain in Chapter 17). In this chapter I am not discussing involution and the role it might play in murder/aggression/death, etc. Clearly, however, a full use of both Freudian and perennial insights into death, aggression, masochism, and sadism would make use of innate biological aggression, Thanatos (as I use it), and involution (which is the way Freud uses "Thanatos"). This would give us a much more detailed picture of the dynamics of trying to extricate oneself from samsara by killing the self of another. The basic conclusions I have drawn in this section would, as far as I can tell, remain unchanged, but naturally the specifics would be more encompassing and more precise.

death and death terror become all-significantly interwoven into the final motivation, and this fact alone has real explanatory power in regard to human viciousness, as Rank, Lifton, et al. have pointed out.

Thus, whatever natural aggression may be innately present in humans, the significant point is that it is amplified through conceptual domains, and part of that amplification includes the heightened apprehension of death, which, when turned outward, explodes into really vicious aggression and hostility, and in proportions not given instinctually. And *that* murderous hostility is pre-eminently the substitute sacrifice, a killing of others to magically buy off the death of the self. The original death terror becomes death-dealing, and *there* is the human source of joyous murder.

Murder: a new way to magically avoid death by offering up another being's life as a substitute sacrifice. Thanatos arises moment to moment and must be handled; and if the individual won't submit to the true sacrifice of his separate self, he will always be open to morbidly substituting somebody else's instead. And the history of mankind, beginning precisely at the membership stage, is the history of the wholesale substitute sacrifices and murderous wastages that have specifically marked the animal called *Homo sapiens*.

MURDER IN MYTHOLOGY

We have already discussed the *esoteric* meaning of the ritual sacrifice or Mass Communion: the separate-self sense is sacrificed in union to the Great Goddess (level 6), is undermined and released, there to be resurrected in trans-personal communion with subtle Oneness. And we have seen that the same rite could, and usually did, serve as a substitute function, and in a viciously graphic fashion: it was a literal, exoteric, human sacrifice to the Great Mother—not a mystical acceptance and therefore transcendence of death, but rather a magical and literal attempt to deny death. Not true sacrifice, but substitute sacrifice. Not Atman, but the Atman project.

To understand precisely how the symbolic heart of the true sacrifice, or "emptying awareness of self," can be converted by a separate self, unwilling to surrender, into substitute forms of personal immortality, power, and cosmocentricity, we need only look to the Maki ceremonials of the inhabitants of the Melanesian island of Malekula, in the New Hebrides. For the Maki ceremonial "serves on the one hand the aims of the community, inasmuch as it magically fosters the fertility of the race, but on the other hand the personal fame and ambition of the individual, since it is a rite of a strongly competitive kind, in which the men of the village, breeding up and sacrificing numberless boars, vie for status both in this world and in the next."[69]

The "overkill" of substitute sacrifices in the ceremony itself is striking, "since in the course of a ceremonial as many as five hundred pigs may be offered in a day." Five hundred! The man slashing through a field of animals, hacking all to shreds, wallowing through a gorge of flesh and intestines, crimson on the ground. "It is clear," says Campbell, "that any man who takes seriously the salvation of his eternal soul must be considerably occupied with the [substitutive] spiritual exercise of breeding, trading, and reckoning his pigs, which, indeed, serve as money in Malekula . . . just as in the higher cultures gold supplies the basic standard of all monetary worth."[69] The connecting link, as we have seen, is money as an immortality symbol.

"The offered beast is a [magically] captured quantum of divine power, which, through its sacrifice, is integrated with the giver. The giver climbs, so to say, on the rungs of his sacrifice. And the Maki is a great ladder of such rungs."[69] And a ladder one must keep climbing—salvation is always in the future, and therefore always requires more sacrifices. For Thanatos, Shiva, and Sunyata must be appeased. "The guardian," as these natives themselves put it, "stands upright in the midst of the path of fire, then rushes forward to consume us; but it is content to eat the boar."[69]

It is content to eat the boar instead—there, perfectly, is the substitute sacrifice. And if a boar is not enough, then another human being. Otto Rank summarized it perfectly: "The death fear of the ego is lessened by the killing, the sacrifice, of the other; through the death of the other, one buys oneself free from the penalty of dying, of being killed."[26] The whole point being, as Becker put it, "the offering of the other's body in order to buy off one's own death." And all motivated by the unconscious desire to actually transcend into real and timeless immortality.

At this point in history, then, of heightened temporal or farming consciousness and the blossoming Atman project, homicide and war came into being as wholesale vehicles of substitute sacrifice, the negative side of the Atman project. It is quite revealing, therefore, to find that one of the most predominant themes of the mythologies of the farming cultures everywhere is that of the coming into the world of death and of sex. And from whence death?

Those pre-sexual, pre-mortal ancestral beings of the mythological narrative lived the idyl of the beginning, an age when all things were innocent of the destiny of life in time [the uroboric age]. But there occurred in that age an event, the "mythological event" *par excellence,* which brought to an end its timeless way of being and effected a transformation of all things. Whereupon death and sex came into the world as the basic correlates of temporality. And the particular point [registered nowhere in mythologies prior to this point] is that death comes *by way of a murder*. A fundamental complementarity is vividly recognized between not simply birth and death [as in the earlier myths of the hunting societies], but sex and murder. [My italics.][69]

Thus, simple life and death, being and non-being, so characteristic of the typhonic level, have now—on the membership level—been elaborated upon and transformed into the more complex opposites of sex and murder. That is to say, Eros and Thanatos have taken on new forms: Eros as life into Eros as sex; Thanatos as death into Thanatos as murder—and all as correlates of the blossoming world of temporal extension and farming consciousness.

But to set this in perspective, let us quickly note that the precipitating mythological event—the sacrificial murder of the god—which brought this temporal world of death and sex and murder into being, is nowhere in mythology yet spoken of as an agonizing Fall of Man. The murdered god, in fact, was said to have been buried to rise again as corn, wheat, and other food crops for the necessary sustenance of all, so that frequently, in fertility rites, the murdered victim was cut up and buried in the fields as a magic re-enactment of the primordial murder itself. So although the divine murder brought some hardships into this world, it wasn't all guilt, terror, and sin. It was a mini-Fall, lying roughly halfway between the beginning Fall of the typhon and the final Fall of the mental-egoic level. And the myths of all three periods point to just that.

THE WAR MACHINE—SACRIFICE RUN RIOT

The mythology of sacrificial death, perverted from a symbol to a sign, and pressed into action on a large-scale basis by the separate-self sense, is the substitute function and substitute attempt at transcendence known to us all as war.

Murder as self-preservation: offering up another person's life as a magical attempt to perpetuate one's own through substitute sacrifice—what an incredible twist on Sunyata! And yet, without any doubt whatsoever, "the logic of killing others in order to affirm our own life unlocks much that puzzles us in history,"[26] from scapegoating to mass war to Roman arena games to Nazi blood sacrifices. All men and women intuit that the skull will grin in, and war is a simple arrangement for the skull to belong to the other guy.

So we see again: when people become objects of the negative Atman project, they become *victims*, substitute sacrifices, scapegoats—and war, the mass potlatch of death-dealing for immortality, is merely wholesale victimage in outright form. And victimage, as Robert Jay Lifton put it, is simply "the need to reassert one's own immortality, or that of one's group, by contrasting it with its absolute absence in one's death-tainted victim." So could Kenneth Burke point out that the heart of man's social motivation is the "civic enactment of redemption through the sacrificial victim." And Eugene Ionesco summed it up beautifully: "As long as we are not assured of immortality, we shall go on hating each other in spite of our need for mutual love." Hating each other, and killing each other. Indeed, Mumford has really built his extraordinary study of history, politics, and technics around the phenomenon of sacrifice itself, and the special *necessity* of mass sacrifice and war in maintaining the social equilibrium of the state.

For what is at stake in war is not food, not properties, not even ideologies directly, but one's own version of the Atman project: one's qualifications for immortality power and death transcendence. And the more the enemy drops, the more immortal the conqueror feels. "Fortunate and favored, the survivor stands in the midst of the fallen. For him there is one tremendous fact; while countless others have died, many of them his comrades, he is still alive. The dead lie helpless; he stands upright amongst them, and it is as though the battle had been fought in order for him to survive it. . . . It is a feeling of being chosen. . . . He is stronger. . . . He is the favored of the Gods."[74]

What a pathetic way to earn one's feelings of cosmocentricity, especially since it is still only a substitute for real transcendence. But such precisely is the urge that lies behind all substitute sacrifice, on any scale, from prejudice to mass war. Moment to moment the separate self intuits Thanatos, Shiva, and Sunyata—it intuits that it is illusory and death-bound, that death will in fact grin in, and if it grins in on someone else first, then the pressure is off for a while.

If luck, as Aristotle said, is when the arrow hits the fellow next to you, then scapegoating is pushing the fellow into its path—with special alacrity if he is a stranger to you. A particularly pungent phrasing of the logic of scapegoating one's own death has been given by Alan Harrington: it is as though the sacrificer were to say to God after appraising how nature feeds voraciously on life, "If this is what you want, here, take it!"—but leave *me* alone.[26]

The substitute sacrifice.

And the simple fact is that, around the third millennium B.C., especially in Sumer—those early city-states of Ur, Uruk, Kish, Lagash, and all—modern, massive warfare of one state against another was born. A royal chronicle of that period reads:

> Sargon, King of Agade, the city of Uruk he smote and its wall he destroyed. With the people of Uruk he battled and he routed them. With Lugal-zaggisi, King of Uruk, he battled and he captured him and in fetters he led him through the gate of Enlil. Sargon of Agade battled with the man of Ur and vanquished him; his city he smote and its wall he destroyed. E-Ninmar he smote and its wall he destroyed, and its entire territory, from Lagash to the sea, he smote. And he washed his weapons in the sea.[70]

Here, just here, at precisely the height of the membership stage, modern warfare as we know it was invented, and it was simply a new reflex of the Atman project—the attempt to become God by grasping at substitute and token immortality, cosmocentricity, and power. "In the words of a great Orientalist, the late Professor Hans Heinrich Schaeder . . . , it was exactly here, with this epochal crisis in the history of mankind, that the world-historical process of which we ourselves are a part took its rise, its special theme, and its characteristic being: *the programmatic exercise of power by men over men.*" As Schaeder himself put it, "the exercise of power is governed everywhere by the law of intensification, or as the Greeks would say, 'greed for more than one's share.'"[72] Greed, Eros, trishna, grasping—the right arm of the Atman project, searching through the finite realm for infinite satiation, and necessarily failing that, being driven to ever greater "intensifications." As the Maki would go through five hundred pigs a day in substitute sacrifice, the new war machines would churn up as many humans in a matter of minutes.

Therefore, on our list of the new modes of substitute activities, we find the *beginnings* of the war machine: a new form of substitute power and pretend immortality, bought at blood-red prices. I say "beginnings" because it got worse with the rise of the mental-egoic structure. But I think, although somewhat painfully, that with Duncan, Burke, Rank, Becker, Lifton, and so many others, we have to look steadily and unflinchingly at war, and draw the only obvious conclusion possible. For the staggering and terrifying thing about war is that, despite the loathsome things said of it on the one side, and, on the other, despite the noble causes and holy reasons and high ideals brought in to prop it up, one fact stands alone: war has been popular. It has thus served a necessary function, and served it well. And it served the cultural Atman project, the attempts to make egos into gods, power-soaked and blood immune. We all know the statistic: for every one year of peace in mankind's history, there have been fourteen years of war.

And why its popularity? I believe the central reason is very straightforward: war, just like money, is a simple and easily accessible immortality symbol. Both war and money have been equally popular throughout history because neither requires much talent to gather or use. They are much, much easier to come by than are other immortality symbols, such as a pyramid or mummification. Thus, money and war were the cultural forms of the Atman project that were most accessible to vast numbers of the common folk. Both gold and war placed immortality prospects in the hands of the average citizen, and thus kept alive the cultural arm of the separate self's Atman project. For not only could you traffic for immortality in the marketplace, you could traffic for it on the battlefield. And historically, *both* have been the necessary glues for complex societies—one positive, one negative, covering both sides of the Atman project. We have already discussed the necessary role of money in civilization. Let us, then, without belaboring the point, simply note as well that the "ability to wage war and to impose collective human sacrifice has remained the identifying mark of all sovereign power throughout history."[26]

9 Polis and Praxis

The typical relationship of the alimentary uroboros involves food. The typical relationship of the body-typhon involves emotional-sexuality. These, however, are relationships that are shared, to one degree or another, with the rest of nature—that is, they are subhuman capacities. But the typical relationship of the membership-self involves *verbal communication*. And it was the emergence of verbal membership and inter-subjective communication (via language) that allowed and constituted the existence of what the Greeks would eulogize as *polis*. Polis was the first arena of truly human relationship, the relationship found nowhere else in nature, the relationship that *specifically* defined the new species of *Homo sapiens*. No wonder that the two most famous definitions of man are: "Man is the animal *symbolicum*" (Cassirer) and "Man is the animal of *polis*" (Aristotle).

Now I use "polis," which is the Greek word for city-state, in its original and idealistic sense, as being a *shared human community,* and a community based on unrestrained *communication* (via language). In the best sense, polis is simply the arena of membership, a higher form of unity based on transcendent symbol exchange. You and I are now *exchanging* ideas (although unilaterally due to the medium of print; better to imagine that we are talking about all this), and that exchange is an act of verbal communication and inter-subjective sharing quite beyond the subhuman capacities of the rest of nature and the subhuman capacities of our own organisms. Polis, then, is the arena of the membership-self.

Now the activity in polis is called *praxis*. Praxis means, in the narrow sense, "practice." But as traditionally used, by Aristotle for instance, praxis is much more than that; it is purposive, enlightened, moral behavior pursued in the company of polis. It is *meaningful* and *concernful* activity, not based on subhuman wants and desires, but based upon mutual human recognition and unrestrained communication. Apart from engaging in uroboric food and typhonic sex, our life as truly human individuals is a life of social practice and social activity, a life which takes us beyond the animal body and introduces us into a shared human community of symbols, discourse, communication, goals, and ideals. I can only become truly human in polis, or symbolic community, and I can only exercise my humanity in praxis, or social engagement and sharing with fellow communicators. And *all* of this is rendered possible by language, which *allows* inter-subjective exchange of ideas, so that when you and I truly communicate, you and I literally enter each other's psyche in a sharing of understanding. The arena of that sharing is polis; the exercise of that sharing is praxis. It is a shame that polis has been debased to mean "politics" and praxis to mean "moralism"—they really contain much more noble ideas than all that.

For Aristotle, praxis, or enlightened and moral social activity, was not to be confused with *techne,* or technological activity. Both depend upon rational and linguistic mentality, but beyond that they are radically different. The reason is basic and profound: techne deals with the manipulation of subhuman levels, with material goods, with nature, with food production, with empirical (animal sensory) investigations, with technological innovations, and so on. But praxis deals with human interaction and exchange of shared understandings. It is not the use of mind to probe nature, but the use of mind to meet another mind. Techne is level 3/4 assaulting level 1/2. Praxis is the exercise of level 3/4 in communion with another level 3/4: human to human, not human to subhuman. And, as Habermas has said, the catastrophe of modern times (and of modern sociological and psychological theory) is that praxis has been reduced to techne.[178]

Now polis consciousness, or membership consciousness, *transcends* (but *includes*) the needs and characteristics of the subhuman stages which preceded it in evolution. With polis-praxis, consciousness takes on its first truly human characteristics, and shows itself to be more than (but not apart from) the laws of physics, biology, nature, plant, and animal. The membership mind, since it was beginning to transcend the body, was ushered into an entirely new and "superorganic" realm, whose laws are written with symbols other than those of physics and biology. Man was no longer living solely in the world of nature, but also in the world of culture; no longer just instincts, but also verbal learning; no longer nature, but history. This was an entirely higher realm, that of polis, and it possessed entirely higher laws, those of social praxis.

Combine it all in this fashion: the difference between nature and history, physics and psychology, animal and culture, impulse and discourse, instinct and intention, biological survival and ethics, is the difference between body (level 1/2) and mind (level 3/4). And thus mankind, in developing a true (if initial) mentality, came into possession of history, intention, culture, discourse, and ethics. Came, that is, into possession of polis-praxis. One need not agree with Rousseau's philosophy to appreciate his statement that "this passage from the state of nature to the state of society [polis] produces a very remarkable change in man, in substituting justice for instinct in his conduct, and giving to his actions the morality [praxis] which before they lacked."[112]

We simply note, then, that polis-praxis consciousness contained an extraordinary potential. And so extraordinary was this potential that it has tended to produce two wildly opposed views on the nature of polis, the state, and social community in general. On the one hand, because of the monumental potential embodied in polis-praxis, its simple existence has always brought forth Utopian views, some very profound, most wildly romantic. On the other hand, because nowhere in history has polis-praxis lived up to the potential embodied in free and unrestrained communication, its practical failure has always brought forth scathing critiques of society in general and the state in particular. This whole arena of argument is generally called "political science" or "social theory."

Bertrand Russell once commented that what ought to be taught in school was not logic, but how to avoid its use, since almost everybody gets it wrong. I sometimes feel the same way about social theory and political science, and thus tend at this point to simply avoid its use. I follow instead that sound commandment, "Thou shalt not commit a political science."

But, of course, something must be said, however pitiful, and therefore I shall commit generalizations and platitudes, for these simplicities will suffice perfectly to allow us to sketch the broad profile of consciousness evolution which alone is our present task.

We begin by repeating that each stage of evolution transcends but includes its predecessor. This is certainly true for humans as well. We have seen throughout this volume that each stage of human evolution, although it transcends its predecessors, must include and integrate them in a higher unity (failure to do so = neurosis). Another way to say this is that the human individual is a *compound individual* (Whitehead, Hartshorne)—compounded, that is, of all the levels of reality that have unfolded prior to man's present stage, and capped by that present stage itself. "Man," said Gregory Palamas, "is the concentration into one whole of all that is, the recapitulation of all things created by God. Therefore he was produced last of all, just as we also (in our turn) round off what we have to say with a conclusion."[375]

In this volume, we needn't become overly precise about the exact nature of the earlier levels of evolution which are encapsulated and compounded in man. To begin with, I have already (for convenience) collapsed all sorts of lower levels into "one" stage—that of the uroboros, which we defined mythically as the "recapitulation of all lower levels." On the more precise side, I have elsewhere presented an exhaustive breakdown of all these various levels (see *The Atman Project*). For our more general purposes, we can instead rely on the common-sense breakdown of the stages of evolution: matter to plant to lower animal to higher animal to man (or to mind, which is as far as evolution on the whole has proceeded thus far).

The first hominids, although already higher animals themselves, were just emerging out of, and recapitulating, all the lower levels of evolution—matter, plant, and lower animal—and this stage we called, in a most general fashion, the uroboros (level 1). The higher-animal stage, as it began to pass clearly into the first human species, we called typhon (level 2). And the mind—as embodied in language communication—we called mythic-membership (level 3). The whole point in using these very general terms was not to imply that, for example, during uroboric times man was *only* material and vegetal and reptilian, but that he had to pass *through* all that (especially in his own ontogenetic cycle), and was thus initially embedded *in* all that and dominated *by* all that.

At any rate, by the time we arrive at the mythic-membership-self, that self is already a compound individual of all the previous levels of evolution—matter and plant and reptile (uroboros), higher mammal and image formation (typhon), as well as the new and "capping" verbal mind (membership). Thus man at this stage contains uroboros and typhon and mythic mind all encapsulated *in one organism*. Most importantly, *each of these levels continues to function and continues to live in man*. That is, each of these levels in man expresses its needs and maintains its own existence through *systems of relationships or exchanges* with the *corresponding* levels in the outer world. Thus: man's physical body (pleroma and alimentary uroboros) depends for its existence on a system of literal exchanges with other physical, mineral, and vegetative bodies, epitomized in the act of eating, or food exchange. His higher animal body (typhon) is a system of exchanges with other living animal bodies, epitomized in the act of human biological sex, but including all emotional intercourse in general. His linguistic (membership) mind is a system of symbol exchanges or communication with other minds. All of these systems of exchange are nothing but the various levels of the Great Chain as they appear, enwrapped and enfolded, in the human compound individual.

Notice, too, that each successive level of exchange represents a higher evolutionary growth and therefore expresses a higher-order attempt at unity (or a higher-order Atman project). The uroboros seeks unity by joining itself with physical food; the typhon seeks a higher unity by bodily joining itself with another typhon (i.e., biological coupling or sexual intercourse and feeling exchange in general). These are all subhuman unities, however. The first specifically human form of unity is comm-unity, or verbal communication in a polis-society of inter-subjective understanding and practical discourse (praxis).

The human being, then, is a compound individual of all lower levels of reality, capped by its own particular and defining level (at this point in history, it was membership-language). And society, or polis, is simply a *compound* of these compound individuals. Likewise, praxis is the activity of compound individuals in that compound society. The compound society and compound individuals are profoundly inseparable, however, because each is built upon the *systems of exchanges* that are compounded in the first place, and *exchanges,* by definition, do not occur in isolation. It is ridiculous to speculate about the *mentality* of a "noble savage" existing "uncorrupted" by society, for mentality is initially the third level of exchange (the verbal-symbolic), and without that social exchange, there is *no* mind from the start: there is only food and sex—savage, to be sure, but noble only in the eyes of the incurably romantic.

We have now said enough to form our first generalization on "political science" (we will present one more later): It is only in polis-praxis and communicative exchange that humanity first becomes truly human, and finds, in that elevated humanness, potentials not given to nature at large.

Now it is just this new potential of polis-praxis that underlies the various social utopianisms, idealisms, and traditionalisms. One version of the potential of the polis-praxis was stated in its most memorable form by Edmund Burke:

> The state ought not to be considered as nothing better than a partnership in a trade of pepper and coffee, calico or tobacco, or some other such low concern. It is to be looked upon with other reverence; because it is not a partnership in things subservient only to the gross animal existence of a temporary and perishable nature. It is a partnership in all science; a partnership in all art; a partnership in every virtue, and in all perfection. . . . Each contract of each particular state is but a clause in the great primeval contract of eternal society, linking the lower with the higher natures, connecting the visible and invisible world, according to a fixed compact sanctioned by the inviolable oath which holds all physical and moral natures each in their appointed place.[112]

If you at all understand the Great Chain of Being, you will easily understand that quote.

The same type of idealistic potential runs through the works of Plato, Kant, Green, Bosanquet, and Hegel—although, of course, they vary extensively in details. Hegel, for instance, maintained that the individual is truly himself only in some society, while Bosanquet went so far (i.e., too far) as to claim that society is more real than any of its members. But aside from its extremisms, the initial insight of this position is certainly understandable.

Central to this idealistic trend (a trend I share in part—I will soon amend it with our second generalization) is the recognition that polis or comm-unity is, indeed, a higher form of *unity,* and therefore has the potential for overcoming the fragmentation of various splinter groups. Erik Erikson stated this tenet in a now classic form:

> History provides a way by which the pseudo-species mentality of warring groups can become disarmed, as it were, within a *wider identity.* This can come about by territorial unification: the *Pax Romana* embraced races, nations, and classes. Technological advances in universal "traffic," too, unite: seafaring, mechanized locomotion, and wireless communication each has helped to spread changes eventually contained in a sense of widening identity which helps to overcome economic fear, the anxiety of culture change, and the dread of a spiritual vacuum.[119]

In its more extreme moments, however, social idealism seems to produce something akin to ecstatic raving, especially when its proponent concludes he himself is part of the greatest society ever to exist. Hegel, for instance, falls into almost manic enthusiasms whenever he mentions the State in general and the German State in particular. That he could have lived to meet Herr Hitler.

But that is not a comment on Germany; it points out the perfect inadequacy of pure idealism. The great difficulty with idealistic social theories, ranging from Burke to Hegel, is a uniform blindness to the fact that the state's *potential* for goodness is almost matched by its *potential* for brutality. And to understand this brutality, we need a second major generalization to set next to our first.

We noted that the human compound individual consists of various systems of exchanges, which, at this point in history, included material-food, emotional-sex, and verbal communication (levels 1, 2, and 3). Each of these systems of exchange occurs across an appropriate interface; the exchange itself consists of a *cycle* of reception, assimilation, and release. Society, as a compound of these compound individuals, is thus an amalgamation of *all* these exchanges. It therefore includes, as a *minimum,* various *institutions* for maintaining and reproducing the life of each of these levels of the human compound individual, thus:

Level 1. The technological production and economic exchange of material entities, whose paradigm is food, and whose sphere is physical labor.

Level 2. The production and exchange of biological life, whose paradigm is emotion and sex, and whose sphere is emotional intercourse (from feeling to sex to power).

Level 3. The production and exchange of ideas, whose paradigm is discourse (language), and whose sphere is communication (praxis).

As we proceed to higher levels of evolution, we will add higher exchanges to this list (at the mental-egoic level, for example, we will see the social necessity to facilitate mutual exchange of self-recognition, whose paradigm is reflexive self-consciousness, and whose sphere is mutual personal esteem). But this simple list will serve our general purpose. The point is that, although the polis-praxis is a potential that *concludes* this list, it must *include* all of the list—include, that is, institutions for *all* the various levels of exchange, bottom to top, food-farming to sex-marriage to thinking-education.*

Now obviously the polis-praxis, as a compound of compound individuals, can—like any other compound—not only function but misfunction, not only grow but degenerate, not only serve but oppress. Specifically, we need only note that *any* system of exchange—from material labor to emotional intercourse to conceptual communication—can be restricted, oppressed, repressed, and distorted by the *social environment in which the exchange ought ideally and freely to occur.* ("Freely" means "appropriately," not "excessively.") Most often, this distortion and disruption is instigated by those individuals, whether citizens or empowered leaders, who ought otherwise be the guardians of undistorted exchange and relationship. This disruption then tends to become institutionalized, so that it reproduces itself without conscious intention (by force of social inertia).

The archetypal champions of unrepressed relationship in each of these spheres are Marx (social labor, uroboros, level 1), Freud (emotional intercourse, typhon, level 2), and Socrates (verbal discourse, membership communication, level 3). And, of course, a complete social theory would add (as I will later suggest) such higher spheres and "champions" as ego-esteem (level 4; Locke†); psychic intuition (level 5; Patanjali); subtle oneness (level 6; Kirpal Singh); and ultimate transcendence (level 7/8; Buddha/Krishna/Christ).

---

* By "bottom to top" I mean all the levels of the Great Chain that have evolved, on the *average mode*, for any given society.

† I have listed Locke here for his emphasis on egoic freedom; later, I will mention Hegel for his studies on the master/slave relationship; these are subjective choices; the reader might have his or her own favorites for the various levels. Other eminent analysts of level 4 include Kierkegaard, Sartre, Carl Rogers, Hobbes.

For our simpler purposes, all we need do is set forth our second generalization: If the polis-praxis is expressive of a higher evolutionary achievement—and it is—it is also the executor of a potential crippling, not only of its own level but of *all other levels as well*. The state—as Marx, Freud, Socrates, and Christ discovered in their own spheres—can be brutally oppressive of everything from religion to ideas to sex to labor.‡

The *reasons* for oppression, the specific *means* of oppression, and the actual *structures* of oppression are legion, and furthermore they vary in each sphere of exchange. In fact, so complex is this topic that at this point even generalizations and platitudes fail us, and to go beyond them I would definitely have to commit a political science. But again, something must be said, and therefore what I propose to do is to drastically narrow the discussion—without, I hope, forgetting its broader background outlined so far—and center on one particular institution, usually embodied in one particular individual: the institution of *kingship*.

This actually serves our *generalized* purposes very well. First of all, kingship is an epitome (and caricature) of polis, as Louis XIV would soon explain (*"L'état, c'est moi"*). Second, it is also a possible concentration of every form of oppression and exploitation. Third, the *psychology of subservience* to kingship is a paradigm of subservience in general, and is therefore, as we will see, a paradigm of *willing* subjugation and oppression. To demonstrate the basics of what is involved, I will limit the discussion to the exchanges of level 1, or uroboric food and material and goods. In subsequent chapters we will expand the discussion to include higher spheres. Finally, in keeping with our policy of generalized observations, I will hold the discussion on a popularized level.

DIVINE KINGSHIP

Very little is actually known about the origins of mankind's first kings. Actual kingship—as opposed to simple tribal chieftainship—began sometime in the low-membership period, perhaps as early as the tenth millennium B.C., for the king's tomb at Eynan (about a dozen miles north of the Sea of Galilee), dated about 9000 B.C., is the earliest yet found.[215] And of course kingship itself truly blossomed during the high-membership period, in the hieratic city-states of Egypt and Mesopotamia. Other than that, precise details are lacking; or rather, an agreed reading of what archaeological data we do possess is lacking.

‡ Religion: levels 5–8; ideas: levels 3–4; sex: level 2; labor: level 1.

Understand that the invention of kingship is a phenomenon of une-
qualed impact. Politically, it was probably the single greatest change in
mankind's consciousness that had ever appeared; its repercussions were
awesome—and its effects are still with us today.

Kingship was not merely an estate for governing a people; it was not a
practical measure, practically conceived, for organizing and ruling a society. The king was not merely an especially bright fellow chosen to make
decisions for the masses and given the power to represent them as a whole.
He was not given just respect and the simple power of decision—for mankind, at this point, had much more to give, many more possessions and
much more by way of accumulated wealth. Mankind, through the invention of farming, now had a *surplus* in terms of food, of goods, of monies,
of wealth. In the previous typhonic societies, the small amounts of goods
and wealth that existed were shared equally among all peoples—the societies were ones of giving and sharing.

But now, in the emerging societies of the great city-states, there existed
a massive surplus—in goods, foods, monies—and, quite simply, this surplus
was in large measure given to the king and his court. A massive redistribution of goods began, goods which moved from the people on the whole to
a small and select few, a redistribution quite unheard of before this time.
No longer were the produced goods and wealth of a society to be shared
equally among those who actually produced them. They were, instead,
channeled through the hands—the often greedy hands—of an elite. Never
before in history could a few accumulate the produced wealth of the many.
Never before, in other words, could widespread material exploitation and
oppression exist. And students of mankind's political unhappiness, brutal
ity, and exploitation have always agreed that the tangled mess we call political oppression began precisely here, in the great city-states, with the first
great kings. Something awesome was afoot here, something from which we
have never quite recovered, something which, in the end, might prove to
be the death of us all.

Kingship: what on earth happened? How could it happen? And why?

As I said, the origins of kingship are shrouded in obscurity and almost
lost to anything but speculation. But one thing is quite certain, and one
thing is universally agreed upon: the first kings were gods.[70, 153, 201, 215]

This in itself is fascinating, but we must be careful here, for there are
actually two different questions concealed in the simple and agreed conclusion that "the first kings were gods." Namely, were the first kings *actually*
gods, actually in god consciousness or superconsciousness (say, of the subtle level)? Or were the first kings merely perceived as gods or god-like
beings by the simple and unsuspecting farmers and peasants? Were they
gods or god figures? Boddhisattvas or politicians?

Campbell, for one, feels strongly that many of the first god-kings were
actually enlightened or "absorbed and lost in God," and this enlight-

enment "characterized the actual holiness of the sacrificial kings of the early hieratic city-states."[70] I believe that is possible but not probable. It is possible because, during this membership period, a few highly advanced individuals were indeed enlightened to subtle Oneness, and there is no reason the king could not be among them. It is not probable, however, because the only evidence Campbell presents for the actual holiness of the kings is that they almost universally submitted themselves to literal human sacrifice. Campbell thinks that is evidence of the Great Goddess, whereas, as I earlier explained, that is perfectly characteristic of the Great Mother. Campbell's own evidence convinces me that the early "divine" kings were mythically viewed as consorts of the Great Mother, and we know what happens to such consorts: "When the time arrived for the death of the god," explains Frobenius, "the king and his Venus-spouse were strangled and their remains placed in a burial cave in a mountain, from which they were supposed then to be resurrected as the new, or 'renewed,' heavenly spheres."[153] That is a perfect Great Mother ritual—magical/mythical renewal rites, human blood sacrifice, the dead and resurrected god, etc. That's simple magic-logic, not transcendence.

What is admirable about these early "divine" kings, however, is not their transcendence but their unswerving dedication to the mythic world view. These earliest kings, frequently submitting themselves to ritual regicide, served an integral function in the society at large, and tended to be *subservient* to that function. That subservience is glaringly epitomized in the sacrificial rites, where, no matter how barbaric they were, nonetheless the king voluntarily submitted himself to what mythic mentality thought was a necessary function: he died for his polis. To paleologic, the god-king-consort of the Great Mother *had* to die, or life itself would dry up. The king, too, devoutly believed this, and submitted to his civic duty. So while the earliest "divine" kings may not have been truly Divine, nonetheless they weren't yet conniving politicians.

The early god-kings, then, were ritually immolated at the end of a span of years, in subservience to mythic polis. But it is quite obvious that the great politico leaders of the later military dynasties did no such thing. What they wanted, in fact, was just the opposite: *never* to go away, but to achieve substitute immortality here on earth and thus be worshipped as a Divine God-King. And such is precisely what happened. In fact, it was even in a fairly brief span of years that the early communities and city-states of the ritually immolated god-kings gave way to the dynastic-militaristic states headed by tyrannical politicos who were nonetheless viewed as "divine kings." And, according to Mumford, it was just this "divine" kingship, coupled with human sacrifice and a military machine, that produced the hellish terror of the murderous megamachine in whose shadow we still stand. Here, according to Mumford (and he is by no means alone in this opinion), was the precise point—during the rise of the very first dynastic/political states—that massive warfare came into its own. And slavery—it never really existed on any large scale prior to this time. And exploitation. And arrogantly elitist class distinctions. And massive oppression of the many by the few. This, at least, is historical fact. This is the legacy of "divine" kingship and the dynastic state. And this is nothing less than "the colossus of power gone mad, a colossus based on the dehumanization of man that began, not with Newtonian materialism, Enlightenment rationalism, or nineteenth-century commercialism, but with the first massive exploitation of men in the great divine kingships of the ancient world."[26]

Consider: how can you aspire, as a king, to build an immense empire, pile up power and amass wealth, corner the farmed surplus and channel it into war, fashion a heaven on earth for yourself and a handful of royalty—how can you possibly do that when your number comes up in a few years? If you are due for the sacrificial knife in a matter of years, undertaking a lifetime of military and political conquest somehow just doesn't appeal to you.

The *first* thing that had to change, therefore, in order for politicos to step into the office of "divine" kingship, was to get rid of that nasty sacrifice business.

But simply to get rid of the sacrificial rites would have been much too difficult; perhaps too obvious as well. No, the first politico king had to come up with something better than that. And indeed he did: grabbing an idea whose time had come, the "divine" king convinced those around him that a substitute sacrifice of *somebody else* would do just as well. And such is precisely what happened: in Sumer (probably around 2500 B.C.) priests were already being used as substitutes in the life-renewing rites. Frobenius explains:

And when the time arrived for the death of the god, the king and his Venus-spouse were strangled and their remains placed in a burial cave in a mountain, from which they were supposed then to be resurrected as the new, or "renewed," heavenly spheres. And this, surely, must represent the earliest form of the mythological and ritual context. Already in ancient Babylon it had been weakened, in as much as the king at the New Year Festival in the temple was only stripped of his garments, humiliated, and struck, while in the marketplace a substitute, who had been ceremonially installed in all glory, was delivered to death by the noose.[153]

And at that point, the king's vision was released, for the first time in history, to a world of temporal possibilities. Still seen as a god by the pious, but with the appetites of any other idiot, the "divine" king was in a position to fulfill the wildest fantasies of the Atman project: power, immortality, cosmocentricity, omnipotence. And with a rapidity that is astounding, the basic mold of the standard political tyrant was set. The warrior kings, in short, cut themselves off from subservience to community. Instead of serving society, they arranged the reverse: a replacement of social sacrifice with undiluted personal ambition.

And since this personal ambition was located precisely at the center of the *power networks* of the polis (i.e., at the *decision points* of the systems of exchanges, material, emotional, communicative, insofar as they were given to decision), it could distort, oppress, and exploit those exchanges for personal benefit—and there is the crux of the matter.

Because we are, as agreed, temporarily limiting this discussion to the distortions of material exchanges (level 1), let us recall that the single most distinguishing social activity of this period was the farming production of a surplus, and this surplus—besides being the product of a true expansion of consciousness—served also as a promise of surplus time, surplus futures for the separate self, promises of immortality. This food surplus, time surplus, future surplus could be represented by money—"time is money"—and thus a person "could traffic for immortality in the marketplace."

Now it has long been known that the first large amounts of surplus productions (grain, gold, etc.) were often given as offerings to the "divine" kings in the first great temple compounds of the Near East. The largest part of the reason for this undoubtedly was an extension of the fetishistic and substitute sacrifice—giving to "god" in order to magically avoid catastrophe and gain boons ("Give me something good in exchange," said the Crow ritual). And thus the *temples,* in their *exoteric* function, soon gave way to *banks.* And the sacrificed surplus gave way to *accumulated* wealth and *taxes.* It is uncontestedly true that "the first banks were temples, the first to issue money were priests or priest-kings."[61]

Now a banker is simply a substitute priest, for he deals in the currency of immortality symbols rather than timeless transcendence itself. Thus, many of those whom we today call priests (or preachers) are actually bankers—they promise not timeless release but everlasting self-preservation. At any rate, as the early temples became the first banks, the early priests became banker-priests and then just bankers. And the bankers worked for the "divine" kings.

The ironic fact is that as the kings and priests (bankers) came to control and own the surplus, they were not just given some excess foodstuffs and some shiny metallic coins. They were given nothing less than control over the immortality symbols of the community, for that is precisely what the surplus itself was: immortality power. Thus, the kings and priests, the politicos and tyrants, were given the inner strings to the Atman project of each and every individual in the society. That, and that alone, is the key to, and nature of, socio-political power. And the "divine" king now had the key. Today we are agreed that the picture looks something like this:

> that once mankind got the means for large-scale manipulation of the world, the lust for power began to take devastating tolls. This can be seen strikingly at the rise of the great civilizations based on divine kingship. These new states were structures of domination which absorbed the tribal life around them and built up empires. Masses of men were forced into obedient tools for really large-scale power operations directed by a powerful, exploitative class. . . . Power simply got out of hand—or rather, got pressed into the service of a few hands—and instead of isolated and random [substitute] sacrifices on behalf of a fearful tribe, ever larger numbers of people were deliberately and methodically drawn into a "dreadful ceremony" on behalf of the few. . . . This new arrangement unleashed on mankind regular and massive miseries that primitive societies encountered only occasionally and usually on a small scale. Men . . . only succeeded in laying waste to themselves with the new plagues unleashed by their obedience to the politicians.[26]

THE PSYCHOLOGICAL FUNCTION OF THE KING

We are faced, then, with a very general and somewhat simplistic question: why would men and women willingly submit themselves to what must be called such "oppressive rulership"? Why such loyalty to authority figures that were all too often tyrannical madmen? And even if the rulers were benevolent, why such slavish devotion? For throughout history these rulers were more often than not worshipped as god figures, whether they were actually demonic, beneficent, or even blandly non-qualifiable. Notice that we are not talking about leaders who were *actually* god-conscious (such as numerous Dalai Lamas, Gandhi, perhaps a very few of the early god-kings, etc.), but about why people want, need, and desire to *subject* themselves to god figures in the first place, whether such figures are in fact godlike or not. That is, we have already looked at the outward form of oppression (the power loci in the compound society ambitiously exploiting the various levels of exchanges in its compound individuals); we look now at its inward form (the personal and psychological acquiescence to, and even embrace of, such exploitations and distortions). For as it turns out, in seeking to be *subjects,* men and women unwittingly sought *subjection.* And in order to have the former, they tolerated the latter.

Why did people go from an economy of simple sharing among equals to one of pooling via an authority figure who has high rank and absolute power? The answer is that *man wanted a visible god always present to receive his offerings, and for this he was willing to pay the price of his own subjection.* . . . Once men consented to live by the redistribution of life's goods through a god figure who represented life, they had sealed their fate. There was no stopping the process of the monopolization of life in the king's hands.[26]

Hocart's example: "The Fijians had invisible gods, sometimes present in the priest or in an animal; but they preferred a god always present, one they could see and speak to, and the chief was such a god. That is the true reason for a Fijian chief's existence."[26]

We are thus forced to move our question back a notch: why do people want a visible god figure? For if people demand god figures, and if all too often oppressive scoundrels assume the role, then people are, in effect, *demanding* oppression. As Brown put it, people have historically been politically enslaved, but on the deepest psychological level, the slave is somehow in love with his chains. And if this is true—or partially true—then no amount of social reform, let alone Marxist revolution, will truly alleviate the problem. If people want to throw themselves at the feet of Heroes, they will do whatever thing, no matter how enslaving, the Hero wants—especially if times go a little bad. A verse from the American depression: "We care not if Thy flag be white or red; Come, ruthless Savior, messenger of God; Lenin or Christ, we follow Thy bright sword." Whether one chooses the sword of "Onward, Christian Soldiers," or adopts the hammer and sickle of Lenin, psychologically the motivation is the same: the demand for a visible god figure.

What, then, is the nature of this need? Many answers have been offered, and of those many suggestions, the following are the ones I consider most pertinent; i.e., they are all partially but significantly involved: The god figure exists to receive gifts and offerings (via substitute sacrifice); to provide necessary leadership; to ensure prosperity; to provide communal unity. Most psychologists have maintained—and I think this is especially pertinent—that the god figure is a receptacle of projections from the individual unconscious ("the shadow"). This involves a type of "transference" to the god figure of an unresolved need for parental (fatherly) love. Children unrealistically (magically and mythically) see their parents as being titans, capable of protecting them, embracing them, elevating them, supporting them. What wonder if the king served (and still serves) such a purpose for the childish masses?

Finally, it has been suggested that kingship itself, apart from its otherwise crude functions, served as an *initial* evolutionary advance of civilization and consciousness. Kenneth Clarke, for instance, said something like "One cannot help wondering how far the evolution of civilization would go had it depended upon popular will." And thus: "Only in the kingly court could man test his boundaries and potentials." The point is that kingship and courtly life were a concentration of cultural activity, and, however misused it often was, it tended to serve as a reservoir of potential polis and praxis, and thus served the evolution of civilization and consciousness. From this special vantage point (which is an important but still partial view), the king served as the original bearer of *individualized* or egoic consciousness. The king was the first egoic self (a self we will examine in the next few chapters), and for that reason deservedly stood out from his fellows and announced the shape of future evolution. In this sense, anyway, the king was rightly viewed as a Hero.

But all these various reasons are not mutually exclusive. In my opinion, they all contributed to the awesome respect frequently given to the king figure by the masses. I would, however, like to add one more reason, and a reason that really embraces, though not replaces, all of them.

As we have frequently said, all sentient beings intuit their prior and real Atman consciousness or Buddha Nature. But the normal individual cannot live Atman directly, since that would demand death and transcendence. On the one hand, then, he binds to himself as much as possible of Atman intuition by creating a substitute self which appears Atman-like (cosmocentric, etc.). On the other hand, he creates and latches on to a whole host of objective substitute gratifications. But these activities are never totally successful, however, and so the individual transfers his Atman intuitions to others in the environment. He knows *somebody* is God, but since it doesn't seem to be him, it must be somebody else. And he *needs* to see visible god figures in order to keep alive his Atman intuition. In order to maintain contact with Atman intuition, people will transfer it to any place (internal or external) where it can survive. In modern man, it symbolically resides mostly in his own ego and his own heroes—and the smaller the one, the bigger the other.

In short, men and women *need* visible Atman figures because they have forgotten that they themselves *are* Atman. And until that recollection is made, men and women will always be slaves to heroes. Psychologically, and therefore politically.

I believe this transference of Atman intuition was one of the major forces behind the creation of "divine" kings. The god-king was a demanded and visible substitute or symbol of unity consciousness, god consciousness, Atman consciousness. People have always demanded such, and the clever king-hero has always known just how to manipulate this need: "By proclaiming themselves gods of empire, Sargon and Rameses wished to realize in their own persons that mystic or religious unity . . . which could alone form the tie between all the peoples of an empire. Alexander the Great, the Ptolemies, and the Caesars will, in their turn, impose upon their subjects the worship of the sovereign. And so . . . its mystic principle . . . survived in the empire."[26]

At any rate, this need to create receptacles for the positive Atman transference was certainly one factor in the historical support of the "divine king," the great mana figure that, even to this day, dominates political history. And just as a child creates visible gods out of his parents, even if they beat him, so men and women want masters, even if they enslave them. Because people needed a visible god-hero, they willingly submitted to virtual slavery in his behalf. *"And there never has been, historically, any fundamental change in the massive structure of domination and exploitation represented by the state."*[26]

That, of course, is something of an overstatement, but it does point up the fact that, of our two generalizations on the potentials of the polispraxis, the second one—that of significant oppression—has by and large carried the day. The great noetic network of social praxis was, almost from the start, infected in strategic places by diabolic power, and power that, by virtue of its location in the hierarchy of the compound society, could distort and oppress, to one degree or another, the material, sexual, and communicative exchanges in its compound individuals. And by diabolic I mean not only intentional evil but also that type expressed in the saying that in order for evil to triumph, it is only necessary that good men and women do nothing.

In the most general sense, then, this diabolic activity (and "innocent" inactivity) saw the focus of effective social praxis switch from the mutualities of the clan, the group, the community, the polis, to the king, the hero, the head of state, the state itself. And these heroes—some divine, most demonic, some collective, most singular—began to carve out the face of history with the silent support of the enthralled masses.

And history is about to begin.

IV
THE SOLAR EGO

10 Something Unheard Of . . .

We are now on the brink of the first glimmerings of the modern era. All the essentials are present: a farming consciousness, the state, rank, money, war, kingship, mathematics, writing, the calendar, a proto-subjectivity in consciousness. All that is needed is the decisive transformation in consciousness to set the modern world. . . .

It's incredible when you start to think about it, but sometime during the second and first millennia B.C., the exclusively egoic structure of consciousness began to emerge from the ground unconscious (Ursprung) and crystallize out in awareness. And it is just this incredible crystallization that we must now examine, the last major stage—to date—in the collective historical evolution of the spectrum of consciousness (individuals can carry it further, in their own case, by meditation into superconsciousness). It was that transformation which set the modern world.

We have heretofore followed the evolution of consciousness up to and through the high-membership period, which we generally and roughly dated at around 4500–1500 B.C. But these dates—like all the dates we have given—are just that: general and rough. For the roots of any given structure of consciousness can usually be traced back quite a way prior to its full-fledged emergence; and likewise, each structure itself not only contains the roots of the next structure, but also continues to exert its profound influence, as itself, far beyond its own high and evident period. Further, and most important, even when a given structure is no longer a *stage* of evolution, it remains as a lower *level* in the compound individual of the next stage, just as we of today still contain uroboros, magic, and myth in our own makeup (a fact beautifully expressed in our own brain structure, where the neocortex envelops or compounds the limbic and reptilian brains).

We are simply tracing out the historical and prehistorical periods where the average mode of self was a particular level of consciousness. This is not to say that, in any given period, certain individuals do not deviate from the average mode—for indeed they do. During the mythic-membership period, for example, there invariably were a small percentage of people that *never* evolved past the uroboric or typhonic stages—they appeared "retarded," "asocial," "backward." And there were those who *regressed* to the typhonic or uroboric or infantile autistic stages—the "insane," the "madmen," the "possessed." There were those, on the other hand, who transcended into realms of the superconscious, into higher unity consciousness. And finally, there were those who precociously evolved ego or proto-ego structures. These latter individuals were—to use the term somewhat differently than in the last chapter—*heroes,* which in this context (the context I will stress in the next few chapters) means *one who first tries out the next major structure of consciousness.*

Just as with the overall membership period, it is very useful to subdivide the egoic stage into major periods. Because the egoic structure is so close to us—*is* us—we have infinitely more historical details with which to work, and thus we can subdivide it innumerable times in innumerable ways, from spatial perspectives to art styles to cognitive forms, from technological to philosophical to political styles. All of those subdivisions are valid and important—and have been undertaken by various scholars—but for our much simpler purposes, we will just use a chronological breakdown into three general periods: the low, the middle, and the high ego periods.* For the West (Europe and Near East), the dates are—low: 2500–500 B.C.; middle: 500 B.C.–1500 A.D.; high: 1500 A.D.–present.

The low egoic period was a time of transition; the breakdown of the membership structure, the emergence of the egoic structure; the resulting rearrangement of society, philosophy, religion, and politics. This early period continued until sometime during the first millennium, when an unmistakably "modern ego" tentatively emerged. Gebser marks this point (the beginning of the "true mental-ego," what I am calling the beginning of the

---

* Not to be confused with early, middle, and late ego as set forth in *The Atman Project.* For correlations, see the footnote on page 10.

middle egoic period) with the appearance of the *Iliad,* Jaynes with the *Odyssey,* others might like to mark Solon of Greece as most outstanding (sixth-century-B.C. Greece: Solon, Anaximander, Thales, Pythagoras—people *we* of today can understand with little difficulty). At any rate, from the sixth century B.C., the world was never the same—this middle egoic period lasted until around 1500 A.D., with the Renaissance, and shortly after, Galileo and Kepler, and then Newton, and . . . suddenly we arrive at the present, still in the high egoic period. Since we are concerned with the emergence or evolution of structures of consciousness, we will naturally concentrate on the hallmarks of the low egoic period (2500–500 B.C.), the period of the emergence of egoic awareness.

While we celebrate each step in the growth of consciousness, we may rightly lament the accompanying increases in the capacity for destructive and evil activities. As we have frequently seen, there is a price to be paid for each growth in consciousness. New capacities, new potentials, new insights are opened—but new terrors and new responsibilities follow in their wake. And nowhere is this more evident than with the emergence of the mental-egoic structure. On the one hand, it was a tremendous growth experience—it marked a transcendence over the dimly conscious, still somewhat pre-personal, mythic and diffuse structure of the membership stage. It opened up the possibility of truly rational and logical thought (in typhonic times, the environment was starting to become an object of awareness, and thus it could be "operated upon," usually by magic; in membership times, the body was starting to become an object, and thus could be "operated upon" or farmed—its impulses delayed, its instincts controlled; in egoic times, the thought processes themselves start to become objects of awareness, and thus thoughts could be operated upon, which eventually results in "formal operational thinking," or logic, as Piaget showed). The ego brought introspection and self-analysis, penetrating science and philosophy. Most significantly of all, it marked the final emergence from the subconscious realm, which meant that the self could now return to the superconscious in ways and to a degree never before quite possible. Although very few egos *did* attempt Return, the possibility was at least present—as Buddha, Shankara, Lao Tzu, and Christ would soon tell (we will return to this point shortly).

Alas, however, for the other side of the story. With the ego level we reach a stage of evolution where the separate self is so complex and so "strong" that, in breaking free of its earlier and subconscious ties to cosmos, nature, and body, it could turn on these previous stages (which now were also levels of its own compound individuality) with a vengeance never before evidenced. For the ego—lying precisely halfway between the subconscious and the superconscious—was in a position to deny its dependence on both. And in ways never really seen before, the ego did not just transform up and out of the typhonic and membership stages, it violently *repressed* them. The ego rose up arrogant and aggressive, and—blown sky high by its Atman project—began to sever its own roots in a fantasy attempt to prove its absolute independence.

I will often concentrate on the disastrous consequences of the Atman project wrought by the hands of this new substitute self. For what we don't realize today is just what the typical self of every previous stage failed likewise to comprehend: *this* is not the highest and greatest mode of consciousness which can be attained—there lie ahead the realms of the superconscious, and the pitiful ego, by comparison, is as a speck of nothingness. But this speck, emerging by its own truly heroic and commendable efforts out of the chthonic subconscious, turned then to lay waste to both its roots in the subconscious and its future in the superconscious. It attempted—and succeeded—in repressing access to both realms, and imagining success, began to remake the cosmos in its own image.

EGO BIRTH: A MYTHOLOGICAL LOOK

As usual, let us first touch bases with Jean Gebser:

> We have two reasons for choosing the designation "mental" [our mental-egoic] to characterize the structure of consciousness still prevailing [from the time of the *Iliad* to the present]. First, the word harbors an extraordinary abundance of relations in its original root, which in Sanskrit is *ma,* and from which secondary roots such as *man-, mat-, me-,* and *men-* have been derived; all the words formed from this root express definite characteristics of the mental structure. Secondly, this word is one which stands at the beginning of our Western culture, for it is the first great word in the first great line of the first great song of the first great Western pronouncement. This word "mental" is contained in . . . the accusative of *Menis,* with which the *Iliad* begins . . . —a statement which, for the first time within our Western world, not only evokes a picture but describes a ceremonious act directed by man (not exclusively by the gods), in an ordered or causal course of events.
>
> Thus, we are dealing with directional thinking, which comes tentatively out into the open. If mythical thinking [or paleologic] . . . was an imaginative, symbolic projection, which took place within the confines of the circle with its polarity, directional thinking is radically different. It is no longer polarized, that is, enshrined in and mirroring

polarity; it is object-oriented and hence turned toward the objective world.[159]

"This process," concludes Gebser, "is a happening so extraordinary that it literally shook the world. By means of this event [emergence of the mental-ego], the protective circle of the soul—the incorporation of man in the [mythic-membership] embrace of a world-soul, wherein he lived in polar relationship with nature, cosmos, and time—has been blasted. The ring has burst; man steps from the plane into space, which he will attempt to conquer in thought. Something unheard of has happened, something which has changed the world in its very foundations."[159]

Changed the world in its very foundations—the change was simply this: according to the Great Chain of Being, the next stage of evolution, after the mythic-membership, would be the final differentiation and crystallization of the mind out of the body. In order for this to occur, the self had to struggle against its previous embeddedness and immersion in nature, in the body, in the remnants of participation mystique and uroboric dissolution. It had to struggle against (or rather *transform*) those factors that acted to reduce consciousness to pre-personal impulses.

In general mythological terms, the self had to break free of the Great and Chthonic Mother, and establish itself as an independent, willful, and rational center of consciousness. As Neumann so carefully explained, "Ego consciousness has, as the last-born [i.e., the last major structure yet to evolve in consciousness], to fight for its position and secure it against the assaults of the Great Mother within and the World Mother without. Finally it has to extend its own territory in a long and bitter struggle," a struggle that led to nothing less than the emergence and emancipation of mental-egoic consciousness.

If we now look closely at the collective mythologies of the beginning of this egoic period, what we discover is unequivocally clear: *an entirely different form of myth begins to emerge,* a myth never before seen to any great extent. The easiest way to introduce this new myth is by recalling the typical structure of the old Great Mother myths. In those myths, as we explained, the individual (i.e., the self structure of that period), involved with the Great Mother, usually comes to a tragic end—killed, mutilated, castrated, sacrificed. The Great Mother is always the victor—the self never triumphs over the Great Mother, but is always reduced to one of her mere satellites, remaining a pre-personal "momma's boy."

But in the new myths, we find an extraordinary occurrence: the individual triumphs over the Great Mother—breaks free from her, transforms her, defeats her, or transcends her. And this is the "Hero Myth," the myth that *is* this period of history. Thus: "Toward the close of the Age of Bronze [c. 2500 B.C.] and, more strongly, with the dawn of the Age of Iron (c. 1250 B.C. in the Levant), the old cosmologies and mythologies of the goddess

mother were radically transformed . . . and set aside in favor of those
male-oriented, patriarchal mythologies of thunder-hurling gods that by the
time a thousand years had passed, c. 1500 B.C., had become the dominant
divinities of the Near East."⁷¹

It is for just this reason, Campbell explains, that "the early Iron Age lit-
eratures of both Aryan Greece and Rome and of the neighboring Semitic
Levant are alive with variants of the conquest by a shining hero of the
dark and . . . disparaged monster of the earlier order of godhood, from
whose coils some treasure was to be won: a fair land, a maid, a boon of
gold, or simply freedom from the impugned monster itself."⁷¹

Now there are several fascinating aspects to this historical emergence of
the Hero Myth—the myth of the individual Hero triumphing over the
Great Mother or one of her consorts, such as the old serpent-dragon-
uroboros, or over a Great Mother derivative, such as Medusa with serpent-
monster hair, or over a Great Mother offspring, such as Typhon. The first
aspect is that *the Hero is simply the new egoic structure of consciousness,*
which, coming into existence at this time (the low egoic period), is naturally given living expressions in the mythology of this period. And the true
hero myths do not emerge before this period because there were no egos
before this period. Campbell, for instance, specifically states that the *beginning* of the Great Mother transformation is c. 2500 B.C.—the date we
chose for the beginning of the low egoic period.

Now the second important aspect of the egoic Hero Myth is the nature
of the monster that is slain, captured, or subjugated. We will very shortly
return to this topic in detail, for there are a handful of fascinating points
all intertwined in this fateful battle. But for the moment, we need only
note that the slain monster is the Great Mother, or one of her symbols, or
one of her consorts. And the "treasure hard to attain" that the serpent
monster guards and tries to conceal is simply the ego structure itself. This
is significant, for the serpent is really the uroboros, the structure which,
with the Great Mother, kept the ego immersed and encoiled in unconsciousness. The dragon guards the ego—and that's what the Hero must lib-
erate. Prior to this time in history, the Great Mother (with her old uroboric consort, holdover from the dawn state of mankind) sacrificially
swallowed up egos and returned them to herself in subconsciousness,
thereby preventing, as we saw, the necessary emergence of egoic consciousness. But somewhere during this period, the Hero clutched his egoic
self out of the jaws of the Devouring Mother and secured thereby his own
emancipation.

Such, then, is the nature of the fiercely individualistic and "shining hero
of the dark and disparaged monster of the earlier order of godhood."
There is now little question that "the counterpart for the Greeks was the
victory of Zeus over Typhon, the youngest child of Gaea, the goddess
Earth [or biological and chthonic earth Mother]—by which deed the reign

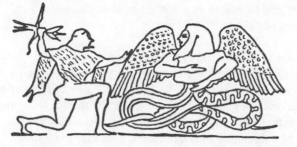

Fig. 22. Zeus defeating the Typhon, a classic Hero Myth. The mental-ego finally emerges from the typhonic realms.

of the patriarchal gods of Mount Olympus was secured over the earlier Titan broods of the great . . . mother."[71] Furthermore, "the resemblance of this victory to that of Indra, king of the Vedic pantheon, over the cosmic serpent Vritra is beyond question."[71] And they all represent the budding principle of the individual hero over the old "force of the cosmic order itself, the dark mystery . . . , which licks up hero [mental-egoic] deeds like dust: the force of the never-dying serpent [uroboros], sloughing lives like skins, which, pressing on, ever turning in its circle of [mythic] return, is to continue in this manner forever, as it has already cycled from all eternity [seasonal time], getting absolutely nowhere."[71]

That is the nature-mythic circle which, in Gebser's words, was blasted apart by the emergence of the heroic ego; *that* was the "happening so extraordinary that it literally shook the world." And just *that* was the something-unheard-of which crashed into existence during this period, the "something which has changed the world in its very foundations." In the West, says Campbell:

> The principle . . . represented by the freely willing, historically effective hero not only gained but held the field, and has retained it to the present. Moreover, this victory of the principle of free will, together with its moral corollary of individual responsibility, establishes the first distinguishing characteristic of specifically Occidental myth: and here I mean to include not only the myths of Aryan Europe (the Greeks, Romans, Celts, and Germans), but also those of both the Semitic and Aryan peoples of the Levant (Semitic Akkadians, Babylonians, Phoenicians, Hebrews, and Arabs; Aryan Persians, Armenians, Phrygians, Thraco-Illyrians, and Slavs). For whether we think of the victories of Zeus and Apollo, Theseus, Perseus, Jason, and the rest, over the dragons of the Golden Age, or turn to that of Yahweh over the Leviathan, the lesson is equally of a self-moving power greater than the force of any earthbound serpent destiny. All

stand *"first and foremost as a protest against the worship of the Earth and daimones of the fertility of Earth."*[71]

In short, the characteristic core of the newly emergent hero myths and philosophies of this period was simply the personal, "freely" willing ego. For "the accent of the same old basic mythic themes dramatically moved from the side of the ever-repeated archetype to that of the unique individuality . . . : and not only to his particular individuality, but also to the entire order of values that may be termed properly personal. . . . It is this dramatic, epochal, and—as far as our documentation tells—unprecedented shift of loyalty from the impersonal to the personal [that] is comparable to an evolutionary psychological mutation."[71] My own feeling, as I have frequently said, is that this movement was absolutely desirable, for one has to move from the impersonal to the personal on the way to the trans-personal. But as for this being "an evolutionary psychological mutation," I certainly agree—and those, as we saw, were also Gebser's precise words as well.

But Campbell and Gebser are not alone in their reading of the anthropological, mythological, and psychological record of mankind's history. Neumann is at pains to carefully demonstrate that only after the escape from the Devouring Mother, only after the heroic battle with the dragon, "only then is [mankind] born as a personality with a stable ego." Neumann is specific: "Through the masculinization and emancipation of ego consciousness the ego becomes the 'hero.' The story of the hero, as set forth in the myths [of this period], is the history of this self-emancipation of the ego. . . . The development of the conscious system, having as its center an ego . . . is prefigured in the hero myth." And this is so because the hero is simply the "bearer of the ego, with its power to discipline the will and mold the personality." Finally, this means "not only that man's ego consciousness has achieved independence; but that his total personality has detached itself from the natural context of the surrounding world."[311]

And, of course, Julian Jaynes has just delivered himself, in *The Origin of Consciousness in the Breakdown of the Bicameral Mind,* of what amounts to a reformulation, somewhat extreme, of this whole transformation. Nevertheless, it is based upon a careful, even brilliant, reading of mythology, and therefore we can quickly mention it. According to Jaynes, mankind prior to the second millennium B.C. "did not have any ego whatsoever." But between the second and first millennia B.C. (i.e., somewhere in the low egoic period), "the great transilience in mentality had occurred. Man had become [self-]conscious of himself and his world. . . . Subjective consciousness, that is, the development on the basis of linguistic metaphors of an operation space in which an 'I' could narratize out alternative actions to their consequences, was of course the great world result."

Let us, then, join with all these scholars—whose backgrounds and orientations are, we might note, quite different—and accept as very probable just that fact: sometime in the second and first millennia B.C., what we know as the egoic structure of consciousness emerged out of the mythic-membership level of consciousness. The heroic emergence of the ego level: something, indeed, quite unheard of. . . .

MYTHIC DISSOCIATION

But we come now to a crucial footnote to this story of the emergence of the heroic ego, a footnote that historically almost became an entire text in itself, and a perverted text at that. We said that the ego, in the necessary course of its emergence, had to break free of the Great Mother or biological nature embeddedness. That is all well and good—the ego, in fact, did manage to break free of its attachment and subservience to the Chthonic Mother—the realm of typhonic and mythic embeddedness—and establish itself as an independent, willful, and constellated center of consciousness, a feat represented in the Hero Myths. But in its zeal to assert its independence, it not only *transcended* the Great Mother, which was desirable; it *repressed* the Great Mother, which was disastrous. And there the ego—the Western ego (the story was somewhat different in the East†)—demonstrated not just an awakened assertiveness, but a blind arrogance.

No longer harmony with the Heavens, but a "conquering of space"; no longer respect for Nature, but a technological assault on Nature. The ego structure, in order to rise arrogantly above creation, had to suppress and repress the Great Mother, mythologically, psychologically, and sociologically. And it repressed the Great Mother in *all* her forms. It is one thing to gain a freedom from the fluctuations of nature, emotions, instincts, and environment—it is quite another to alienate them. In short, the Western ego did not just gain its freedom from the Great Mother; it severed its deep interconnectedness with her. A severe lesion grew up, not just between ego and nature (Great Mother), but between ego and body (a lesion we will examine in the next chapter).

† For two basic reasons: the East developed and implemented on a large scale techniques for transformation into the superconscious realms, which acted as a counterbalance to and release from the exclusive tyranny of the ego; on the other hand, masses of Eastern peoples never truly developed beyond membership societies, with heavy emphasis on pre-egoic ties and communal values.

Fig. 23. Great Goddess Kali, India. Kali, when viewed in her highest form as wife of Shiva, is a perfect example of the assimilation of the old Great Mother image into a new and higher corpus of Great Goddess mythology—precisely what did not happen in the West (with the possible but rather tepid exception of Mary, who nevertheless was thoroughly expunged by the Protestants). For Goddess Kali is usually pictured with all the old symbols of the devouring Great Mother—sacrificial knife, skulls, blood, the serpent—but in her worship by the true saints and sages (e.g., Ramakrishna), and in her pure metaphysical form, she was always the Great Goddess, never demanding human blood sacrifice but always calling for the interior sacrifice of the separate-self sense. Notice, in that regard, the halo of subtle-level light surrounding her head—something which is never found in Great Mother icons. The beauty of this scheme is twofold: (1) The old mythology of the Great Mother is maintained in most of its forms, but it is integrated and transformed in a higher mythology which serves actual sacrifice in awareness, not substitute sacrifice in blood. (2) The old and terrifying imagery of the devouring Great Mother is retained as a reminder that the

This repression had profound and severe repercussions, about which we will often editorialize. For the moment, and in keeping with our mythological survey, we need only note that, once the Great Mother myths were transcended by the Hero Myths, the Great Mother was not integrated into subsequent mythology (as ideally it should; recall that each stage of evolution ideally transcends but includes, negates but preserves, its predecessors, and failure to do so = pathology). Rather, the themes, moods, and structures of the Great Mother corpus were simply *left out* of subsequent mythology. So left out, in fact, that it would take the genius of Bachofen, in only very recent times, to simply discover just the existence of this older maternal mythology.[16] This is what Campbell means when he says "the old cosmologies and mythologies of the goddess mother were *transformed* and in large measure even *suppressed*." The transformation we applaud; the suppression we lament. (It is an indignation at this suppression that runs so strongly through all of Campbell's works, with the result, it seems to me, that he occasionally then misses the importance of the transformation per se.)

But even Neumann, arch-champion of the Hero Myth, clearly recognized that the heroic thrust went way too far, and "with this, the great revaluation of the feminine begins, its conversion into the negative, thereafter carried to extremes in the patriarchal religions of the West."[311] So extreme, in fact, that in these religions there isn't even an explicit *mention* of the Great Mother, let alone an appreciation of her necessary, if admittedly lower, functions. And one cannot integrate what one doesn't even admit exists in the first place.

The point is that, where the egoic self ought to have gone from mythic *identification* with the Great Mother to mythic *differentiation* from the Great Mother (which *allows* subsequent *integration;* you cannot integrate that which has not been differentiated in the first place), it went instead into mythic *dissociation.* It went too far, as it were, and turned transcendence and differentiation into repression and dissociation: the dissociation and alienation of the Great Mother.

My final point is that, when the Great Mother is repressed, the Great Goddess is concealed. These are *not* the same archetypes, as I explained in Chapter 7. The Great Mother is representative of level 2/3, the Great Goddess of level 6; and the Hero Myths, as I have explained them, refer specifically to the victory of level 4 over level 2/3 (the Great Mother). However, when the Feminine Imago is rejected *in toto,* the higher wisdom, or Sophia, which often finds its natural expression in the Great Goddess, is

---

life of the separate self is indeed surrounded by pain, suffering, and ultimately death, and that one must transcend the self to transcend that anguish. Kali, then, is the perfect Great Goddess: she preserves but transcends the Great Mother, and thereby integrates the lower with the higher.

likewise denied expression. And one may—it is a terrible realization—look in vain through Judaeo-Christian-Islamic religion for any authentic trace of the higher touch of the subtle Goddess herself. And *that,* we will see, would become a perfect and terrifying comment on an entire civilization.

11 The Slaying of the Typhon

With the emergence of the ego level, the self had finally succeeded in differentiating itself from the Great Mother and Mother Nature. At the same time, we saw that the process was carried to extremes in the West, with the result that there was not just a differentiation between ego and nature, but a dissociation between ego and nature. In just the same way, there was not just a *differentiation* of mind and body—which was a necessary and positive step in evolution—but a *dissociation* of the mind from the body. And I am saying that these two dissociations are *one:* the alienation of the self from nature (and the Great Mother) is the alienation of the self from the body.

Now in order to facilitate this discussion—which in itself is complex enough—I will lump the typhonic and membership structures together and simply refer to them collectively as the "typhonic realms." This is perfectly acceptable, as long as we remember that it is a simple generalization. These two structures, the typhonic and the membership, are indeed quite different, but *in comparison with the mental-egoic structure,* they have much in common. For instance, both are dominated by the Great Mother, both lack a conclusive differentiation of mind and body, both are still in-

termeshed with nature and instinct, both tend toward impulsiveness, and
so on. But above all, we note that both of these structures lack a conclusive differentiation of mind and body—that is, the mind is still "in" the
body (totally so in typhonic times, partially so in membership times).
Thus, I will refer to these two structures collectively as the "typhonic or
bodily realms," the realms wherein mind and body are still pre-differentiated (while, of course, continuing to refer to them *individually* as *the*
typhon level and *the* membership level). For what we want to follow is the
fate of the body as the ego-mind finally emerges—and what we will find is
that where the organism should have differentiated into mind and body, it
tended instead to *dissociate* into mind and body.

What I am saying, then, is that in Western history, the typhonic realms
and the Great Mother were buried together, and the new substitute self,
the ego—however otherwise representative of a major growth in consciousness—rose up viciously assertive in its new vision of cosmocentricity
and death immunity. We have already examined the suppression and
repression of the Great Mother; we turn now to the suppression and dissociation of the typhon (the typhonic realms).

Fortunately, our work has already been done for us in a remarkable
book called *The Next Development in Man*, by L. L. Whyte.[426] Hailed by
scholars from Mumford to Einstein, *The Next Development* is basically
about one phenomenon—a phenomenon which Whyte calls the "European
dissociation," which is a "particular form of disintegration of the organizing processes in the individual which, though arising from a tendency la-
tent in a physiological characteristic to all races [which we will shortly ex-
plain], attained its most marked form in the European and Western
peoples during the period from around 500 B.C. [there again we are at
sixth-century-B.C. Greece] until the present time. During these two and a
half millennia this dissociation became a permanent element in the European tradition and the distinguishing mark of European and Western
man." The European dissociation is basically the dissociation between the
mind and the body—once again: not just a differentiation, but a dissociation.

Now, according to Whyte, the European dissociation between ego and
body rests upon a dual specialization of the whole organism. For the organism can, on the one hand, act spontaneously in the present, but on the
other, it can preserve records of past actions. These two different capacities are not necessarily in conflict, but they can tend to drift apart:

> The recording faculties of the brain tend to emphasize the records
> of the past, while the transmissive processes of the nerves link the or-
> ganism with the challenges of its present environment. There thus
> develops a tendency for systems of deliberate behavior, which make
> greater use of the organized records of the past, to separate them-

selves from the immediate responses. . . . This dual specialization is useful and does not damage the integrity of the organism, so long as the operation of these two partial functions is kept in balance.

Whyte explains this "dual specialization" from many angles. On the one side, the memory-recording side, lies the world of mental concepts, delayed behavior, controlled responses, deliberate and voluntary actions, reasoning—everything we refer to generally as mental-egoic. On the other side lies the world of immediate responses, dynamic processes, spontaneous present activity, instincts, present and immediate feelings—everything we refer to generally as the body. "In the early stages of the development of this dual specialization the contrast between the two modes was not excessive and the balance was adequately maintained."

We will presently give a quick summation of the history of the generation of the European dissociation as seen by Whyte, but for the moment let us simply note that there gradually arose, by the second and first millennia B.C., the great imbalance and ultimate separation of the two systems. Through an aggravation of the dual specialization of the organism, and a simple burst in growth of the mental component, the organism drifted into two antagonistic systems: mental-delayed-static vs. bodily-spontaneous-dynamic. "Gradually the contrast of the two functions produced an organic lesion; deliberate behavior was organized by the use of static concepts, while spontaneous behavior continued to express a formative [and dynamic] process; that special part of nature which we call thought thus became alien in form to the rest of nature; there grew up a disjunction between the organization of thought and the organization of nature." More precisely:

> The demands of communication led man first to emphasize permanent elements, but man, like nature, is a system of processes. This inescapable contrast prejudiced organic harmony. The whole-natured behavior of primitive and ancient man broke up into two ultimately incompatible systems, neither of which could employ the entire human being: the system of spontaneous behavior, of immediate responses to present situations, relatively unaffected by the rational organization of past experience; and the system of deliberate behavior, of delayed responses based on the systematized experience of the past to the relative neglect of present stimuli.
>
> Moreover as the intellect extends its scope it tends to dominate the entire system and to force to one side, and in doing so to distort, the forms of spontaneous behavior. Because the immature intellect has a static prejudice and is therefore partially divorced from the processes of the organism it cannot itself provide a general co-ordination capable of uniting deliberate and spontaneous behavior. Conscious and

unconscious, reason and instinct, are divorced, with consequent mutual distortion.

In short, "in the European dissociation reason and instinct are at war." And it is not the *existence* of reason or instinct that is the problem, but the *conflict* between the two, as Whyte himself frequently points out. As Neumann put it, "Our cultural unease or dis-ease is due to the fact that the separation of the systems [mind and body]—*in itself a necessary product of evolution*—has degenerated into a schism [dissociation] and thus precipitated a psychic crisis whose catastrophic effects are reflected in contemporary history."[311] It is not, then, the existence of the ego per se that is regrettable, but the inability to integrate the newly emergent ego with the prior typhonic realms, the realms of instinct, emotion, feeling, and body-self activities.

Historically, according to Whyte, this European dissociation came about this way: "During the first period [of human evolution as outlined by Whyte] men were . . . living from hand to mouth in small communities, either nomadic or sheltering in caves, and hunting or collecting their food [i.e., the times of the typhon]. This period covers part of the Paleolithic Age and closes about the time of the first neolithic arrow heads and pottery. The differentiation of individual behavior and of social organization had not then proceeded far [and] verbal symbolisms played only a small role. Even at the end of the period the most advanced communities had only a limited faculty of speech and few general conceptions." Note that Whyte (like Jaynes) does not see language playing any significant role in the typhonic self.

This period of "non-verbal" hunting and gathering ended, according to Whyte, around 9000 B.C., and the period 8000–4000 B.C. (our "low-membership stage") Whyte views as preparatory for the rise of the high civilizations, c. 4000–1000 B.C. (our "high-membership stage"). Of the entire membership period, Whyte states:

The millennia from 8000 to 1000 B.C. include so many different forms of society from the neolithic communities to the ancient civilizations that no single generalization can cover them all. Nevertheless, if these societies are considered from a biological point of view one tendency is evident throughout this period. Compared with the relatively static and simple forms of primitive [typhonic] man, a quicker development is now in process towards a more complex differentiation of behavior, both within the life of each individual and in the different functions of the individuals within the community. The responses of primitive man to his environment were relatively swift, that is, they followed the stimulus either immediately or after only a short delay. His memory was too short and his attention too uncertain to permit him to plan far ahead, and his power to dominate the environment was correspondingly restricted. . . . But with the advantages of urban life [membership] ancient man was able to exercise faculties that had previously had little opportunity; he developed new tools for action and new words for thought . . . and so gradually evolved the complex and extended patterns of deliberate behavior characteristic of civilized society. . . . In contrast to the relatively quick responses of primitive man, a considerable part of the whole of human activity is now composed of the systems of deliberate behavior . . . , which include deliberate planning and rituals extending over months or even years (compared with the days or weeks covered by the plans of primitive man). . . .

Speech, script, and conceptual thought are now of rapidly growing importance in the organization of society. The concept, or idea, has become one of the main instruments of social co-ordination, and ideas begin to be linked in sequences which permit reasoned attention to be given to novel situations, and so lead to the long-delayed deliberate responses which result from sustained thought.

That was also the single, major distinction we made: the membership-self was marked by language and temporal extension, with consequent delayed gratifications and deliberate long-circuited reactions, as opposed to the impulsive and immediate reactions so characteristic of the previous typhonic self.

"Nevertheless," and Whyte is at pains to emphasize this point, "though the social tradition was already complex and far reaching in its modeling of the earlier instinctive [typhonic] and traditional [membership] forms of life . . . , the general control of the individual's behavior and the factors determining choice in situations of difficulty or conflict were not yet the subject of general attention, and hence also not yet the subject of verbal formulation as an accepted part of the tradition. There was still no need for a general conception of man as an independent person with the faculty of choice in accordance with his individual character." Still, that is, no ego. "Man is still a part of nature, though already thoughtful; thoughtful, but not yet about himself; an individual, but still displaying normal organic integration."

But then, historically, that incredible "something unheard of." According to Whyte, "a momentous change opens the third [or egoic] period; the passing of the ancient world and the development of rational self-consciousness. The transformation coincides with the collapse of the Bronze Age civilization and the expansion of life which resulted from the use of iron. During the centuries from 1600 to 400 B.C. the processes of history acquire a wholly novel shape . . ." We add, therefore, yet another scholar who sees rational, egoic self-consciousness emerge sometime during the

second and first millennia B.C. There is no doubt in Whyte's mind that
the growth of self-consciousness and rationality was a highly desirable
achievement; and yet he, too, clearly saw the fateful consequences of such
a step. Thus, in the same sentence that I just broke off, Whyte finishes with
an incredible sentiment, "for now [1600–400 B.C.], if ever, is the fall of
man."

What happened? In essence, the answer given by Whyte is strikingly
similar to that given by Jaynes (*sans* hallucinations and brain physiology),
and the fact that they developed their ideas independently (Whyte wrote
thirty years ago; Jaynes does not mention or footnote him) simply lends
support to the thesis itself. And the thesis, in its *general* form, can be put
simply: the ego arose in the "breakdown" of the membership mind. We
have already heard Jaynes's special version; Whyte's runs thus:

"Everyone," he begins, "who pauses to consider the significance of this
moment in the story of man [emergence of the ego] must be held in awe
by the grandeur of the transformation that was consummated in so short a
time." And this transformation to the mental-egoic level was made possible, even mandatory, by one significant fact: "The processes which organized human behavior had, it seems, been ready for a swift reorganization;
the [previous membership] pattern had become unstable and now settled
rapidly into a new shape."

In the pagan age man could think out practical problems without
finding himself involved in any general or persisting conflict. Thought
and action were never far from immediate instinctive needs, no
dualism of incompatibles had yet become dominant in human nature
or in man's thought about himself, and though decision on a particular course of action might sometimes be difficult, such difficulty
seemed to lie in the nature of things rather than in his own nature.

Yet this primitive condition was bound to sooner or later be
disrupted, either by increasing differentiation of thought and of deliberate behavior, or by the clash between different modes of life
brought into contact by the improved methods of communication.
When this occurred the old assurance collapsed, instinctive [ty-
phonic] and traditional [membership] systems ceased to be adequate
to organize behavior, man became uncertain what to do, and so un-
sure of himself.

But this, as Jaynes would later put it, was the pause that profaned.
"This hesitancy," Whyte continues, "meant that instinct and tradition [ty-
phon and membership] having proved inadequate the individual was
being compelled to rely for guidance on his own mental processes. Instead
of being aided primarily by instinctive responses to external stimuli and by
mimicry of the forms of a stable social tradition, the individual was now

increasingly dominated and controlled at moments of decision by the special forms of his own thought processes. This dominance of the individual's own mental processes means, in unitary thought, that his attention was drawn to these processes. Instinctive and traditional responses to the outer world no longer sufficed to organize the whole of behavior, decisions had now increasingly to be made in accordance with forms internal to himself. Thus man became self-conscious. The individual became aware of his own thought."

Social and cultural life was simply becoming too complex for the somewhat rigid membership structure to adequately handle. First in specific heroes, but then in more and more average individuals, membership translation failed and transformation to the egoic structure occurred, so that, by the time of the end of the low egoic period, whole societies of self-conscious, "freely" willing, individual personalities were starting to emerge. For the ever-increasing "circumstances of human life demanded that individual choice, based on personal consideration of the problems of behavior, should to an increasing degree dominate behavior. The attention of the individual was drawn more and more to his own thought as well as to external stimuli, and he became aware of himself as a thinking and feeling person endowed with the faculty of choice. . . . He had to become aware of himself as a person."

All of this, of course, is a greatly simplified summation of Whyte's views, and I do not mean to rush lightly over what are rather complex transformations. But even if we went into all the details, his conclusion would still be awaiting us: "The process which we are considering may be regarded as the development of individual personality [and] it was only during the first millennium B.C. that this degree of self-consciousness became widespread."

At this point, then, let us look more closely at the nature of this new substitute self, the mental-egoic. For according to Whyte, there is one common characteristic that underlies a significant portion of egoic activities. It is a very simple characteristic: many of the mental-egoic activities are, in large measure, based on the *past*. That is to say, they are based on the memory records of past actions, past experiences, past events. As you are now thinking about all this, you are working largely with memories—for it is from memory, from the past, that you draw words, names, and concepts.

That in itself is not a bad thing—it is through the use of memory that mankind was able to pull itself out of its slumber in the subconscious. Odd as it sounds, memory is a form of transcendence, for it allows one to rise above the fluctuations of the moment. As mankind's self began to shift away from the body and toward the mind, toward thought and language, it began likewise to shift toward memory. The ego is in part a memory-self, and that is what allows it to rise above the fluctuations of the body. Even

Bergson clearly recognized that mental "consciousness signifies, before everything, memory."*

All of which is fine. There are only two basic problems with the ego. One, after the ego is formed, it is very, very difficult to transcend. The ego is so stable, so "permanent," so "strong" that it not only escapes the subconscious, it also tends to deny the superconscious. The ego has to be very badly bounced around by life before it will open itself to transcendence. Nonetheless, the ego is a desirable and necessary "halfway house" between subconsciousness and superconsciousness. Two, the very characteristics of the ego (its memory components) tend toward several complications, foremost among which is the European dissociation. For thought operates largely with the past, and there is one thing certain about the past: it is static.† Thus, thought tends to be at odds with the simpler world of instinctive impulsiveness. Thought therefore tends to set itself apart from nature. And so, as the individual began to identify with the recording and thinking and memory aspects of the organism, he began to form a conception of himself as a static, permanent, persistent self; and that thought-self tended to feel separate not only from the impulsive world around it, but also from the spontaneous aspects of its own body.

"This is the curse laid on *homo sapiens*," explains Whyte. For during the early development of the mind and intellect, during, that is to say, the low egoic stage, "intellectual man had no choice but to follow the path which facilitated the development of his faculty of thought, and thought could only clarify itself by separating out static concepts which, in becoming static, ceased to conform either to their organic matrix or to the forms of nature. . . . Thought thus became alien in form to the rest of nature." The ego, then, which otherwise was a magnificent growth in consciousness, tended also to form (initially) as a separative lesion in awareness. Whyte is at pains to point out that thought doesn't *have* to operate with only

---

* It is true that the superconscious states are trans-mental-memory; the point is that they are *not* pre-mental-memory: plants and animals are pre-memory. When sages such as Krishnamurti criticize memory outright, they fail to distinguish pre-memory and trans-memory, they fail to see that memory is a necessary but intermediate stage on the way to trans-memory Consciousness as Such.

† I don't mean to imply that thought operates *only* with the past. For the most noble use of the mind is in its capacity as a *creative* tool of future potentials, potentials not given in the past or the present. Creativity by definition transcends the given (the past and the present), and that is the mind's highest achievement. But this creativity is a capacity generally given only to a rather advanced and mature intellect; the initial, immature, and ordinary intellect merely ruminates over the past and the present. and replays its old records; that is what I am talking about. This is very similar—I would even say identical—to Whyte's distinction between the "immature and static intellect" and the "mature and process intellect." His point is that it is not thought per se that causes the European dissociation, but immature/static thought that does so. And, says Whyte, the early mental-ego was, rather necessarily, caught in such static, fixed patterns.

static concepts—thought can form *process* concepts (which is really what Whyte's book is all about). Whyte will have nothing to do with the romantic fallacy and the glorification of the body over the mind, despite the use to which his work has been put by modern gestaltists, sensory-awareness advocates, "experiential therapists," and so on. It's just that, initially at least, thought *tends* to clarify itself via static forms.

And it is not so very difficult to see how this all occurred, and why. For all we have to remember is that the ego was the new substitute self, and like all substitute selves, it had to pretend to fulfill the desire for some form of cosmocentricity, immortality, and everlastingness. And the ego did just that with *its own thought processes*.

Whyte himself is very well aware of the deeper issues involved in the emergence of the ego in the European dissociation. For the creation of permanent, static, fixed entities—especially the static self concept—is based on the fear of change, of flux, of dynamic and process reality. Beneath the creation of the "existent entity 'I,'" says Whyte, is simply "the demand for permanent entities, substances which in themselves do not change. The immature intellect, being unable as yet to cope with process, creates these persisting entities for its own convenience."

Whyte then drives precisely to the heart of the matter. For there is a reason lying behind the desire to create "permanent entities," and Whyte knows just what it is: "this [newly emergent] self-awareness led also to a more vivid sense of the precariousness of the individual life. To become self-aware is to become conscious of the perpetual threat of nature to the security of the self and of the inescapable fact of death. . . . Once alone and afraid man fears . . . the action of the whole [i.e., he fears true unity consciousness, for that entails the death of the separate-self sense], and *instead desires eternal* [*everlasting*] *life*."

There is a very clear definition of the Atman project! And further, since the ego cannot "escape from the sense of separation," it looks instead for something that, in Whyte's own words, "*as recompense promises immortality*." Thus, this search for everlastingness and immortality is merely a substitute for true unity with the Whole, and "to be made content with so spurious a substitute was the inevitable price of man's misunderstanding of his own nature and of his part in the whole." The inevitable price, we would say, of the sleep of his Buddha Nature.

Thus, we can start to see why the thought process, the concepts, the ideas, and the memories were so important: in its drive to a promised immortality, the new self sense, in a fashion never before so grandiose, seized upon the characteristics of the world of thought. For thought, being initially static, seemed to offer something that neither nature nor flesh would: *permanence*. The word "tree," for example, stays the same while all actual trees change, mature, and die. Thought promises eternity by delivering its substitute: permanence. No wonder Rank could say that all ideologies

were immortality projects. Therefore "man's thought—still betraying its secret desire for permanence"—became the executor of the Atman project,
the attempt to become cosmocentric, immortal, forever cheating death
through the crystal unchanging world of concepts. And thought, the static
mental-ego, simply *dissociated*, as a *substitute sacrifice*, the changing and
impulsive world of the *body*—hence the European dissociation. "The god
of his own thought," concludes Whyte, "was henceforth man's chief source
of inspiration." The self sense, in flight from death, abandoned the body,
the all too mortal body, and took substitute refuge in the world of thought.
We are still, as it were, hiding there today.

Having used thought to transcend the body, we have not yet learned to
use awareness to transcend thought. That, I believe, will be the next development in men and women.

12 A New Time, a New Body

The great growth in consciousness represented by the ego was, it appears, something of an explosion as well, and one has the feeling that mankind was as a child given its first bicycle—it could move much faster but spent most of its time crashing into curbs. The ego brought so many changes, so many potentials, and so many disasters that the debris from that explosion is still falling around us. And part of that explosion was a *new mode of time,* and a *new mode of body*. The time was historical, linear, conceptual; the body, devitalized and deformed.

THE DISCOVERY OF HISTORY

We start with time, for the ego level brought with it, as it emerged from the typhonic realms, a mode of linear and historical time which had never before existed. It is quite true that the mythic-membership structure, principally through the vehicle of the non-present (i.e., language), had a fairly vivid comprehension of an extended temporal world of past, present, and future—in fact, we discussed the creation of this temporal world (of farming futures) in some detail, specifically in the sense that an extended time series was part and parcel of farming consciousness and its brand of death denial and immortality strivings. But this extended temporal world was of a very peculiar nature, a nature that, in fact, prevented time from being *everlastingly* "linear" without discernible end (as is historical, egoic time). Mythic-membership time was certainly an extended series, but it was *seasonal*. It was cyclic. It was embedded in the nature myth of cyclic return, ebb and flow, winter to summer and back to winter and back again to summer, forever in circles, "getting," said Campbell, "absolutely nowhere."

This was temporal without doubt, and temporal enough to promise the needed futures for farming immortality—next season and next season and next season—but a temporal world that *ultimately* was without direction, except perpetually around in circles. It was moving, but to no special destination; it was going, but not meaningfully; it was the time of the merry-go-round, matching the celestial spheres that temporally circled forever and ended up where they started. "Nature was seen in her imagined purity of endless cycles of sun risings and settings, moon waxings and wanings, seasons changing, animals dying and being born, etc. This kind of cosmology is not favorable to the accumulation of either guilt or property, since everything is wiped away with the gifts and nature is renewed with the help of ritual ceremonies of regeneration."[26]

And so, apparently, it was in mythic-membership cultures. Annual regeneration rituals acted as both an immersion in the nature myth of cyclic return and as a substitute expiation of the fear and guilt inherent in being any sort of a separate self. It was a buoyant feeling many people still get with New Year's celebrations—the feeling that all can be wiped clean, that karma can be magically ignored, that a fresh start is possible. In earlier times, however, these rituals of regeneration (which do remain today as New Year's Eve) were probably more of an entire baptism of the soul and total (but temporary) alleviation of the sense of sin that clings tenaciously to any type of self sense. The whole point is that this world's awareness was *circular* and cyclic; it did not consciously accumulate; the awareness of last year's mistakes was simply washed away and baptized with amnesia. But, of course, last year's karma accumulated nonetheless, so that despite the unavoidably appealing innocence of the situation, which has swayed more than one scholar, the principle involved was really that of "where ignorance is bliss, 'tis folly to be wise." But this ignorance was not a matter of choice or design—it was simply the limit of comprehension attainable by circular, natural awareness.

Sometime during the low egoic period, however, consciousness began to separate from and rise above this simply natural mode of seasonal time.

"Hence the new mythology brought forth, in due time, a development away from the earlier static view of returning cycles. A progressive, temporally oriented mythology arose, of a creation . . . at the beginning of time, a subsequent fall, and a work of [hierarchic or evolutionary] restoration, still in progress."[71]

The point, now uncontested, is that prior to the low egoic period, history as the chronicle of the events of a society just did not exist at all. To ask an individual living during the mythic-membership period, "What is the history of your peoples?" would be like asking, "What is the history of winter?" Anthropologists have long recognized that only progressive cultures keep histories. And the earliest form of history is dated c. 1300 B.C., right in the middle of the low egoic period; and the "father of history," Herodotus, stands in fifth-century-B.C. Greece—the beginning of the middle egoic.

> More exact evidence is found in the inscriptions on buildings. In the typical inscription previous to this date [1300 B.C.], the king gave his name and titles, lavished praise on his particular god or gods, mentioned briefly the season and circumstances when the building was started, and then described something of the building operation itself. After 1300 B.C., there is not only a mention of the event immediately preceding the building, but also a summary of all the king's past military exploits to date. And in the next centuries, this information comes to be arranged systematically according to the yearly campaigns, and ultimately bursts out into the elaborate annual form that is almost universal in the records of the Assyrian rulers of the first millennium B.C. Such annals continue to swell beyond the recountal of raw fact into statements of motive, criticisms of courses of action, appraisals of character. And then further to include political changes, campaign strategies, historical notes on particular regions. . . . None of these characteristics is seen in the earlier inscriptions.[215]

"This is," concludes Jaynes, "the invention of history. . . ."

Like each and every growth in consciousness, the apprehension of historical time was, to put it crudely, both good and bad. Good, in that the evolution of consciousness necessarily moves from pre-temporal to temporal to trans-temporal, or from pre-historical to historical to trans-historical. The comprehension of historical realities was, in itself, a perfect advance in consciousness, a fact that only decadence theorists would deny. Historical consciousness, as today's reflection on yesterday, is the paradigm of reflexive thinking in general, of philosophy, of science, of psychology. Historical consciousness is the epitome of polis-praxis.

Bad, however, in that the vast new world of historical horizons—

stretching out beyond seasonal circles—played directly into the often power-crazed appetites of the heroic ego. Power seeks nothing more than to expand itself, and to continually *accumulate* that expansion. And whereas seasonal/cyclic time is not favorable to such accumulation, since it "starts all over" next season, historical time—stretching out linearly beyond all seasons—is the perfect home for power drives seeking unlimited addition. "It is obvious," says Campbell, "that a potent mythical formula for the reorientation of the human spirit is here supplied [in the newly emergent historical myths]—pitching it forward along the way of time, summoning man to an assumption of autonomous responsibility for the renovation of the universe in God's name, and thus fostering a new, potentially political philosophy of holy war."[71] And if one then wishes to leave God's name out of it altogether, then secular war will do just as well—and that, we will see, is precisely what happened.

This dangerous situation was drastically aggravated by the fact that the ego's heroic emergence was otherwise corrupted by its often violent repression of the body, of nature, and of the Great Mother. Since nature/body is the *referent* of seasonal time, and since *mind* is the referent of historical time, the severance of the mind from the body meant a corresponding severance of history from nature. This was not the transcendence of nature via history, which is the purpose of the latter's existence, but the dissociation of nature and history, which tends to deform both. For once the ego was cut loose from seasonal nature and from the body, it had no *felt* roots in which to *ground* its otherwise higher-order awareness. It then seemed perfectly acceptable to the ego to begin a premeditated assault upon nature, regardless of the *historical* consequences of such activity, because history and nature were no longer integrated in a mutually dependent fashion. Likewise, the ego failed, almost from the start, to comprehend that an attack upon nature was already *an attack upon its own body* (level 1/2 of the compound human individual), so that the whole project was, in the deepest and truest sense, finally suicidal. That this ecological interdependence of human body and natural environment only became obvious in this century—that is to say, 4,000 years after the ego's emergence!—shows precisely how deep-seated this prejudice was.

The point is that the newly emergent ego, placing its faith in dissociated thought and "ungrounded" history, set its Atman project on a tangential pitch into the disembodied future. History, mind, culture, and thought were all thus contaminated with the European dissociation. The ego's Atman project, its search for substitute gratifications and immortality designs, demanded and acknowledged *only* a time that kept going linearly straight ahead, carrying its immortality dreams with it.

Thus, while the apprehension of the historical mode of time was in itself a growth process, it was applied instantly and *exclusively* to the dissociated egoic structure. To the ego, then, history was a chronicle of the ego's power-laced feats, and not a chronicle of the evolutionary steps toward Atman—one of those steps being, of course, the death and transcendence of the ego itself.

Thus, if everything were "wiped clean" in seasonal regeneration, as had often been the case in mythic times, the ego's immortality projects would go with it. In its more intensified awareness of death, the ego needed *more time*. It had *goals* to ensure its everlasting permanence, and those goals were energized by the restless but displaced search for true release in Atman. By cutting itself loose into a linear and progressive world of time, which was not just trans-naturic but anti-naturic, anti-ecological, and open-ended forever, the ego's essentially unquenchable and unfulfillable desires had room to pitch forward everlastingly.

For all these reasons, the heroic ego fashioned the illusion that it would not just see, but live to dominate, its future. And thus the ego began to see its entire *past* in this light. Small wonder that, at even the earliest point that historical reality was discovered, it was infected with the egotistical notion that history was, first and foremost, *a chronicle of the ego's accomplishments* and heroic feats. The first recorded histories were, as we saw, tales of *egoic* (kingly) victories and triumphs and daring feats, usually in battle, always boastful.

We of today are still caught in that egotistical view of history. But the actual truth concealed in the new mode of historical time was the truth that consciousness is our destiny and awakening our fate; the truth that the world is indeed going somewhere, *meaningfully:* it is going toward Atman. The problem is that the ego per se is *not* going there—it is not itself going to Atman, but is merely one of the steps on the way. In my opinion, the sooner the mental-ego realizes that history is a tale of its own demise, the sooner it will cease misinterpreting that tale as an exclusive chronicle of its own feats.

A NEW BODY

The separate self, then, had a new mode of time—but it also had a new mode of body, and I would like to dwell on this new body, the alienated and dissociated body. We saw that historically the typhonic realms did not just differentiate into mind and body, but dissociated into mind and body, and our point now is that as the organism dissociated into the egoic pole and the somatic pole, *both* poles were *deformed*. Not transformation, but deformation—and there is our topic.

In an important discussion, L. L. Whyte himself pinpoints the crux of

Fig. 24. The Devil. We will see throughout this text that the god(s) or sacred images of one stage of development become the demons, devils, demiurges, or disparaged gods of the next stage of evolution. That, I suggest, is the supreme law of mythological development—and not there alone, for the same principle applies to any system of psychological growth. The reason is that what is natural and appropriate at one stage becomes archaic, regressive, and infantile at the next. Thus, from the higher stage, the lower stage—which was once worshipped and revered—is now looked upon as something to struggle against, to subdue, even to scorn.

We come, then, to the classic Devil as portrayed in late Western mythology, and—it is no surprise—the Devil is simply the old typhonic structure. Fig. 24 is really an absolutely perfect representation of Satan. First, it is clearly typhonic—half man, half animal, accent on animal. In fact, it is strikingly reminiscent of the Sorcerer of Trois Frères. That Sorcerer, which was the supreme god to the typhonic hunters, is now the supreme demon to the mental-ego; but such is natural development. Second, this figure also shows the serpent-uroboros, and it is correctly portrayed as having evolved only through the lower three chakras—food, sex, and power —which is perfect typhonicism. And third, it is hermaphroditic or Great Mother infused. While the serpent per se is often depicted as the Devil, Satan reaches its arch-personification in the typhon, because the typhon contains both the serpent-uroboros and the lower aspects of human nature (emotional-sexuality and magic).

Ideally, the lower stages should be transcended, transformed, and integrated in and by the higher stages. The higher stages do indeed have to initially struggle against the lower levels and often do intense battle with them, in order to emerge from their exclusive and lower-order motivations and identifications. But the battle can go too far, as I am suggesting it did in the West, producing not just differentiation but dissociation, not just transcendence but repression. The East developed the mental-ego, did battle with the uroboros and the typhon (e.g., Indra's triumph over Vritra), but the battle ended in differentiation and transformation, not dissociation and repression. In the East, therefore, all the old myths of the Great Mother, of the serpent, and of the typhon, were taken up and integrated in a new and higher mythology. True, the old gods and goddesses were viewed as demons or lesser god figures, but their existence was acknowledged and then made subservient to, and even manifestations of, the higher God figures. The East had its satan figures—but they were viewed as lower manifestations of God and as protectors of the Dharma, as long as one didn't worship them in and by themselves.

Only in the West, then, where the dissociation of ego-mind and body-typhon was often severe, did the typhon (now cut off from conscious participation) assume truly menacing proportions (as Satan) and appear to take on an ultimately and absolutely evil significance. The simpler truth buried in this cosmic satanic terror was that Satan was the body-typhon personified; that growth demanded a struggle against the regressive pull back into exclusive and obsessive body-consciousness; and that Satan-typhon when pursued in and by itself was necessarily an "evil" or a hindrance to the emergence of the higher structures. What the West overlooked, however, was the maxim "Give the Devil its due." Satan was not integrated into the new mythology of the Sun Gods (nor was the Great Mother), and this paralleled, precisely, the alienation of the body by the heroic ego. "Give the Devil its due" really means that the typhon serves an appropriate if limited function, and when exercised in an appropriate, functional, and non-obsessive fashion, serves the reproduction of the pranic level of the human compound individual. The typhon dissociated, however, shows up in obsessive overindulgence, on the one hand, and repressive puritanism and life blockage, on the other. The most overt but by no means sole manifestations of this are, respectively, witch sabbaths (Fig. 25) and witch hunts (Fig. 26). Psychologically it manifests itself, on the one hand, in hedonism, obsessive genital-sexuality and the perversions, exclusive aestheticism, dominance of the pleasure principle, degenerate emotionalism; and, on the other, in hyper-intellectualism, schizoid mentality, arid abstractionism, history divorced from nature, ego terrified of body.

the matter: "The fundamental division is between deliberate activity organized by static concepts [the early ego] and the instinctive and spontaneous life [impulsive body]. The European dissociation of these two components of [the] system results in a common distortion of both. The instinctive life lost its innocence, its proper rhythm being replaced by obsessive desire. On the other hand rationally controlled behavior was partly deflected towards ideals which also obsessed the individual with their allure of perfection and disturbed the rhythm of tension and release."[426] Incidentally, "the rhythm of tension and release," which Whyte so stresses in his discussion of both instinct and concepts, is simply that *cycle of exchange* (intake, assimilation, and release) which we defined as the basic activity of *each level* of the compound individual, food to sex to thought.* His point, to use my terms, is that the dissociation of the mental and bodily levels of exchange disrupts and deforms both exchanges, charging them with obsessive and overcompensating activities, activities which are driven by the dissociation of the systems themselves, not by any intrinsic characteristics of the individual systems.

The result is that both components of the organism are deformed (the body, or level 1/2, and the mind, or level 3/4), and the same deformity and drivenness reappears in both dissociated components. "This similarity," Whyte concludes—and I would like to greatly emphasize this—"is not accidental. In splitting the . . . system in a given manner, the same form of distortion appears in both dissociated components. In this case the periodicity of whole-natured process is transformed into a dual obsession; it matters little whether the aim is union with god or woman, the ecstasy of the pursuit of [substitute] unity or truth, of power or pleasure—the sustained intensity and lack of satisfaction proves the European [dissociation] stamp."[426] More specifically:

> The European soul [that is, the ego alienated from the body] never truly loses itself in God; the mind never finds ultimate truth; power is never secure; pleasure never satisfies. Bewitched by these illusory aims which appear to promise the absolute [the Atman project], man is led away from the proper rhythm of the organic processes to chase an elusive ecstasy. Morbid religiosity, hyperintellectualism, delicate sensuality, and cold ambition are some of the variants of the dissociated personality's attempt to escape its own division. The oscillation from emotional mysticism to rationalism, and from rationalism to a materialism of power, which mark the history of Europe, do not represent any essential change. They only express the successive oscillations of the search for novel stimulation within the limits set by the basic dissociation.[426]

* to psychic to subtle to causal.

The idea is that the compulsive emphasis on body sensuality and sexuality on the one hand, and the ego's obsessive drive for power or abstract truth or future goals on the other, are both often characteristic of the dissociated self because, however otherwise different, they both play off the same split, the same fragmentation. This implies that the alienated ego, on the one side, and hyper-genital sexuality and sensuality, on the other, are correlative deformities of the organism. Indeed, Whyte himself says as much on several occasions. Historically—and let me remind the reader that this discussion ultimately refers to anthropological data and historical occurrences—Whyte sees the rise of egoic idealism and deliberate sensuality-sexuality as two aspects of the same European dissociation, which occurred, as we saw, during the low egoic period:

> Instinctive modes of behavior had been woven by primitive tradition into a system of life which, during the ancient civilizations [of the membership period], was relatively stable. The instinctive tendencies were . . . held in balance by a physiological control, similar in character to the organic control in less developed mammals. But as the ancient civilizations acquired more powerful technical methods and the community, or at least some of its members, were assured of immediate survival, a new and unsettling factor entered. Since instinctive fulfillment gave satisfaction, favorably placed individuals could devote their surplus in material security [the farming surplus] to the deliberate pursuit of instinctive pleasures. The organic balance of the instincts, which had been adequate to maintain a proper co-ordination of behavior while social conditions were still primitive, doubly failed in this new and more complex situation. It not only failed to establish adequate responses to new and pressing situations, but it could not even maintain a proper balance of the instinctive life, now that the individual was aware of what gave him satisfaction and possessed the instruments with which he could deliberately exploit and intensify this satisfaction.[426]

"But parallel with this new deliberate sensuality," concludes Whyte, "upsetting proper co-ordination and therefore accompanied by sadism and masochism, there developed also the new deliberate idealism. . . . Both the sensuality and the [obsessive idealism] were new, and represented [in part] the dualistic and therefore distorted [exchanges of both levels]."

Furthermore, with the rise of the dissociation between the body and the ego, "Eros degenerates [regresses] into what is generally understood by the concept of sex, the specialized pleasure principle of the isolated internal tendencies [characteristic of the typhonic level]. Egoism and sex, which are normally developed and fulfilled within the life of the whole, are then exposed as isolated tendencies seeking exhaustion in death [the substitute sacrifice]." The mythology of sex and murder, which began in the mythic-membership period, is now *retained, intensified,* and *compounded* due to its repression—it explodes with a compulsive vengeance in (dissociated) egoic times. The obsession with sex and violence is still with us to this day because the dissociated ego is still with us. For all the disastrous consequences of both, we have outgrown neither.

I am dwelling on the fact—the fact that the dissociated ego and hypersensuality are correlative deformations of the total body-mind—because that is essentially the point argued by Norman O. Brown in his reformulations of psychoanalysis. The burden of Brown's work, as I would reconstruct it, is basically to trace the radical changes in the ego and the body as the separate self begins to awaken to its own mortality—to death, Thanatos, and Sunyata. For, in recoil from death, the separate self begins likewise to shrink back from life—to try to dilute life, dilute its own vitality, sequester its own energies. And this results in nothing less than the radical deformation of the total organism.

"Children, at the age of early infancy which Freud thinks critical, are unable to distinguish between their souls and their bodies."[61] There is

Fig. 25. A rather blatant form of devil worship. This was part of a witch's sabbath, but the interesting item about this particular carving is that the practitioners are well dressed, civilized, cultured—too cultured, in fact, the point being that an excessive zeal to embrace the mental realms and deny the animal aspects of the human compound individual was precisely what led to the alienation of the typhonic realms and their subsequent obsessive-compulsive allure. To put it rather dramatically, when Zeus killed the Typhon, instead of transforming and integrating it, he set in motion the causality of fate that sealed this woman's misfortune—and not hers alone, as Freud would soon discover.

Brown's starting point, and it is, of course, the infantile typhon: the general period wherein mind and body are not yet differentiated (the mind itself hardly exists at all, and what mental aspects do exist are still embedded in the body). For my own part (and apparently against Brown), this is not an *ideal* state—the ideal state is one of mature *trans*-differentiation, wherein mind and body, once differentiated, are now integrated. Brown eulogizes the primitive state of pre-differentiation, and speaks as if the mind and body are here perfectly one, whereas in fact there is hardly any mind to speak of—no language, no logic, no concepts—and the self is basically *nothing but* a bodyself. When we say that mind and body are at this stage undifferentiated, we mean mind has not yet developed, and what mind there is, is still stuck in the body. Nonetheless, the essential point is that the individual has to emerge out of this pre-differentiation state, this infantile typhon, and that emergence is stressful and fraught with consequences. Those dramatic consequences are what Brown has traced.

Now although at this early typhonic stage the mind and body are pre-differentiated, the typhon itself is beginning to separate from the environment (and the old uroboric stage)—it is therefore faced with primitive forms of dread, anxiety, and the terror of death. According to Brown, the body-ego (or typhon) is both in flight from death (Thanatos) and under sway of what he calls the *causa sui* project—the attempt to be father of oneself, cause of oneself, god to oneself (in our words, the Atman project). Thus the typhon, in flight from death and under sway of the *causa sui* or Atman project, has to begin to take steps to shield itself from the terrible vision of its vulnerability, its mortality, its helplessness. It has somehow to screen out or repress the terror of it all. We might say that at this point, if repression did not exist, it would be necessary to invent it. There is simply no other way the separate self could face its own emergence out of the uroboric slumber—except by repressing death, and its reflex terror, and *all aspects of life that threaten death.*

The typhon has to be careful—it has to proceed with caution. And as the membership level emerges, with its vehicle of extended time, the nightmare begins to stretch out in all directions, past and future. In order to survive, then, with a minimum of terror, the self has to begin to simply close its eyes; to numb itself; to tighten down its own activities and sequester its own vitality. *To avoid death, it has to dilute life*—I think it is that simple. But the idea is not mine; it belongs to the existential psychologists, particularly Brown and Becker: "The situation of the child is an impossible one, and he has to fashion his own defenses against the world, has to find a way of surviving it . . . We have achieved a remarkably faithful understanding of what really bothers the child, how life is really too much for him, how he has to avoid too much thought, too much perception, too much *life*. And at the same time, how he has to avoid death that rumbles behind and underneath every carefree activity, that looks over his shoulder as he plays."[25]

Thus, the infant self has but one choice: in Becker's words, he "has to repress *globally,* from the entire spectrum of his experience, if he wants a warm sense of . . . basic security. He must repress his own . . . compromising bodily functions that spell his mortality, his fundamental expendability in nature. . . . In other words—and this is crucial enough to bear stressing one final time—the child 'represses himself.' He takes over the control of his own body as a reaction to the totality of experience, not only to his own desires. As Rank so exhaustively and definitively argued the child's problems are existential."[25]

Fig. 26. Witches being hanged in England. The witch hunt is the precise and formal inverse, or mirror image, of the witch sabbath. Both the witch and the witch hunter suffer from the same *dissociation of mind and body, but they take up stances on opposite sides of the boundary (the actual boundary, of course, is within their own organisms). The witch is obsessed with the typhon, the witch hunter terrified of it. The witch hunter, unable to transform and integrate his or her own typhonic drives, is horrified at their very existence, and thus is dedicated to the extermination of any individuals who—in actual fact or not—appear to be typhonically driven "by Satan." Modern Protestantism owes much of its existence to the alienated Satanic fantasy produced by the European dissociation, for without that neurotic schism the whole motivation of their proselytizing fury would evaporate. But witch hunting is not an exoteric Christian monopoly—it is part of everything from scapegoating to prejudice: proof of the axiom that one hates in others those things, and only those things, that one hates in oneself.*

The infant self, upon impact with death, simply recoils and shrinks back both from the Great Environment at large and from its own internal but unmanageable vitality. It does this by itself. It is a self-repression (which is later compounded and extended by society's enforcing specific "surplus repressions"). This is very similar to the notion of "vital shock" described by Sri Aurobindo and Bubba Free John. Yet this recoil or vital shock, this shrinking away from the vitality of the whole-body being, means that the separate self at this stage is simply starting to shrink back from itself—starting, that is, to separate itself from itself, to split or dissociate itself into "safe" fragments versus "unsafe" fragments, and we see here the very beginning of the European dissociation, the divorce between the "permanent" ego and the mortal fleshy body.

It all boils down to a simple fact: the separate self has to begin to sequester and dilute the vitality of the organism, to dilute life to a point that it doesn't threaten death, to *dilute the energies of the organism itself* to a cautious level of low intensity.

Now this organic energy has been called by many names. Bergson termed it élan vital; to the Hindu it is prana; Lowen, bioenergy; Freud, libido. In a broad sense, it is simply emotional-sexual energy, the energy pre-eminently of level 2, the typhonic force. It is this prana or typhonic bioenergy that has to be sequestered and restricted through self-repression. And, according to Brown, this has one major result:

In attempting to restrict and sequester its own vitality, the organism focuses and limits its libido to a very few select areas and regions of the body—the genital being the most notable. The result is that the normal ego then enjoys true vitality and intensity only during genital orgasm (and sometimes not even then—impotence and frigidity, for example). That is the only time the ego can "let go" and allow the circulation of real intensity, vitality, and bliss. In this very special sense, genital sexuality is what Freud called a "well-organized tyranny"—not so much because of its simple existence (and here I disagree profoundly with Brown), but because the body's full vitality and intensity is restricted to *just* that activity. More specifically, I would say that the maintenance of exclusive genital prana beyond its *normal and necessary* developmental period represents the refusal to accept its death and discover *higher* states of whole-body ecstasy, ecstasy beyond the genital. But the general point is as Brown says: "The special concentration of libido in the genital region . . . is engineered [or at least maintained] by the regressive death instinct, and represents the residue of the human incapacity to accept death."[61]

"So one of the first things a child has to do," as Becker summarizes the whole problem, "is to learn to 'abandon ecstasy.'" *L'enfant abdique son extase,* said Mallarmé. Oddly enough, he abandons ecstasy, dilutes élan vital and libido, just because it threatens *death*—"it is too much," as Maslow said. And so now we drive to Brown's major point: "The sexual organizations, [the restrictions of vitality to certain activities and areas of the body, are maintained] by the infantile ego in order to repress its bodily vitality . . . , to sequester by repression its own unmanageable vitality (id)."[61]

That, however, is just the half of it. Since the self is in flight from death, it must, as we just saw, begin to devitalize and neutralize the intensity of the organism. By deadening the body, the self can pretend to gain some sort of distance from it, mortal flesh that it is. The ego can, that is, split itself from the body by deadening the body's hold on it. By attempting, as it were, to kill the body, the ego-self can pretend to be aloof from the flesh, free of its mortality and death taint, unfettered by the body's vulnerability and finiteness. By repressing or devitalizing the body, the self can pretend to ignore it into docility. For the body to be buried, it first must be killed. And, according to Brown, it is exactly this "negation that gives us a soul [dissociated] from the body."[61]

Henceforth, self-identity is retracted from the whole-body being and restricted exclusively to the ego. The organism is split, the body is out. "By a process of 'narcissistic self-splitting,' the intellectual ego, in Schilder's terminology, is split from the body-ego [typhon]."[61] I repeat: the error is *not* the differentiation of mind and body, but the dissociation of mind and body. Brown, at any rate, is very much aware that *both* the disembodied ego and the deformed (restricted) body are correlative distortions of the total organism. The devitalized body, he says, is simply "the bodily counterpart of the disorder in the human mind."

As Brown points out—and this is really the only point I would like to impress upon the reader's mind—the inevitable legacy of all this is *"the radical deformation of the human ego and the human body."* For there, finally, we have returned to Whyte's main point, which was that "the dissociation of these two components [ego and body] of an organic system results in a common distortion of both." But let me quickly point out that, in their various writings, Brown and Whyte are talking about not just what happens in infants today, *but also what happened to a collective mankind about 4,000 years ago.* If all of this is even approximately correct, we arrive at an extraordinary historical conclusion. If there was a change of mind at the beginning of our modern egoic era—and there was—there also occurred a change of body. And Norman O. Brown knows it: *"There is a revolution in the body at the beginning of modern times."*[62]

Mankind had simply progressed to the point where the rapid growth of consciousness allowed it to reach far beyond the physical bounds of the body. At the same time, it was confronted with an ever more intense realization of, and reflex against, death. Instead of integrating the previous typhonic or body realms with the newly emergent ego, the ego simply repressed the typhonic realms, dissociated the mind and body, and thus distorted and deformed both. And the whole endeavor was underscored by the growing realization that the body is mortal and decaying, a perfect threat to the egoic immortality project of static ideology and disembodied history. In Greece, a saying sprang up: "the body, a tomb." As far as we know, that phrase *never* existed in history before the dawn of the egoic period.

I am not, of course, suggesting that prior to the egoic era none of the above-mentioned conditions existed in any form; and I am certainly not suggesting that, for example, genital sex didn't exist—obviously it did. The point is only that the ego, in intensified flight from death, devitalized and diluted the organism and its energies. In a global way, it repressed and deformed the body—"the body, a tomb"—which also restricted and deformed its own mentality (*because* the mind is a part of the *compound individual,* and any distortion of any level reverberates throughout the whole). The ego then either shrank in terror from the body, or compulsively exploited it for pleasure and orgasmic release, as Whyte demonstrated.

And the consequences were absolutely fateful: "The divorce between soul and body," says Brown, "takes the life out of the body, reducing the organism to a mechanism." It devitalizes it, *mechanizes* it. The body became a *mechanism. The rational ego and the mechanistic body*—indeed, we are here on the trail of the very beginning of modern psychology, science, and philosophy, all supported not just by the change of mind at the beginning of our era, but also by "the revolution in the body at the beginning of modern times."

In this dehumanized human nature man loses contact with his own body, more specifically with his senses, with sensuality and with the pleasure-principle. And this dehumanized human nature produces an inhuman consciousness, whose only currency is abstractions divorced from real life—the industrious, coolly rational, economic, prosaic mind.[61]

The rational ego. The mechanistic body. The modern era.

13 Solarization

We come now to a fascinating point: the transition or transformation from body to mind—which, as we have amply seen, occurred during the low egoic period—was almost universally represented as a transition from earth to heaven,[311] and also as a transition from darkness to light.[76] Why?

Furthermore, the transition from body to mind was often paralleled by a transition from matriarchy (and Great Mother) to patriarchy (and Sun Gods).[70, 71] Why?

These two questions are the center of this chapter.

And—as an intriguing, controversial, nagging, but always insistent side issue—we will see that both of these questions inevitably converge upon that mythic character, now world famous, now entrenched in the modern psyche, now undeniable in its influence, but now as elusive as ever: the extraordinary figure of Oedipus, son of Laius, king of Thebes, and of Laius' wife, Jocasta—the same Jocasta that would soon be Oedipus' own wife—with mythically world-wrenching consequences. In a special sense, we will begin this chapter with Oedipus; and with Oedipus, we will end.

ONTOGENETIC CLUES

We start with the second question: why was the transition from body to mind so often paralleled by a transition from matriarchy to patriarchy? I realize that to many scholars the answer seems all too obvious. To feminists, it is a simple case of sexist repression: any such relatively abrupt move from matriarchy to patriarchy must have been sexist to the core. But if the patriarchy was sexist, wasn't the previous matriarchy also sexist, and for precisely the same reasons? If the former was sexist, so was the latter, in which case sexism drops out as a definitive and causal issue. On the other hand, to many (male) historians, the transition was a case of the (covertly assumed) supremacy of the masculine principle: the society of the Great Mother was pre-personal, instinctive, and often subhuman when left to its own devices. It therefore took a masculine principle to supersede it. But even if that were partially true, why *deny* the feminine principle in the process? That is, is there no "feminine" principle other than that represented by the Great Mother? Might there not be a higher, "solar" femininity to equally match the solar masculinity of the patriarchy? If so, why was *that* higher feminine principle denied access in the patriarchy, as it most definitely was? In short, I think the issue is much more complex than both sides will admit—and we will explore just these complexities.

We can begin our investigation by examining modern ontogenetic development for *clues* to, but not determinants of, what *might* have occurred in that transition from matriarchy to patriarchy. And we have already introduced one such clue: we suggested that the Great Mother and the typhonic realms were inseparably linked. In large part, this seems to be a simple biological given: the first imprint of life is birth from a womb and nursing at a breast. Further, as the infant begins ontogenetically to emerge from its pre-personal, uroboric fusion state, the first thing it consciously encounters is the mother—and not just the mother, but the Great Mother, the World Mother. The outside world is "the mother's body in an extended sense," said Melanie Klein.[233] "Originally, the whole world is the mother and the mother is the whole world," said Brown.[62]

Modern developmental psychology (e.g., Loewald, Margaret Mahler, Jane Loevinger, Louise Kaplan) tells us that the self starts out embedded in, or unconsciously one with, that which it will *later* apprehend objectively as the Great Mother (that initial and primitive oneness is the uroboric fusion state). But once the self emerges, *as typhon,* from this primitive uroboric fusion, and differentiates itself *from* the Great Mother, *then* the Great Mother likewise comes into objective existence—and the self at this stage is therefore faced with an intense struggle and conflict *with* the Great Mother (which is why the Great Mother so dominates the typhonic realms, but is not objectively *recognized* in uroboric realms).

On the one hand, the infant self is driven by a strong desire (Eros) to *regressively* unite with the Great Mother and thus sink back into the relatively undisturbed "narcissistic pleasure" of the uroboric state (where *both* the self and the Great Mother disappear into subconscious fusion).[126] On the other hand, the stronger the self becomes, or the more it matures (as typhon), the more it can resist this regressive form of unity (i.e., the more it can resist a lower and regressive level of the Atman project: oral fusion, food, alimentary uroboros).[106] But by all accounts, this is an intense struggle. As Jane Loevinger summarizes the evidence: "This primal [uroboric] unity between [great] mother and child is gratifying, but the strong early tie to mother, and particularly regression to it from later stages [typhonic], is also threatening, since it implies return also to an earlier, less differentiated stage of [self] development [namely, the uroboros]."[262]

The essential point, and the only point we really need to emphasize, is that the reactions of the infant self to the Great Mother are essentially *identical* in both sexes. That is to say, the female infant originally desires reunion with the Great Mother in precisely the same way the male infant does.[311] This is obviously *not* a genital desire at this early stage, but rather a simple passing back into that originally appealing uroboric slumber and fusion. In psychoanalytical jargon, the earliest relations of male libido and female libido to the pre-Oedipal mother are essentially the same.[232] Likewise (to cover the negative aspects), the Great Mother to *both* sexes is also a source of terror, dread, and death impact (wherever there is other there is fear; the first other is the Great Mother).[384] Thus, the whole relationship is basically one of desire for regressive unity, mixed with real existential struggles, with life and death, vulnerability and death impact, love and desire—all felt similarly by both sexes.

The point is that the very deepest imprints are indelibly left on the psyche of *both* the male and the female by the Great Mother image, and in a way that is biologically impossible for the father image. As Louise Kaplan so carefully explained, "mother is the one partner with whom the baby plays out the separation drama." The father image does not significantly enter into the typhonic stages; or rather, it plays only a decidedly secondary role. Father, at these early stages, is not yet invented. (The child is often aware of the penis, but, as we will soon see, the penis is thought ultimately to belong to the Great Mother.)

This early situation, naturally, soon changes. As the infant matures, and begins moving through the membership stages toward the ego levels, the Great World Mother increasingly gives way to the *individual* and *circumstantial* mother. Unlike the Great Mother, who is initially all of a piece with the outer world, the circumstantial mother is perceived as a purely separate individual, given a particular name, set apart from other individuals, and possessing all sorts of individual characteristics. The Great Mother was the whole world ("whole" means level 1/2—there are no higher levels at this early stage); the individual mother is simply the most important figure among numerous figures that begin to crowd awareness. Further—and most important—the individual mother is *verbal;* she interacts with the child on a mental (membership and eventually egoic) level, whereas the Great Mother was a pre-verbal mood. What is more—and here is where the drama commences—the individual mother is usually involved with a particular and individual male—the father.

The stage then shifts, therefore, from a *dyad* of self and Great Mother to a *triad* of self, individual mother, and father. No longer two players on the stage, but three. Thus begins the drama of the "separation of the parents"—the classic Oedipus and Electra complexes. But, as both Freudians and Jungians point out, this separation of the parents, with true Oedipal-Electral overtones, only seriously begins during the verbal membership period, and only *culminates during the early egoic period* (ages four to seven years in modern society).[126, 311] It is only at this point, at this early egoic level, that the father image (as a cultural authority figure) decisively leaves its imprint on the psyche.[311] So this shift—and I am drastically simplifying it as between only two major stages, whereas in fact it is extremely complicated—is from the typhon-Great Mother to the ego-mother-father.

But this, indeed, is quite a change. For one thing, let us note that the Great Mother is the phallic Mother or the hermaphroditic Mother—the mother that is both male and female, the serpent mother, the uroboric mother. And this is not the case only for mythology—modern depth psychology has discovered that the whole of early child development is permeated by an atmosphere of hermaphroditic or bisexual feelings (these are loaded terms—their technical meaning will soon become clear). The basic point is this: because, in the infant's awareness, the Great Mother eventually gives way to both the individual female mother and the male father, it *appears* that the male (penis) father and the individual (female) mother *both* come *from* the Great Mother. That is, the magical primary process of the typhonic level imagines that the Great Mother actually contains *both* the male and female genitals. That is probably the most basic reason that the Great Mother is everywhere portrayed mythologically (and ontogenetically) as being the *phallic Mother,* the hermaphroditic mother (and here the Great Mother *also* shows her original fusion with the uroboros, as the *serpent*-phallic-mother).

At the same time, the infant typhon itself contains precocious desires and impulses that are not yet differentiated into male vs. female genitalia (i.e., male and female sexual tendencies are not yet differentiated).[141]

Figs. 27A and 27B. The uroboric Great Mother. Structurally a typhon (i.e., half human, half beast), the Great Mother figure represents both her developmental connection with the uroboros as uroboros, and her hermaphroditic constitution, where the uroboros is then symbolic of the phallus. Fig. 27B is the more primitive, because the uroboros is literally connected to, or undifferentiated from, the mother, whereas in Fig. 27A the uroboros is differentiated from, but still closely associated with, the mother. But in both cases, the uroboros represents the Great Mother's close connection with both the alimentary stage (level 1, or uroboros as uroboros per se) and the emotional-sexual stage (level 2, or uroboros as symbol of the phallus of the hermaphroditic mother).

Thus, the early bodyself or typhon is, like the Great Mother it now confronts, hermaphroditic; i.e., both self and Great Mother are initially and primitively bisexual.

Very soon in child development, this original hermaphroditic situation begins to differentiate and clarify itself—on both sides. On the subjective side, the child awakens to his or her actual sexual identity—male *or* female genitalia. On the objective side, the phallic Great Mother breaks down into the individual mother on the one hand and the phallic father on the other. But the original and primitive state of bisexuality is said to be very difficult to surrender, for when a person awakens as a separate sexual being (male *or* female), he or she awakens as a "half person" who *needs* another "half person" to complete a bodily unity (that precisely is the typhonic sex drive). Note that for Plato, as for Genesis, the separation of the sexes was connected with the fall of man.

It is this difficult (but absolutely necessary) awakening to the reality of sexual differentiation that eventually leads up to, and *in part* propels, the classic Oedipus and Electra complexes, under the general formula known as the "separation of the parents," wherein the young child "falls in love" with the parent of the opposite sex, and generally feels rivalry with the same-sexed parent; hence the attempt to "separate" them. For the phallic Mother has differentiated into the female mother and the phallic father; that primitive hermaphroditic unity has differentiated into a *higher* recognition of actual sexual differences, and the individual Oedipal/Electral complexes are driven by an attempt to find a *similarly higher* form of unity (Atman project) at this new level of differentiation. Thus, the child zeroes in on the parent of the *opposite sex,* there to find its "missing half" and thus complete a new and higher unity of opposites: no longer body plus Great Environment (level 2 plus level 1), but male body plus female body (level 2 plus level 2)—and a half step up the Great Chain of Being, a higher level of the Atman project.

The child thus begins developing this emotional-sexual level of being (the typhonic level). Now this development is not geared *solely* toward the opposite-sexed parent—it is actually a development on the whole. It is a *general* growth and exercise of emotional-sexuality—or simply *feeling* in general—which is so globally characteristic of the body realms. Nonetheless, the evidence strongly suggests that the opposite-sexed parent is a definite focal point of this emotional-sexual development. This is apparently why strong frustrations or rejections by the particular parent, at this crucial stage, can so cripple emotional-sexual relations in general, often for the rest of one's life. Thus, the emotional-sexuality of the child begins to develop on the whole, but it often is focused on, and even explicitly desiring of, the opposite-sexed parent—so much so that specific genital desires for actual bodily union often emerge. And this complication leads, more or less, to both disaster and the possibility of new growth.

For notice, as the child soon does, that *actual* body unity is not really possible. Put rather crudely, there are now *three* people on the stage (ego-mother-father) and only *two* opposite genitals. That is to say, someone is going to get left out of this body union. The so-called primal scene—when the child sees (or fantasizes) the parents in intercourse—is found related to so many emotional problems for just that reason. The primal scene is terrifying because the child is now odd person out. The child's desire to establish itself in body unity is dashed to hell right there in front of its eyes. Mommy and Daddy are as one body-being in love, and the child is always left out. The infant will have to wait until later in life, when, with his or her spouse, the long-sought body union will finally be consummated, whereas an unconscious allegiance to the original family romance—with its necessarily unfulfilled desires and deep resentments at being odd person out—is said to constitute the core of many neuroses.

Now this might sound, of course, rather tragic and cruel—the poor child getting left out and all—but the crucial fact is that it is precisely *by getting left out* of this body unity that the child is forced to construct a *higher-order* unity, a unity that is not of the body but of the mind.

We can summarize this as follows, beginning with the male: The male child wants to possess the mother so as to complete the body unity; i.e., he wants to see himself with his mother, and thus he wants to "oust" the father—this is the "separation of the parents," with jealousy, anger, and upset toward the father. The child wants to pry the parents apart and thus step in himself with the mother and close the body circle. This is of course impossible, and so, through a rather complicated course whose details need not concern us, the child takes the next-best thing and *identifies* with the father, since the father *already* possesses the mother. The boy more or less surrenders the desire to *possess* the mother and seeks instead to be *like* the father ("identifications replace object-choices").[126]

But identification is a *mental* accomplishment. The child can identify with the father only by using concepts, roles, and so on. And this means a fundamental transformation has occurred from body union to mental union. The child does not take the actual father into his body, he takes the father image into his ego. (This is also part of the formation of the superego, the internalized parent.) This overall identification helps the child form a higher-order self, a properly mental self, and a stronger ego capable of more than body-bound desires.

Essentially the same thing occurs in the female child, except of course the roles are reversed. The female child, as a result of an increasingly differentiated consciousness, wants to form a new (and higher) unity by possessing the father: she (like the male) no longer is content to merge subconsciously with the hermaphroditic Great Mother. Rather, she wants to differentiate and separate the actual parents and herself step in to replace the individual mother in the new body union. Eventually finding that impossible, she instead takes the next-best course and mentally *identifies* with the individual mother, since the mother already possesses the father. This likewise is a move from body union to mental union (or identity), and it assists in the creation of a truly mental self, a strong ego, and a superego. It also helps to create a *mental-femininity,* as opposed to the chthonic Great Mother, because the individual mother is a *verbal* and mental being. This is of crucial importance: the chthonic (body-bound) Mother ideally gives way to mental-femininity (what we will be calling "solar-femininity").

All of that is fairly straightforward, if complex, but there is yet another side: remember that the child was originally hermaphroditic or bisexual—that the boy, for example, has a bodily-feminine side as well (that is, romantic inclinations toward other males). Thus part of the boy ends up wanting to *possess* the father. And so part of the boy ends up *identified* with the mother. So likewise with the girl: she in part desires mother and identifies with father. Now although this entire scenario is fairly complicated, the end result is simple enough: each child winds up incorporating into its mental-self structure the images and concepts of both parents, male and female. The general point is that, while the body *tends* to be dominated by the Great Mother, the mind is definitely structured by *both* the mental-mother and the mental-father, or mental-feminine and mental-masculine (or again, solar-femininity and solar-masculinity).

At the same time all of this is occurring, the superego is finalized ("the super-ego is heir to the Oedipus complex"): the mother-parent and the father-parent (both *mental* imagos) are internalized as authoritarian pockets in the ego. On the positive side, this internalization helps, as we said, the formation of a higher and mental self. On the negative side, the superego potentially (and usually) contains overly harsh injunctions and prohibitions, demands and taboos. If certain body impulses are deemed unacceptable to the superego, it has the power to *repress* them and, at the same time, to make the ego still feel guilty for having them in the first place. To take the parent into the ego is to keep part of the ego a child; the individual can now not only praise himself but blame himself; feel not only pride but guilt. And we would do well to remember that side of the new superego: a major source of body repression and a major source of morbid guilt.

A HINT FROM MYTHOLOGY

Let us now introduce a simple but universal mythological equation: the body is Earth, the mind is Heaven. Now this particular "heaven" is not to be confused with a truly Transcendent Heaven (level 6/7), any more than the Great Mother is to be confused with the Great Goddess. This heaven is not anything so lofty as a Dharmakaya or Buddha Realm or Christian Paradise. Rather, this particular heaven simply represents the ascendance of the mind (level 4) over the body (level 1/2)—it is precisely the *heaven of Apollonian rationality* (not ultimate transcendence). Thus, in this particular motif, the mind was Heaven, the body was Earth, and the transcendence of the latter by the former was everywhere celebrated in the

Hero Myths of this period. The Hero, then, was Ego-Mind-Heaven, all representative of level 4 in the Great Chain.

With this equation, we can state the results of our ontogenetic clues in this fashion: the Earth is ruled fundamentally and most significantly by the Great Mother, but Heaven is potentially ruled by *both* the mental-feminine and the mental-masculine.

But the new mental-egoic Heaven, which came into historical existence around the second or third millennium B.C., was ruled only by the father, the masculine, the male. Why? Before answering, we need a few more clues.

AWAY FROM THE CHTHONIC

Let us first note that, to the extent that the chthonic Great Mother was representative of body, earth, food, magical fertility, and emotional-sexuality, its *transcendence* was necessary and desirable. We are *not* talking about the transcendence of the feminine principle per se—there is solar-femininity (or mental-femininity), there is the Great Goddess, and so on. We are talking about the Great Mother, as she was represented in myth and ritual, even during the matriarchy itself (which rules out male sexism in this regard). The mythological fact is that the natural association of the Great Mother with the body realms showed her necessarily associated with the chthonic, the dark, the vegetal and animal, the humid. "That the worship of the Earth and Death Goddess is often associated with swampy districts has been interpreted by Bachofen as symbolic of the dark level of existence on which, uroborically speaking, the dragon [uroboric mother or phallic mother] lives, devouring her progeny as soon as she has produced them. War, flagellation, blood offerings, and hunting are but the milder forms of her worship."[311] Further:

> The Great Mother in this character is not found only in prehistoric times. She rules over the Eleusinian mysteries of a later day, and Euripides still knows Demeter as the wrathful goddess, riding in a chariot drawn by lions, to the accompaniment of Bacchic rattles, drums, cymbals, and flutes. She is shadowy enough to stand very near to the Asiatic Artemis and Cybele, and also to the Egyptian goddesses. Artemis Orthia of Sparta required human sacrifices and the whipping of boys; human sacrifices were likewise required by the Taurian Artemis; and the Alphaic Artemis was worshipped by

women with nocturnal dancing, for which they smeared their faces
with mud [blood].[311]

The conclusion is that "no 'barbaric' goddesses are here being adored
with 'sensual' and 'Asiatic' practices; all these things are merely the
deeper-lying strata of Great Mother worship. She [has the] power over
the fruitfulness of earth, men, cattle, and crops; she also presides over all
birth, and is thus, at one and the same time, goddess of destiny . . . ,
death, and the underworld. Everywhere her rites are frenzied and orgiastic;
as mistress of wild animals, she rules all male creatures, who, in the form
of the bull and lion, bear aloft her throne."[311]

This is perfectly obvious even in the Greek rituals associated with De-
meter and Persephone. "In a festival celebrated in memory . . . of De-
meter and Persephone, suckling pigs were offered in a manner suggestive
not only of an earlier human sacrifice but of one precisely of the gruesome
kind that we have observed in Africa and among the Marind-anim of
Melanesia [the ritual sacrifice of the young maiden and her consort, followed by their cannibalistic disposal, sacrifices to the Mother]. The Greek
festival, called Thesmophoria, was exclusively for women, and, as Jane
Harrison has demonstrated in her *Prolegomena to the Study of Greek
Religion,* such women's rites in Greece were pre-Homeric; that is to say,
survivals of the earlier period, when the . . . bronze-age civilizations of
Crete and Troy were in full flower and the [sun] gods, Zeus and Apollo,
of the later patriarchal Greeks had not yet arrived to reduce the power of
the great [mother]."[69]

These rites are pristine examples of the nature and function of the Great
and Devouring Mother; they can be studied in their historical settings or,
more interestingly, if less accurately, in the novels of modern writers who
have researched this period (and this archetypal level) and used it for dramatic effect (see especially John Farris, *All Heads Turn When the Hunt
Goes By,* and Thomas Tryon, *Harvest Home;* both are highly recom-
mended; they also have the added attraction of clearly recognizing that the
Great Mother, and not the father, is ultimately responsible for bodily castration and dismemberment). The rites, in various historical forms, are everywhere typical; they involve human or animal sacrifice (usually pigs),
serpent-phallic worship, eating of dismembered entrails (or symbols
thereof), and orgiastic hysteria. This latter association of the Great Mother
with emotional-sexual energy is especially evident in the rites themselves,
even in their later and toned-down versions. "In celebration of these anni-
versaries, the priestesses of Aphrodite worked themselves up into a wild
state of frenzy, and the term Hysteria became identified with the state of
emotional derangement associated with such orgies. . . . The word Hysteria was used in the same sense as Aphrodisia, that is, as a synonym for the
festivals of the [Great Mother]."[311]

No wonder that "the supersession of the stage of the Great Mother is not a fortuitous historical occurrence, but a necessary psychological one"[311]—necessary, that is, if such body-bound, chthonic, orgiastic consciousness is itself to be superseded by a higher mentality. At the very least, as Jane Harrison's classic study would put it, "a worship of the powers of fertility which includes all plant and animal life is broad enough to be sound and healthy, but as man's attention centers more and more on his own humanity, such a worship is an obvious source of danger and disease," so that the new and higher mentality came "first and foremost as a protest against the worship of the Earth and the daimones of the fertility of Earth."[71, 186]

THE NEW MENTALITY

At the least, then, the transformation to the new mentality—the heroic ego—was an appropriate move away from the chthonic, the Earth Mother, the subhuman body. Whatever else we may decide, let us not overlook that essential truth. But, indeed, the new mentality was not just away from the chthonic Mother and toward a new and higher mental-femininity as well as mental-masculinity; it rather was a move solely dominated by the mental-masculine, and this will definitely concern us.

For there is no overwhelming structural reason that the new mentality, the heroic ego, could not be feminine as well as masculine; no reason that Heaven couldn't be ruled by mental- or solar-femininity as well as solar-masculinity. The basic point is only that both femininity and masculinity should be released from their embeddedness in the chthonic Earth Mother and opened to the mental sky. I think that the most central and benign forms of the Hero Myth are open to just that interpretation, because even with its patriarchal trappings, the "treasure hard to attain"—which, we saw, was fundamentally the freed ego structure—is usually represented by a *feminine figure*. Granted, it is the male who rescues the female figure (this is the patriarchal version, after all), but the essential point is that both the male and the female figure are released from their entrapment in the chthonic dragon and devouring earth matriarchate. "With the freeing of the anima from the power of the uroboric dragon, a feminine component is built into the structure of the hero's personality. He is assigned his own feminine counterpart, essentially like himself, whether it be a real woman or his own soul, and . . . *this feminine element is the most valuable part* of the [release from the serpent-mother]. Herein, precisely, lies the difference between the princess [higher solar-femininity] and the

Great Mother [chthonic power], with whom no relations on equal terms are possible."[311]

In other words, the new heroic mentality, rising victorious out of the chthonic Mother, was ideally a solar-masculinity/solar-femininity. But where ideally we should have had the sons and daughters of Heaven, we had only the sons of Heaven. Why?

THE NATURAL PATRIARCHY

Why, then, the patriarchy? I am going to suggest that it was neither pure sexism, on the one hand, nor pure male superiority, on the other, but rather a complex mixture of both male-sexist attitudes and male-appropriate behavior, coupled with an even stranger mixture of female oppression and willing female compliance in her planned fate of irresponsibility. That is, it is highly unlikely that a phenomenon as widespread and far-reaching as the patriarchy was *solely* a product of brutal insensitivity and vicious inhumanity, coordinated on a worldwide basis to simultaneously put half of humanity into ruinous bondage. Rather, it was surely the product of a mixture of natural tendencies and unnatural inclinations, and I would like to briefly touch on both.

We start with the natural tendencies that might have disposed the heroic mentality to be initially masculine. It used to be psychologically fashionable to maintain that male and female behavior were innately different, with the male supposedly being more aggressive (but otherwise unemotional), assertive, and active, and the female being more passive, pacifist, and non-aggressive (but otherwise emotional). More recently, psychological fashion has tended to shift to the opposite extreme; it is not uncommon to hear educated people maintain that *all* sexual role differences are purely cultural, and that in their essential psychology, male and female are equivalent. For my part, I think both are true; it depends upon whether one means male and female body, or male and female mind.

That is, I believe the male body and female body, by virtue of their different structures and biological functions, are innately wired toward just those sex differences that are caricatured as the stereotypical male (active, aggressive but otherwise unemotional, etc.) and the stereotypical female (passive, non-aggressive but otherwise emotional, etc.). However, the human mind, to the extent it can transcend its initial embeddedness in the body, does indeed tend to *transcend those sexual differences*. The more male and female grow and evolve, the more they transcend their initial body differences and discover a mental equivalence and balanced identity.

This is, in a sense, a form of higher mental androgyny (not physical bisexuality, which is a regression to the polymorphous typhon). Conversely, the less evolved (and intelligent) a person is, the more he or she displays stereotypical male or female characteristics, defined by the animal body from which the self has not yet differentiated. I think recent research shows very clearly that the most developed personalities display a balance and integration of both masculine and feminine principles, and are thus "mentally androgynous," whereas less developed individuals tend to display the stereotypical attitudes of their particular sex.[344] The more you grow, the less you are male or female, until, at the limit of growth, there is "in Christ neither male nor female."

Nonetheless, this would definitely place something of an extra burden on the initial development of a truly solar-femininity, a true feminine heroic ego. Since the ego-mind must differentiate itself out of the body, the innate body wiring could not help but leave its imprint on the initial mental unfolding. And since the female body wiring tends toward passivity and emotionalism, so the initial feminine mind would tend toward emotive mentality, "intuitive" (feeling-toned) modes of cognition, paleologic, and so on (hence the widespread belief in "woman's intuition," which is not transcendent insight but emotional hunch. Frances Vaughan, in *Awakening Intuition,* acknowledges the existence of "woman's intuition," but points out that it is emotional intuition, not spiritual intuition). This type of mentality would include a quick mastery of language, but *not* of logic or higher rationality. Even today, girls develop language skills earlier than boys, but find it hard to move on to logic, mathematics, formal operational thinking, etc.[344] The point is that, however valuable this feeling-toned mentality might be for other purposes, it probably was more of a hindrance than a help to the female in the emergence of a logical, rational, and trans-chthonic mentality.

The masculine principle, on the other hand, whose initial body base would so easily be amplified into war and aggressive exploitation, had, for just those less than admirable reasons, an edge in developing the more beneficial forms of active mentality known as logic, reason, and conceptual understanding; that is, a free and non-chthonic mental ego. If that is true, it clearly would be a prime natural *tendency* for the heroic ego to emerge as the heroic male ego, and, I believe, that indeed was partly the case.

Another natural tendency has long been recognized by anthropologists. As Ruth Underhill pointed out, "the mysteries of childbirth and menstruation are *natural* manifestations of power. The rites of protective isolation, defending both the woman herself and the group to which she belongs, are rooted in a sense and idea of mysterious danger, whereas the boys' and men's rites are, rather, a *social* affair."[69] That is, to put it rather crudely, since the female-mother image already was naturally embedded in the birth-body-earth realm, then when the development of mental culture occurred, it tended to fall into the realm of the fathers. Because the feminine principle was already associated with Earth, the Heavenly transformation was left, in large measure, to the masculine principle. "Hence the fundamental correlation between heaven and masculinity."[311] In this sense, anyway, it is not surprising that "all human culture, and not Western civilization alone, is masculine in character, from Greece and the Judaeo-Christian sphere of culture to Islam and India."[311]

This also helps explain the otherwise perplexing fact that "there is a broad resemblance between the mother figures of primitive, classical, medieval, and modern times; they remain embedded in nature. But the father figure changes with the culture he represents." Thus: "'The fathers' are the representatives of law and order, from the earliest taboos to the most modern juridical systems; they hand down the highest values of civilization, whereas the mothers control the highest, i.e., deepest, values of life and nature. The world of the fathers is thus the world of collective values; it is historical and related to the . . . cultural development within the group. The advocacy of the canon of values inherited from the fathers and enforced by education manifests itself in the psychic structure of the individual as 'conscience' [superego]."[311]

And that, of course, brings us back to a distinctive feature of the ego: in being formed largely through social-mental communication with others, it bears the heavy imprint of its earliest and most significant social transactions, an imprint generally known as the superego (conscience and ego-ideal). And since socio-culture was now, for all intents and purposes, the world of the fathers, so likewise was the superego now largely patriarchal. Thus, and historically there can be little doubt about this, "'Heaven' and the world of the fathers now constitute the superego, one of the most important aids in the ego's struggle for independence."[311] (We explained the latter point in the beginning of this chapter: mental identifications help replace body-bound urges.)

But, having said that much, we must now conclude by emphasizing that the superego also brought a new capacity for inner dissociation. The superego is indeed part and parcel of the new and higher mental self; but, for just that reason, it can help repress, deny, and dissociate the lower realms (in particular, the uroboros and the typhon, aggression and emotional-sexuality). The transcendence of the lower realms is necessary and desirable; their repression, however, is pathological and morbid, and represents nothing more than a strategic failure to integrate the roots of consciousness. Repression is a fanatic denial of evolution, a denial that one's own brain-mind is composed of reptilian stem (uroboros) and limbic system (typhon) as well as neocortex (ego-mind), a denial that one's feet are of the earth and one's body of the serpent-typhon. Repression, finally, is an insult and a cruelty to those stages, primitive but necessary, upon whose early successes our consciousness now rests.

The repression of these primitive energies does not result in their annihilation; the insult of repression results merely in their outrage, and their subsequent forced entry into consciousness through disguised, painful, symptomatic, pathological, and morbid forms. The enraged serpent and typhon, cut off from participation in consciousness, lash back wildly as wounded beasts. And we will find that, from this point on, history is no longer defined by irrationality, but by violent irruptions of irrationality.

But society is not necessarily built on repression; in that regard I believe Freud was profoundly wrong. Society is built on the ascent, transformation, and true evolution of consciousness, which is a natural unfoldment of higher potentiality, and not the forced labor of the old uroboric-typhonic serpent. Society is a higher task that no amount of beating could equip the reptile to handle. To say that mental life is fundamentally built upon the repression of animal life is to say animal life is built upon the repression of plant life and plant life is built upon the repression of dirt—it gets the whole Chain of Being precisely backward. Freud's thesis seems to make sense because he took one link in the Chain—that of typhonic emotional-sexuality—and defined it as the only real link in the chain, whereupon all others—especially the higher ones, such as mind, ego, society, and culture (not to mention religion)—appear to be nothing but a sneaky rearrangement of this lower link. This rearrangement obviously must be forced, and therefore it naturally appeared to Freud that the higher is built upon a forced repression and squeezing of the lower.

What is true is that the higher, once it emerges from the ground unconscious, *can* repress the lower. The ego/superego *can* repress the typhon, and this is what concerns us. In particular, let us simply note that the egoic repression of emotional-sexual energies results in their morbid expression; pre-eminent among these morbid expressions—and crucial for the understanding of the historical era beginning at this time—are excessive and unrestrained aggression, on the one hand, and morbid and unrelenting guilt, on the other. Historically, the patriarchy brought both. And this leads us directly to the next topic.

THE UNNATURAL PATRIARCHY

I believe the above factors (apart from the repression) were the more or less natural characteristics that inclined the first egoic hero to be masculine. But notice that these characteristics were ones of function, *not* of status. Nonetheless, the temporarily preferential *function* of the masculine principle was parlayed, through oppressive exploitation, into a preferential *status* of the masculine principle. A simple difference of function became a difference of status, and resulted finally in the ignobility of *"taceat mulier in ecclesia,"* the Jew's daily prayer of thanks at not having been born a woman, an incredible insult for which the stereotypical Jewish chthonic Mother extracts daily revenge in the form of morbid guilt. This sexist oppression is unnatural and criminal—or whatever purely derogatory terms one prefers—and it is to these unnatural inclinations that we must now look.

The motives for oppression are not uniform, because there are fundamentally different types of oppression—oppression of material labor, of emotional-sexuality, of communicative exchange, of spirituality. The motive for oppression depends, in part, upon the type of oppression involved. The type of oppression involved is determined by ascertaining, as carefully as circumstances allow, which level of exchange is being denied to which otherwise qualified group(s) of individuals.

Speaking in the most general terms, there is no question but that historically the major sphere of consciousness denied access to the feminine principle by the newly emergent patriarchy was that of socio-cultural communication; i.e., free mental exchange, free access to heaven, free ideation. The feminine principle was denied access to the newly emergent mind.

And we do not have far to look for the motive of that particular type of oppression. For we have seen that the natural course of evolutionary events that ought to have led to the differentiation of mind and body, had (in the West) already gone somewhat amuck in the European dissociation of mind and body. Under the strain of the responsibilities of the newly emergent mental ego; under the impact of a new and keener apprehension of mortality; under the stress of an increasing vulnerability; under a preference for static thinking; under a surge in power drives and aggravated aggression—in short, under a new twist in the Atman project that saw immortality in abstract thought and cosmocentricity in unfettered egoic expansion—under all that, the two systems, mind and body, fell apart. And here is the immediate point: because historically the body was equated with femininity and the mind with masculinity, then the inward and psychological dissociation of the body from the mind meant an outward and sociological oppression of the feminine by the masculine.* Since the body was perceived as a threat to the egoic Atman project, the feminine was viewed as a threat to masculine, egoic, communicative heaven. In short, when Adam fell, he fell in two—Adam, Jr., and Eve; male and female; heaven and earth; psyche and soma. And Adam, Jr., was a sexist.

This is carefully hidden in the Genesis account by calling the first

---

* The point is that the oppression, repression, and/or exploitation of nature, body, and woman all occurred *for the same reasons;* nature, body, and woman were viewed as *one entity,* an entity to be suppressed. Put differently, all three were substitute sacrifices of and by the male ego—the *same* substitute sacrifice.

human "Adam," as if the proto-human were male. But, since Eve came out of Adam and was initially contained in Adam, the only possible conclusion is that the *original* Adam was not male but bodily hermaphroditic or bisexual. That is to say, Adam, Sr., was really the primordial hermaphrodite, the phallic Mother, the great Chthonic Earth Mother, out of which, as we saw, emerge the individual female mother and the individual phallic father. The final release of the feminine principle and the masculine principle from the Chthonic Mother occurs with the emergence of the true mental ego: free Adam and free Eve. In the Genesis account, free Adam emerged; free Eve did not.

To understand this, let us simply recall that the new ego was under sway of the European dissociation—the split between mind and body. And since there was not just the transcendence of the body but its repression, there was not the transformation of the maternal-chthonic but its suppression. This suppression of the maternal-chthonic seemed to multiply its appearance everywhere (via projection), and thus efforts to cancel it were redoubled, with the net result that the feminine principle *in toto* was suppressed. That is, the masculine principle alone, not the feminine principle as well, was released from its chthonic origins. The mental-feminine was not released from the body-chthonic; Adam emerged freely from the Great Mother, while Eve was identified *solely* with the Great Mother, with body, with emotional-sexuality. "Away from the maternal unconscious" was confused with "away from the feminine altogether."

This is clear even in the Genesis myth itself. While in the garden of Eden, Adam is totally under sway of chthonic masculinity—that is, he is indeed the phallic mother. He dotes around with vegetables and animals; he won't work, won't farm, won't cultivate; he has no culture, no mental endeavors, no mind. While romantics claim this to be ultimate Paradise, we have seen that it was really the state of pre-personal immersion in nature and instinct. When Eve enters the scene, she too is chthonic or nature-embedded, leading essentially the same life as instinctual Adam. But after the fall, Adam takes up knowledge, mentality, farming, discipline, culture, and self-consciousness—he is released from the fate of pansies and fruits and subhuman sleep, and takes up a properly human profile. But Eve does nothing of the sort—she remains chthonic. Cast out of the Garden, she is nevertheless prevented from entering cultural discourse. She is *only* to mother, to sex, to cook, to bodily procreate, to bodily seduce, to bodily toil, to bodily comfort. She is *not* to think, to plan, to speak up, to counsel, to philosophize, to calculate, to cultivate. And this is what I mean when I say free Adam emerged from chthonic Eden, but not free Eve (this will become more apparent in a moment).

The historical fact—not even hidden in mythology—is that the feminine principle *in toto* was excluded from the newly emergent world of rational mind, of culture, of free communicative exchange, of Apollonian heaven.

The primary injunction to the female was to be seen but not heard; i.e., not talk; i.e., not participate in mental communication. Solar-femininity, conscious-femininity, mental-femininity—this was denied. Thus, the Daughters of the Sun never emerged, and the female was socially identified solely as a daughter of the earth, chthonic, mysterious, dangerous, a threat to reason, a threat to heaven. Henceforth, woman's basic role, besides chthonic mother, was great seductress, and she had to learn to play one or the other well (and often both at once, an impossible task; thus, in marriage, after the woman gave birth to a child, she was automatically the chthonic mother, and the husband often then looked elsewhere for a great seductress—hence the so-called double standard of sexual conduct).

In Genesis, because Eve is forced, unlike Adam, to remain chthonically bound, she appears *solely* in the trappings of the chthonic Mother, the phallic Mother, the uroboric-typhon, the serpent-bride, whose characterization, as far as it goes, is perfectly true to the chthonic form: an emotional-sexual woman *structurally* coupled with a sneaky phallus (serpent), with no mention of actual masculinity. "Now the serpent was more subtil than any beast of the field which the Lord God had made. And he said unto the woman, Yea, hath God said, Ye shall not eat of every tree of the garden?" (3:1).

And so it came about, in this half-twisted patriarchal tale, that among the very first recorded words that man ever said to the Lord his God were: "The woman whom thou gavest to be with me, she gave me of the tree, and I did eat" (3:12). The great seductress, she made him do it. And among the very first recorded words of this Lord God to woman were: "I will greatly multiply thy sorrow and thy conception; in sorrow thou shalt bring forth children; and thy husband, he shall rule over thee" (3:16). No liar, that God. And to Adam: "Because thou has harkened unto the voice of thy wife, in sorrow shalt thou eat all the days of thy life" (3:17). Adam was punished for listening to Eve's *voice;* i.e., for *allowing femininity to enter the mental-communicative field.*

How quickly, and how violently, this oppression occurred, we can only guess. That, in some ways, it was physically implemented (in addition to its being psychologically generated) is certain. The whole oppressive side of the patriarchy was prefigured in certain men's lodges and secret societies, organizations in which, as Neumann showed, the mental ego first emerged, but organizations through which, as Father Schmidt suggested, sexist oppression was first instituted. These "men's festivals not only were addressed to an ignoble, immoral aim, but strove for it through ignoble and immoral means. The aim was to . . . establish through intimidation and the subjection of the women, a cruel ascendency of the males."

The means were Hallowe'en burlesques, in which the players themselves did not believe, and which, consequently, were lies and impostures from beginning to end. And the ill effects that issued from all this were not only disturbances of the social balance of the sexes, but also a coarsening and self-centering of the males, who were striving for such ends by such means.[69]

And thus, in Campbell's words, "it may well be that a good deal of what has been advertised as representing the will of 'Old Man' actually is but the heritage of a lot of old men, and that the main idea has been not so much to honor God as to simplify life by keeping woman in the kitchen."[69]

PATRIARCHAL IMMORTALITY

But, of course, good or bad, right or wrong, natural or unnatural, the patriarchy must have served the Atman project, and served it well. And indeed it did.

"Social organization came to be focused in the patriarchal family under the state's legal protection. It was at this time that biological fatherhood became of dominant importance because it became the universal way of assuring personal immortality."[26] Phallic patriarchy: a new and crucial form of the social Atman project. As Becker explains:

> Rank called this the "sexual era" because physical paternity was fully recognized as the royal road to self-perpetuation via one's children—in fact, it was one's bounden duty. The institution of marriage extended from the king to his people, and every father became a kind of king in his own right, and his home a castle. Under Roman law the father had tyrannical rights over his family; he ruled over it legally; as Rank was quick to observe, *famulus* equals servant, slave.[26]

Patriarchy became a new and easily accessible symbol of individual immortality, a new twist on the Atman project. In the Roman law of inheritance, "the notion was that, though the physical person of the deceased had perished, his legal personality survived and descended unimpaired on his Heir or Co-Heirs, in whom his identity (so far as the law was concerned) was continued." Thus, and this precisely clinches it, "in the old Roman Law of Inheritance, the notion of a will or testament is inextricably bound up, I might almost say confounded, with the theory of a man's posthumous existence in the person of his heir—the elimination of the fact of death."[62]

The point is that the average male (father) had immortality symbols not only in whatever property, money, gold, and goods he could amass, but

also in his progeny, especially his sons, his heirs. For his heirs were his
subjects while he was alive and his "posthumous existence" when he
"died." His heirs were his property and his subjects, by law. "Today we
are shocked when we read of the ancient Greek who blinded his sons for
disobeying him and going off to war—but their lives were literally his personal property, and he had this authority and used it."[26] For the simple
fact is that there was (and still is) an "intimate unity of patriarchal family
ideology with that of kingship."[61] And this occurred for a fairly
straightforward reason: as more and more people began to emerge as
egoic, individual, heroic personalities, with the concomitant forms of the
Atman project, they needed new forms of cosmocentricity and immortality
symbols—and *looking at the life of kings, they found it*. The massive
properties and accumulations of the kings, and the obedient subjects and
servants of the kings, announced the "good life." Thus, "with the rise of
kingship men came to imitate kings in order to get power."[26]

Thus, every man's home was his castle, and he the supreme ruler of it.
He had immortality symbols not only in his property and gold, but also in
his family, his wife, his progeny—his subjects and his heirs. "As Heichel-
heim showed, the Iron Age, at the end of which we live, democratized the
achievements of the Bronze Age (cities, metals, money, writing) and
opened up the pursuit of kings (money and [subject-heirs] and immortality) to the average citizen."[61] And, naturally, "the new patriarchy
passed not only family immortality to the son, but also gold, property, and
interest—and the duty to accumulate these in turn."[61]

So it was that, through a new structure of self (egoic) and a new set of
substitute objects, the pursuit of kings—property, gold, and subjects
(heirs)—was opened to the average citizen at large. Or rather, to the average Adam at large. Eve remained in the kitchen, without property, without
gold, and without subjects. In fact, she herself, *being* a subject, formed
part of the oppressed base upon which the immortality projects of the
male ego were now built. How deep this male terror still runs! The feminine threatened, not only masculine mentality, but egoic immortality. Look
no further for the causes of the masculine terror of "feminine power,"
causes still rampant today, causes still "ignoble and immoral" in their
means and their ends.

SOL INVICTUS

Thus, for various reasons, some sexist, some not, the monumental transition to the heroic mental ego was left largely to the masculine principle.

But it is extremely important that, in throwing out the bath water of sexism, we do not throw out the baby of actual transformation with it. The *truth* concealed in the patriarchy, however otherwise entrapped, was the higher-order self known as mental ego, characterized by self-consciousness, and established by a truly evolutionary mutation in consciousness. And it is this truth we must eventually celebrate, even as we redress its imbalances.

We saw that this higher truth—the emergence of free mind (level 4)—was everywhere represented in mythology with the coming of Heaven and the Hero-gods of Heaven. The most dominant heavenly orb is, of course, the sun, and thus the new heroic gods were, in all cases, Sun Gods. The Sun was simply representative of the *light of reason*. It was representative of Apollonian rationality. (It was *not* representative of the ultimate Clear Light Void, just as the heaven in which it existed was not representative of Dharmakaya, but rather of mind. The Sun represented "enlightenment" in the European sense, Voltaire's rationality, and not in the Eastern sense, Buddha's transcendence.)

The point is that the Hero of these myths brings not only ego-mind, *but also light*. The light was not physical light, and not Ultimate Light, but the light of mental clarity, which was dramatically symbolized by the blaze of the Sun shining in the mental heaven. Thus, we add another link to our equation: Hero = Ego = Mind = Heaven = Light = Sun.

This is precisely why "the most widely disseminated archetype of the dragon fight is the sun myth, where the hero is swallowed every evening by the nocturnal sea monster dwelling in the west, and who then grapples with its double, so to speak—the dragon whom he encounters in this uterine cavern. He is then reborn in the east as the victorious sun, the *sol invictus;* or rather, by hacking his way out of the [chthonic] monster, he accomplishes his own rebirth. *In this sequence of danger, battle, and victory, the light is the central symbol of the hero's reality. The hero is always a light-bringer and emissary of the light*" (my italics).[311]

In this way, too, can we understand "the victory of the son, who becomes a matricide in order to avenge his father, and who introduces the new age of the patriarchate with the help of the *paternal-solar principle*. We use the word 'patriarchate' . . . to signify the predominantly masculine world of [heaven], sun, consciousness, and ego. In the matriarchate, on the other hand, the . . . earthy, body-bound world of the unconscious reigns supreme, and the predominant feature here is a preconscious, prelogical [mythic], and preindividual [*not* transindividual] way of thinking and feeling."[311]

Similarly, "the celestial orb to which the monarch is now likened is no longer the silvery moon . . . but the golden sun, the blaze of which is eternal and before which shadows, demons . . . take flight. The new age of the Sun God has dawned, and there is to follow an extremely interesting [mythological] development, known as *solarization,* whereby the entire system of the earlier age is to be . . . transformed, reinterpreted, and in large measure even suppressed."[71] The *transformation* of the old chthonic and telluric mythologies (via solarization) was part of the growth of consciousness; however—and this bears repeating one more time—the *suppression* of those mythologies (and the realms they represented) was a catastrophe that still affects us all. We have, male and female alike, even to this day, still to come to adequate terms with our chthonic roots. And that leads us to our last topic.

OEDIPUS

With the above understanding, we are in a position to return to our initial point of departure in this chapter, and attempt closure: the basic nature and meaning of the Oedipus (Electra) myth, the myth that has weighed so heavily on our collective psyche, the myth selected by Freud as *the* defining myth of human consciousness. We don't have to be dogmatic fans of Freud to be impressed by the fact that the greatest psychologist of this century chose *one* particular myth as *central* to human nature. Freud certainly overstated the case, but something of profound significance is going on here. What follows is my reinterpretation and reconstruction of the essential significance of the Oedipus myth.

The actual details of the myth itself are simple enough: Oedipus, without knowing it, commits incest with his mother and murders his father, and when he discovers his crime, blinds himself out of guilt. The meaning is straightforward: on the surface, Oedipus seems merely an innocent seeker and sufferer, making his way through a life that includes a rather nondescript killing and a not unordinary love affair. But beneath the surface, in the subconscious (or "offstage"), Oedipus loves, not just a woman, but his Mother, and kills, not just an adversary, but his Father, and when Oedipus discovers his crime—when he makes it conscious for the first time—the guilt drives him to self-inflicted blindness.

Oedipus is the myth of consciousness torn between the old chthonic matriarchate and the rising solar patriarchate. Oedipus rebels against the solar-father principle of a higher and more demanding mode of awareness, and seeks instead a union with the old comfort of the chthonic earth, an emotional-sexual incest with the Mother, an immersion in her domain. Oedipus, in other words, is *not* a true ego hero—he does *not* conquer the old chthonic attraction, but rather succumbs to it. He does *not* make the final transformation from telluric body to solar mind, from instinct to ego, from pleasure to reason, but, rebelling against and finally murdering the higher solar principle, he regresses back to the embrace of Mother Earth.

And this is clinched by the fact that, upon regressing to the status of a son-lover of the Great Mother, Oedipus suffers the tragic fate of *all* phallic consorts of the Mother: castration, sacrifice, and dismemberment. Oedipus puts out his own eyesight, blinds himself, using as a weapon the clasp symbolic of the old matriarchal system. But notice: this is not so much a bodily castration as a higher castration of eyesight, which is everywhere symbolic of knowledge, light, and solar reason. Oedipus destroys, castrates, his own individual ego-mind, and returns to the pre-personal bodyself of mother nature, where he is therein "disposed like dust." Thus, to perfectly cap the story, Oedipus, in his old age, blind and infirm, vanishes mysteriously into the bowels of the Earth. Bachofen, in his singularly brilliant fashion, concludes that Oedipus "is one of the great human figures whose agony and suffering lead to more gracious and civilized behavior, who, still embedded in the old [chthonic] order of which they are the products, stand there as its last great victims, and at the same time as the founders of a new age."[16, 311]

What lends such genius to Sophocles' telling of the Oedipus tale is that the *actual* desires and feats of Oedipus are too stark, and too full of impact, to occur *consciously* to Oedipus. They therefore transpire in the story without his knowing it. This perfectly represents, with ingenious dramatic flair, the fact that his desires are subconscious. Thus, when they are finally made conscious, when Oedipus realizes what he has done, the resultant guilt is devastating. No wonder Freud was totally overwhelmed with its message, and no wonder he saw its universal significance. For the universality of the myth is simply due to the fact that each and every individual must, in his or her own development, pass through the Oedipus (Electra) drama. As we suggested in the first part of this chapter, the Oedipus complex is directly concerned with a shift of the Atman project *from* the body *to* the mind: a transformation from seeking unity via the body (in emotional-sexual intercourse) to seeking unity via the mind (in communicative intercourse), a miniature version of moving from chthonic matriarchate to solar patriarchate. To *fail* in this transformation upward is simply to suffer the fate of Oedipus: morbid guilt, emotional-sexual incest and desire, self-dismemberment, masochistic death.

If you want the most accurate but drastic simplification of Freud, it is this: a "neurotic" has an "Oedipal problem," and an "Oedipal problem" means that the *mind* is fixated in (or repressive of) certain aspects of the *body* (oral, anal, phallic), and therefore suffers from this fixation/repression in the form of symptoms. We already saw that failure to transform and integrate the lower levels of evolution results in neurosis. Freud simply summarized all the lower levels as *body* (libido), and saw its repression as the core—the Oedipal core—of all neurosis. This is not the only source of anxiety and neurosis, but it is central enough, and pre-eminent enough, to make Freud's thesis central to any comprehensive theory of human compound nature.†

The point is that Freud could find the Oedipus complex at the center of every psyche because it stands pivotal in the universal but difficult transformation from body to mind, from serpent-typhon to egoic self, from Sphinx to Man. The riddle of the Sphinx is no riddle at all—the Sphinx is half animal and half human; i.e., it is a typhon. And it was precisely the typhon-Sphinx that gave Jocasta to Oedipus as his wife—i.e., that helped unite Oedipus with his own Great Mother and thus seal his subhuman fate.

To say a person has Oedipal problems means he/she is *unconsciously* seeking union (seeking Atman release) via the body, via sex, via emotional discharge, and, rebelling against the demands of a higher solar mentality, the person remains, to this day, among the "figures . . . who, still embedded in the old order . . . , stand there as its last great victims."

† Needless to say, the Freudian Oedipus complex has nothing to do with the actual nature of the higher spheres, levels 4–8. It is pivotal *only* in the transition from body to mind, from level 1/2 to level 3/4, with direct emphasis on the contributions of level 2. As usual, I am no fan of Freud beyond the lower levels.

14 I and the Father Are One

We come now to the second strand of evolution during this mental-egoic period, the strand of evolution that involves not the *average mode* of consciousness but the *most advanced* mode of consciousness. For with certain of the most highly evolved souls of this period, with such sages as Buddha, Krishna, Christ, and Lao Tzu, the ultimate causal realm itself was penetrated, the realm of the Dharmakaya (and Svabhavikakaya, since we are treating them together, as explained below), the realm beyond even the personal God or Goddess, the realm of the unmanifest Void. This was an understanding quite beyond anything produced prior to the general mental-egoic period, and it simply meant that *consciousness on the whole* had evolved so far that the truly advanced heroes of the time could then, as it were, jump the rest of the way to ultimate Atman itself. Notice that the first great "axial sages," such as Buddha and Lao Tzu, began to emerge around the sixth century B.C.—the very beginning of the middle egoic—but rarely, if ever, before.

In other words, with these types of highly advanced sages, the growing tip of consciousness moved from Sambhogakaya religion (level 6) to Dharmakaya religion (level 7/8). The differences between these religions (and their respective levels of consciousness) are both profound and easily recognizable. We will be examining these differences in detail throughout this chapter, but as an introduction, notice:

In the Sambhogakaya, or the subtle realm, a transcendent oneness—one God, one Goddess—makes itself evident to the soul, and the soul communes, in sacrificial awareness, with that archetypal oneness. In the Dharmakaya, the causal realm, the path of transcendence goes even further, for the soul no longer communes with that oneness or worships that oneness—it *becomes* that oneness, in a state the Muslim mystics call the Supreme Identity. That is, in the subtle realm, there is a slight remnant of the subject-object dualism, a subtle distinction between the Creator and the creature, between God and the soul. But in the Dharmakaya, the subject and object become radically identical; the Creator and creature become profoundly united—so united, in fact, that both disappear as separate entities. They are both, God and soul, dissolved in and returned to the radiant ground of the prior Void, or unobstructed and all-pervading Consciousness as Such—what we earlier called superconsciousness and the ultimate Whole.

In short, if the subtle realm is the realm of one God, the causal is the realm "beyond God," the realm of a prior Godhead, Ground, Source, or Void, out of which the personal God/dess emerges. If the Sambhogakaya one God was viewed (and rightly so) as the Creator of the worlds, the Dharmakaya Void could say, as Osiris/Ra would, "I am the divine hidden Soul (Atman) who created the god(s)." And if the Sambhogakaya was "our Father who art in Heaven," the voice of the Dharmakaya Void could say, "I and the Father are One."

MOSAIC AND CHRISTIC REVELATION

These transitions are very easy to trace, even in the West. When, for example, Moses descended from Mount Sinai (the mountain motif is representative of transcendent height), he brought with him the Sambhogakaya, a revelation given to him via voice or subtle-level nada illuminations (the burning bush, the voice of God, etc.). This religion clearly understood that there is a Creator (in this case, God the Father) that perfectly transcends the material worlds yet gives form to them. This was the religion of Moses, and before him (to lesser degrees), of Abraham and Isaac and Jacob. It was a religion of the subtle realm.

It was, in short, *monotheism,* or One God revelation. Now we already saw that this subtle-level oneness (level 6) was occasionally intuited in mythic times, usually in the form of the Great Goddess, but that these early intuitions were, by all accounts, rather crude. The Great Goddess, for instance, was usually held to be a pre-eminent One among many, not One without a second. That is, there were still polytheistic trappings to that religion, carry-overs from the naturic realm. But the clear rise of monotheism signaled an end to all forms of exclusive polytheism (and animism), and expressed the first unequivocal revelation of One Divinity.

The first clearly monotheistic God emerged in Egypt. It was not Ptah, Ra, Osiris, or Isis, but Aton—revealed to and by Iknaton, king of Egypt c. 1372–54 B.C., of the XVIIIth dynasty; son and successor of Amenhotep III. And, according to scholars from Freud to Campbell, Aton—or at least the monotheistic conception—was carried from Egypt into Sinai by the historical person known as Moses. Moses itself is an Egyptian name, and no matter what dates are finally assigned to Moses, he was almost certainly born an Egyptian noble. Freud, for one, thinks Moses was a member of the court of Iknaton himself, although there is some difficulty with the dates here.[149] At any rate, the monotheistic conception was carried by Moses into the desert (headed for Israel and the Promised Land), where, at the mountain known as Jabal Musa (Arabic: "Mount of Moses"), or Mount Sinai, this Atonic inspiration was either added to, or capped by, an actual communion with the Divine God itself (precisely as told in Exodus), epitomized by fire, by light, by angelic archetype, and by voice (nada, mantra). But then, for reasons that are far from clear (some say because Moses was murdered due to the strict discipline he imposed on his peoples), the name of a local volcano god, Yahweh (Jehovah), was substituted for the name Aton, and the basic God of Western civilization was set.

This monotheistic religion was, as far as it went, a correct reflection of the Sambhogakaya realm: a higher God exists, which is Fire and Light, which can be contacted in revelation and prophetic ecstasy, which confers meaning on personal destiny, which must be contacted through discipline and struggle, but which remains *ultimately* an Other—ultimately a Creator separated from all creation, a God separated from the world and from the soul. It is possible to deeply commune with this God, but not absolutely become one with it. But those are all more or less true insights into the subtle realm.

Notice that, even according to the biblical tale, the first thing Moses confronted, when he returned to his people from Mount Sinai, was the old pagan religion, the religion of sorcery, nature gods, and the chthonic mother (golden calf), the religion of emotional-sexual rituals and body trances. Even at their very peak, these rituals disclose only the psychic or Nirmanakaya realm, as we saw with shamanistic religion. In other words, Moses, bringing the evolutionarily higher religion of the Sambhogakaya, had to confront, battle, and transcend the old Nirmanakaya religions. And, to judge from the Old Testament, this was no easy confrontation—in fact, if Moses was murdered, this would be my first guess as to why.

Similarly, Christ's revelation was an evolutionary advance, a revelation of the Dharmakaya, a revelation that "I and the Father are One." (This was the same revelation that the Upanishads brought in India—*Tat tvam asi,* "Thou art That," you and God are ultimately one, a message not clearly found in the earlier Vedas, which were Mosaic-like in revelation.) But Christ now faced the old Mosaic law of the *external* One God of the Sambhogakaya, which he criticized as being partial, so that he was ultimately crucified because "you, being a man, make yourself out God." That is, he was crucified because he dared to evolve *from* the Sambhogakaya—where the subject-object dualism remains in a subtle form, and where therefore the dualism between Creator and creature remains in a subtle form—*to* the Dharmakaya—where subject and object reduce to prior oneness, and where therefore God and soul reduce to prior Godhead, or the Void of the Supreme Identity.

With the extraordinary discovery and final release of the Gnostic Gospels (*The Nag Hammadi Library*),[350] it now appears certain that the essence of Christ's teaching, the esoteric side, was a pure gnosis, which in Sanskrit is precisely *jnana* (the same root: gno = jna). Jnana (or prajna) is simply the insight that discloses the Dharmakaya. Prajna (pro-gnosis) is exactly what gave Buddha his enlightenment; jnana is exactly what disclosed Brahman-Atman to Shankara, and so on. Small wonder that in these Christian gnostic texts we find such instructions as: "Abandon the search for God and the creation and other matters of similar sort. Look for him by taking yourself as the starting point. Learn who it is within you. . . . To know the self is to know God. . . ." It is also obvious, from these texts, that Jesus' primary religious activity was to incarnate in and as his followers, in the manner, *not* of the *only* historical Son of God (a monstrous notion), but of a true Spiritual Guide helping all to become sons and daughters of God: "Jesus said: 'I am not your master, because you have drunk, you have become drunk from the bubbling stream which I have measured out. . . . He who will drink from my mouth will become as I am.' "

Elaine Pagels points out that there are three essential strands to the esoteric message of Christ, as revealed in the gnostic gospels: (1) "Self-knowledge is knowledge of God; the [highest] self and the divine are identical." (2) "The 'living Jesus' of these texts speaks of illusion and enlightenment, not of sin and repentance." (3) "Jesus is presented not as Lord but as spiritual guide."[321] Let us simply note that those are precisely tenets of Dharmakaya religion.

The point is that Christ clearly left an esoteric circle of gnostic disciples, which eventually would include John, Mary Magdalene, Theudas, Marcion, and the great Valentinus. "And while the Valentinians publicly

Fig. 28. The Heart of Christ. This is not the physical heart, nor is it the subtle-chakra heart—it is the causal and ultimate Heart, precisely as described by Sri Ramana Maharshi and Bubba Free John, and intuited via identity by all Dharmakaya sages.

confessed faith in one God, in their own private meetings they insisted on discriminating between the popular image of God—as master, king, lord, creator, and judge—and what that image represented—God understood as the ultimate source of all being. Valentinus calls that source [level 7] 'the depth' [Abyss or Void]; his followers describe it as invisible, incomprehensible primal principle. But most Christians, they say, mistake mere images of God for that reality."[321]

But the gnostic understanding was even more profound than that. It was not that the ordinary Christian notion of God the Creator was *wrong,* but that it was *partial.* "For Valentinus, what Clement and Ignatius [early exoteric Christian bishops] mistakenly ascribe to God actually applies only to the *creator* [level 6]. Valentinus, following Plato, uses the Greek term *demiurgos* for creator, suggesting he is a lesser divine being who serves as

Fig. 29. Gautama Buddha; Cambodian sculpture, eleventh century A.D.
Gautama Buddha (sixth century B.C.*) was one of the first Eastern sages—*
and probably the greatest of the historical Oriental sages—to clearly and
unequivocally grasp the Dharmakaya. His profound insight was almost an
exact analogue of Christ's, although the cultural manifestations and philo-
sophical accouterments were naturally quite different. That is, they both
discovered the deep structure of the Dharmakaya, but the surface structures
through which they expressed this understanding were rather different, re-
flecting the differences in historical conditioning, personalities, cultural
contingencies, languages, philosophical background, etc. Notice the seven
serpents, representing the seven major levels of being through which Bud-

the instrument of the higher powers [of level 7/8]."[321] There is a perfect understanding of one of the differences between God the Creator (Sambhogakaya) and the Void-Source (Dharmakaya). When the early gnostic Marcion suggested that there must be two different Gods [level 6 vs. 7], he was right. And Valentinus, like Christ before him, knew it: "It is not God [or level 7], he explains, but the [subtle-realm or level 6] demiurge who reigns as king and Lord [creator], who gives the law and passes judgment on those who violate it—in short, he [the subtle-realm demiurgos] is the 'God of Israel,'" the God of Moses, the God the Father of the subtle and archetypal realm, the Sambhogakaya. All of this appears to be very clear to the early gnostics, and it expresses a sophistication and precision of spiritual understanding that is most impressive—in particular, it demonstrates a profound grasp of the hierarchy of the superconscious spheres.

For Valentinus, achieving gnosis involved going *beyond* God the Creator, or the subtle-realm demiurgos-god. To reach level 7, one must go beyond level 6; to reach Godhead, one must go beyond God altogether. This

---

dha's consciousness passed prior to, and as a condition of, his supreme enlightenment. Notice, too, that these are serpents, representing the absolute sublimation and return of kundalini consciousness to its highest and prior Abode beyond mind, body, world, and self. Finally, notice that the serpents are not at the sixth chakra (or even the seventh), as they were in Pharaonic times, but rather reach beyond the brain centers altogether. This is no longer the subtle level, but the causal. Precisely the same serpent locations can be seen in Vishnu and Nagarjuna (Figs. 34 and 31). But it is very important to realize that the depiction of the serpent power lying beyond the brain-mind is not necessary for the true sages—nor are halos of light (as in the saints of the subtle level)—because the whole point of the sage is that he or she has transcended altogether the chakras, whether high or low. Thus, while yogis (level 5) are almost always depicted with the third eye and/or a serpent at the sixth chakra; and while saints (level 6) are almost always depicted with halos of light and/or a serpent at or slightly beyond the seventh chakra (at the crown of the head), the sage (level 7/8) is almost always shown with neither (as in Fig. 30 or 33). I have included this picture of Buddha, as well as of Vishnu and Nagarjuna, because they all point out that when true sages are occasionally pictured with the serpent power, the serpent(s) is always shown exaggeratedly extending way beyond the brain-mind—beyond the sixth or seventh chakras—representing their ultimate transcendence. Finally, I chose this picture as a way to say a fond goodbye to our old friend the serpent. For that uroboros—which we saw at the very Dawn State of mankind, coiled at the base of the Great Chain, ruling over the slumber in Eden—is here depicted in its final release and ultimate evolutionary return to Source, rising beyond the personal organism altogether and returning to its prior Abode.

*Fig. 30. Bodhidharma (sixth century A.D.), founder of Ch'an (Zen)
Buddhism, the school of religion that, with the possible exception of its
cousin Vajrayana, has historically produced the greatest number of enlightened practitioners, East or West (i.e., individuals clearly established in the
Dharmakaya). Bodhidharma and his heirs—Hui-neng, Ma-tsu, Huang-Po,
Lin-chi (Rinzai), Tung-shan, Ts'ao-shan, Yun-men, Dogen, Hakuin—
embodied the first clear and substantial grasp not only of the Dharmakaya
but of the Svabhavikakaya. Bodhidharma is shown here practicing "pi-
kuan"; kuan is the Chinese equivalent of the Sanskrit prajna (gnosis).*

involved, in fact, a *release* (apolytrosis) *from* God the Creator—"In this
ritual he addresses the demiurge, declaring his independence, serving notice he no longer belongs to the demiurge's sphere of authority and judgment, but to what transcends it." This involved as well a reception of transcendent knowledge, or gnosis: "Achieving *gnosis* involves coming into
direct contact with the true source of divine power—namely, 'the depth' of
all being. Whoever has come to know that Source [level 7] simultaneously comes to know himself."[321]*

The Christian mystic Behmen was eloquent on these points, and in a
fashion that shows perfectly how similar gnostic Christianity is to *all* Dharmakaya religions, including Buddhism: "Whoever finds it [the ultimate,
level 7/8] finds Nothing and all Things. But how finds he *Nothing*? He
that findeth it findeth a supersensual Abyss [the Void], which hath no

---

* "My being is God, not by simple participation, but by a true transformation of
my Being. My *me* is God" (St. Catherine of Genoa). "See! I am God; See! I am in
all things; See! I do all things!" (Dame Julian of Norwich). And best of all: "The
Ground of God and the Ground of the soul are one and the same" (Meister
Eckhart).

ground to stand on; and he findeth also nothing is like unto it and therefore it may fitly be compared to *Nothing,* for it is deeper than any *Thing.* And because it is Nothing, it is therefore free from All Things, and is that only Good, which a man cannot express or utter what it is, there being Nothing to which it may be compared, to express it by."

But this is not a transcendent vacuum. The Void means seamless, not featureless; it transcends but includes *all* manifestation. Therefore Behmen continues: "But in that I lastly say: *Whosoever finds it finds All Things.* It hath been the Beginning of All Things; it is also the End of All Things. All Things are from it, and in it, and by it. If thou findest it thou comest into that ground from whence All Things are proceeded, and wherein they subsist."

To make a very long and very complicated story brutally short, this higher evolutionary religion never took official root in the West. From Christ to Valentinus to St. Denys to al-Hallaj to Giordano Bruno to Eckhart, such insights were savagely opposed and eventually uprooted, often by execution. There were two basic reasons for this.

Fig. 31. Nagarjuna (c. second century A.D.*), a spiritual descendant of Buddha and founder of Madhyamika Buddhism. Nagarjuna was the first great sage to not only see but fully enunciate in dialectical fashion the Dharmakaya-Void, thus drawing out and extending on the Buddha's original insight. His influence, direct or indirect, on subsequent religious thought in the East was profound. All major Mahayana Buddhist sects trace their lineage to him (including Bodhidharma and Padmasambhava). Just as important, however, his thinking/contemplation had a far-reaching influence on Shankara, founder of Vedanta Hinduism (all great modern Indian sages acknowledge Shankara as the master historical teacher of India). The simplest way to understand Nagarjuna's metaphysic is to say it resembled a cross between Kant and Schopenhauer: the mind imposes phenomenal categories upon noumenal Reality, but by clearing awareness of conceptual elaboration and subject/object duality, the absolute Noumenon itself could be intuited via prajna. But for Nagarjuna, as for all sages, this was not mere philosophy but direct realization (satori, enlightenment, liberation).*

One, the new and higher Dharmakaya religion simply appeared to be wrong to the Sambhogakaya believers. How could one be asked to "go beyond God" or even "renounce God"? Was that not blasphemy, heresy, deviltry? The Sambhogakayins, of course, were mistaken (or partially mistaken), but it is easy enough to see that it was often an honest mistake, despite its usually cruel consequences.

Two, the more politically motivated individuals—the early bishops and banker-priests—correctly realized that a God beyond God meant an end to their power, which was based on God number one. Already we see this in Clement, Bishop of Rome (c. 90 A.D.). "Clement argues that God, the God of Israel [level 6], alone rules in heaven as divine Lord, master, and judge. But how is God's rule actually administered? God, he says, delegates his 'authority of reign' to 'rulers and leaders on earth.' Who are these designated rulers? Clement answers that they are bishops, priests, and deacons. Whoever refuses to 'bow the neck' and obey the church leaders is guilty of insubordination against the divine Master himself."[321] And so would go the wretched chronicle of exoteric religion in the West.

The point of all this is that, in the orthodox religions of the West, the spheres of the Divine and the Human never evolved to the natural point where they become one. Orthodox Western religion stopped at the Sambhogakaya realm, and never truly grasped the Dharmakaya. Thus, the *separation* of God and Man, or Creator and creature, which is natural and unavoidable at the lower levels of evolution, was never overcome in a higher synthesis and transformation, either in theory or in practice. The flowering

Fig. 32. Padmasambhava, founder of Tibetan Buddhism (c. eighth century A.D.). Padmasambhava was to Tibet what Bodhidharma/Hui-neng was to China: bearer of the first significant intuition not only of Dharmakaya but also of Svabhavikakaya (although Lao Tzu preceded Bodhidharma in China by a thousand years, his school never took root as an actual means of practice).

of the Dharmakaya was left, by and large, to the East, to Hinduism, to Buddhism, to Taoism, to Neo-Confucianism. But no wonder that members of Dharmakaya religions are so puzzled and even exasperated at the dualistic view of reality still remaining in the Sambhogakaya religions of the West. And add this dualistic split between God and Man to the European dissociation of Man and Nature (mind and body), and you arrive perfectly and completely at the orthodox Western world view, which the Zen scholar D. T. Suzuki whimsically but unerringly described as: "Man is against God, Nature is against God, and Man and Nature are against each other."

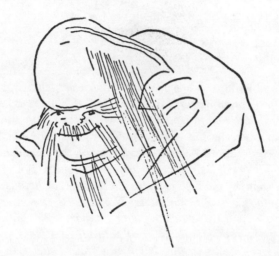

Fig. 33. Lao Tzu (c. sixth century B.C.*), the first major explorer of the Dharmakaya in China. Although Lao Tzu, founder of Taoism, was the first important Chinese to penetrate the causal realm (which he called the "Tao"), his school never flowered as a method of actual practice and real sadhana, but tended—perhaps because he was too far ahead of his time in China—to degenerate, in the hands of his less evolved followers, into forms of magical-mythical rituals or, at best, into mere yogic (level 5) techniques (so-called "Hsien Taoism" versus "Contemplative Taoism"). But Lao Tzu himself stands forever as part of a historic elite: Christ, Buddha, Lao Tzu, and the Upanishadic author(s)—the first great explorers of the Dharmakaya. The very best of Lao Tzu was, however, taken up almost entirely by Ch'an (Zen) Buddhism, so that, in Zen, the best of the Buddha and the best of Lao Tzu not only lived on but flowered magnificently. Such, exactly, was the brilliance of Zen: Buddha and Lao Tzu combined and preserved.*

Fig. 34. Lord Vishnu. Note again the seven serpents way beyond the brain-mind. But the real reason I have included this figure is out of homage to the authors of the major Upanishads, who, along with Buddha, Christ, and Lao Tzu, represent the earliest great explorers of the Dharmakaya realm. However, I cannot present a drawing of the Upanishadic authors, because their historical existence is lost to antiquity. We simply do not know the real names, much less the actual historical details, of the great sages that composed the Upanishads. Nonetheless, the doctrines of the Upanishads are popularly associated with the names of various sages, perhaps factual, perhaps mythical: Aruni, Yajnavalkya, Balaki, Svetaketu, and Sandilya. But one fact is certain: beginning around the sixth century B.C., a corpus of writings—the Upanishads—was set forth in an eloquent and brilliant fashion; so brilliant, in fact, that Max Müller stated that the Upanishads embodied "a system in which human speculation seems to have reached its very acme." But more than that—it was not just speculation, but the result and product of a brilliant penetration and understanding of the causal and ultimate realms of existence: an actual awakening to the very Brahman-Atman itself. The Upanishadic insight would eventually mature into the brilliance of Shankara, and from there to Sri Ramana Maharshi. In homage to those original but historically silent sages, we include this figure. In subsequent chapters, I will often represent this entire strand of Dharmakaya exploration with the name of Krishna (simply because, through the Gita, he became the most popular Indic sage).

THE EVOLUTION OF RELIGIOUS EXPERIENCE

If we pull together everything we have seen on the nature and levels of growing-tip consciousness, or most advanced consciousness, we arrive at an outline of the hierarchic *evolution of religious experience,* which is at the same time an outline of the successive levels of the superconscious sphere. It looks like this:

Nirmanakaya—level 5; shamanistic trance, shakti, psychic capacities, siddhi, kriyas, elemental forces (nature gods and goddesses), emotional-sexual transmutation, body ecstasy, kundalini, and hatha yoga

Sambhogakaya—level 6; subtle realm; angelic and archetypal visions; One God/dess, the Creator of all lower realms (levels 5 through 1), the demiurgos or Archetypal Lord; saintly religion of halos of subtle light and sound (nada, mantra); nada and shabd yoga, savikalpa samadhi, saguna Brahman

Dharmakaya—level 7; causal realm; unmanifest Void, Empty Ground, the Godhead; unity of soul and God, transcendence of subject-object duality, coalescence of human and divine; the Depth, the Abyss, the Ground of God and soul; I and the Father are One; jnana yoga, nirvikalpa samadhi, nirguna Brahman

Svabhavikakaya—level 8; culmination of Dharmakaya religion; identity of manifest and unmanifest, or identity of the entire World Process and the Void; perfect and radical transcendence into and as ultimate Consciousness as Such, or absolute Brahman-Atman; sahaja yoga, bhava samadhi

Now there are a couple of points about that outline. First of all, I have throughout this volume avoided extended discussions of the differences between level 7 and level 8, or the Dharmakaya and the Svabhavikakaya. I have instead usually treated them as one level (level 7/8), and called that level Atman, Spirit, the ultimate Whole, the superconscious All, ultimate unity consciousness, Godhead, occasionally "God" in an absolute sense, occasionally just Dharmakaya. The reason is that, although the differences between level 7 and level 8 are important and profound, they are altogether beyond the scope of this volume (I have, however, explained these differences in *The Atman Project*). Suffice it to say that the Dharmakaya is the asymptotic *limit* of the spectrum of consciousness, and the Svabhavika-kaya is the always prior and present *ground* of *every* level of the spectrum. The former is the Source of all levels, the latter is the Suchness (tathata) of all levels; the former is the highest of all levels, the latter is the Condition of all levels. But, as I said, for our simpler purposes, we can usually view them as one major "level," level 7/8, Atman, Godhead—which is both One and Many, Source and Suchness, Only and All.

Second, if we look historically at the use of the figures of the Great Goddess, God the Father, and the Void/Godhead, we find invariably that they seem to line up alongside the various levels of religious experience in a definite way. I am not going to press this point, but simply offer it for what it might be worth. For example, we have seen that the first insight into subtle Oneness was often represented by the Great Goddess, but that this insight was crude, initial, and still contaminated by polytheism; that is, still tied to lower levels in general and level 5 in particular. Even to this day, level-5 yogis worship pre-eminently the Great Goddess. The point is that the Great Goddess usually, and on the average, represented the *culmination* of level 5 and the *beginning* of level 6.

With the coming of the patriarchy, this subtle Oneness was seen more clearly in the form of monotheistic religions—Aton, Jehovah, etc. As the patriarchy itself matured—by the time of the middle egoic—this subtle One God was surpassed by the Void/Godhead, wherein "I and the Father are One." Thus the patriarchal God the Father represented the *culmination* of level 6 and the *beginning* of level 7.

We can summarize it all this way: *historically,* the Great Goddess begins in the Nirmanakaya and disappears into the Sambhogakaya; God the Father begins in the Sambhogakaya and disappears into the Dharmakaya; the Void/Godhead begins in the Dharmakaya and disappears into the Svabhavikakaya (and the Svabhavikakaya is the Ground and Condition of them all). Thus:

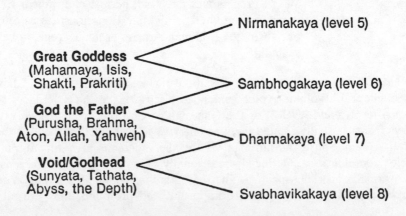

Nirmanakaya (level 5)

Great Goddess
(Mahamaya, Isis,
Shakti, Prakriti)

Sambhogakaya (level 6)

God the Father
(Purusha, Brahma,
Aton, Allah, Yahweh)

Dharmakaya (level 7)

Void/Godhead
(Sunyata, Tathata,
Abyss, the Depth)

Svabhavikakaya (level 8)

I am not saying religion necessarily evolves from Goddess to God the Father to Godhead; I am saying it evolves from Nirmanakaya to Sambhogakaya to Dharmakaya to Svabhavikakaya, but that *historically* the Goddess, God the Father, and the Godhead have typically aligned themselves with that hierarchic evolution in a recognizable and equally hierarchic fashion. That alignment might have been sexist, natural, accidental, or whatever. Since I have found these parallels to repeat themselves almost universally, I offer them as suggestive guides.

Finally, this hierarchy of religious experience—level 5 to 6 to 7 to 8—is not just a historically interesting movement. It has two other related meanings: one is the path of future evolution on the whole, the other is the path of present-day meditation. To take the latter first: a careful survey of reports of present-day meditation shows that advanced meditation discloses, in the same order, the very same higher structures† of consciousness first discovered in historical succession by the past *transcendent* heroes of the various epochs. That is, the person today (level 4) who begins and eventually completes a well-rounded meditation goes first into shamanistic intuition (5), then subtle oneness (6), then causal emptiness (7), then final and complete enlightenment (8).[11, 48, 59, 64, 67, 164, 226, 275, 430]

Second, because we are now *collectively* at the precise point in history (level 4) where the exoteric curve (1–4) is *starting* to run into the esoteric curve (5–8), our analysis suggests that future evolution on the whole will begin to run into the same higher structures first glimpsed, in successive fashion, by the esoteric heroes of past ages—and it will do so in the *same order*. If our analysis is generally correct, this fact will necessarily provide a most powerful, *general,* sociological prognosticative tool. And this analysis is supported, not just by the hierarchic ordering of past transcendent heroes, but also by the hierarchic disclosures of present-day meditators.

The point is just this: Future evolution on the whole (i.e., the average mode of consciousness) will likely follow the same hierarchic path first glimpsed, stage by stage, by the successive transcendent heroes of the past, *just as* meditation today follows the same hierarchic path, because what all three—past transcendent heroes, present-day meditators, and future evolution on the whole—are following is simply *the higher levels of the Great Chain of Being.*

We will return to this topic in later chapters and draw out some of its implications. My simple point here is that, in mapping out the higher stages and levels of consciousness, we have two very different sources of information: one is present-day accounts of the stages of advanced meditation, and one is the *historical* accounts of esoteric (most advanced or growing-tip) consciousness as it evolved and unfolded in its various stages in the transcendent heroes of the past. In *The Atman Project,* I suggested

---

† I.e., similar in deep structure, not necessarily (not even usually) in surface structure.

the stages of the former; in this volume, we have traced the stages of the latter. That the hierarchic stages of both are apparently quite similar in deep structure is, to me, a striking fact of no small consequence. *And,* if these two correlations hold up, it will strongly suggest that the third strand —future evolution on the whole—will follow the very same course in the very same order.

PATERNAL IMAGES

Finally, we have a small piece of unfinished business: in keeping with our policy of carefully differentiating average-mode consciousness from most advanced consciousness, we must address the existence of the average "paternal image" of the solar patriarchy and distinguish it from the conception of God the Father or even the Godhead itself. That is, just as we distinguished between magic and psychic (in typhonic times), between the Great Mother Image of biological dependence and the Great Goddess of subtle Oneness (in mythic times), so must we now carefully distinguish between the Paternal Image of cultural authority (in the egoic patriarchy) and the Progenitor Source (whether God the Father or the Godhead itself).

The basic Father Image itself arose as a simple correlate of *mental* existence, because "the fathers"—for reasons both sexist and natural—represented culture, mental communication, law, and authority. As we saw, the emergence of this solar-paternal-mental principle from the old chthonic deep was everywhere embodied and celebrated in the myth of the heroic ego triumphing over the Great Mother of the previous mythic age.

For the same reasons, individuals, both male and female, depended upon the fathers for the transmission of mental culture and mental security. And thus, in times of stress, the average individual naturally (but wishfully) had recourse to thoughts of a great father protector, a personal-god father.

No wonder that, during this period, cultural rituals and exoteric religious activities were geared toward "god the father." The whole exoteric religious atmosphere was a substitutive prostration to the "king of kings," "the shah of shahs," the "great ayatollah," the fetishistic father image who could promise (but not deliver) relief from guilt, mortality, and separate-self existence. No matter that there existed a truly transcendent Divinity, called "God the Father" (or higher yet, the "Godhead") by the actual saints and sages of this period. The fact is that the masses had little or no true understanding of subtle or causal Godhood, and thus they fell into mental manipulation of the *cultural father image,* but an image appropriately blown up to cosmic proportions as a Great Big Daddy who personally watches over egos. That is, although the great majority of early mental-egos prayed and prostrated to "god the father," most did so not as a direct path to Atman but as a new form of the Atman project, as an attempt to expiate guilt, secure immortality, gain boons, and veil the skull of death. Many immature egos, to this day, continue this same fetishistic practice, in the form of evangelicalism, proselytizing fury, political power plays, and so on.

The immediate impetus for this sprang primarily from the immense psychological impact of the father authority figure. That is to say—and I think there can be little doubt about this—the god of the masses (then and now) was a simple *projection of the paternal superego,* for, as Freud said, "I could not point to any need in childhood so strong as that for a father's protection." Thus, up to this point, the existence and function of the father-god has, like that of the biological mother-goddess and that of emotional magic, a more or less naturalistic explanation. And, up to this point, I agree entirely with those explanations, and am even willing to argue them against all alternative explanations.

But beyond that average, paternal, and egoic self, certain highly evolved sages had access to actual and ultimate realms of the superconscious, culminating in the Perfection of the Dharmakaya/Svabhavikakaya. Specifically, through various gnostic disciplines, the translations of the egoic level were superseded, the *death* of the ego was accepted, and transformation into superconsciousness began, a transformation intense enough that, if completed, resulted in either disclosure of or actual union with God. This is precisely why Buddha introduced the conception of *anatta,* which means "no ego" or "ego death," and made it *the* fundamental tenet of his system. Likewise Christ said that he who does not hate his own psyche, or ego, cannot be a true disciple. And the exact symbolic meaning of Christ's crucifixion was the crucifixion or death of the separate self, in all forms, followed by the Resurrection of ultimate unity consciousness (I and the Father are One) and the Ascension to radical release in and as Godhead.

For various reasons, mostly metaphorical, the saints and sages often spoke of these higher realms as "God the Father" or "the Godhead," the idea being, as Kant would put it, that as a father is to his sons and daughters, so the Absolute is to all humans. But it does not follow that because some sages, such as Christ, Eckhart, or Teresa, spoke of "God the Father," this was merely a projection of the superego. It does not follow because, if this were true, there could be no difference between Christ or Krishna or Buddha and any average egoic self caught in simple parental projection. But since, whatever else may be said, there is a *structural* difference between Buddhas and egos, the reductionistic argument collapses. The obvious conclusion is that there is a radical difference between the mental father figure (level 4) and the Transcendent God or Godhead (level 6 or 7), and the two can be confused only by ignoring the incredibly complex subtleties involved, subtleties which this book—and countless others—have attempted to explain.

While we may be wrong, it cannot be so established on the basis of reducing Buddhistic/Christic vision to a parental superego projection, since the two have radically different structures (finite vs. infinite, mental vs. causal, temporal vs. eternal, large vs. dimensionless, individual vs. selfless, etc.). Yet that reductionistic argument is the *only* one that has been advanced; it is also the *only* one that *can* be advanced within a scientistic, physicalistic, empiricistic framework (in order to "account" for the universal conception of a Transcendent Source). However, since that argument has totally collapsed, the field is now open to properly transcendent interpretations. That is, with the collapse of reductionism, there isn't a respectable intellectual challenge to the perennial-philosophical interpretation. Yet all scienticians, such as Sagan, Monod, etc., implicitly (and unconsciously) assume the Freudian-reductionistic argument, without the slightest chance of being able to prove it. That is, when asked, *"Why* the universal announcements, from Christ to Buddha to Lao Tzu, of an ultimate Transcendent Ground?" they answer instantly in Freudian, wishful, and projective explanations, violating and collapsing the structural differences they are asked to explain.

As a type of summary, we can put together all the various "mythos figures" that we have examined in this volume, from the lowest to the highest, as shown in Fig. 35.

As we earlier said, the esoteric and exoteric modes and images definitely interact, especially sociologically. Not only did many sages metaphorically speak of "God the Father" *because* this was the patriarchy; their pronouncements reciprocally (but not necessarily intentionally) supported and reinforced the patriarchy. When the mystic sages spoke of "God the Father," or "I and the Father are One," or "Purusha (male-father Creator) is the ultimate," and so on, it was instantly reduced to ordinary dimensions and everyday symbols by the masses of egoic listeners, and thus was funneled into the typical egoic self, where it merely reinforced the paternal superego. Our Father in Heaven illicitly tended merely to support our father, despotic and sexist king of his castle.

This tended as well to support and reinforce many types of oppression (economic, sexual, communicative), because the ruling cultural fathers claimed (as many today still do) the authority of the actual God the Father (or true Transcendent Source), when, of course, they had no such imprimatur at all. But by claiming the divine authority of transcendent God, the cultural fathers were more easily able to support their own political authority and political ambitions—they played off the fears and the pa-

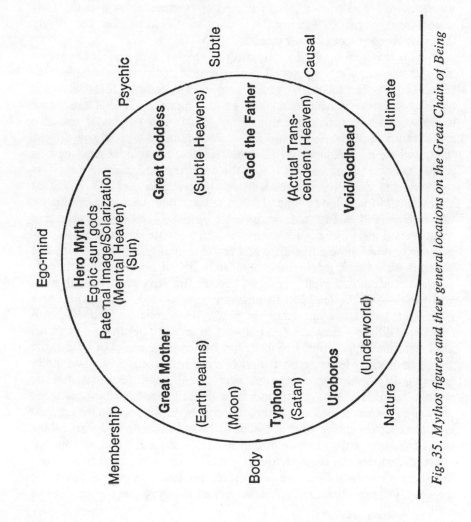

Fig. 35. Mythos figures and their general locations on the Great Chain of Being

ternal projections of the egoic masses, catering to those fears *and* reinforc-
ing them by setting the stakes in a Cosmic Framework, "the divine right of
kings." And this political authority, as scholars from Reich to Marcuse
have explained, was an authority stamped into the paternal superego of
each and every citizen from birth, simply because the superego was then
forged in an atmosphere of political domination. As Reich put it, ideology
was anchored in character structure. And so it came about that the conscience of the superego was not the true voice of God in man, but merely
the internalized voices of other men.

It is my strongest hope—if I may end this chapter with a short editorial—
that, as the male once rescued consciousness from the chthonic matriarchate, the female might today help rescue consciousness—and her
brother—from the patriarchate. And as the innate but initial masculine
mode seemed appropriate for the former, the innate but initial feminine
mode seems appropriate for the latter. We of today face a new dragon
fight, and we need a new Hero Myth. The dragon we now must fight is
simply the egoic structure itself, and the new "treasure hard to attain" is
centauric and psychic awareness (or simply level 5 in general). And that
attainment will take a new type of Hero, a Hero that, centuries from now,
will be eulogized as I have done the solar ego. We need today to develop
intuition and alert but passive awareness, as we yesterday needed so des-
perately to develop assertive logic and active mentality. The new Hero will
be centauric (which means mind and body united and not dissociated),
whole-bodied, mentally androgynous, psychic, intuitive *and* rational, male
and female—and the lead in this new development most easily can come
from the female, since our society is *already* masculine-adapted. But until
males stop killing themselves (and others) in order to be strong and silent;
until females stop encouraging just that behavior as evidence of a "true
man"; until chauvinists settle their accounts with their own masculinity
and stop defensively exploiting their sisters; until angry feminists stop, on
the one hand, reactivating chthonic "female only" matriarchal obsessions
and, on the other, trying to co-op patriarchal obnoxiousness; until feminist
intellectuals stop asking what it means to be truly female and start asking
instead what it means to be neither male nor female but whole and human
—then the patriarchy, the mental-ego, which has served its necessary, useful, but intermediate function, and which, for that, we have much to be
thankful, will nevertheless soon prove, quite literally, to be the death of us
all.

15 On Becoming a Person

EXCHANGE DISTORTION

We have seen that the human being is a *compound individual,* compounded of matter, prana, verbal-membership, ego, soul, and spirit. The material body is exercised in labor; the pranic body is exercised in breath, sex, and feeling; the verbal-membership mind is exercised in communication (and the beginning of praxis); the ego, in mutual personal recognition and exchange of esteem (the culmination of praxis); the soul, in psychic and subtle transcendence; the spirit, in absolute absorption in Atman.* That is, each level of the compound human individual is exercised in a complex system of ideally unobstructed exchanges with the corresponding levels of the world process at large.

Furthermore, humanity actually and literally *reproduces* itself on each level by an appropriate exchange of the elements of that level. Humanity reproduces itself materially through the exchange of food secured by physical (technic) labor from the natural environment. It reproduces itself bio-

---

* Because, by this point in history, only the first four levels had emerged on a large scale, we will largely, but not entirely, limit our discussion in this chapter to just those first four levels; the interested reader can extrapolate, beyond our discussion, to the higher levels, since the same principles are involved.

logically via breath and sex. It reproduces itself culturally via verbal or symbolic communication, and so on.

But all of these levels are not *manifest* in individual humans from birth. Rather, the human compound individual *begins* its growth and development by adjusting to the physical world, then to the emotional world, then the verbal, then the self-reflexive, and so on (until growth stops in its case).[436] While these developments often parallel or overlap one another, nonetheless each is built upon, and rests upon, the foundation afforded by its immediately junior level.

Thus the higher rests upon the lower—but the higher is *not* caused by or constituted by the lower.[375, 435] The higher does not come *from* the lower; it comes *from* the ground unconscious *via* the lower.[436] The mind, for instance, emerges from the ground unconscious by way of the body, and only eventually learns to differentiate itself from and thus transcend the body. This differentiation would be impossible if the mind were merely constituted *by* the body. The higher could not transcend the lower, i.e., could not be higher, if it were only an arrangement *of* the lower. To maintain otherwise is to embrace the reductionistic fallacy.

And because the higher *does* transcend the lower, the higher can "repress" the lower. For example, sex cannot easily repress sex, but mind *can* repress sex, simply because mind is more than sex and higher than sex and can thus "come down on" sex.

Now the capacity for repression (defense mechanisms in general) exists to one degree or another on almost every level of the spectrum, but it doesn't become really extensive until the verbal-membership level, and it doesn't become truly "powerful" until the egoic level.[126, 139] For our simplified purposes, I will usually assume that truly "powerful" repression issues basically from the mental-ego—we have, for instance, seen that the European dissociation, the repression of the body-global by mind, didn't occur on a large scale until the middle egoic period.

To say that the higher can repress and distort the lower might make it appear that the lower has no capacity to distort the higher. In one sense, it is true that, for example, sex cannot repress mind. But the lower can "infect" the higher in two basic ways: (1) It can, as it were, erupt and thus disrupt higher functioning. (2) If the lower is fundamentally distorted itself, it can partially pass on this distortion to the higher. The first point is fairly self-evident; the second occurs as follows:

Because the lower tends to emerge first in development, a distorted lower *inclines* the higher to subsequently reproduce the distortion in its own domain. That is, since the higher emerges from the ground unconscious *through* the lower, then if the lower is distorted, it inclines the higher to similar distortion (through what we might call "emergent contamination"). Because the higher both comes through and then rests upon the foundation of the lower, a "tilt" in the first floor tends to cause a similar "tilt" in the second, and so on. But this is not an absolute causality: not only is the lower distortion only partially passed on, but the higher level, by virtue of its transcendence, can often redress the imbalance.† More often than not, however, a distortion in the lower predisposes the higher to similar distortions or, at the very least, predisposes the higher to spend much of its time overcompensating for the lower defect (e.g., Adler's "organ inferiority," masculine protest, etc.).

But now we reach a dilemma. We said that an individual human being generally develops level 1, then 2, then 3, then 4, etc. We said the distortions of a lower level (say, level 2) could be passed on to a higher level (to 3, then 4, etc.). But we also said that the capacity to distort and repress the lower levels doesn't "powerfully" exist *until* the egoic level (4). How, then, could level 2 pass on its distortions to level 4 if level 2 isn't distorted until after level 4 exists?

In part, the answer is simple: once the ego emerges, it can repress and distort the lower levels, and these distortions then "boomerang" back to the ego. The ego can cripple its foundation, which then tends to cripple the ego. Also, to temporarily break out of our generalization, the lower levels *can* be distorted by factors other than the ego: environmental deprivations, severe and repeated trauma, crude types of self-repression, early defense mechanisms (as outlined by psychoanalytic ego psychology), and so on.

But the other part of the answer is more intriguing: we said that the mental-ego is the primary instigator of powerful repression. And so, obviously, until the ego emerges in a particular individual (e.g., as long as the individual is still an infant or young child), that individual will only be open to lesser and cruder forms of self-induced repressions. However, even though this individual (child) does not yet possess an egoic structure, it is surrounded by, and brought up by, individuals who *do* possess *egos*. And these egos *can* distort and oppress the exchange functions of the lower levels in the as yet egoless individual. And thus, when the ego does eventually emerge in this individual, it *will emerge upon foundations already distorted by the egos in its environment,* and will partially reproduce those distortions in its own domain.

This doesn't mean one individual can directly *repress* another. It means one individual can *oppress* another. This oppression has several consequences, which we will explore in this chapter; two of them are: (1) the oppression can distort the lower levels in the oppressed, so that when the mental-ego emerges, it emerges through and on a fractured foundation;

† Thus, e.g., a distortion in the third level most immediately affects the fourth, less so the fifth, even less the sixth, and so on. Not only is each subsequent level further removed from the original distortion, it has more opportunity to redress the original distortion. But all levels (except 7/8) can be distorted, and the closer one level is to a distortion in a lower level, the more likely it is to reproduce it.

(2) the mental-ego, as it emerges in the atmosphere of oppression, can it-self *internalize* the originally external oppression, and internalized oppres-sion *then* leads to repression.

This does not mean all repression has its source in oppression. The situ-ation is much more complex than that. Most significantly, when the new ego emerges, it emerges ready and anxious to repress itself in an effort to avoid death and Thanatos. *All levels do this to one degree or another,* but, to keep with our generalization, this self-repression reaches "powerful" proportions with the ego. *Most* egoic repressions are self-repressions. The ego will create and suffer repression even in the most idyllic surroundings, simply because *all* egos are in flight from death and must repress death. Nonetheless, when specific oppressions are *added to* this fundamental self-repression, then the ego suffers *surplus repression.* And so we amend our formula: internalized oppression is surplus repression.

It works like this: The mental-ego, we saw, contains an important com-ponent called the "superego," or the "internalized parents." According to standard theory, the superego itself is composed of the ego-ideal and the conscience. The ego-ideal contains all the positive injunctions, goals, de-sires, rules, and assertions forged by the young ego in its *relationship* with verbal significant others (especially the patriarchal authority figure). This includes a *network of permissions* as to what one may think (mind), feel (emotion), and do (physical) *in order to keep this desired relationship.* To follow the injunctions is to feel *pride.*[436]

On the other side, the conscience is composed of all the negative com-mands and prohibitions forged by the young ego in its relationship with verbal significant others (especially the patriarchal authority figure). This includes a *network of taboos* as to what one may *not* think, feel, or do. To violate the taboos is to *violate the relationship* with the significant other, and thus to experience *guilt.*[436]

Thus, the originally *external* relationships between the young ego and significant others become *internalized structures* of the ego itself—that is (in part) the superego, the ego-ideal, and conscience.[262, 263] And these in-ternalized relationships, injunctions, and taboos, are then carried every-where by the ego, as part of its makeup, whether the significant other is actually watching or not, present or not, even alive or not.[36] The parent—especially, at this historical point, the patriarchal father—becomes an internal structure of the ego. Thus the paternal superego.

Now the ego will, as we said, automatically instigate a fair amount of repression entirely on its own. But a harsh superego will simply compound the problem. That is, harsh parental (societal) oppression, when in-ternalized, will lead the ego to extra repression, surplus repression. That is, any impulse, thought, or activity deemed taboo by the internalized su-perego will be repressed, alienated, dissociated—and that is *surplus* repres-sion, repression over and beyond that which the particular ego would, by itself, find necessary to instigate. In this fashion, a person who is a member of an oppressive society—who is "in" that society—eventually finds that that society is now "in" him, and he then perpetuates on his own person just those alienations originally external to him. In this fashion the sins of the mothers and fathers are visited on the daughters and sons, "even unto the third and fourth generations." There is, for example, no doubt that the paternal superego, with an excessive burden of guilt and body-taboo, contributed to the European dissociation.

In Chapter 9 we saw that with the rise of polis, the various levels of being could be externally *oppressed*. Here, we see that with the rise of the mind (membership and especially egoic), the various levels of being can be internally *repressed*. These are *correlative* potentials for distortions in and of the human compound being, and they cross paths most noticeably, but not solely, at the superego, where the internalization of society's oppression leads the individual to surplus repression.

SOME RECONSTRUCTIONS

Here are our generalizations so far: (1) the higher comes *through* the lower but not *from* the lower; (2) a distorted lower *inclines* the higher to reproduce similar distortions in its own sphere; (3) but does not absolutely *cause* the higher to reproduce the distortions (the higher can to some degree reverse, amend, compensate, etc.); (4) the individual can defensively *repress* or distort, to one degree or another, any or all of his own levels of exchange (physical, emotional, mental, etc.);‡ (5) an exter-

‡ As I said, this can occur, to one degree or another, on all levels, but it becomes particularly "strong" with the ego/superego. I.e., there can be surplus repression on lower levels, but it is crude and weak in comparison with egoic. As for defenses, I have in mind precisely the hierarchy of defenses outlined by psychoanalytic ego psychology: denial, introjection/projection, undoing, reaction formation, conversion, identification, displacement, repression (proper), rationalization. That hierarchy of defenses fits perfectly the first four levels of being, starting with the alimentary uroboros (denial, introjection/projection) and ending with the ego/superego (repression [proper], rationalization). All of those defenses are first and foremost *self-induced defenses*, but *all* of them can be surplus-induced by oppressive/traumatic environments, by simple role-modeling of alienated parents or peers, by operant conditioning, and so on.

In my opinion, there are only two major problems with the psychoanalytic theory of defenses. First, of course, it leaves out all the higher levels of being, and thus leaves out as well all the defenses against the higher levels (the ego defends against transcendence as strongly as it defends against the id). Second, psychoanalytic theory fails to grasp that each level of the human compound individual possesses a boundary

nal (powerful) other can *oppress* and distort an individual's levels of exchange; (6) internalized oppression is surplus repression. These generalizations are all we need to reconstruct the essentials of such theorists as Marx and Freud without their reductionistic tendencies. Let me give a few brief and simplified examples:

Marx's central investigations always centered on, to use his words, "relations of production appropriate to a given stage in the development of the material forces of production. The totality of these relations of production constitutes the . . . real foundation [of society]."[292] That is, Marx was interested first and foremost in the various forms of the exchanges of level 1, or matter—exchanges centering on material production, food, capital, land, property, economic activity, and physical labor. And Marx concluded that "the mode of production of material life conditions the general process of social, political and mental life."[292]

In particular, Marx felt that economic *exploitation,* in one form or another, meant an *alienation* of natural labor, and that the alienation of labor produced an alienation of thought and feeling—produced what Marx called "false consciousness."

This is most easily understood from the popular writers on Marxist thought, especially when they touch on the topics of oppression and exploitation. In a sense, Rousseau was one of the first "Marxists" when he stated: "The first who, having fenced off a plot of ground, took it into his head to say *this is mine* and found people simple enough to believe him, was the true founder of civil society"[358]—but "society" in a "bad" sense (notice he says "*simple* enough," i.e., stupid enough). The point, as Becker puts it, is that "primitive equality was ended by private property, which led to the differential personal ownership of wealth."[26] Thus, as Robinson notes, "for Hegel as for Marx, the historical fact of alienation was directly linked to the institution [and exploitation] of private property. In the *Philosophy of Right* Hegel had expounded in thoroughly Marxian fashion the connection between capital accumulation and the

---

or interface, and that introjection and projection can and do occur across the boundaries of *any* level. That is, introjection/projection, while certainly characteristic of the oral-uroboros, is not *just* uroboric. Introjection/projection is not simply a primitive and low form of defense; it is cross-level, universal to the levels of the hierarchy, not to one stage of the hierarchy. The failure to grasp this point forces psychoanalysis to say that *all* internalizations are regressions to the oral stage, which is simply not the case. This confusion occurs because psychoanalysis takes the skin boundary of the organism as *the* fundamental boundary, whereas it is merely the most visible. There are emotional boundaries, membership boundaries, egoic boundaries, psychic boundaries, etc., and *each* supports traffic in internalization (introjection) and alienation (projection). And while, for example, a few of the mental-egoic introjects are regressive (aspects of the superego, e.g.), the vast majority are not. I think any analyst will tell you that the psychoanalytic theories on introjection/internalization/identification are the most confused in the field (all the other defenses are fairly well worked out), and the above, in my opinion, is precisely why.

growing impoverishment of the workers, culminating in the rise of a 'vast industrial army.' "[351] For "these new states were structures of domination which absorbed the tribal life around them and built up empires. Masses of men were forged into obedient tools for really large-scale power operations directed by a powerful, exploitative class. It was at this time that [individuals] were firmly compartmentalized into various special skills which they plied monotonously; they became automaton objects of the tyrannical rulers."[26]

Now humans as "automaton objects," *adjusted* to a social reality that is oppressive and false, is approximately what Marx meant by "false consciousness" and "alienated individuals." The point is that *if physical exchange is distorted* (through massive and undeserved private property for the few, through the concentration of vast amounts of money, capital, goods, etc., in the hands of a rich elite, and so on), *it forms a distressed base upon which feeling and thinking are built* (in both rich and poor alike, although, of course, in drastically different directions: the poor toward impoverishment, the rich toward decadence). And as feeling and thinking *adjust* to that false base, as levels 2 and 3/4 equilibrate to the distortions in level 1, they tend to reproduce that falseness in their own spheres. Thus, as a simple example, the *mentality* of the savagely poor tends toward depression; the rich, toward elitism.* In general, philosophy caught in this trap produces what Marx called "ideology"—philosophy which springs from, and reinforces, oppression and exploitation and nonemancipation. This led Marx to the famous statement that whereas most philosophers merely think about the world, the real need is to change it.

The point is that physical exploitation does not simply deprive one of appropriate material exchange, but tends, often profoundly, to mold the shape of senior levels in the compound human individual. *Upon alienated*

---

* To be more precise, we can view the Great Chain in terms of Maslow's needs hierarchy, and then put the point this way: (1) Material exchange distortion—the excessive concentration of material goods in the hands of a few—deprives the poor of satisfying physiological and safety needs, and this *holds* their consciousness to the lower levels; at the same time, it allows the rich to exploit and overindulge those needs—a degenerate and decadent use of the material level which, ironically, also tends to hold *their* consciousness fixated in the lower realms, but in a reverse way. (2) These *material* distortions—in rich and poor alike—then tend to reproduce themselves on higher levels, but again in reverse ways. In the poor oppressed, this reproduction leads to thoughts and feelings of depressive helplessness, hatred or bitterness, low self-esteem, etc. In the rich elite, it leads to thoughts and feelings of overblown, undeserved, and unrealistic self-esteem, to imperialism, elitism, socialitism, etc. (Please remember that all of these are tendencies, not causalities.)

The point is that *both* rich and poor alike are alienated by distorted material exchange. Obviously so the poor; but also the rich, who, in resting their material affluence on the necessary deprivations of others, sever themselves from the moral totality of mankind and set in motion that "causality of fate," described by Hegel, where the alienation from others results inexorably in the alienation of self.

labor tends to emerge alienated feelings and thoughts (in both rich and poor alike). And that, I think, is one of Marx's enduring insights.

There are, however, four central inadequacies to general Marxist theory. First, there is an over-commitment to materialism (taken from Feuerbach), which leads Marx to see history as almost nothing but the unfolding of material forces ("dialectical materialism") aiming at undistorted and unobstructed material exchange, free of obsessive private property and material exploitation. While that is probably (and hopefully) true enough for level 1, it has only a slight direct bearing on the motivations of level 2, less so on level 3, even less on level 4, etc. (It is important on these levels, but only insofar as they are contaminated by distortions from the lower.) But to reduce history to dialectical materialism is to reduce the Great Chain of Being to level 1.

Second, this materialistic over-commitment often predisposes Marx to the notion that the lowest level of being—food, matter, economic labor, and production—doesn't just influence the higher levels (of mind, philosophy, and religion), but causes and creates them. Hence his oft-quoted statement to the effect that it is not the consciousness of men that determines their existence, but their material and economic existence that determines their consciousness. He doesn't see that the higher comes through the lower and is thus often affected by it: he thinks that the higher comes *from* the lower and is causally produced by it.

Third, Marx often fails to understand that the effects of material distortions can, although with some difficulty, be largely overcome at and by a higher level. As a crude example, think of the number of individuals under severe material oppression that have risen above these distortions to produce enduring and even brilliant philosophical/mental insights (not to mention spiritual breakthroughs): Homer, for one (some say he was a slave, and blind as well); Marx, for another (he lived in bitter poverty most of his life). This is in no way to condone exploitation; it only goes to show that material production does not absolutely, not even pre-eminently, determine consciousness.

Fourth, if traditional Marxism understands well the brutality of outward oppression, it gives scant heed to the more profound mechanics and brutality of the internal demand for oppression. It is ridiculous to suggest that, in such extreme cases of exploitation as literal slavery, the victim is secretly responsible. But in so many lesser and more subtle forms of exploitation, the oppressed are indeed "in love with their chains." The Frankfurt school—aided by psychoanalytic insight—spent its early years redressing just that imbalance, and showing that, in many aspects of oppression, the oppressed secure their own chains and hand the key to their future oppressors—"the hidden unconscious tie," said Marcuse, "which binds the oppressed to their oppressors."[351] Now we have already discussed the reasons for this in Chapter 9, and we needn't repeat what was said. The point, simply, is that the self is *already* anxious to repress itself, and since the internalization of oppression helps produce extra repression, the self is *partially* a willing victim from the start. Take, then, as a sharp summary, the following from Marcuse: "There is such a thing as the Self [which is, for us, Atman]—it does not yet exist [or has not yet emerged in collective consciousness] but it must be attained, fought for against all those who are preventing its emergence and who *substitute* for it an *illusory self* [the substitute subject], namely, the subject of voluntary servitude in production and consumption, the subject of free election of masters."[282]

So much for our simplistic reconstruction of Marx. But material oppression, as chronicled by Marx, is not the sole means of manipulation and exploitation, whether internally or externally imposed: it is merely the most ontologically primitive and therefore the most visible. The "next level up" in the compound individual is that of emotional-sexuality, and there, too, distortions and scars can be inflicted, by oneself and by others, with equally profound repercussions.

This, of course, was Freud's great province: the distortions of sexuality. However, he tended to the same type of reductionism as Marx. But where Marx saw level 1 (matter) as all-encompassing, and made material production paradigmatic,† Freud saw level 2: only the id (prana) is *fundamental,* and *from* it come all higher and mental structures. Sex, for Freud, was paradigmatic.‡ From the id, via repression, sublimation, etc., come ego, psyche, and civilization. The same error we saw in Marx: theoret-

† I.e., Marx made food paradigmatic.

‡ Freud was indeed interested in levels 3 and 4, but he tended to make level 2 paradigmatic (he collapsed levels 1 and 2 as one level, the id; he was, however, aware of their separate existence, because his first two instincts were hunger and love, or oral-uroboros and typhon-sex; or again, his self-preservation instincts—food—and species-preservation instincts—sex). Although level 2 was paradigmatic for Freud, he eventually lessened this reductionistic "libido psychology" with the tentative introduction of "ego psychology" (in *The Ego and the Id*), although it was really Anna Freud's *Ego and the Mechanisms of Defense* and then Hartmann's *Ego Psychology and the Problem of Adaptation* that began to turn the reductionistic tide—and, incidentally, to simultaneously rob psychoanalysis of its perverse shock value. Early psychoanalysis was so much "fun"—"Wait 'til they hear what we have to tell them!" exclaimed Freud on his first visit to America—simply because, like a naughty little boy, it tried to see something "dirty" under every mental and cultural production, and succeeded nicely until the reductionism itself became flagrantly self-contradictory, and the higher levels were slowly, but begrudgingly, readmitted—a concession Freud was almost bitter about. No more fun. . . .

Incidentally, the same thing happened to Marxist theory. Marxist theory was shocking and novel—it was "fun"—only if it could claim that all higher levels came preeminently from material/economic exchanges. The early Marxists even accused the Freudians of ideology, believe it or not, because the Freudians reduced everything only to level 2 and didn't go all the way to level 1! But when Marx and Engels thought their position through more carefully, they necessarily began to waver and say that higher levels (mind, philosophy, religion) were only strongly influenced by material exchange. They consequently lost their shocking and novel edge—rightly so, but it did take the fun out of it. And, of course, it left the Marxist system in a shambles: it's like saying, "Everything but everything comes from level 1. Sort of."

ically squeezing and twisting the lower in hopes of extracting the higher.

The fact is that, as the membership mind emerges from the ground unconscious, it emerges *via* the emotional-body (id) and then "rests" upon it. Thus emotional urges do indeed "underlie" mind and culture, as Freud said; they do not, however, cause or produce them. And because mind and culture are not produced by a repression or twisting of emotional-sexuality, then, as Reich and Marcuse would soon point out in their own (quite different) ways, *Culture as such is not incompatible with sexuality.*"351

Nevertheless, because the membership mind does emerge via emotional-sexuality, the mind can be "scarred" by distortions in the sexual sphere, and these distortions are indeed frequently (but not solely) induced by an oppressive society and then internalized as a surplus repression. That is, oppressive (and internalized repressive) distortions *in emotional intercourse* can partially reproduce themselves in communicative intercourse. In short, upon distorted emotionality *tends* to rest false membership.

Finally, let us simply suggest—without elaborate explanation—that membership itself can be internally distorted and repressed as well as externally strained and oppressed; and further, the internalization of this oppression leads to surplus repression. The result of any of these falsifications is the distortion of communicative exchange, the distortion of membership, the crippling of praxis. Go to the next level: upon this distorted, alienated, and false membership tends to rest fraudulent self-esteem or false ego (although, like all higher levels, the ego can to some degree reverse or overcome the distortions of lower levels in general, including, in this case, membership). Bateson's work on double binds, as well as the whole theoretical stance of "communication psychiatry," offers much evidence on how distorted membership tends to induce and support fraudulent ego.23, 359

Lastly, the ego itself, whether initially false or not, can likewise be repressed, oppressed, and/or surplus-repressed. The result is ego-splitting, the dissociation of ego into persona vs. shadow, or the simple division of personality (seen most dramatically in multiple personality neuroses, although similar if milder dissociations occur in almost all character disorders). In general, the result is a distortion of the exchanges of self-esteem, egoic integrity, and accurate self-recognition.

And so proceed the various types of exchange distortions that can occur *on every level** of the compound individual by virtue of its living in a compound society: self-repression, external oppression, and internalized surplus repression.

But the notion of egoic "self-esteem" and mutual self-recognition, which I just introduced, leads us directly to our next topic.

* Except 7/8.

A REAL PERSON

We mentioned, in Chapter 9, that with the emergence of the mental-egoic structure (historically and ontogenetically), a *new level of exchange* comes into being: the mutual exchange of self-recognition, whose paradigm is reflexive self-consciousness, and whose sphere is mutual personal esteem.

This, of course, is a decisive and far-reaching development, a development that *historically* began during the low-egoic period and came tentatively into its own during the middle-egoic.† But instead of extensively discussing this development as it unfolded historically, we need only point to the works of Hegel and Habermas (specifically, Habermas' reconstruction of Hegel), because in their various writings they have already established a formidable theoretical foundation for precisely those points which seem to me so significant. Although we can only mention a few of these points in this short section, it should be said that I consider the Habermas/Hegelian reconstruction to be absolutely essential to an understanding, not only of this period in history, but more importantly of this entire level of exchange as it today emerges and lives itself out in the ontogenetic development and maturation of the human compound individual. That level is, of course, the level of egoic esteem and exchange of mutual self-recognition based upon communication free of domination and distortion.

In this section I will briefly mention four of the basic points of the Habermas/Hegelian position (as I would reconstruct it) most pertinent to our present discussion.

The first is the insight that "the identity of self-consciousness is not an original one, but can only be conceived as one that has developed."[292] While that might today seem an obvious point, no philosopher prior to Hegel understood it. That developmental view is, of course, the backbone of our own presentation.

The second point is that egoic self-esteem is actually a *system of mutual exchange;* it is not a self-contained act of invulnerability; even less is it a securing of narcissistic feelings, as maintained by Freudians. For one cannot gain egoic self-esteem without others, and it is actually the *exchange* of esteem with others that *constitutes* true self-esteem. That is, true self-es-

---

† L. L. Whyte on this historical period: "The attention of the individual was drawn more and more to his own thought as well as to external stimuli, and he became aware of himself as a thinking and feeling person endowed with the faculty of choice . . . he had to become aware of himself as a person."[426]

teem proceeds "on the basis of mutual recognition—namely, on the basis
of the knowledge that the identity of the 'I' is possible solely through the
identity of the other who recognizes me, and who in turn is dependent
upon my recognition."292

Self-esteem, in fact, is the *opposite* of "self-assertion," for "self-assertion severs itself from the moral totality," it revokes and denies "the complementarity of unconstrained communication and the mutual satisfaction
of interests." And the one who *severs* this *exchange process* experiences
"in the repression of the lives of others the deficiency of his own life, and
in his turning away from the lives of others his own alienation from himself." The conclusion: "Personal identity can be achieved only on the
basis of mutual recognition"292—and there is our next-higher level of exchange (level 4).

The third point is that mutual recognition and communicative exchange
cannot be reduced to lower levels, as empiricists, Marxists, Freudians,
scienticians, etc., attempt. Habermas makes this point by carefully distinguishing between what we would call level 1/2—nature, labor, the body,
property, techne, etc.—and level 3/4—communication, praxis, language,
interaction, mutual self-recognition, etc.177 On this distinction Habermas
demonstrates sharp differences in epistemology, methodology, and structures of cognitive interest:

> Habermas develops this distinction [between 1/2 and 3/4] at a
> number of levels. At a "quasi-transcendental" level, the theory of
> cognitive interests distinguishes the technical interest in prediction
> and control of objectified processes [1/2] from the practical interest
> in maintaining distortion-free communication [3/4]. At a methodo-
> logical level, a distinction is drawn between empirical-analytic inquiry
> [suited only to 1/2] and hermeneutic or critical inquiry [which
> specifically takes as "object" 3/4]. At the sociological level, subsys-
> tems of purposive-rational action are distinguished from the institu-
> tional framework in which they are embedded. And at the level of so-
> cial evolution, the growth in productive forces and technological
> capacity [level 1] is distinguished from the extension of interaction
> free from domination [3/4].292

In simpler terms, when Habermas says that praxis cannot be reduced to
techne, that hermeneutics cannot be reduced to empirical-analytic inquiry,
that symbolic interaction cannot be reduced to work-labor, that communicative exchanges cannot be reduced to material exchanges—all of that
is simply to say that level 3/4 cannot be reduced to level 1/2—mind cannot be reduced to body.

The fourth point is that the lower levels nevertheless form the substratum for the higher exchanges, and thus interact and interconnect with

them. To give only one example, we will limit our discussion to physical labor (level 1) and personal self-esteem (level 4). The Habermas/Hegelian point is that as mutual personal recognition is first formally stabilized, it is stabilized upon the substructure of labor and property. (In my view, it is stabilized upon *all* the lower levels, 1–3, but we are limiting this example to level 1 exchanges and their influences upon the newly emergent personal ego of level 4.)

Thus, in this example, "Hegel establishes an interconnection between labor [level 1] and interaction [mutual recognition, level 3 but especially level 4] by way of 'the legal norms, on which social intercourse based on mutual recognition is first formally stabilized.' The institutionalization of mutual recognition between *legal persons* is a matter of 'individuals recognizing each other as proprietors in the possessions produced by their labor or acquired by trade.' "[292] In other words, *legal* or institutional/conventional recognition of, and respect for, egoic *personhood* was interrelated with, and initially (but not solely) built upon, private property and the recognition of private property. "Thus the possessions arising from the labor process [level 1] function as [a] substratum of legal recognition [of personhood]."[292]

The point is that "the exchange of equivalents [level 1 possessions], formally institutionalized in the [legal] contract, becomes the model for the reciprocity on which interaction [exchange of mutual egoic recognition] is based. In this way the result of the 'struggle for [personal] recognition,' the *legally recognized self-consciousness*, incorporates the results of the labor process by which we free ourselves from the immediate dictates of nature."[292] Notice that that is a point we have made with *every* level of consciousness: each successive level includes but transcends, incorporates and goes beyond, all its predecessors. It is no surprise, then, that Hegel and Habermas maintain that the egoic exchange of mutual self-recognition *"incorporates* the results of the labor process by which we *free ourselves from* [or transcend] the immediate dictates of nature."

With these thoughts in mind, I want now to leave the specific points of the Habermas/Hegelian reconstruction, but tie their central features into the historical developments which began to occur during the newly emergent egoic period.

As it was only by law that nonviolent recognition and protection of *property* existed, so it was by social-legal convention that aggravated violation of *personhood* was prohibited. No more need goods be owned merely by the strongest, most aggressive, or most apelike, for a legal person had a legal right to own the goods that resulted from his own physical exchanges (or were secondarily acquired by trade). And this meant that individuals *had* to mutually *recognize* each other in an exchange of esteem if the law were not to be violated. A *person* had *property,* and the respect of property demanded the recognition and respect of personhood.‡ And neither persons nor legalized property existed much before the egoic period.[85, 215, 252, 417]

The available evidence clearly suggests that, beginning in the low-egoic period, and concretizing in the middle-egoic, the father (this is still the patriarchy) became the first significant and widespread owner of personal property.[26] And the father's property was protected, not by his muscles, but by a *corporate consciousness* embodied in law.[292] The king no longer "owned the world"—the individual father, as "king of his castle," wrestled back some of his property from the warlord.

Likewise—and more important—the father, legally possessing property, became for the first time in history a *legal person,* a "legally recognized self-consciousness" or ego.[26] This meant, first, that individual self-consciousness—the heroic ego which evolution had labored so long and hard to produce—was recognized and protected by rights of law, and all who recognized law recognized personal self-consciousness and entered into a mutual exchange of that consciousness. And second, a legal person was one who could not rightfully become a *slave,* or the material *property* of another person. Put differently, a legal person was, among other things, his *own property.* As Locke would soon put it, "Every man has a property in his own person." Or, in today's slang, every person could be his own self.

In short, each legal person, each egoic "I," both was his own property, his own self or "me," and could own appropriate external property, or "mine." That is, *each "I" had its own "me" and "mine."* I realize that to those spiritually oriented, this seems very egotistical and self-centered; but we must remember that evolution was just now moving up from the prepersonal toward the personal, from the animal and subhuman to the individual and personal, and egoic "I-me-mine" was a necessary correlate of this evolution ("I-me-mine" disappears in superconsciousness, but only *after* it has served its intermediate purpose).

The point is that consciousness was heroically struggling to break free from its infantile embeddedness in instinctual nature, struggling to rise above that domain where "dog eat dog" establishes ownership and where "might makes right" establishes ape law. What was deplorable, but perhaps initially unavoidable, was not that egoic "I-me-mine" became legally recognized, respected, and protected, but that this right was not extended to more people. Not that father was a person, but that mother wasn't; not that father was legally protected, but that slaves weren't—there was the tragedy. This tragedy is corrected, not by depriving some of personhood, but by first extending personhood to all.

‡ Fichte: "The right of exclusive possession is brought into being through *mutual recognition:* and it does not exist without this condition. All property is grounded in the union of many wills into one will."[99]

That a legal person had and was his own property meant that his egoic self-consciousness was socially sanctioned and mutually recognized in exchanges of esteem. It meant that his center of awareness was no longer necessarily fused and lost in nature, on the one hand, or given overtly to a human master, on the other. Nor could his personhood be violated by other persons within the acknowledgment of law. (It need hardly be mentioned that there are today large numbers of peoples, governments, and institutions that have not yet reached even this simple and minimally acceptable definition of humanness.)

In the same way, a legal person was a *sanctioned source of his own actions*. "A Person," said Hobbes, "is the same that an Actor is." Thus, the Latin *persona* means "actor's role"—the ego is initially and necessarily an appropriate collection of personae, a complex of social roles for appropriate interactions, actions mutually recognized as significant, appropriate, "legal." Hence a slave, according to Roman law, had no persona—he was not his own person; he was not a person at all (or, his person was the property of the master).

Now just as a legal person can own himself, so a legal person has the potential to *author* his own actions. Neither instinctual nature, nor conformist membership, nor king, nor mythic nature gods—none of these totally owned the new legal ego, and thus none of them was the overbearing author of the ego's actions. As Hobbes said, "For that which in speaking of goods and possessions is called an Owner, speaking of actions, is called Author." Thus a slave, according to Roman law, not only had no persona, he could not legally act or author his actions (he couldn't vote, etc.). The new legal ego, as self-owner, was also self-author. That is to say, it had the *potential* to organize, to some degree, its own autonomy: to choose itself, to free itself from dictates of nature (id) and king (superego), to assume responsibility or authorship for its actions. As today's psychological jargon has it, to be a real person.

A real person: historically, we have seen that a real person (1) had and was its own property; (2) could potentially author its own actions; (3) existed as a system of exchanges of mutual recognition and esteem with other actors/authors/persons. *None of this existed on a large scale prior to the middle-egoic period,* and all of it signaled a momentous evolutionary achievement. In essence, it represented the interlocking and exchange of the newly emergent self-reflexive consciousness, an inter-subjective union and sharing of the legally recognized self-consciousness, a new and higher form of unity on the way to Unity.

In a sense, each child growing up today has to pass through this same process of building up an "I, me, and mine." The child has to become his own person, or his own property, and his own author, or responsible agent of his own actions. First, he has to become his own property by prying his selfhood out of its initial embeddedness in the material environment, in

maternal fusion, in animism, magic, and myth. He has to transfer the ownership of his consciousness from others to self. Second, he then has to assume responsibility for that ownership. He has to become author of his actions, and cease giving authorship of his life to mother, to father, to king,
and to state. To be a real person is to assume ownership and authorship,
and thereby pass from pre-personal slavery to personal autonomy. In
short, the establishment of free egoic exchange.

Now the disruption or distortion of egoic exchange (historically or ontogenetically), through either repression or surplus repression, leads to a
splitting of the ego into those personae which are acceptable and those
which are unacceptable, unwanted, or feared.[222] The unacceptable personae are alienated as the "shadow," or "subconscious personae" (sometimes called "sub-personalities," although I mean it in a definitive sense as
alienated personae).[436] A subconscious persona, or shadow, becomes a
"hidden face," a "secret personality" that perpetually surprises, distorts,
and edits the conscious communications of the ego. A shadow persona is
the way an individual hides communication from himself; it is a personal
text whose authorship is denied; a voice whose ownership is rejected; an il-
legal front. A shadow persona is the way an individual refuses to own and
author his life's text, his own self. The shadow is a source of unconscious
editing, misinterpretation, and mistranslation of (parts of) one's *linguistic*
self and its *narrative* history.[436] The shadow is a hermeneutical nightmare,
the seat of intentional if unconscious misinterpretation.*

And therefore the shadow represents personal actions and communications whose *meanings* are not understood consciously by the individual himself; his shadow thus appears as a *symptom.*[436] These shadow
symptoms baffle him, confuse him—they're "all Greek," all foreign language, to him. He doesn't know what they *mean* because he has unconsciously misinterpreted his own life text and its narrative history. This is
why I directly and absolutely link the shadow to hermeneutical concerns—
hermeneutics is, recall, the science of interpretation: what is the *meaning*
of *Hamlet?* of *Crime and Punishment?* of your own behavior, your actions,
your life? Realize at once that there is *no possible empirical* way to establish these answers.[316, 433] Give me a scientific-empirical proof that you
have *the* precise meaning of *Hamlet*, of *A Streetcar Named Desire,* of last
night's dream. The point is that, once we reach levels higher than those of
the senses (1/2), once we reach membership and mind (3/4), we are dealing with structures of meaning that no empirical-sensory evidence can decide, and therefore we are forced into (or rather privileged to use) sym-

---

* Why does an individual hide communication from himself? He hides those aspects of communicative exchange *which appear to threaten the death of the ego or
verbal self-concept.* He substitutively sacrifices those aspects, "kills" them, tosses them
out, alienates them, in order to preserve his egoic immortality project. That is, the
shadow is a substitute sacrifice of the mental-egoic form of the Atman project.

bolic, mental, and communicative discussion and *interpretation* to decide the crucial issues—and there is hermeneutics. No wonder Habermas (and others) draws such a strong line between empiric-analytical inquiry and hermeneutical inquiry—it is the difference between inquiry based on modes that are subhuman vs. those properly human.[156, 177] The reason most orthodox Western psychology cannot tell you one interesting point about the meaning of your life is that it has proudly restricted itself to empiric-analytical inquiry, i.e., inquiry *based on* sensory, objectified, subhuman modes and processes. The liberating insight is that an individual's life as a mental being is a life of trans-empirical, hermeneutical exchange.

And thus, *when* a person hides communication from himself, via the shadow, he simultaneously hides from himself the *meaning* of various aspects of his life, behavior, thoughts, and feelings. The shadow becomes his seat of misinterpretation, bad hermeneutics, a false reading of his life's text. And this is why the shadow simultaneously generates various "symptoms"—actions and feelings the individual does not understand, does not comprehend, does not interpret correctly—and thus actions and feelings that seem alien to him, alienated from him, threatening, frightening, afflicting.[436]

Do not confuse the shadow with the id (typhon). The id is emotional-sexual energy; the shadow is a largely verbal and syntactical structure.† While all id repressions tend to support and energize correlative shadow structures (i.e., I can hide sex from myself only by hiding some aspects of communication from myself), a shadow repression can occur without significant reference to the id (i.e., I can hide vast and significant aspects of mental communication from myself without hiding sex from myself). Nevertheless, once a persona narrative is alienated and dissociated from the ego (to become shadow), it is invariably contaminated with, and "merged" with, uroboric and typhonic discharges, and the whole complex then forms the basic core of neurosis—or, more precisely, character disorder.

We now reach a crucial point. *Self-esteem* cannot occur if the ego is dissociated into acceptable personae vs. shadow personae, for then one cannot accurately or honestly *recognize* oneself, and therefore one cannot accurately and honestly *recognize* others. Because one cannot clearly see all of oneself, one cannot enter into mutual self-exchange fully and honestly—one hides from oneself, and thus from others; and others, in turn, are hidden. The whole *flow* of *mutual* self-recognition, which actually *constitutes*

---

† Here I decisively side with Jung, Lacan, and others, and against the earlier Freud: the "unconscious" is not just non-verbal energy and images. It can and often does contain highly structured and linguistic systems, the shadow being one of them. The id (typhon) *is* pre-verbal, and consists of sexual and aggressive drives; the shadow is linguistic and hermeneutical, and consists of meaningful but dissociated narrative units.

self-esteem, is disrupted and distorted. It's almost as if you were landed in a foreign country with a conniving and deceitful interpreter (the shadow), and then proceeded to try to establish meaningful relationships with others, relationships upon which your own self-esteem will soon rest. *And,* you never suspected or confronted the interpreter. *And,* you were the interpreter.

The ego unconsciously caught in this trap thinks it is communicating truthfully and openly to others and to itself, but because it is actually hiding the shadow from itself, it communicates not so much lies as half-truths. The whole flow of communicative exchange is thus shot through with "hidden texts" and sabotaged by unconscious editing, deleting, and distorting. The individual is no longer transparent to himself or to others, and this opaqueness confounds all attempts at self-esteem, at integrity, at accurate self-recognition, and at mutual self-appreciation. In narrating its self-text in half-truths, it reads in itself only half-esteem.

This state of affairs is reversed only when the ego includes in its life text the story of the shadow—when it befriends the shadow and re-accepts its narrative as a legitimate tale in the whole history of the ego. Or, to say the same thing, when the shadow is turned from an outlaw into a legal persona, part of the "legally recognized self-consciousness."

At the same time, this means that the ego is willing and capable of *interpreting* the shadow correctly, of consciously grasping its *meaning,* and of integrating this meaning into the larger meaning of one's personal life history itself.[436] I shall make no further point of this, but take it as perfectly obvious that the central core of any meaningful psychotherapy is the hermeneutical interpretation. Even psychoanalytical therapy is absolutely based on what it explicitly calls "the interpretation"—the ego begins its reconciliation with the shadow by learning to correctly interpret the symptoms (depression, anxiety, etc.) *in which* the shadow is now hiding. The therapist, for instance, might say, "Your feelings of depression are really masked (hidden) feelings of anger and resentment"—he helps the client reinterpret his symptoms to discover the shadow distortion which gives rise to the symptoms in the first place. When, and if, the interpretation and "working through" is completed, the *meaning* of the shadow symptom is more transparent to the ego, and thus it is capable of adding that shadow meaning to its hermeneutical stock—it can befriend the shadow because it can now *understand* the shadow. "We have met the enemy, and it is us!"

This shadow interpretation often involves "digging into one's past" simply because one must dig into the narrative *history* of one's life text in order to discover at what page of that unfolding text one first began to (unconsciously) misinterpret, edit, and distort that text via shadow authorship. To *see* that page clearly is to see the genesis of the shadow, to see the first lines of the deceitful story written then and henceforth by a shadow author. *From there,* one can more easily *reconstruct,* and *reinterpret,* the misinterpretations and hidden tales of that shadow persona, so that, ultimately, the two narrative tales—egoic and shadow—are reunited in a larger and more accurate interpretation of the meaning of one's entire life text. No more shadow, no more symptoms. Freud was so totally taken by "recovering past memories" simply because one must recover shadow authorship—"we will remember the past, or we will be doomed to repeat it."

In short, the ego has to *accept authorship* of the text of the shadow and *accept ownership* of the communications coming from the shadow. The ego, that is, has to become a "real person": to assume ownership and authorship and thus move toward autonomy and integrity, toward higher unity on the way to Unity. In a simplified sense, that is the essence and goal of humanistic/existential therapy: "On Becoming a Person" (Rogers). What a collective mankind began to do some three thousand years ago is what every individual born ever since must likewise attempt: to establish an egoic "I-me-mine," to become a responsible actor, owner, and author.

But, as always, let us end this section by setting the "egoic person" in the proper perspective, that is, in the context of the Great Chain of Being. For the problem with the personal ego is that, like all forms of separate self, it does not recognize itself as but one moment in a much larger arc of evolution; a *necessary and desirable* moment, to be sure, but an intermediate and temporary moment nonetheless. For the new ego, and its new possessions, remain in the last analysis merely new substitute subjects and new substitute objects, new twists in the Atman project, new power plays for immortality. This has always been understood by the mystic sages, and is probably best described in the writings of that modern sage Krishnamurti. For, as he points out, ultimate reality (Spirit) subsists as "choiceless awareness," a superconscious awareness that is not particularly or exclusively attached to any subject or object whatsoever.[240] In Zen, this ultimate state of awareness is known as *wu-hsin* (*mushin*), which means the "non-blocked" or "non-fixed" mind, the mind that, like a rushing stream, does not hesitate, stumble, or block, but cascades freely and equally over all manifestation.[387] As the *Diamond Sutra* would soon put it, "The awakened mind is not fixed anywhere nor does it exclusively abide." It springs freely from, and returns cleanly to, the Dharmakaya.

But *property* and *persons* are, beyond their temporary usefulness, nothing but "stick points" or "blockages" to higher consciousness. They are ways of defending and fortifying the separate self against transcendence. Or rather, they are attempts to gain transcendence in ways that prevent it and force substitute release through their exploitation and fortification. When Hui-neng summarized the entire essence of Zen as "Inwardly, no identity; outwardly, no attachment," he was pointing to these two major wings of the Atman project—the substitute subject and substitute object,

both energized by the ever-present intuition of Atman displaced to intermediate dimensions. And the individual, seeking ultimately this resurrection of the superconscious All, in the meantime substitutes the inward
world of ego and the outward world of property, and exploits them both in
the attempted Return.

Thus, for many individuals—both then and now—the ego and its possessions (I, me, and mine) served not just a temporary moment in the
Atman project, but rather the *sole* form of the Atman project. Evolution
ceased in their case, and both persons and property became wildly over-
burdened with the Atman project. The *persona,* otherwise so necessary,
came to be a *permanent self:* "Persona finally acquires the modern sense
of the personality as the *real self.*"[62] The ego-persona remained as the actor's role, but the actor couldn't take the mask off. The show must go on;
thus, the words "Not I, but Christ," as befitting ultimate authorship, have
become meaningless. "To be a real person" then means "to avoid superconsciousness."

And this is Rank's last major era, what he called the "psychological
era,"[26] the era that has reached a fevered pitch in modern America, where
psycho-babble is the Newspeak and "gut reactions" count above all else
and where one can get away with murderous hypocrisies if one merely
prefaces them with "Here and now, I am feeling . . ." The psychological
era is simply the era of the fixated ego, the era where the personal self
alone is supreme, the era in which we now live, where, looking deep within
the soul, we find nothing, we can find nothing, but ourselves. Our persons.
Our property.

GUILT, TIME, AND AGGRESSION

We earlier argued that, whatever natural aggression is innately present in
humans, the important point is that it is amplified through conceptual domains, and that amplification—itself *not* genetic—constitutes the specific,
morbid, excessive aggression known only to man. The most significant part
of that cultural and conceptual amplifier is a component known as "death
impact," for the heightened apprehension of death drives the self-system
into wildly defensive maneuvers, most common of which is simply turning
death terror *outward* into death dealing, into the really overblown potlatch
of murderous hostility which so often has characterized mankind. The new
and heightened self-consciousness of the ego seemed, in many ways, to
continue this course: more self-aware, therefore more vulnerable, therefore more potentially capable of joyous murder.

It starts with guilt and time.

Throughout this volume we have been stressing the fact that different modes of time inhere in different levels of consciousness. Furthermore, each level of consciousness embodies a particular mode of separate-self sense; each mode of separate self faces a new and different type of death fear (Thanatos); and the repression of these different modes of death seizure, at each level, energizes that level's distinctive mode of time. From the simple passing present to the extended present to cyclic/seasonal time to historical/progressive time: each mode was constructed as a transcendence of its predecessor, but it was also constructed and burdened by a self in flight from death and demanding some sort of extended temporal world through which to project its thoughts of immortality and death denial.

And since *guilt*, in its very widest sense, is simply the guilt of emergence, the guilt of being a separate self, the guilt connected with the apprehension of death, then it comes to the same thing to say, as Brown does, that "time has to be constructed by an animal that has guilt and seeks to expiate."[61] That fears death and seeks escape—for *that* demands time. Death, guilt, and time—three sides of one existential terror.

Now Brown's historical point—and it is the one I want here to emphasize—is that the transition from the archaic (magic-mythic) period to the modern (egoic) period involved a change both in the structure of time and in the structure of guilt, and that these changes were correlative.[61] While these correlations might seem somewhat obvious to us by now, nobody before Brown really noticed the extraordinary linkages between time, guilt, death, and death repression, and they deserve to be stated clearly, if very briefly.

"Archaic man experiences guilt, and therefore time," he begins. Again, the connection is that guilt, fear, and anxiety are all ultimately bound up with death, and the denial of death energizes time. Brown's statement means: "Archaic-mythic man was already self-conscious enough to feel guilt, to fear death *and* repress death, and therefore he imaginatively projected his self through time in an effort to protect and preserve it."

But the guilt and corresponding time of this archaic-mythic period were different from those of the modern (egoic) era, according to Brown. First of all, he points to Eliade's widely accepted distinction, which we already discussed, between mythic time and modern time: "Mythic time is cyclical, periodic, unhistoric, [whereas] modern time is progressive (historical), continuous, irreversible." Second, he draws the necessary connection: "Eliade's distinction between archaic and modern time . . . is to be understood as *representing different structures of guilt.*" Thus: "In modern man guilt has increased to the point where it is no longer possible to expiate it in annual [seasonal and cyclic] ceremonies of regeneration. Guilt is therefore cumulative, and therefore time is cumulative [historical]. Archaic society had no history. Cumulative guilt imposes on modern societies a historical destiny."[61] I would not put it quite so negatively—history was not just an increase in guilt but also an increase in consciousness—but the essential point is as Brown says: different structures of guilt mean different structures of time.

Brown agrees that this transformation from archaic-mythic time/guilt to modern-egoic time/guilt occurred with patriarchal societies and especially patriarchal religion. He also neatly connects this new time/guilt structure with the concomitant rise of private property and possessions. "Cumulative [historical] time, which disrupts the old solution to the problem of guilt [which was mythic-seasonal expiation rites], organizes a new solution, which is to accumulate the tokens of atonement, the economic surplus." The point, which need not detain us, is that this transformation from mythic drives to egoic drives brought a new form of economic drive as well, the drive of "conspicuous consumption" in an attempt to bolster the newly emergent self-esteem needs.

We see, then, that the new ego brought a new time into the world, and a new guilt (and a new economy). Brown continues and establishes the crucial and fateful consequence: "The new equally guilt-ridden schema of possession inaugurates the predatory pattern which Veblen described, and transforms archaic masochism to modern sadism."[61] That is, the new egoic structure brought with it the possibility of a new and intensified form of aggression, itself a reaction to a more intense mode of guilt.

Aggression and mass homicide, in the form of war, generally began (as we saw) with the early mythic-membership structure. And the war machine itself was constructed toward the end of the membership period, around the third millennium B.C. in the city-states of Sumer—Kish, Lagash, Ur, and all. Everything we said then about the nature of murderous aggression still holds true, and is meant to be applied to this egoic era as well, but in an even more pervasive and intense fashion. For one cannot help but notice that, during the egoic period, the war machine in many ways is totally out of control. The sacred or semi-sacred restraints are gone (or perverted into "holy wars"); wars increasingly are fought over ideas and not over simple property or goods, and thus the sheer and senseless destruction of all goods, people, and property becomes perfectly acceptable—not goods, but abstractions, are now the objects of war; the new self sense, drunk with power and cut loose from its organic and typhonic roots, merely marches through piles of disfigured finite objects, securing thereby its token Atman feelings. Of course, not all—not even most—egos are like this; but *nothing*, absolutely nothing, existed like this before the egoic, heroic, individualistic period. Take Tiglath-pileser I (1115–1077 B.C.). "He no longer joins the name of his god to his name," begins the horrifying chronicle:

His exploits are well known from a large clay prism of monstrous boasts. His laws have come down to us in a collection of cruel tablets. Scholars have called his policy "a policy of frightfulness." And so it was. The Assyrians fell like butchers upon harmless villagers, enslaved what refugees they could, and slaughtered others in thousands. Bas-reliefs show what appear to be whole cities whose populace have been stuck alive on stakes running up through the groin and out the shoulders. His laws meted out the bloodiest penalties yet known in world history for even minor misdemeanors. They make a dramatic contrast to the juster admonishments that the god of Babylon dictated to . . . Hammurabi six centuries earlier.[215]

"Why this harshness?" asks Jaynes, and "for the first time in the history of civilization?" His answer is substantially the one we are proposing: "The very practice of cruelty as an attempt to rule by fear is, I suggest, at the brink of subjective [egoic] consciousness."[215]

Just so, the murderous impulses of the tyrant-king were not simply *imposed* on the world at large, for the world at large often embraced them eagerly. The new ego, being even more self-conscious than its mythic-membership predecessor, was more vulnerable, more guilty, more death-terrorized, and therefore more joyously willing to deal in massive substitute sacrifices. It was not just that the king crusaded in wars, it was that the people ecstatically supported his wholesale slaughters. "Hence," said Mumford, "the sense of joyful release that so often has accompanied the outbreak of war." As Rank put it, at stake is the community's *immortality account,* and the more you can rob others of immortality by killing them, the greater grows your own immortality account.

And why do we not violently revolt at the loss of those in our own ranks killed in war? "We mourn our dead without undue depression," said Zilboorg, "because we are able to celebrate an equal if not greater number of deaths in the ranks of the enemy." And by thus replenishing our immortality account, the pressure is off for a while, and in the wake of this joyous release our "love" for each other's egos grows. Duncan was viciously correct: "As we wound and kill our enemy in the field and slaughter his women and children in their homes, our love for each other deepens. We become comrades in arms; our hatred of each other is being purged in the sufferings of our enemy."[26] And so would proceed the new egoic Atman project, attempting, on the one side, to gain cosmic self-esteem and, on the other, to replenish or avenge the shortages in its immortality account—by whatever means available.

SUMMARY: EXCHANGE DISTORTION AND THE EGOIC ATMAN PROJECT

We have seen (in this and the last few chapters) that the new egoic structure, as a true evolution of consciousness, brought new and expanded *potentials*. It brought a new level of exchange, that of mutual self-recognition
and esteem. It brought a higher mentality; the possibility of rational comprehension; self-reflexiveness; a grasp of historical time; a final transcendence of nature and the body; formal operational thinking; a capacity
for introspection; a new form of, and potential respect for, morality; legally recognized self-consciousness; and the beginning of the sanctity of
personhood. These might not have been universally implemented and respected, but the *potential* for such exchanges was clearly present.

The new egoic structure also brought, *necessarily,* new terrors. The self-
conscious ego was more vulnerable; more aware of its mortality; more
guilty in its emergence; more open to anxiety.

And the new terrors *inherent* in the ego, when coupled with the new
powers of the ego, resulted in the *possibility* (not necessity) of even more
brutal terrors exercised *by* the ego: new substitute sacrifices, mass homicide, oppressive exploitation, massive slavery, class alienation, violent
inequality, hedonistic overindulgence, and wildly exaggerated substitute
gratifications—all of which could cripple the levels of exchange both in
oneself and in the others who happened to fall under one's influence or
power.

This can all be summarized very succinctly: just as the ego is (to date)
the highest or "capping" level of the average human compound individual,
with the power to distort, oppress, and repress not only *its own* level but
all lower levels as well, so the egoic Atman project could exploit not just
its own level but *all* the lower levels of being in an attempt at substitute
gratification, token transcendence, and symbolic immortality.

I am not going to burden the reader with endless lists of specifics.
Rather, I will simply suggest the essential and unifying idea; namely, the
egoic Atman project could exploit (and thus distort):

1. Material exchanges: attempting to possess unlimited wealth and
property, money and gold, goods and capital, as immortality symbols.

2. Emotional-sexual exchanges: attempting to squeeze transcendent sat-

isfaction out of orgasmic release and hedonistic overindulgence, or emotional excess in general.

3. Verbal-membership exchanges: attempting to verbally propagandize for one's own ideology and one's own version of symbolic immortality; attempting to distort ideally free communicative exchange in order to control membership consciousness and gain symbolic omnipotence; communicative distortion through defensive and substitutive maneuvers.

4. Egoic self-esteem exchanges: attempting to rob others of equal recognition and esteem by forcing one's own ego to be "number one," recognized above all others, cosmocentric and all-glorified.

Further, the distortions of any of these exchanges—distortions ultimately driven by the Atman project, driven by the attempt to make the self appear immortal and cosmocentric through whatever level—can disrupt and distort any or all of the other levels of exchanges, in oneself and in others, as we outlined in the first part of this chapter. If the distortion is on a lower level, it can *incline* the higher to reproduce the distortion; if the distortion is on a higher level, it can *induce* (via repression) a distortion of the lower. A powerful *other* can oppress exchanges in self; the self can repress its own exchanges; and internalized oppression results in surplus repression.

There can be no doubt that the primary and immediate aim of any sane and humane social theory would be the relaxation and relief of oppression and repression, at every level of exchange in the compound individual. Without in any way detracting from that aim, let us nevertheless conclude with the reminder that, although *some* of these evils (of oppression and repression) are only potential and not mandatory to the egoic level, nonetheless they are all *tendencies possible* to the egoic level—in anybody. Granted they can be lessened and humanized; but the final point is that wherever there is exclusive ego, there is the egoic Atman project—and just that is the ultimate problem.

As long as the egoic forms of the Atman project are present, just those types of exchange distortions, oppressions, repressions, inequalities, and injustices are guaranteed—both master and slave need them. No wonder—to give only one short example—that Otto Rank said that economic equality is "beyond the endurance of the democratic type" of person. And, I would add, the socialist type as well. The democratic ego and the socialist ego are still egos, and egos by structure house the *tendency* and the *power* for exploitation, repression, and oppression. As a frightening Czechoslovakian saying has it, "In democracy, man exploits man; in communism, it's the other way around."

The reason equality is "beyond the ego" is that if *everybody* has the same amount and type of visible immortality symbols, then those symbols miserably fail their consoling purpose—we are all then equally immortal, which is to say, none of us is immortal. Because we cannot find true and real transcendence and timelessness, we are reduced to stealing what immortality symbols and tokens of transcendence as we may from our fellow human beings. This is one of the factors that lead to exploitation (the king and state can always grab faster than a citizen alone can), and social inequality (some citizens can, however, grab faster than others), and radical class stratification (quick grabbers on top, slow ones on bottom). "Modern man cannot endure economic equality because he has no faith in self-transcendent . . . symbols [that is, in *real* transcendence]; visible physical worth is the only thing he has to give him [substitutive or symbolic] eternal life."[26] And that type of analysis is true on *all* levels of exchange, material to emotional to verbal to egoic—we will find true Atman, or we will deliver the exchanges of all levels into the hands of the Atman project.

I suppose that Buddha, with his own penetrating insight into the necessary relationship between attachment, fear, and hatred, could probably have put it all very simply. For according to Buddha, hatred and aggression arise wherever there is attachment (clinging and grasping), for one mobilizes to defend one's attachments. Aggression, in this sense, is *property defense.* Even in the animal world, aggression almost always occurs as a simple defense of territorial property. But man alone of all the animals has a *property* in his *person,* and thus a new form of aggression: man alone will lash out blindly to defend his egoic immortality status and "save face" (save the mask). Each attachment, each property, whether internal as self or external as possessions, acts as a stick point or lesion in choiceless awareness that will fester with the stench of hostility. This lesion, this person/property defense, this new twist in the Atman project, can fuel both oppression and repression, for one aggresses internally and externally to protect the person/property.

And mankind will never, but never, give up this type of murderous aggression, war, oppression and repression, attachment and exploitation, until men and women give up that property called personality. Until, that is, they awaken to the trans-personal. Until that time, guilt, murder, property, and persons will always remain synonymous.

16 The Dawn of Misery

Some aspects of the picture we have painted of the mental-egoic structure are not, alas, very pretty. Even less pleasing is the realization that the picture itself now contains, as tiny specks in the corner, the faces of you and me. For we moderns are all, all, living in the world of the egoic structure; it frames our very countenances, as it were, and sets the limits of our perspectives.

Yet once again I remind the reader that it is not the existence of the egoic structure itself that constitutes our cage, but only the exclusive identification of our awareness with that structure. The structure itself houses numerous benefits—a logical and syntactical brilliance that soon would bring forth medicine, science, and technology. But we will not let this structure work *for* us because it *is* us—we have rather totally identified with it, and thus we have burdened the ego with the Atman project and corrupted the ego's productions with demands that they could not fulfill. We have, for instance, placed upon technology the preposterous demand that it make this earth into a heaven, which means, in effect, that it turn the finite into the infinite. In the frantic and driven attempt to blow the finite up to infinite proportions, we have merely blown the finite up. We dislike its boundaries immensely, and instead of our truly transcending them, the now unconscious urge to transcendence drives us merely to disfigure and destroy them. And *that,* indeed, is the dismal state of affairs, the nature of our present age, the genesis of which we have briefly traced in the last few dozen pages.

But this dismal state of affairs, this egoic atmosphere of guilt, doom, and despair, is not simply a state that I am reading *into* the anthropological records; it is one I am reading directly *from* those records. For the anguished cry that is the ego has come not from a few modern-day romantics or transcendentalists, but from a collective mankind during the second and first millennia B.C. As if men and women knew precisely what was happening, knew precisely that the day of the Fall had dawned, knew that the ego was emerging out of its ancient slumber in the subconscious—as if they knew all that, the written records and the mythologies of that time scream out in psychological anguish, and in ways *never* before voiced or recorded. That "something unheard of" was announcing its presence throughout the civilized world.

> Wherever I turned there was evil upon evil.
> Misery increased, justice departed,
> I cried to my god, but he did not show his countenance;
> I prayed to my goddess, she did not raise her head.[70]

That from poor Tabi-utul-Enlil, around 1750 B.C., Babylonia, fifteen hundred years before Job. And it wasn't that Enlil was not pious or god-devoted:

> Prayer was my practice, sacrifice my law,
> The day of worship of the gods, the joy of my heart,
> The day of devotion to the goddess, more to me than riches.[70]

It was just that somehow, for some reason, Enlil was too awake, too self-conscious, too vulnerable, too aware of his mortal dilemma to pass it off on mythic god figures. No longer magical and mythic protectors, but simple anguish—there is Enlil's fate. And he, bless the poor man, knows it.

> The man who was alive yesterday is today dead;
> In a trice he is given to grief, of a sudden, crushed.
> For a day he sings and plays;
> In a moment he is wailing like a mourner.[70]

There is nothing like this in any literature or records of any sort prior to this general period. But now, in the second and first millennia B.C., the records exploded in grief, doubt, sorrow:

> Lo, my name is abhorred
>   Lo, more than the odor of birds
>   On summer days, when the sky is hot.

> To whom can I speak today?
>> Brothers are evil;
>> The gentle man has perished.
>> With wretchedness I am laden.
>> Wickedness smites the land;
>> It has no end.
> Death is before me today:
>> Like the home that a man longs to see,
>> After years spent as a captive.[70]

"There is no trace whatever of such concerns in any literature previous to [these] texts. . . ."[215]

The ego, indeed, was a monumental growth in consciousness, but it was one that therefore demanded a monumental price as well. A price that, judging from the literature of the time, could only be called dreadful, awesome, damning. "And so," Campbell explains, "at last, after all those myths about immortality and of kings who set and rose as the moon; . . . after the high and holy fairy tales of creation from nothing, magical verbalization, masturbation, or the intercourse of divine beings, the early pranks of the gods upon each other and their creatures, floods, miscreations, and the rest—now, at last: *the one point not previously conceded even so much as a place on the agenda,* namely the moral problem of suffering, moved to the center of the stage, where it has remained ever since."[70]

Campbell calls this climactic point *"the great reversal,"* since it was the time, the *first* time, that "for many in the Orient as well as in the West, [there occurred] a yearning for release from what was felt to be an insufferable state of sin, exile, or delusion."[70] If you look at Fig. 1, the "great reversal" is precisely that point at the very top of the circle where the outward path reverses to the inward path. And that point is basically where we are today, at the top of the curve, halfway along the path of evolution. For that point of the "great reversal" is "where we have remained ever since," as Campbell noted.

The ego, then, lies at the extreme point of vulnerability, halfway between the Eden of the subconscious and the true Heaven of the superconscious.* And thus we can call the egoic period the time of the great reversal, or we can call it what theologians ever since have: the Fall of Man. "For," to repeat the sober words of L. L. Whyte, "now, if ever, is the fall of man."

Now, if ever. But what happened? What precisely occurred? Did the gods desert man? Or did man turn his back on the gods? Did humanity simply suffer a collective nervous breakdown? Whatever it was, it marked

---

* Here and in subsequent chapters I use the word "Heaven" in its purely transcendent and superconscient sense, as covering the levels 6–8, and not as the egoic heaven of level 4.

Fig. 36. Ixion. Etruscan bronze mirror, fourth century B.C. *"In the period of Pythagoras in Greece (c. 582–500?* B.C.*) and the Buddha in India (563–483* B.C.*), there occurred . . . the Great Reversal. Life became known as a fiery vortex of delusion, desire, violence, and death, a burning waste. . . . In the Buddha's teaching, the image of the turning spoked wheel . . . thus became a sign, on the one hand, of the wheeling round of sorrow, and, on the other, release in the sunlike doctrine of illumination. And in the classical world the turning spoked wheel appeared also at this time as an emblem of . . . life's defeat and pain."*[72] *Ixion, bound by Zeus to a blazing wheel of spokes, is simply the egoic structure, and the wheel itself is the round of samsara. The Buddha's message:*

> *Ye suffer from yourselves, none else compels,*
> > *None other holds you that ye live and die*
> *And whir upon the wheel, and hug and kiss its spokes of agony,*
> > *Its tire of tears, its nave of nothingness.*

nothing less than, to borrow Whyte's phrase, "a profound transformation of human nature at that time."

There is, of course, no simple answer to this rather complex problem. Instead, what I would like to do is briefly outline four major factors that almost simultaneously contributed to a sense of the Fall.

First, the egoic structure, as a highly conscious and self-reflexive entity, *necessarily* was (and is) opened to *natural* guilt and existential dread. As Whyte put it, "This was the attraction of man's attention to a novel field, the mental processes occurring in himself. The outward-looking pagan became introspective; man became aware of moral conflict, aware of himself, and aware of his own separation from nature. Knowledge of conflict led to self-consciousness and to the sense of guilt."[426] This was *not* a neurotic guilt. That is, it was not a guilt that could be avoided, or a guilt whose existence signaled misperception or shadow distortion. Rather, it was a simple, natural result of the emergence of self-consciousness, as Neumann said: "With the emergence of the fully fledged ego, the paradisal situation is abolished. [This] is experienced as guilt, and moreover as original guilt, a fall." In short, the ego necessarily takes "its own emergence as guilt, [and a knowledge of] suffering, sickness, and death as condign punishment."[311]

As if that weren't bad enough, there was the possibility of adding to this natural guilt the surplus guilt of neurotic disorders—the surplus guilt resulting from the surplus repression at the hands of the paternal superego. For example, excess conceptual aggression can be bound by the superego and retroflected back onto the self system, with results that range from neurotic guilt to anxiety disorder to phobic response.[126, 328, 429] But this is simply one example of the second contributing factor, which in general refers to all the "things that can go wrong"—all the exchange distortions which we outlined in the last chapter. These, added to the natural terrors of the egoic structure, merely doubled its discomfort.

The third contributing factor is, in some ways, the most significant. As individuals (egos) awoke from their immersion in magical and mythical gods and goddesses—the simple, exoteric, naturalistic, infantile images of motherly and fatherly protection—they *consciously* felt, as never before, their *actual alienation* from real Godhead and true Spirit. The average individuals living in the magical and mythical periods were even *more* alienated from Spirit than was the ego, but in their ignorance and slumber they did not have to acutely face their actual alienation.†

† That is, they were on a lower level in the Great Chain—they were farther away from the *limit* of evolution (level 7), which contains a conscious realization of Spirit, even though they were, like all entities, nevertheless already grounded in Spirit (level 8). This is why we differentiate between Spirit as the highest of all evolutionary levels (Dharmakaya) and Spirit as the Ground of all evolutionary levels (Svabhavikakaya). Only with this ultimate paradox—Goal *and* Ground—can one even intelligently discuss

But when these mythic individuals awoke as truly separate and self-conscious beings, they were faced on the one hand with a *loss* of their infantile mythic protectors, and on the other with a realization of their prior and actual alienation from very God. They did not *lose* a real God consciousness, as romantics and theologians fancy; what they lost was their immersion in simple mythic-parental images. Nonetheless, they began also to *correctly* intuit, more than ever, their actual separation from Spirit, and this double separation must have been a source of acute agony in the more sensitive and intelligent souls of the period, such as poor Enlil, and later, Job.

But not all egos are sensitive and intelligent, and as we move now to the fourth factor contributing to a sense of the Fall of Man, the "hard-headedness" of the ego comes to the foreground. As we have often stated, the great and enduring accomplishment of the heroic ego was its capacity to withstand the assaults of the uroboros, typhon, Great Mother, magic and myth, assaults which threatened to disperse consciousness and return it to chthonic darkness and subconsciousness. The very strength of the heroic ego, however, often led it to an erroneous, even illusory, assumption; namely, that it was perfectly self-sufficient and independent. This was the state of affairs that was so deplored by Whyte, Brown, Campbell, etc., and the state I have gone out of my way to criticize.

Now the ego could pull this chicanery only by repressing, or forcefully closing its eyes to, not only the lower levels of consciousness, from which it had finally emerged, but also the higher realms, which should have been its destiny. It sealed out subconsciousness *and* superconsciousness. There thus arose that peculiarly Western egoic mood: cool, rational, abstract, isolated, bravely over-individual, solid, shy of its emotions, shyer of God. This ego—and it really underwrote an entire civilization—was built upon a denial of necessary Earth and a refusal of actual Heaven. And in this doubly defended consciousness (repressing the Below and denying the Above), the new ego, with its visions of cosmocentricity, proceeded to remake the Western world.

It might be objected, of course, that this type of brave new ego would *not* contribute to a sense of the Fall of Man, but rather, swaggering like John Wayne in the midst of mere mortals, bring conviction, optimism, and even cheer into the world: man (i.e., rational ego) can do anything! In a sense, that objection is certainly true; besides, the ego *does* serve its necessary and appropriate phase of evolution, and while in that phase it tends to play, more or less appropriately, the swaggering adolescent, sure it can do anything, and punching the world out to prove it. But that attitude, if it

---

the undisputed fact that all individuals are already enlightened *but* they have to practice mightily and evolve and progress steadily through meditative stages (hierarchy) *in order* to realize that fact. Spirit is *both* the highest rung on the ladder *and* the ladder itself. Nothing less than that paradox will suffice in any discussion of Spirit.

persists into adulthood, especially older adulthood, becomes a source of cynicism, skepticism, doubt, and despair. Just as there are more things in heaven and earth than are dreamt of in your philosophy, so there are more levels of consciousness in heaven and earth than are dreamt of by your ego. To the extent that consciousness does not continue its natural progression beyond the ego, to the extent the ego *fights* to prevent this letting-go, then to just that extent the ego deprives itself of higher wisdom, higher fulfillment, and higher identity, and in their place tend to rest bitterness, dilemma, regret, and despair. And so also with the civilization built by, and upon, that ego. . . . This fourth factor is actually the Greek concept of *hybris,* the "pride that goeth before a fall," and this egoic *hybris* was surely part of the atmosphere of the Fall of Man.

SUMMARY: THE FALL

The Great Reversal, or "Fall of Man," as it occurred *historically* (we will examine another meaning of the Fall in the next chapter), was primarily the awakening of self-conscious knowledge that correctly disclosed, among many other things, that men and women were *already* and *priorly* alienated from true Spirit and real Atman. This was not an *actual* Fall from spiritual Heaven (7/8), but a move up from Earth (1–3), a move that carried the realization that men and women (and *all* things) were *already* Fallen, or apparently separated from Source and Spirit (i.e., were not yet *consciously* in real Heaven or Atman consciousness). To this true awakening (factor 3) were added natural guilt (factor 1), neurotic guilt (factor 2), and guilty pride (factor 4)—all cascading over each other in a nightmare of terror. The texts from just that period, the second and first millennia B.C., show just that horrifying moral atmosphere—in both East and West alike.

And so, what type of myth soon came to be crucial, if not central, to this atmosphere of the dreadfully wrong? Surely the archetypal myth of the egoic period is that of King Etana of the city of Kish, which, in a condensed fashion, contains all four factors crammed into a short and simple narrative. The tale is straightforward: The good King Etana, on the back of the great Solar Eagle (solarization), sets out to ascend to real Heaven (6–8) and find therein eternal release (superconsciousness). Higher and higher they climb (evolve), past the lower heavens (of the old gods and goddesses) and toward the highest summit (Atman). But then Etana panics and screams out to the eagle, "O my friend, do not climb further!" At that, Etana and the eagle begin falling downward. "For two hours they fell; two hours more . . ." The document, which is broken and fragmented at the end, finishes off:

> A third two hours . . .
> The eagle fell . . .
> It was shattered on the earth . . .

And the last scattered lines tell of the king's widow in mourning. . . .[70]

The Fall of Etana, the Fall of Man—real Heaven could not yet be reached, and yet men and women are aware of its existence; the (apparent) gap between humanity and true God is painfully understood; immersion in the old gods and goddesses (the lower heavens) cannot help; the necessary ascent or solarization itself brings self-conscious panic, fear, and guilt; the story concludes with the shattering fate of all egos. And around the world, during just this period, the deserted men and women, Etana each and all, waited in quiet and puzzled desperation, aware of their impending fate, and spending their time trying to deny it.

And there, I think, the Western world still waits.

V

THE CONTEXT

17 Original Sin

In my opinion, there is one and only one way in which a scientific evolutionary theory can join hands with a truly religious or spiritual view, and that is by seeing that there was not one major Fall of Man—there were two. Let us take them one at a time.

THE SCIENTIFIC FALL

The Fall that we have concentrated on in this volume was the Fall—actually composed of a series of mini-Falls—from the archaic state of uroboric and "paradisical" immersion, the state wherein environment, consciousness, and body were all largely undifferentiated. And that Fall did indeed occur; it began in typhonic times, intensified in mythic times, and exploded in the modern egoic era. Mankind had finally emerged from its slumber in subconsciousness and awakened as a self-reflexive and isolated awareness. That event was actually an evolutionary advance and perfect growth, but it was *experienced* as a Fall because it necessarily carried an increase in guilt, vulnerability, and knowledge of mortality and finitude.

That was *not* a Fall out of some prior high estate; it was not a Fall from a *trans*-personal Heaven but a Fall out of the *pre*-personal realm, the realm of earth, nature, instinct, emotion, and unselfconsciousness.

Further, that Fall (out of subconscious Eden) was not the actual *creation* of mortality and finitude (as so many romantic myths and scholars maintain); it was rather the conscious *awakening* to a world *already* mortal and finite. It was not Original Sin per se; it was the Original Apprehension of Original Sin. In point of fact, in the pre-personal state of Eden, Adam and Eve were *already* separated from Godhead—they simply could not realize it. That is, in uroboric-typhonic times, men and women were already mortal and finite; they were born, suffered, and died; they were already *in* the world of maya, sin, and separation. They simply did not have to *consciously* face that fact. They slept the life of the lilies of the field, which is not timeless eternity but simple naïveté; yet in that "paradisical" ignorance they were nonetheless ground up, mortified, and recycled, but without ever having to, or ever being able to, recognize their actual condition, their actual samsara of birth, death, separation, and sin.

The eating from the Tree of Knowledge, then, was not itself Original Sin. It represented the acquisition of self-consciousness and of true mental reflection, and with that evolutionary knowledge men and women *then* had to face their prior alienation. They still were born, still suffered, still died— but now they *knew* it, and had to bear just that new and agonizing burden. This is why we said the eating from the Tree of Knowledge was not Original Sin or Original Alienation, but the Original Apprehension of Original Alienation. By eating from the Tree of Knowledge, not only did men and women realize their already mortal and finite state, they realized they had to leave Eden's subconsciousness and begin the actual life of true self-conscious responsibility (on the way to superconsciousness, or Actual Return). They did not get thrown out of the Garden of Eden; they grew up and walked out. (Incidentally, for this courageous act, we have Eve to thank, not blame.)

I know it is a popular belief that men and women *historically* fell out of some High Estate, and that Eden was therefore a trans-personal bliss. But the only possible definition of trans-personal Heaven is a state wherein *all* souls are consciously awakened and enlightened as the Whole, as Atman, as Buddha Nature. I have found not the slightest scrap of believable evidence that such Heaven ever existed on earth in the dim past. Even Joseph Campbell, who, with so many other spiritual scholars (Huston Smith, etc.), appears to place the Golden Age of spirituality in the Bronze Age (or generally in a past historical epoch), would not make the claim that that was the Heaven—wherein *all* souls were *perfectly* enlightened—from which men and women fell and of which highly esoteric mythology speaks (we will examine *that* Heaven in just a moment). And therefore, mankind did not historically fall *down* from Heaven; it fell *up* and out of the uroboros and the subconscious, and *into* self-consciousness and the pain and guilt involved therein.

Of course, scientific evolutionary theory supports us entirely in that view, although the scientist would state it in a slightly different way. He would say—as Carl Sagan already has—that the Fall occurred more or less when man went from subconscious (or semi-conscious) ape to self-aware human, who could then reflect on his fate and worry about it—hence, the Fall. Although there are all sorts of logical problems with that *strictly* scientific account (evolution via "natural selection" cannot account for evolution at all; it is based upon either deriving the higher from the lower or deriving the higher from thin air), it at least is in the same ball park with the view I have espoused. It agrees with our account of *"what* occurred," even though it cannot tell us *"why* it occurred." Since we are in this chapter talking about two different Falls, let me call this Fall—which was crystallized in egoic times (about 4,000 years ago)—the "scientific fall," since it is in essential agreement with the *what* of the scientific view of evolution, an agreement we gladly embrace.

The "scientific fall" is *identical* to that point we earlier called the "Great Reversal"—that point where men and women awoke as self-conscious egos and thus fell out of their slumber in subconscious nature, magic, and myth. By calling it the "scientific fall," I do not mean to cast aspersions on the *what* of science—far from it, I am agreeing with the scientific record of evolution to date, which, on the whole, shows us that historical Eden was definitely a pre-personal immersion in nature. The scientific fall, the Great Reversal, the emergence of the ego, occurred, we have seen, around the second millennium B.C.

INVOLUTION AND EVOLUTION

What, then, of the "theological fall" from a true Heaven? What of an actual "Original Sin"? Did that *ever* occur? What is its meaning?

In my opinion, the only possible way to make sense of original sin, or the theological fall, is to perfectly bypass exoteric religion and follow exclusively the insights of esoteric religion; that is, Christian mysticism (gnosticism), Vedanta Hinduism, Mahayana Buddhism, etc., as well as the philosophers, East and West, who have clearly understood mystical or transcendent truths. For if we follow their initial leads, not only original sin and alienation but the entire nature of evolution itself will become transparent.

To begin with, we need only recall that *all* esotericism subscribes to the view that reality is hierarchal, or composed of successively higher levels of reality (or, more accurately, levels of decreasing illusion*), reaching from the lowest material plane to the ultimate spiritual realization.[375] This is the universal Great Chain of Being, a rather condensed version of which we have presented in Fig. 1. For quick reference, and because this is what we will be discussing in this chapter, I remind the reader that some of the major links in the Great Chain are: (1) physical, material nature, (2) the biological body, (3) the lower mind (verbal-membership), (4) the advanced mind (egoic-conceptual), (5) the lower soul (or psychic level, the Nirmanakaya), (6) the higher soul (or subtle level, the Sambhogakaya), (7) the Spirit (as Limit, Dharmakaya), and (8) the Spirit (as Ground, or Svabhavikakaya).

According to this cosmology/psychology, the ultimate Brahman-Atman periodically "gets lost"—for the fun and sport (lila) of it—by throwing itself outward as far as possible: to see how "far out" it can get.[419] Beginning at level 7/8, or beginning as Spirit-in-itself, Spirit throws itself outward (and "downward") to *create* (via "kenosis"†) level 6, or the subtle realms, and then throws itself out again to create level 5, then 4, and so on until all the various levels are created as manifestations, expressions, or (kenotic) objectifications of ultimate Spirit itself.[436]

But in doing so, in initiating this great sport and play, Spirit temporarily "forgets" itself and thus "loses" itself in successively lower levels.[411] That is, since Spirit successively "forgets" itself in each descending level, each level actually consists of successively *decreasing* consciousness.[441] The Great Chain thus descends from superconsciousness to simple consciousness to subconsciousness.[11] And further, since each successive level has *less* consciousness than its predecessor, each level cannot consciously

---

* We say "levels of decreasing illusion" instead of "levels of increasing reality" because *all* levels, in themselves, are ultimately nothing but illusions, there being *only* Spirit at all times. Nonetheless, to say that all levels are *ultimately* illusory is not to say they are *equally* illusory—and just that fact gives us the hierarchy, levels 1–7, which we non-technically call "levels of reality" or "levels of increasing reality." But the hierarchy of the levels is a fact totally overlooked by a plethora of "new age" philosophers, physicists, and psychologists, who, understanding that *all* phenomena are mere shadows, fail entirely to grasp the *relative* differences between the *types* of shadows themselves.

† "Kenosis" is a Christian concept meaning, approximately, "self-emptying." Spirit creates the world by giving or emptying itself into and as the world, but without in any way whatsoever ceasing to be entirely and wholly itself. Creation is no privation to Spirit, nor is creation apart from Spirit, nor does Spirit need creation. Creation neither adds to nor subtracts from Spirit, and Spirit remains prior to, but not other to, creation. This view thus differs from pantheism, monism, and monotheism—it is a doctrine of "non-duality" (advaita). Pantheism maintains creation is *necessary* (it confuses the sum of all shadows for the Light beyond all shadows); monism denies relative reality to creation; and monotheism claims a God radically apart from creation—all are subtly dualistic. Finally, kenosis is precisely the doctrine of maya.

grasp or fully *remember* its predecessor.[120] That is, each level *forgets* its senior level(s). Thus, each level's creation amounts to an *amnesis* or forgetting of its higher predecessor—we can even say it is created *by* amnesis of its senior, which was created by amnesis of *its* senior, and so on—and the whole chain, of course, rests ultimately on the forgetting *of* Spirit *by* Spirit.[486]

Each level, then, is created by a forgetting of its senior level, so that ultimately all levels are created by a forgetting of Spirit. And thus, *all* levels are *already* forgetful of their Source, their Suchness, their Origin, and their Destiny—all are already living in (apparent and illusory) separation from Godhead, living in alienation, in sin, in suffering. Even the highest soul itself, level 6, is alienated, fallen, sinful—*because* its very existence tended initially and exclusively to occur by and through a forgetting of Spirit (7/8). And, of course, how much more so for the lesser levels (5–1).[64]

This whole "downward" movement, whereby Spirit playfully loses and forgets itself in successively lower levels, is called *involution*.[419, 436] We will see why it is called "involution" in a moment; for now, we need only note that in involution, each level is (1) a successive "moving away" from Godhead, (2) a successive lessening of consciousness, (3) a successive forgetting or amnesis, (4) a successive stepping down of Spirit, (5) a successive increasing of alienation, separation, dismemberment, and fragmentation, (6) a successive objectification, projection, and dualism.

But, we hasten to add, this is ultimately only an *illusory* moving away, or an illusory fall, because each level is still *nothing but* Spirit at play.[63] Each level is an illusory separation from Spirit because each level is really a separation of Spirit by Spirit through Spirit. The *reality* of each level is only Spirit; the *agony* of each level is that it *appears* or *seems* to be separate from Spirit. Spirit is not *lost* at each level, just *forgotten;* obscured, not destroyed; hidden, not abandoned. This is a great game of hide-and-seek, with Spirit being It.[210]

Nonetheless, each level, because it has forgotten Spirit, appears isolated, alienated, finite, separated, bounded, fragmented. And the crucial point, worth repeating in a sentence or two, is that each level does not just forget Spirit, it necessarily forgets *all* its higher predecessors, which connect it, mediately, to Spirit. That is, as each successively lower level is created, it forgets its senior and superior level. This is so, we saw, because the lower cannot fully and consciously embrace the higher without itself becoming the higher. That is, if a lower level could fully embrace a higher, it would not, by definition, be lower.

The point is that, as involution proceeds, not only Spirit but each senior level is *forgotten*. In a sense, then, they are rendered *unconscious*. And thus, at the end point of involution, *all* the higher levels are unconscious. The only level left in awareness, or the only level to actually exist in a manifest fashion, is that of matter, or physical nature, level 1.

All the higher levels, up to and including Spirit, are thus rendered unconscious. And the sum of these higher but unconscious structures is simply the *ground unconscious*. In the ground unconscious, the Ursprung, there exist all the higher structures in a *potential* form, ready to unfold into actuality, or emerge in consciousness. Involution, then, is the *enfolding* or in-turning of the higher structures into successively lower ones, and evolution is the subsequent *unfolding* into actuality of this enfolded potential.[436]

In short, once involution is complete, evolution can begin. As involution was the enfolding of the higher in the lower, evolution is the unfolding of the higher from the lower. But "from" is the wrong word: it is not that the higher actually *comes from* the lower as a cause from an effect. The lower can never produce the higher. It is rather that the higher comes *from* the Ursprung, where it already exists as potential. But, as I often hinted in previous chapters, when the higher emerges it does indeed pass *through* the lower. It must do so, because the lower already exists, and the higher reaches existence only by passing through it.

Thus, for example, when body-life (level 2) emerges, it emerges *from* the Ursprung but *via* matter (level 1); the mind emerges *from* the Ursprung *through* the body, and so on. Each senior level emerges from the ground unconscious via its junior level. This is why, as we saw, the exchanges of the higher levels, although they are not produced by the lower, can be partially deformed or distorted by the lower. That is, in the compound human individual, the distortion of the lower levels can partially deform the exchanges of the higher—and this deformation is what so concerned Marx, Freud, etc. This occurs *not* because the higher is produced by the lower or comes from it, but simply because it comes through it and then rests upon it. It's like a chick and its egg: the chick emerges by breaking *through* the eggshell, and the chick can be deformed in the process (if the shell is brittle, hard, etc.). But to say the higher comes *from* the lower, or ego comes from id, or consciousness is produced by matter, is like saying the chick is made of eggshells.

At any rate, at the end of involution, all the higher structures exist, as enfolded potential, in the ground unconscious (*put there* by successive forgetting and amnesis during involution), and are now ready to unfold in evolution. This overall cycle is represented in Fig. 33. On the right is involution, with the structures placed in brackets to indicate their being rendered unconscious through amnesis. On the left is evolution, the successive unfolding of these structures in the reverse order that they were enfolded.

If we look closely at the scientific record of evolution to date, we cannot help but be impressed by the accuracy of the Great Chain of Being: the match is perfect to date. As far as science can tell, the order of the evolutionary tree began with simple matter, the physical universe (level 1), which itself emerged approximately 15 billion years ago with the Big

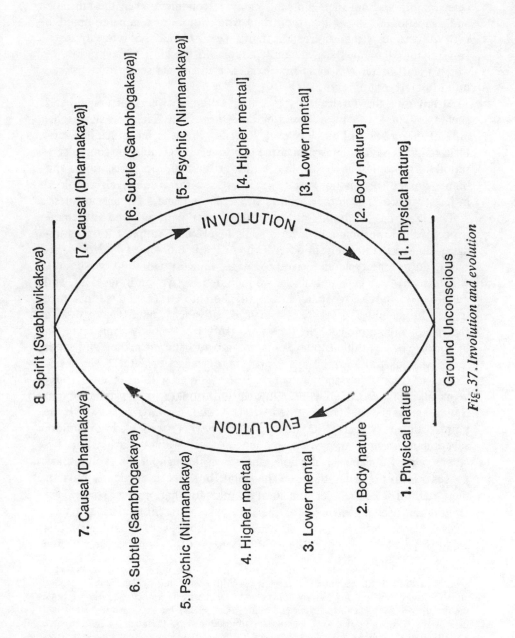

8. Spirit (Svabhavikakaya)

[7. Causal (Dharmakaya)]

[6. Subtle (Sambhogakaya)]

[5. Psychic (Nirmanakaya)]

[4. Higher mental]

[3. Lower mental]

[2. Body nature]

[1. Physical nature]

INVOLUTION

EVOLUTION

Ground Unconscious

7. Causal (Dharmakaya)

6. Subtle (Sambhogakaya)

5. Psychic (Nirmanakaya)

4. Higher mental

3. Lower mental

2. Body nature

1. Physical nature

Fig. 37. Involution and evolution

Bang.‡ Prior to that time, according to astronomers, the material universe simply was not there. In fact, many astronomers, even the atheistic and agnostic, are saying that their data would more or less be compatible with the various religious creation myths (e.g., Genesis, Shintoism, etc.). In our view, the Big Bang is simply the explosive limit of involution, at which point matter was flung into existence out of its senior dimensions, or, ultimately, out of Spirit.

At any rate, the physical universe, after billions of years, arranged itself such that simple life forms could emerge *through* it. This was the beginning of the pranic or body-life level, level 2, which, in more detailed esoteric maps, is said to consist of three sub-levels: vegetable, or simple sensation ("protoplasmic irritability"); lower animal, or perception; and higher animal, or emotion. And, indeed, these three sub-levels unfolded in just that order, each representing successive advances in consciousness.

The laborings of the life-prana level(s) eventually allowed the emergence of the lower mind, or level 3. This level, in its simplest form as images, emerged tentatively in some primates but blossomed in *Homo sapiens,* during the typhonic period of magic imagery (totally body-bound, which is why, in a *general* fashion, we included the typhon in level 2), and culminated as *verbal* mentality in the membership era (which we therefore treated in general as level 3). Level 4, or advanced mind, emerged with the rise of the heroic ego, the first mind truly free of body. And there, so to speak, rests evolution today, poised midway between matter and God.

As we look at the evolutionary process, even just to date, it's hard not to notice its most outstanding feature: its *holistic* growth. In fact, over fifty years ago a remarkable but little-known philosopher by the name of Jan Smuts published a book entitled *Holism and Evolution,* in which he pointed out, very clearly, just that fact. Everywhere we look in evolution, said Smuts, we find a succession of higher-order wholes: each whole becomes part of a higher-level whole, and so on throughout the evolutionary process. I am not going to argue the point, but take it as plainly obvious that "natural selection" per se cannot account for that process. Natural selection can account, at best, for the survival of present wholes, not their transcendence into higher-level wholes. To the average biologist, this sounds shocking, but the conclusion, of those whose specific field is the

‡ Recent evidence suggests 7–9 billion years ago for the Big Bang, which makes it even more difficult to account for emergent evolution with statistical probabilities. Scientists used to say that because evolution had a virtually *unlimited* amount of time, the emergence of higher life forms and man could easily be explained by statistical likelihoods. That unlimited time was drastically reduced by the strong evidence of a 15-billion-year limit, a limit that severely (and in the opinion of some, fatally) strained probability figures. Cutting that limit in *half* will, I predict, completely destroy the statistical argument, which will leave science unable to account for the how or why of evolution. I.e., there is a "force" driving evolution that far outdistances statistical probabilities—and that force is Atman telos.

theory of scientific knowledge, is straightforward: "Darwin's theory . . . is on the verge of collapse. . . . He is in the process of being discarded, but perhaps in deference to the venerable old gentleman, resting comfortably in Westminster Abbey next to Sir Isaac Newton, it is being done as discreetly and gently as possible, with a minimum of publicity."[375] The point, in a phrase, is that the orthodox scientific theory of evolution seems correct on the *what* of evolution, but it is profoundly reductionistic and/or contradictory on the *how* (and why) of evolution.

But if we look upon evolution as the reversal of involution, the whole process becomes intelligible. Where involution proceeded by successive separations and dismemberments, evolution, as the reverse, proceeds by successive unifications and higher-order wholes. Where involution proceeded by successive forgetting or amnesis, evolution proceeds by successive remembering or anamnesis (Plato's "recollection" or "remembrance," Sufi *zikr,* Hindu *smara,* Buddha's "recollection," etc.). Further, anamnesis and holism are actually the same thing: to remember is really to re-member, or join again in higher unity.[431] Evolution *is* holistic, because "to evolve" is simply to re-member that which was dis-membered, to unify that which was separated, to re-collect that which was dispersed. Evolution is the re-membering, or putting back together, of that which was separated and alienated during involution. And evolution, as a successive remembering or joining together in higher unity, simply continues until there is *only* Unity and *everything* has been remembered as Spirit by Spirit.

Finally, the "force" of evolution that has so insistently produced *higher-* level wholes—a force which cannot be explained by natural selection—is simply Atman telos itself, as everybody from Aristotle[112] to Hegel[193] to Aurobindo[12] has carefully pointed out. Evolution is not a statistical accident—it is a laboring toward Spirit, driven, not by happy-go-lucky chance, however comforting that notion is to those who deny reality to any level higher than insentient matter, but by Spirit itself. *That* is why evolution is a progressive advancement, and why it proceeds in leaps and bounds that far outdistance statistical probabilities. This perennial view of evolution, in short, does that which Darwinianism cannot: account not only for the what of evolution but the why.

Yet, if we look now at human evolution specifically, how does it occur? What is the form of this evolutionary remembrance? How does one stage give way to its higher successor? The essential point is that evolution on the whole appears in humans as psychological *development* and *growth—* the same "force" that produced humans from amoebas produces adults from infants and civilization from barbarism. Let us very briefly, in a few short paragraphs, review *what* we saw occurring in human evolution, and then apply our new insights as to why and how this development and growth occurred.

The earliest period of human evolution was apparently uroboric—

wherein the self and the natural environment were not clearly and sharply differentiated. That was the primal Eden of instinctual harmony with nature, physical and biological nature. It was not that man at this stage was literally nothing but matter or simple animal life; man was already a primate, with proto-symbols and rudimentary images. Rather, man was still immersed in the physical and biological realms, the realms that had already preceded him in evolution, so that, as we earlier put it, although man was not defined by these lower levels, he was immersed in them, one with them, largely governed by them. He was, to that extent, pleromatic and uroboric, recapitulating and still lost in all the lower levels—material, vegetable, animal.

At the next major stage, the typhonic, the self had started to *differentiate* itself from this natural environment. In other words, the typhonic self had *transcended* its embeddedness in the physical and natural world, although it was still magically involved with it (or still somewhat "enfolded" in it, as per "involution"). But the point is that the self had, as it were, peeled the physical-natural world off of itself, and thus "moved up" the Great Chain. Because it could *differentiate* itself from the naturic realm, it could *transcend* those lowest of all levels.

At that typhonic point, however, the self was basically just a *body*. To be sure, it was the most highly evolved body yet to appear, and it did possess a developed mental imagery, the magical primary process. But its entire consciousness was first and foremost body-bound. Thus, although it was no longer "stuck" to the physical and natural world, it *was* stuck to the body, with little or no verbal mind. It was impulsive, body-magical, emotional, pranic.

However, when the verbal mind eventually emerged and evolved (during the membership periods), the self *began* to differentiate from, and thus transcend, the simple body itself. The self—the membership or verbal self—thereby gained a relative freedom from the body's instincts, emotions, and drives (it could "farm" them). The self, now as verbal-mind, began to peel the body off of itself (i.e., differentiate from it). To just that extent, the verbal-mind transcended the typhon-body: it could postpone mere instinctual discharges, operate linguistically upon the world, transcend the simple present of the body's senses by remembering and anticipating, and so on.

At the next stage, the self—now as mental-ego—could finally differentiate itself clearly from the body. Unfortunately, the body was also repressed, which adds a sad kink to the story but doesn't alter the outline in the least. The point is that, at the egoic level, the self had finally emerged through and differentiated from the typhonic body.

Finally, with the full-fledged emergence of the mental-ego, the self became introspective: it was aware of, and thus *somewhat* transcended, its own thought processes. We in the West are at the point where the mind itself is starting, like the environment and the body before it, to crystallize out in consciousness and peel off of the self sense. We are collectively starting, but only starting, to break free of our own thought processes, to cease identifying with them exclusively, to transcend them, and thus to open ourselves to the next step in evolution. We will see, shortly, where that gets us.

For the moment, we return to our original question—why, and how, did one stage of evolution give way to the next? What specifically occurred? Recall that we earlier made a distinction between *translation,* which operates *within* a given stage or level of consciousness, and *transformation,* which is a change of levels altogether. The question then is, why and how did translation give way to transformation at each evolutionary stage?

We already have one clue: we saw that the translations of a given level generally continue as long as the Eros of that level outweighs Thanatos. That was a shorthand notation for saying that as long as the *death* of that level's self sense was not accepted, then consciousness remained *stuck* at that level. And because the self is stuck to that level, identified *exclusively* with that level, it then *defends* that level against death, against transcendence, against transformation. It fortifies its particular level by attempting to arrange all sorts of immortality projects for it—attempting to make it appear cosmocentric, all-significant, everlasting, immortal (according to the standards of that level).

It does this, we saw, not just because it is exclusively attached to its present level and seeks to defend it against all comers, but also because it truly intuits, beyond itself, the Source and Origin of all levels, its own included. It intuits, that is, Atman, Spirit, Godhead, and thus it naturally and unavoidably is drawn to that ultimate estate of True Eternity and Absolute Immortality. But in order to reach that ultimate estate, it must first *die* to its present, limited, and mortal self sense, at whatever level. And until it can accept the death of its present level, it merely applies to that finite level the Intuition of True Infinity. It thus displaces true Atman intuition onto its own mortal self, and wishes to see that mortal and finite self extended to infinite proportions and immortal glory, which, of course, is pure impossibility. That self, like all created and finite entities, will be ground up in the Process of Eternal Sacrifice, and attachment to it yields only suffering in the dissolution and agony in the release.

Why, then, does the self sense not relinquish its present level, accept its death, and thus rise to the next-higher level of consciousness, ultimately to find true Spiritual Eternity? The answer is that the lower is created (in involution, and re-created moment to moment) as a *substitute gratification* for the higher, and ultimately, for Atman itself.[436] The self does not relinquish the lower, so as to find the higher, because it thinks the lower *is* already the higher. Until that substitute gratification is broken, the self actually *chooses* the lower over the higher. As *A Course in Miracles* puts it,

"Who would choose suffering [the lower] unless he thought it brought him something, and something of value to him? He must think it is a small price to pay for something of greater worth. For [suffering, the embrace of the lower] is an election; a decision. It is the choice of weakness [the lower], in the mistaken conviction that it is strength [the higher]."[3] In no other way could the soul abandon the higher for the lower; in no other way could the soul even *want* to leave its original oneness with Spirit.

The point is that, during involution, each and every level is created, not just in a forgetting of Spirit, but as a *substitute* for Spirit. And *therefore,* in evolution, as each level emerges, consciousness exclusively identifies with that substitute gratification *until* it has been thoroughly tasted and found wanting; until that level's Eros goes flat in its appeal; until its desires cease to exclusively allure and motivate. At that point, the *death* of that level is accepted; Thanatos outweighs Eros; translation winds down and transformation to the next-higher structure begins.*

Once on the new and higher level, the self locks into it as the new substitute gratification. The battle of life vs. death switches to this new level, which is then made to appear immortal, god-like, cosmocentric, and so on (according to the standards of that level—as we said, immortality for a typhonic hunter was to live until tomorrow, immortality for a membership farmer was to live until next season, etc.). The whole Atman project shifts to the new level. Since the self cannot (yet) accept the death of this level, it goes about seeking Transcendence in ways that prevent it and allow only substitute gratifications. It applies Atman intuition to *this* level, and so proceeds the drama all over again.

But on a higher level. By accepting the death (Thanatos) of the lower level, the self could *differentiate* from it, thus *transcend* it, and thus *evolve* or *transform* to a higher-order self, more unified, more conscious, closer to Atman, closer to Return. By accepting the death of a lower fragment, the self re-membered a higher-order whole; it ceased merely translating and instead transformed. And so proceeds evolution: remembering more and more, unifying more and more, transcending more and more, dying to more and more. And when all separations have been re-collected, the result is final Wholeness; when all deaths have been died, the result is only God. In this way the Atman project gives way more and more to Atman,

---

* The typical and perfect example of this is the person who overwhelmingly wants money, success, fame, knowledge, etc.—until he finally gets it, whereupon he realizes that's not really what he wanted, a realization that is often quite devastating ("wrecked by success"). But if he understands this, and can accept the death of that old desire, then he is open to pursuing the next-higher level of substitute gratifications, until he tastes them, finds them also ultimately lacking, accepts their death, and so on. The levels of substitute gratifications are, of course, the Great Chain. In order: material/food/money, sex, power, belongingness, conceptual knowledge, self-esteem, self-actualization, subtle transcendence, ultimate enlightenment.

until there is only Atman, and the soul stands grounded in that Source and Suchness which was the alpha and omega of its journey through time.

ORIGINAL SIN AND THE THEOLOGICAL FALL

This view—of involution and evolution—is not without its firm foundations in the perennial philosophy. To give only one example each from East and West: The great German idealist Schelling, in an oft-quoted passage, maintained that "history is an epic composed in the mind of God. Its two main parts are: first, that which depicts the departure of humanity from its centre [Spirit] up to its furthest point of alienation from this centre [the movement of involution], and secondly, that which depicts the return [evolution]. The first part is the *Iliad,* the second the *Odyssey* of history. The first movement was centrifugal [i.e., outward, dispersive, separative, kenotic, dismembering], in the second it is centripetal [inward, re-collective, re-unifying, re-membering]."[99]† And Ananda Coomaraswamy, speaking of the Eastern view, stated that "the life or lives of man may be regarded as constituting a curve—an arc of time-experience subtended by the duration of individual Will to Life [Eros in flight from Thanatos]. The outward movement of this curve—the *Pravritti Marga*—is characterized by self-assertion [or separation]. The inward movement—the *Nivritti Marga*—is characterized by increasing Self-realization [by "Self," the Hindu means Atman]. The outward path is the Religion of Time; the religion of those who return is the Religion of Eternity."[436]

For this esoteric understanding, original sin is *not* something that the separate-self sense *does*. It *is* the separate-self sense, period—on whatever level (1 through 6) and on whatever curve (involution or evolution). It is not that the separate self has a free choice of whether to sin or not; it is that the very structure of the separate self *is* sin. For sin is simply *separation,* exclusive separation, and original sin is simply original separation—that primal movement of the soul away from Godhead, a movement enacted during involution but re-enacted in this moment and this moment and this by the incessant reactivation and identification with the separate-self sense.[430] And that brings us to the theological fall.

In a special way (which we will shortly amend), the creation itself is a

† Schelling tended to view the original trans-personal center as a historic fact on earth: the ancient uroboric Eden. He therefore thought the ego was the high point of alienation from Spirit, whereas in fact it is only the high point of existential vulnerability, which occurs halfway back to Spirit. That technicality aside, his abstract point is perfectly legitimate.

fall, the theological fall, because it marked the illusory separation of all things from Spirit. As Schelling would have it, "The origin of the world is to be found in a falling-away [involution] or breaking-away from God. . . . Creation is thus a Fall in the sense that it is a centrifugal movement. The absolute identity [Spirit] becomes differentiated or splintered on the phenomenal level, though not in itself [i.e., Spirit only illusorily or "phenomenally" splinters]."[99] Thus, even in historical Eden, original sin or original separation was *not* absent. Men and women were already living in a world of multiplicity, separation, finitude, and mortality. The theological fall had existed for billions of years before mankind even emerged! What was absent in Eden was an awareness of original sin, not original sin itself.

But now our slight amendment: the creation per se is not itself an ineradicable cause of sin. Creation is necessary, but not sufficient, for original sin, which means creation is not *absolutely* tied to sin. There can be no sin without creation, but there can be creation without sin. Specifically, it is not necessary for the universe to disappear in order for humans to be enlightened. The universe is not a disease. The creation is not a fall in the sense that it *prevents* enlightenment, as some sects maintain. We call it a fall—the theological fall—only because it marks the initial illusory separation of all things from God. But that which *prevents* the return to God is not God's creation per se but mankind's ignorance of only God. Creation predisposes all levels to forget the Source—but it is *their forgetting,* and not the existence of the levels per se, that prevents the Return. In a sense, God started the fall; man perpetuates it.

Thus, to Return to Source it is not necesssary to destroy and annihilate the lower levels. It is necessary only to transcend them, to cease identifying *exclusively* with them. Each higher level, in fact, must *transcend* yet *include* each lower level in its higher-order unity and synthesis (remembrance).[436] As Hegel put it, "To supersede is at once to negate and preserve."[193] Thus, e.g., when the mind emerged in evolution, it transcended the body but did not annihilate it; rather, the mind had to include and integrate the body in its higher-order self. Failure to do so is not transcendence of the lower but repression of the lower (neurosis). In true and unobstructed evolution, we take all the lower levels with us, out of love and compassion, so that *all levels* eventually are reconnected to Source. To negate everything is to preserve everything; to transcend all is to include all. We must go whole-bodily to God; failing that, we fall into dissociation, repression, inner fragmentation. Ultimate transcendence is thus *not* ultimate annihilation of the levels of creation, 1 through 6, but rather their ultimate inclusion in Spirit. The final transcendence is the final embrace.‡

‡ To me, the beauty of the twin concepts of evolution and compound individuality is this: My very existence today, although not reducible to or derivable from lower levels, nonetheless depends and rests upon the lower levels, whose early struggles and

Thus, at ultimate enlightenment or return to Spirit, the created world can still exist; it just no longer obscures Spirit, but serves it. All the levels remain as *expressions* of Atman, not substitutes for Atman. Thus, original sin—the theological fall—is not so much separation or creation, but separation forgetful of Source and creation in lieu of Atman. It is not multiplicity, but multiplicity divorced from Unity. Original sin is not per se the existence of time, space, death, and guilt, but the existence of time without eternity, space without infinity, death without sacrifice, and guilt without redemption. *That* is sin, original sin, sin without apparent release—and *that* is what we mean when, in shorthand, we say the creation was a fall, the original fall, the theological fall, the *apparent* separation of all things from Godhead.

The theological fall, then, did occur and is occurring now: all things fell from their Heavenly Estate; all entities fell from remembrance in Spirit. And man, to the extent he fails to consciously assume and live this Source, to the extent he lives as a separate-self sense, participates in the state of original sin or original alienation from Spirit. So we repeat that original sin, for humans, is not something the separate self does; it *is* the separate self and the whole world of multiplicity not consciously lived as One. This is why, indeed, all selves (even in infants) are *born* in original sin; the separate-self sense *is* original sin, not by its actions but by its simple and otherwise even innocent existence.

THE RELATION OF THE TWO FALLS

We have seen two major events, both of which have been described, appropriately enough, as "falls"—the scientific fall and the theological fall. And we put the two falls together in this fashion: beginning approximately 15 billion years ago, the material cosmos—which represents the most alienated form of Spirit—blew into sole existence with the Big Bang, which was really the roaring laughter of God voluntarily getting lost for the millionth time. That was the limit of involution, and it represented the epitome of

successes paved the way for my emergence. For that, I am grateful to them. Likewise, they are thankful to me, for in my own compound individuality, the mineral, the plant, and the animal participate in, or are a part of, higher mental consciousness, something they could never achieve on their own. Ultimately, in the compound individuality of the sage, *all* the lower levels are allowed to participate in absolute enlightenment and bathe in the glory of Spirit. The mineral, as mineral, the plant, as plant, and the animal, as animal, could never be enlightened—but the Boddhisattva *takes all manifestation* with him to Paradise, and the Boddhisattva vow is never to accept enlightenment until *all things* participate in Spirit. There is, to my mind, no nobler conception than that.

the *theological fall*—the illusory separation of all things from Godhead. From that point on, evolution back to Spirit began, an evolution which produced, in the actual course of history and prehistory, successively higher-order levels—mineral, plant, lower animal, primate, man—but *all* were still in a state of original sin, or apparent alienation from Spirit.

And around the second millennium B.C., after some dozen billions of years of struggles and substitutes, evolution produced the first fully self-conscious beings, who, for just that reason, awoke to their vulnerability, separation, alienation, and mortality. They did not create all that; they just became aware of all that. That was the *scientific fall,* "the great reversal," the final emergence from Eden.

That period was doubly painful for mankind, for not only was it aware of its scientific fall—no longer blissfully asleep in nature's subconsciousness—it also was aware of its theological fall—cut off from Spirit and Godhead. Man had finally "come up from the apes" as a self-reflexive being, and was therefore open to anxiety and guilt (the scientific fall); and he *also* became aware of the fact that he was *already,* originally, and priorly divorced from Spirit (the theological fall). As a cruel joke, the scientific fall, and the initial awareness of the theological fall, occurred historically at roughly the same time.

For just that reason, the early theologians and philosophers tended to *confuse these two falls.* They confused the Original Apprehension of Original Sin with Original Sin itself, and thus confused the scientific fall with the theological fall. But follow that through logically: since the scientific fall was a historical move up from the subconsciousness of Eden, and since the theological fall is a prior move down from the superconsciousness of Heaven, to confuse the two is to imagine that mankind was, in the immediate past history of the earth, in a type of superconscious Eden—a perfect self-contradiction, and yet that is precisely what theologians almost universally did. They assumed that there lay in the actual historic past a Golden Age of real Heaven on earth, a high estate of totally enlightened beings which preceded mankind and from which mankind fell, when, in fact, what preceded mankind was apes.

When modern science discovered that unequivocal fact—discovered that the so-called "superconscious" Eden or *historical* "trans-personal" Paradise was really the blissful ignorance of subconscious nature and pre-personal stupidity, all religions based on the confusion of the two falls, based on the mistaken belief in a "superconscious" Eden, were literally devastated by the overwhelming scientific evidence. They are still apologizing for that confusion today, without in any way really understanding it; still battling science, still protesting fact, and still further discrediting their authority and believability with every vehement pronouncement they make. For example, Western theology, not understanding the original confusion itself, has been defensively forced into the logical corner of making it a *matter of absolute faith* to believe in all sorts of historical silliness, such as a superconscious Eden, *because* "they are absurd" (Tertullian).* No wonder it took a mere century for science to logically pulverize that type of belief system—because, indeed, it *is* absurd. The theologians were (and are) trying to protect an ultimate truth—man fell from God—but in confusing the two falls, they were forced into eventually relying on *historical* evidence that simply was not there and thus *never* showed up—and they then retreated defensively into absurd postures in a defiant, totally misplaced act of faith.

The point, rather, is that if we back up *prior* to history and time—prior to the Big Bang, so to speak—the theologians *are* right: mankind (and all things) did fall from real Heaven (with original sin, or *involution,* which is also re-created *now,* moment to moment to moment, as a psychological state of ignorance—what the Hindus and Buddhists call avidya, or ignoring of Spirit, a state overcome by jnana or gnosis, "knowledge of the Supreme and Prior Identity"). *At the same time,* the scientists are also right— mankind came up (but not from) the apes. Those are perfectly compatible views, and both are correct. The union of science and religion is the union of evolution and involution.

COMPARISONS

I am not alone in this overall view. Sri Aurobindo, India's great modern sage, has written extensively on just this viewpoint—Brahman getting lost in involution and then evolving back—from matter to prana to mind to over-mind to super-mind and Atman, and he sees it occurring cosmologically as well as psychologically.[10, 11] Aurobindo, of course, is one of the few geniuses and full mystics (East or West) who also had the opportunity and willingness to study the anthropological and paleontological records compiled so carefully by modern science, and he found those records to be not only compatible with his view but supportive of it. Aurobindo is joined in his view by many other modern Indian giants, Radhakrishnan,[335] Chaudhuri,[84] Gopi Krishna,[165] etc.

On the Christian side, there is Father Teilhard de Chardin, a brilliant paleontologist and biologist (and theologian), who not only believed in evolution, but saw it as a progression of life forms leading from the lowest to the highest, and *therefore* necessarily culminating in what he called the Omega Point, wherein all souls reawaken to God consciousness.[395, 396]

But before Teilhard de Chardin, and certainly of more significance,

* More accurately, but no better, his statement was "It is certain because it is impossible," usually quoted as "I believe it because it is absurd."

there stands the towering genius of Georg Wilhelm Friedrich Hegel.†
Hegel, as is well known, was in some ways repeating and refining the insights of his two intellectual predecessors, Fichte and Schelling (whose
own views we have already mentioned), but with Hegel the idealistic genius reached its peak in the West. To be sure, there have been others more
enlightened, and others of equal or greater intellectual status, but none
combined transcendent insight with mental genius in a way comparable to
Hegel. Although I have not that often mentioned him in this book, his
shadow falls on every page.

I am not going to attempt a summary of Hegel's views; the simplest acceptable summary of his work requires a good short book. I will simply
mention a few of his points that bear most directly on our immediate discussion. In particular, we note that the Absolute for Hegel was Spirit—
"The Absolute is Spirit: this is the highest definition of the Absolute. To
find this definition and to understand its content was, one may say, the
final motive of all culture and philosophy. All religion and science have
striven to reach this point." Further, "The Absolute is not simply the One.
It is the One, but it is also the Many: it is identity-in-difference. . . .
[But] Being, the Absolute, the infinite Totality, is not a mere collection of
finite things, but one infinite Life, self-actualizing Spirit." (C)

Further, this Absolute is not a mere static Being. It is also involved in a
process of Becoming. The Absolute "is the process of its own becoming,
the circle which presupposes its end [Atman] as its purpose and has its
end as its beginning. It becomes concrete or actual only by its *development*
and through its *end*." Now this *development* was, for Hegel, history (evolution), which was both a movement *of* Spirit and a movement *toward*
Spirit, or toward the actualization of Spirit in concrete particulars. History
is thus *driven* by spiritual *telos* (our Atman telos), with its "end" being a
state of "absolute knowledge" where "Spirit knows itself in the form of
Spirit." This end-goal of history is "Spirit's return to itself on a higher
level, a level at which subjectivity and objectivity are united in one infinite
act." (C)

This historical development, or actualization of Spirit by Spirit, occurs,
according to Hegel, in three major stages (stages that correspond precisely
with our realms of sub-, self-, and super-consciousness). The first is that of
Bewusstsein, which is bodily awareness, or the sensory perception of an
external world without any mental reflection or self-consciousness. It corresponds with our subconscious realm (uroboric and typhonic). The sec-

† I started out referencing the different quotes of Hegel from his various books, and
then realized this would be useless for the general reader interested in introductory
material. I have therefore taken most of the quotes in this section from one book, Copleston's *A History of Philosophy,* vol. 7, which I recommend as the best very brief
introduction to his works. More detailed introductions include Findlay, *Hegel,* Mure,
An Introduction to Hegel, and best of all, Stace, *The Philosophy of Hegel.* Finally, a
few of the quotes are Copleston's more readily accessible rephrasings of Hegel's
words; these quotes are followed by a (C); the rest are directly Hegel's.

ond phase is that of *Selbstbewusstsein,* self-awareness and mental reflection—our realm of self-consciousness. More specifically, during this period of self-consciousness there occurs, according to Hegel, "the unhappy consciousness," "the divided consciousness," "self-alienated"—because of the stresses involved in self-consciousness itself. This is our "fallen egoic consciousness," the scientific fall, whose genesis we have traced. Hegel's third phase is that of *Vernunft,* or transcendent knowledge, "the synthesis of objectivity and subjectivity," Spirit knowing Spirit *as* Spirit, which for us is the superconscious.

Thus, for Hegel, history is the process of the self-actualization of Spirit, proceeding through three major phases. It begins with Nature, the lowest realm, which is a "fall from the Idea" (Spirit). Hegel thus often speaks of Nature as a Fall (*Abfall*), in ways very similar to our theological or involutional fall. But Nature is not set against Spirit, nor does it exist apart from Spirit. Following Schelling, Hegel agrees that Nature, even though fallen, is actually just "slumbering Spirit," or "God in his otherness." More specifically, Nature is "self-alienated Spirit." In the second phase, this Spirit awakens in man as self-consciousness, and then, in the third phase, returns through man to itself as absolute knowledge, which is also man's highest knowledge. This absolute knowledge arises when "I am aware, not simply of myself as a finite individual standing over against other finite persons and things, but rather of the Absolute as the ultimate and all-embracing reality. My knowledge, if I attain it, of Nature as the objective manifestation of the Absolute and of the Absolute as returning to itself as subjectivity in the form of Spirit, existing in and through the spiritual life of man in history, is a moment in absolute . . . consciousness, that is, in the self-knowledge of Being or the Absolute." (C)

Yet—and here Hegel's genius truly surpassed his predecessors, East or West—although each stage of development transcends and surpasses its predecessors, it does not discard them or obliterate them. All the earlier fragments and lesser levels, all the prior stages, are taken up and preserved in the succeeding higher stages. Each higher stage *negates,* or goes beyond, but also *preserves,* or integrates, all prior stages, so that they are "not annulled but fulfilled." "The last [stage] is the result of all earlier ones: nothing is lost, all principles are preserved."

This is so, according to Hegel, because each stage of development—each stage of the overcoming of the alienation from Spirit—occurs through a dialectical process of thesis, antithesis, and synthesis, or negation, negation of the negation, and higher resolution. This dialectic was first extensively used by Fichte, but it reaches its peak in Hegel (although, unlike Fichte, he rarely uses the terms thesis, antithesis, synthesis). If I may revert to my terminology, I would explain it thus: each level emerges as a thesis, a being with Eros, and this Eros-being initially dominates all translations and therefore *negates* everything that lies outside its purview or threatens its purview. But this Eros-being soon runs up against its opposite or an-

tithesis ("its contradiction," according to Hegel), which is a *negation* of its
original negation, or a negation of its original lopsidedness and partiality.
This negation, this antithesis or contradiction to Eros, is Thanatos. And as
Thanatos *negates* Eros, it negates Eros' original negation, so that both
Eros and Thanatos of this level are then subsumed in a higher-order synthesis created by transformation—unity on a higher, more inclusive plane.
This new level then becomes the new thesis—it develops new Eros, which
eventually faces new Thanatos, which negates the negation, and transformation to the next-higher level occurs, and so on throughout evolution.
The upshot of all this is that each level is negated but preserved on a
higher level, until all stages are stripped of their partiality and lopsidedness, and only All-Pervading Life remains, free of contradiction, free
of negation, free of alienation.

Finally, and let us say it only once with emphasis, true philosophy was,
for Hegel, the conscious reconstruction of the developmental-logic or
stages/levels whereby Spirit returns to Spirit. "The task of philosophy is
to [reconstruct] the life of the Absolute. That is to say, it must exhibit
systematically the . . . dynamic structure, the teleological process or
movement of the cosmic Reason, in Nature [subconsciousness] and in the
sphere of the human spirit [self-consciousness], which culminates in the
Absolute's knowledge of itself [superconsciousness]."‡

Such for a brief glimpse of Hegel's genius. I would like now to turn to
Nicolas Berdyaev, that towering Russian Christian mystic, for perhaps the
words of a fellow Christian would soothe the emotions of modern-day
Christians bound to see Eden as a real Heaven. In discussing the Fall of
Man, he begins thus: "Paradise was a life of bliss, but was it the fullness
of life? Were all the possibilities realized in it? The Bible story has an exoteric character. It expresses in symbols events in the spiritual world, but a
deeper interpretation of those symbols is essential." Berdyaev then zeroes
in on the precise heart of the historical Eden and Paradise: "Not everything was revealed to man in paradise, and *ignorance was the condition of
life in it. It was the realm of the unconscious*" (my italics). He continues:

> Man's freedom was not as yet unfolded, it had not expressed it-
> self. . . . Man rejected the bliss . . . of Eden and chose the pain and
> tragedy of cosmic life in order to explore his destiny to its inmost
> depths. This was the birth of consciousness with its painful divid-

‡ The only reservations I have about Hegel are: (1) He doesn't seem to understand
the subtleties and complexities of the higher realms of superconsciousness. What he
simply calls Spirit actually consists of several levels (5, 6, 7, 8). (2) This also leads
him to use "Reason" in a rather overreaching fashion; to be sure, he meant "Reason"
as a higher consciousness, not logically bound to Kant's *a priori* categories, but he
falls short of clearly and decisively grasping the nature of gnosis or jnana. (3) His
penchant for the number three prevents him from seeing that many of the developmental dynamics that he masterfully explains actually occur throughout all sorts of
levels and stages far beyond three in number.

edness [the ego realm]. In falling away from the harmony of paradise . . . man began to make distinctions and valuations, tasted the fruit of the tree of knowledge and found himself on this side of good and evil. The prohibition was a warning that the fruits of the tree of knowledge were bitter and deadly. Knowledge was born out of freedom, out of the dark recesses of the irrational. Man preferred death and the bitterness of discrimination to the blissful and innocent life of ignorance.[30]

Men and women could, says Berdyaev, "have fed on the fruits of the tree of life and lived for ever the life of unconscious, vegetative bliss." And in words that are precisely those we have echoed throughout this volume, Berdyaev states, "Paradise is the unconscious [state] of nature, the realm of instinct. There is in it no division between subject and object, no reflection, no painful conflict of consciousness with the unconscious."[30] That is the uroboric state, point for point.

Berdyaev, then, is precisely aware of the nature of the scientific fall—the emergence of personal consciousness from pre-personal, instinctual, uroboric Eden, and *not* from a trans-personal Heaven. No wonder he could say what no other theologian could: "The myth of the Fall does not humiliate man, but extols him to wonderful heights. . . . *The myth of the Fall is a myth of man's greatness.*" Of course! The scientific fall marked the emergence of the ego from the subconscious, a feat of heroic greatness, but it was experienced as a fall because, in Berdyaev's words, "the very existence of [self or egoic] consciousness involves limits and distinctions which cause pain. In our aeon, in the fallen world, consciousness always causes pain."[30]

Would he then have us retreat to Eden? Not at all, because "the world proceeds from an original absence of discrimination between good and evil [subconscious ignorance] to a sharp distinction between them [self-conscious apprehension] and then, enriched by that experience, ends up by not distinguishing them any more [superconscious transcendence]." I assure the reader that I am not reading the "subconscious" and the "superconscious" into Berdyaev's thoughts. He himself uses precisely those words:

After the Fall . . . [self-] consciousness was needed to safeguard man from the yawning abyss below [the Devouring Mother]. But [self-] consciousness also shuts man off from the superconscious, divine reality and prevents intuitive contemplation of God [which, as we saw, was just what the ego often did]. And in seeking to break through to superconsciousness, to the abyss above [the Void], man often falls into the subconscious—the abyss below. In our sinful world consciousness means . . . dividedness, pain and suffering. . . . Un-

happy consciousness can only be overcome through superconsciousness.[30]

As for our three major stages of (1) the pre-personal and subconscious
state, (2) the personal and self-conscious state, and (3) the trans-personal
and superconscious state, Berdyaev is perfect: "There are three stages in
the development of the spirit: the original paradisaical . . . preconscious
[state] which has not had the experience of thought and freedom; division,
reflection, valuation, freedom of choice; and, finally, superconscious
wholeness and completeness that comes after freedom, reflection, and valuation. . . . Both at the beginning and the end ethics comes upon a realm
which lies beyond good and evil: the life of paradise [pre-ethical] and the
life of the Kingdom of God [trans-ethical], the preconscious and the
superconscious state. It is only the 'unhappy' consciousness with its dividedness, reflection, pain and suffering that is on 'this side' of good and
evil."

We can finish this section with a concluding remark from Aurobindo,
for he expressed precisely the same sentiments:

> For actually we see . . . the universe start with a *subconscious*
> [state] which expresses itself openly [but with minimal or "superficial
> awareness"]. In the conscient [self-conscious realm] the ego be-
> comes the superficial point at which the awareness of unity can
> emerge; but it applies its perception of unity to the form and surface
> action [this misapplication of Unity to "the surface form" is precisely
> the Atman project] and, failing to take account of all that operates
> behind, fails also to realise that it is not only one in itself but one
> with others. This limitation of the universal "I" [Atman] in the
> divided ego-sense constitutes our imperfect individualised personality.
> But when the ego transcends the personal consciousness, it begins to
> include and be over-powered by that which is to us *superconscious;* it
> becomes aware of the cosmic unity and enters into the Transcendent
> Self [Atman].[335]

And it is that necessary but tragic awakening of the unhappy consciousness—the divided ego-sense—that we have traced in this volume.

Can we not then see that there were, indeed, two falls? The scientific fall
out of Eden, out of uroboric and typhonic times; and the prior but paradoxically present theological fall out of superconscious Heaven? And that
we had to sustain the first fall in order to reverse the second? We had to
evolve past the ape of subconsciousness in order to rediscover superconsciousness. This being so, then we may all take heart, for it now appears
certain that you and I came up from Eden so that we may all return to
Heaven.

18 In Prospectus: The Future

Throughout this book I have taken an approach that, as far as I know, has never before been explicitly followed. I am referring to the fact that we have, in this volume, traced *two* parallel strands of evolution: the evolution of the *average mode* of consciousness and the evolution of the *most advanced* mode of consciousness. We saw that, in general, when the average mode of consciousness reached the typhonic level, the advanced mode of consciousness—in a few highly evolved individuals or shamans—reached level 5, or the Nirmanakaya. When the average mode reached the mythic-membership stage, the advanced mode—in a few saints—reached level 6, or the Sambhogakaya. And when the average mode reached the mental-egoic level, the advanced mode—in a few sages—reached level 7/8, or the Dharmakaya.*

---

* A technical point: Those familiar with my other works will recall that there is one more major level, lying between the ego level and the psychic level—I call it the existential or centaur level ("centaur" because it represents the stage where mind and body, after being clearly differentiated, are then brought into a higher-order integration. This is the level of humanistic-existential psychology/therapy, of self-actualization, of existential meaning). If we want a more precise and complete parallel be-

Now these advanced stages of evolution—levels 5 through 8—are not just of historical interest. For, if our whole hypothesis is even generally correct, these advanced levels remain still as the *present and higher potentials* of every man and woman who cares to evolve and transform beyond the mental-egoic stage. Our suggestion is that the deep structures of all the higher levels exist in the ground unconscious, waiting to unfold in any individual who today bothers to pursue them, just as they unfolded, hierarchically, in the succession of past transcendent heroes.

This pursuit, this transformation into higher and superconscious levels, occurs in precisely the same way all past transformations occurred: the self has to accept the *death* of its present level, *differentiate* from that level, and thus *transcend* it to the next-higher stage. In our present historical situation, this means to die to, differentiate from, and transcend the mental-egoic structure.

In a sentence, that is precisely what meditation is designed to do: halt the mental-egoic *translations* so that *transformation* into the superconscious realms may begin.[436] And, as I earlier mentioned, any careful study and interpretation of the stages of meditation as it occurs in present-day practitioners shows that the *overall* progress of meditation follows precisely, and in order, the higher stages that we have numbered 5, 6, 7, and 8. That is to say, successful and complete meditation moves first into the psychic realm of intuition (5), then into the subtle realms of archetypal oneness, light, and bliss (6), then into the causal realms of unmanifest absorption (samadhi) and radical insight (prajna/gnosis, level 7), and finally into the ultimate realm of absolute dissolution of the separate-self sense in *any* form, high or low, sacred or profane, and the simultaneous Resurrection of All-Pervading Life and Spirit (which is prior to self, mind, soul, and world, but which embraces them all in non-dual or Unobstructed Consciousness, level 8).[11, 48, 59, 64, 67, 164, 226, 275, 436]

My point is that there is precisely nothing occult or spooky, let alone

tween average and advanced modes, we have to (1) use the centaur level and (2) return to the actual distinction between level 7 and level 8. The point is then this: as the Dharmakaya is the esoteric reach of the ego, the Svabhavikakaya is the esoteric reach of the centaur. Because this book is a generalized and simplified account, I chose not to discuss the centaur, and thus also to treat levels 7 and 8 as one major level. To do otherwise would simply introduce excess data and definitions, but without adding any substantial major conclusions. Nonetheless, to simply go on record, in my opinion the centaur was first reached by a significant number of individuals with the flowering of humanistic understanding of man, perhaps as early as the 1600's in Europe (Florence, especially), but peaking with present-day humanistic-existential psychology. Further, this centaur period (really just starting) roughly corresponds with the first true and complete understanding of the Svabhavikakaya, reached perhaps as early as c. eighth century A.D. in Buddhism (Hui-neng, Padmasambhava), but which likewise is peaking with certain *modern-day* sages, especially Sri Ramana Maharshi, Bubba Free John, perhaps Aurobindo, Sri Rang Avadhoot, Yogeshwarand Saraswati.

psychotic, about true meditation. It is simply what an individual at this present stage of average-mode consciousness has to do in order to go beyond that stage in his or her own case. It is a simple and natural continuation of evolutionary transcendence: just as the body transcended matter, and as mind transcended the body, so in meditation the soul transcends the mind and then the Spirit transcends the soul.

And, if we—you and I—are to further the evolution of mankind, and not just reap the benefit of past humanity's struggles, if we are to contribute to evolution and not merely siphon it off, if we are to help the overcoming of our self-alienation from Spirit and not merely perpetuate it, then meditation—or a similar and truly contemplative practice—becomes an absolute ethical imperative, a new categorical imperative. If we do less than that, our life then becomes, not so much a wicked affair, but rather a case of merely enjoying the level of consciousness which past heroes achieved for us. We contribute nothing; we pass on our mediocrity.

If our overall hypothesis is correct, then what we see in the stages of present-day meditation is the same thing we saw in the stages of the historical evolution of the *advanced tip* of consciousness: we see the unfolding of the higher levels of the Great Chain of Being. And *therefore* we also see the probable *future stages* of the evolution of the *average mode* of consciousness, consciousness on the whole. In simplistic terms, we see humanity's future. For, as a quick glance at Fig. 1 will show, the average stage of consciousness has now, today, reached level 4, or the mental-egoic, and the next major stage of average-mode evolution is that of level 5, the Nirmanakaya, which means that *consciousness on the average,* and not just a few exceptional heroes, can begin an opening to the Nirmanakaya realms.†
At this general point in history, the exoteric curve has started to catch up with, and run into, the esoteric curve. Self-consciousness faces transition to superconsciousness. The average individual at large can *start* to become a transcendent hero.

This, of course, is the very last thing that orthodox anthropologists and psychologists would expect, because, looking back on the stages of humanity's evolution, they conclude that such "religious" stages are all behind us. They point out, as Auguste Comte and others already have, that humanity passed from, e.g., magic to myth to science (Comte's "Law of Three"), and thus science alone, firmly rational and mental, is our only hope of future evolution.

But they draw that conclusion by focusing *only* on the stages of the evolution of average-mode consciousness. As far as it goes, I perfectly agree with that type of analysis. The average-consciousness did indeed struggle

† More precisely, those individuals who are today centauric are now open to psychic levels—but this is a technical point and does not detract in the least from the general argument.

from magic (typhon) to myth (membership) to science (ego); I can hardly be accused of denying that sequence.

But all sorts of evidence, from historical growing-tip evolution to specific present-day meditation studies, points to the fact that the stage *beyond egoic science* (but still including it) is that of psychic intuition (level 5), followed by subtle awareness (6), then causal insight (7), then ultimate identity (8). Scientific anthropologists manage to deny this by *confusing* magic (2) with psychic (5) and myth (3) with subtle archetype (6), and thus whenever true psychic and subtle level features emerge, they naïvely claim regression to magic and myth. Their confusion is fueled simply because the first true psychics did emerge in the magic period and the first true saints did emerge in the mythic era, and thus, lumping these all together, they claim the anthropological record shows we have evolved past all that "religious stuff."

In fact, we have evolved past magic, *not* psychic, and past myth, *not* subtle archetype. With this simple confusion, however, not only do orthodox scholars tend to misread some of the important data of *past* evolution, they also then tend to miss the essence of possible *future* evolution. By confusing and collapsing the higher growing-tip evidence with the lower average-mode mentality, they not only misread aspects of past anthropology, they effectively seal out the possibility of recognizing any higher stages of evolution beyond their own level of mental-egoic rationality.

If these anthropologists/scientists/sociologists would care to re-examine the anthropological and historical record, with an eye to differentiating between average-mode consciousness and advanced or growing-tip consciousness, they would be opened to radically different conclusions. Let them distinguish between deluded magic, which was rampant in typhonic times, and true shamanistic insight, which was growing-tip rare during that period. Let them differentiate the biological and mythic image of the mother, which was dominant in membership times, from a true understanding of Mahamaya, Shakti, and the Great Goddess, which the truly advanced saints of that period intuited. Let them distinguish between the cultural paternal father image, which the average ego worshipped during the patriarchy, and the true Progenitor Source or Heavenly Father of the Dharmakaya, which the most highly evolved sages of that period discovered. Cease confusing the average and median and mediocre mode of consciousness with the growing-tip or highly advanced or truly transcendent mode—and *then* look at history.

The same criticism, however, applies to the romantic transcendentalists, but in a reverse way. They, too, usually confuse average-mode consciousness and growing-tip consciousness, or average lower and truly advanced, but they use that confusion to claim that the past epochs were some sort of Golden Age which we have subsequently destroyed. They confuse magic and psychic, myth and subtle archetype, but in the opposite direction: they claim that the evolution past magic was a loss of psychic levels, and the evolution past the mythic Bronze Age was a loss of subtle-archetypal glory. They rail against the rise of mental-egoic science, and damn the present age with accusatory slander, failing as completely as their scientific antagonists to understand the subtleties involved. Let them rather see the record clearly. Let them, too, distinguish between the truly advanced, transcendental heroes of yesterday and the average mode of un-mistakably primitive and unevolved superstition which totally dominated archaic history. And thus, let them save their proper enthusiasms for to-morrow, where lie the real possibilities of their transcendent visions, and the true hope for Return to Spirit.

In this regard, there is a growing and highly vocal group of individuals who feel we are, at present, on the verge of a New Age of Consciousness. In one sense, I share their enthusiasms, as I will shortly explain. But in an-other, I must demur. True, our hypothesis is that the future of humanity—if it even has such—will eventually carry the evolution of average con-sciousness into level 5, or the beginning of superconsciousness (and even-tually beyond that to levels 6, 7, 8). This would definitely be a cause for immediate rejoicing, except that: (1) There is a vast majority of humanity that has not yet stably reached the rational-egoic level. This majority is still caught in uroboric, typhonic, magical, and mythical desires, bodily self-protective stances, and a general refusal to even recognize or respect *other* personal selves. And one does not and cannot reach the trans-per-sonal without first firmly establishing the personal. (2) National govern-ments—which have a disproportionate hand in present and future history—are today, with a few exceptions, organizations of thinly rationalized ty-phonicism, animalistically self-protective, and therefore perfectly willing to dash to hell the entire world in an atomic holocaust, simply to prove their own cosmocentric ability to do so. (3) In America (and Europe), where the New Age is most loudly announced, a significant majority of individ-uals are suffering from the stresses of these civilizations' failures to support truly rational and egoic structures, and thus these individuals are actually *regressing* to pre-personal, cultic, narcissistic pursuits, as Christopher Lasch has made very clear.[246] Often, however, the cults of Narcissus claim that this regression is actually a pursuit of trans-personal realities, or at least "humanistic" freedom. The "New Age" movement is thus, in my opinion, the strangest mixture of a handful of truly trans-personal souls and masses of pre-personal addicts.

This was perfectly prefigured in the "Dharma Bum" period of the six-ties, when an influential number of otherwise highly intellectual people, in-capable of supporting rational and egoic responsibility in a culture clearly stressful and drifting, began championing typhonic, narcissistic, regressive freedom from the ego level, through pre-egoic license, while intellectually claiming to be actually pursuing the trans-egoic Zen of spontaneous free-

dom. As general cultural malaise spread, many other people began to
share the "Dharma Bum" attitude, turning narcissistically upon themselves, damning culture per se, championing Marxist dogma (religion is
not always the "opiate of the masses," as Marx thought, but it is true that
"Marxism became the opiate of the intellectuals," as a French critic put
it), and in general withdrawing to the pre-egoic abode. They often took as
their heroes a handful of truly trans-personal souls and, confusing pre-personal with trans-personal, pointed to Krishnamurti and Ramana and Zen,
and thus managed to front an otherwise undeniable rationalization for
their regress to Eden.

Even *if* all of that were not true, humanity at large still would not face
wholesale and profound Return to Spirit, or true New Age. It would face,
in fact, the entire second half of evolution—levels 5, 6, 7, and 8, a battle
every bit as difficult and prolonged as that of levels 1, 2, 3, and 4. Yet the
New Age enthusiasts speak as if ultimate consciousness and true Spirit will
spring on us within the decade. It took evolution a terrible 15 billion years
to complete the first half of the Return, and I doubt that the entire second
half could be completed by tomorrow afternoon.

Nonetheless, there is indeed a growing minority of individuals who
are truly and legitimately interested in the higher realms of superconsciousness. Legitimate centers of disciplined meditation are rapidly spread-
ing; true interest in gnostic and Eastern "philosophies" is making its way
into respectable universities; trans-personal psychology and meta-
psychiatry are rapidly attracting able and capable minds; a handful of true
gurus and real spiritual masters are making their influence felt. And all of
this, to me, is evidence that consciousness at large is at least *starting,* however feebly, to look toward the superconscious future. It is nowhere near
that future—but it is *starting,* in my opinion, to move into level 5, and thus
to open itself to all sorts of transcendent concerns, contemplation, trans-
personal theory, and so on.

This interest moves in two stages. The first is intellectual curiosity and
intellectual comprehension; the second is actual practice and actual realization. Fifteen years ago, thousands of people in America began reading
about Zen, talking about Taoism, chatting about Vedanta. This first stage
is a type of "learner's permit," which says, in effect, "It's O.K. to think
about these things; they aren't pathological, morbid, degenerate, regressive, etc." In fact, the initial intuition of Spirit often, even usually, drives
the individual to attempt to grasp, in mental forms, that which is actually
trans-mental. He begins to intuit the transcendent realm, but, since he is
still on the mental level, this intuition tangentially compels him to try to
mentally understand all the finer points of the perennial philosophy—he
reads all the books, listens to all the lectures, goes to all the seminars. He
talks about Zen and physics, Buddhism and Bergson, Hinduism and Hegel.
If he is a professor, he might even write a book or two about Zen and his

own field (usually finding them remarkably compatible). He is laboring to reach the trans-mental through compulsive mental activity—an activity itself driven by his trans-mental intuition.

That is all appropriate and perfectly acceptable, as far as it goes; it is the necessary learner's permit. But as an individual's mental grasping exhausts itself, and he is still not enlightened, he might move into the second phase of *actual practice*. He ceases mental translation, and starts subtle transformation. And this is, more or less, just what happened to many people. We said that fifteen years ago in America, thousands of people began talking, thinking, reading, and writing about Zen (etc.). As one cultural critic put it, "There are two types of people in the world: those who have read Zen scholar Suzuki, and those who haven't." But today there are thousands of people actually *practicing* Zen (or similar meditative/contemplative activities). And *this* is the true beginning, the small start, of a collective move toward the transcendent realms.

For those who have matured to a responsible, stable ego—a "real person"—the next stage of growth is the beginning of the trans-personal; specifically, that of level 5, the level of psychic intuition, the beginning of transcendent openness and clarity, the awakening of a sense of awareness that is somehow more than the simple mind and body. I don't see this happening on a large scale for at least another century, if then.‡ But to the extent it does start to occur, there will be profound changes in society, culture, government, medicine, economics—as profound, say, as the move from membership to ego.

I will not bore the reader with a detailed prognostication, but will only toss out a few platitudes to suggest what might be involved. The Nirmanakaya Age will mean a society of men and women who, by virtue of an initial glimpse into transcendence: will start to understand vividly their common humanity and brother/sisterhood; will transcend roles based on bodily differences of skin color and sex; will grow in mental-psychic clarity; will make policy decisions on the basis of intuition as well as rationality; will see the same Consciousness in each and every soul, indeed, in all creation, and will start to act correspondingly; will find mental-psychic consciousness to be transfigurative of body physiology, and adjust medical theory accordingly; will find higher motivations in men and women that will drastically alter economic incentives and economic theory; will understand psychological growth as evolutionary transcendence, and develop methods and institutions not just to cure emotional disease but foster the growth of consciousness; will see education as a discipline in transcendence, body to mind to soul, and regear educational theory and institutions accordingly, with special emphasis on hierarchic

‡ And that century or so, if all goes well, will see the establishment of centauric societies, or at least significant centauric movements and enclaves.

development; will find technology an appropriate aid to transcendence, not a replacement for it; will use mass media, instant telecommunication, and human/computer linkages as vehicles of bonding-consciousness and unity; will see outer space as not just an inert entity out there but also as a projection of inner or psychic spaces, and explore it accordingly; will use appropriate technology to free the exchanges of the material level from chronic oppression; will find sexuality to be not just a play of reproductive desire but the initial base of kundalini sublimation into psychic spheres—and will adjust marriage practices accordingly; will see cultural-national differences as perfectly acceptable and desirable, but will set those differences on a background of universal and common consciousness, and thus view radical isolationism or imperialism as criminal; will view all people as ultimately one in Spirit, but only potentially one in Spirit, and thus provide incentives for each individual to actualize that Spirit, hierarchically, thus limiting mindless and undeserved "entitlement"; will realize fully the transcendent unity of all Dharmakaya religions, and thus respect all true religious preferences while condemning any sectarian claim to possess "the only way"; will realize that politicians, if they are to govern all aspects of life, will have to demonstrate an understanding and mastery of all aspects of life—body to mind to soul to spirit (if that proves impossible, the role of politics will be severely limited to the management of lower-level exchanges, and a new type of "parapolitics," as in "paramedics," will evolve).

In short, a true Wisdom Culture will *start* to emerge, a culture which (1) uses the body appropriately in diet (uroboros) and in sex (typhon), both free of repression/oppression on the one hand, and obsessive/compulsive overindulgence on the other; (2) uses the membership mind appropriately in unrestrained communication, free of domination and propaganda; (3) uses the ego appropriately in free exchanges of mutual self-esteem; and (4) uses the psychic level appropriately in a bonding-consciousness that shows every person to be an ultimately equal member of the mystical body of Christ/Krishna/Buddha. And that stage, if lived benignly and sanely, will prepare the way for level 6, or Sambhogakaya descent at large. But that, of course, is so far off I needn't even speculate.

The point, rather, is that a significant minority of individuals are today *beginning* the transformation into trans-personal realms. They are already starting to move into level 5 by virtue of actual contemplative practice. A few, of course, will continue this transformation into level 6, and maybe even 7/8. The true gurus and masters have already done just that. All of this is optimistic news. But, naturally, these truly evolutionary souls, moving into the trans-personal, appear to orthodox social critics to be *regressing* to pre-personal realms. This brings us right back to the initial point of this chapter. If one does not take the care to differentiate psychic from magic, subtle from mythic, trans-personal from pre-personal, then naturally *all* trans-personal sages appear to be pre-personally regressing. I have already thoroughly agreed that many who claim to be trans-personally evolving are really pre-personally regressing; that the cult of Narcissus is everywhere upon us. But that has precisely nothing to do with true transcendence or real trans-personal evolution. The problem is that, since both pre-egoic and trans-egoic are, in their own ways, "non-egoic," they *appear* similar, even identical, to the untutored eye. But to confuse them is actually like confusing preschool and graduate school because both are non-elementary school. Or again, it's like confusing amoebas, which are pre-reptilian, and humans, which are trans-reptilian, because both are non-reptilian.

My argument with social/psychological critics, as with anthropologists, runs to both sides: the New Age critics often tend to confuse pre-egoic and trans-egoic and thus end up championing not only truly trans-personal endeavors, which is admirable, but also the most grossly pre-egoic movements, which is perfectly disastrous.* And the orthodox critics, such as Christopher Lasch and Peter Marin, champion the same confusion, but in a reverse way: after presenting excellent analyses of the widespread present-day pre-egoic trends toward narcissistic absorption, they ruin their whole presentations by lumping trans-personal endeavors with pre-personal pursuits.† One is tempted to say, "A plague on both houses," except

---

* E.g., Theodore Roszak, in *Person/Planet*, is so (understandably) eager to see a transformation beyond the present-day ego that he goes critically overboard and condemns the egoic-role society per se. He then ends up championing any and all movements that are anti-egoic, and—you guessed it—this includes not only trans-egoic mysticism but also pre-egoic license, regression, narcissism, self-indulgence, and trivialization. He does not care to differentiate the trans-egoic from the pre-egoic, and thus maintains that any break from egoic society is part of a New Age, whereas, in fact, at least half of what he champions is Dark Age.

Similarly, many New Age critics, understanding well that the higher realms are outside of reason, do not bother to differentiate pre-rational impulses from trans-rational awareness, and thus end up advocating not only transcendence but also regression. Some, in fact, simply leave out transcendence altogether and champion typhonic feeling simply because it is non-rational. It is, to me, a great personal disappointment that so many humanistic therapies, which began with the promising understanding that awareness ought eventually to move beyond the mind, have taken the regressive way to do so, and simply retreated to exclusive typhonic exercises: just body therapy, just feelings, just sensory awareness, just experiential sensation. They are, in and by themselves, perfect educations in subhumanity, and they have the nerve to call it "consciousness raising." It is one thing to recontact the typhon and integrate it with the mind so as to eventually transcend both; quite another to recontact the typhon and stay there.

† Such critics would claim that Christ's unity consciousness was a regression to uroboric breast-union and pleromatic-oceanic womb embeddedness. We said that orthodoxy always confuses psychic (5) and magic (2), subtle (6) and myth (3), but *the* classic confusion—the confusion started by Freud in *Civilization and Its Discontents*—is to equate the causal-level Supreme Identity (7/8) with the pleromatic-

that both are partially correct, and their half-truths need to be brought together in a comprehensive view.

At any rate, while I am encouraged by the glimmerings of a New Age, I conclude with a sober appraisal: we are nowhere near the Millennium. In fact, at this point in history, the most radical, pervasive, and earth-shaking transformation would occur simply if everybody truly evolved to a mature, rational, and responsible ego, capable of freely participating in the open exchange of mutual self-esteem.‡ *There* is the "edge of history." There would be a *real* New Age. We are nowhere near the stage "beyond reason," simply because we are nowhere yet near universal reason itself.

Thus, the single greatest service that trans-personalists, as well as humanists, could now perform is to champion, not just trans-reason, but an honest embrace of simple reason itself. Trans-personalism does indeed *negate* ego and reason, but it must also *preserve* them. And that preservation is conspicuously lacking, not just in the world at large—which is the most significant factor—but also in the writings of the majority of modern-day trans-personalists—which admittedly is a minor factor in the world at large, but one that is all the more disturbing. For these trans-personalists viciously attack the ego and reason without also preserving them, and thus their very writings, however otherwise benignly intended, are simply playing into the larger hands of the pre-rational forces now rampant in the world. They are not responsible for this rampage; my point is that they aren't helping to stop it, either. And it is these pre-rational, pre-egoic forces that now hold the balance of future history.

Thus, if the Holocaust engulfs us all, it will not prove, to use the words of Jack Crittenden, "that reason has failed, but that, for the most part, it has not yet been fully tried."

---

uroboric material fusion (1). The latter is pre-subject/object, the former is trans-subject/object, but because both are outside the stream of exclusive subject/object duality, they *appear* similar to superficial investigations. But their extraordinary differences are so easy to demonstrate: the uroboric fusion state is an identity *only* with level 1: it has no access to the higher levels of language, logic, concepts, psyche, subtle, etc. The Supreme Identity, on the other hand, transcends but *includes* all those levels: in the Supreme Identity, one has *access* to body, mind, world, subtle, psychic, etc., *and* one has access to the Realm beyond them which discloses a Unity with all manifestation, high or low, 1 through 8.

‡ And even better, to centauric self-actualization.

19 Republicans, Democrats, and Mystics

Throughout this book I have suggested that the eventual core of a truly unified, critical sociological theory might best be constructed around a detailed, multi-disciplinary analysis of the developmental-logic and hierarchic *levels of exchange* that constitute the human compound individual. This would include, at the very minimum: (1) The physical-uroboric level of material exchange, whose paradigm is food consumption and food extraction from the natural environment; whose sphere is that of manual labor (or technological labor); and whose archetypal analyst is Marx. (2) The emotional-typhonic level of pranic exchange, whose paradigm is breath and sex; whose sphere is that of emotional intercourse, from feeling to sex to power; and whose archetypal analyst is Freud. (3) The verbal-membership level of symbolic exchange, whose paradigm is discourse (language); whose sphere is that of communication (and the beginning of praxis); and whose archetypal analyst is Socrates. (4) The mental-egoic level of the mutual exchange of self-recognition, whose paradigm is self-consciousness or self-reflection; whose sphere is that of mutual personal recognition and esteem (the culmination of praxis); and whose archetypal analyst is Hegel (in his writings on master/slave relationship). (5) The psychic level of intuitive exchange, whose paradigm is siddhi (or psychic intuition in its broadest sense); whose sphere is shamanistic kundalini; and whose archetypal analyst is Patanjali. (6) The subtle level of God-Light exchange, whose paradigm is saintly transcendence and revelation (nada); whose sphere is subtle Heaven (Brahma-Loka); and whose archetypal analyst is Kirpal Singh. (7/8) The causal level of ultimate exchange, whose paradigm is radical absorption in and as the Uncreate (samadhi); whose sphere is the Void-Godhead; and whose archetypal analyst is Buddha/ Krishna/Christ.*

I had originally intended, in this concluding chapter, to present a detailed outline of just such a comprehensive theory, drawing especially on the works of the Frankfurt School, which, in the hands of such as Habermas, has already laid the groundwork dealing with levels 1 through 4.

On second thought, however, I decided that would be an extremely dense way to conclude a book that has otherwise attempted to deal only in generalities and first approximations. Rather, the more appropriate thing to do, it seemed to me, would be to collapse and center the discussion on the three basic "categories" in which consciousness itself can exist, namely: the subjective, the objective, and the non-dual (or Atman itself). These three categories span the entire Great Chain, and thus our essential points can more simply be made with reference to just these three categories. For men and women in general have access to three basic "worlds"— the objective world, the subjective world, and the non-dual world of Atman—and what we want to examine are the types of social theories that have arisen within these basic categories and, beyond that, to suggest how they can be synthesized in a broader framework.†

To begin with, we simply note that the central problem which has always faced critical social and political theorists is just this: *why are men and women unfree?* And in the West, the answers given have roughly fallen into two large categories. One locates the cause of unfreedom in *objective* forces, the other locates it in *subjective* factors. The first began largely with Rousseau, continued through Marx, and today forms the basis of what is loosely called "liberal" political views, as well as all forms of humanistic psychology and philosophy. That view is: men and women are born essentially free, essentially good and loving, but are initiated into a social and political world—an "objective" world—that itself not only

---

* Specifically, the paradigms for the higher levels are: 6—savikalpa samadhi; 7— nirvikalpa samadhi; 8—sahaja (and/or bhava) samadhi.

† I will thus confine my discussion of a "unified social theory" to just these three categories, remembering always that it is a simple generalization intended only to suggest how seemingly disparate social theories can be brought together without compromising their essentials. Obviously, I believe that a truly and comprehensively unified sociological theory will be based on a developmental-logic and hierarchy of exchange similar to the one outlined in the first paragraph of this chapter (and suggested schematically throughout this volume).

teaches but perpetuates social inequality, oppression, and ill will. Although people are endowed with obvious differences in talent, intelligence, and initiative, there is such a vastly unfair distribution of wealth that this distribution cannot be accounted for solely on the basis of subjective differences, but must be due to an objective political superstructure that allows some favored individuals to exploit and suppress the unsuspecting. To give a trite example, John D. Rockefeller might make up to a million times the amount of money that the average worker earns. Yet John D. doesn't work a million times harder, he isn't a million times smarter, nor braver, nor more courageous. In other words, something *other* than John D. (something "objective" to him) is responsible for much of his success, and that "other" is said to be a state wherein economic exploitation is allowed and even encouraged. In no other way, the theory continues, can one explain the fact that, in America for example, something like 10 percent of the people own 60 percent of the wealth. That 10 percent, like John D., might be bright, intelligent, and full of initiative, but they aren't *that* much more endowed than their fellows. Rather, through a superstructure of economic and political exploitation, a small group can extract from the labors of others a disproportionate amount of wealth. Since there is only so much wealth, however, the remaining masses are left in conditions much less than favorable. And *that*, according to this argument, is why men and women are unfree—they are oppressed, exploited, downtrodden. Something in the objective, outer world imposes unfreedom on its subjects.

The very same argument runs through humanistic psychology and philosophy: men and women are born free, open, and loving, but are simply taught and tutored by a repressive society to hate, to manufacture ill will, and to choke off all loving and cooperative impulses. From this angle, then, people are unfree because they are repressively engineered personalities. Thus, *economically unfree because oppressed, psychologically unfree because repressed*—and there is the first side of the Western answer.

Since the objective world is to blame for unfreedom, then if the situation is to be improved, the objective world must be significantly altered. This group's solution to unfreedom is therefore fairly obvious: lift the oppression by redistributing the wealth, and lift the repression by distributing mental health. Abolish the exploitive political and economic structures, so that all may share freely in nature's bounty—and this political approach runs the spectrum from pure Marxists to socialists to liberals to Democrats. On the psychological side, abolish the repressive family, have done with toilet training, punishments, traumatic experiences, repressive child-rearing practices; teach love and kindness and charity, so as to draw out the innate subjective goodness in all people—and that psychological approach, which is now quite the vogue, runs the gamut from Marcuse to humanistic psychology through encounter groups to Horney and Maslow and Fromm to Dr. Spock and the permissiveness movement. For both the political and psychological wings of this group, evil results from repressing a prior or innate goodness: *evil is the repressed good*. That is, evil is an *objective* twisting of *subjective* goodness.

The second group runs from Hobbes and Burke, with Freud and with the ethnologists, and with the political conservatives and Republicans.‡ Men and women are unfree, not so much because of objective, social institutions, but because of something in their very *natures*. The *subject* is mostly to blame, not the object. Psychologically, this view is best represented by the "horrid instincts" school of thought—Darwin, Lorenz, Freud, etc.—which maintains generally that humans are born, to use Freud's particular phrasing of it, with three and only three desires: for incest, cannibalism, and murder. There is the subjective core of humanity. And it is thus a human's subjective nature, and not his/her objective upbringing, that lies at the heart of unfreedom, cruelty, evil, and inequality. From this precarious angle, the best society and family can do is start early with the veneer: lay on sheet after sheet of control, law and order, rationality, and restriction, and hope somehow to trade innate killers for social conformists. Whereas for the first group, evil was repressed goodness, for this group, *goodness is repressed evil*. That is, for the first group, evil is an objective twisting of subjective goodness; for the second, goodness is an objective control of subjective evil. Man is born nasty, and the good you get out of him is only by suppressing the beast. And if the repression breaks down, the devil breaks out.

Politically, this view therefore maintains that inequality and social injustice are absolutely inevitable, for positive reasons (humans innately possess different capacities, and you can have either equality or equal opportunity, but not both), as well as for negative ones (they also harbor innately evil potentials). Thus, as Edmund Burke would point out, a revolution leading to a different objective social structure would be largely useless, because it would still leave the basic subjective human nature intact. And in fact, it might even be worse: for if the state and restrictive political machinery are part of the necessary veneer over madness and anarchy, then revolution would equal, not liberation, but collective nervous breakdown. If objective institutions are relatively fair, relatively democratic, and relatively humane, then don't tamper with them: thus the political philosophy of conservatism. As orthodox psychiatrists and psychoanalysts do not at all approve of humanistic encounter groups and experiential marathons (since if individuals collectively "take off their masks" and expose everdeeper levels of the subjective self, all that ultimately will emerge is a group of irrational killers), so conservatives do not approve of progressive,

---

‡ Should I repeat that this is a useful, but simplistic, generalization? But a generalization that is broadly accurate enough to lead to several important conclusions about sociological theory on the whole, which is our simplified goal.

liberal reshuffling of social institutions since odds are high that things will only get worse (standard example: French Revolution under the banner of "enlightenment").

Thus, for the first group—which we will call the Humanist-Marxists— men and women are unfree because the subject, the "true self," is repressed and oppressed by objective factors. For the second group—which we will call the Freudian-Conservatives—men and women are unfree because the "true self" *must* be repressed and oppressed: the *subject* is to blame. Enter, then, our third group, represented by the mystics, and we find that men and women are unfree because there exists a belief in the existence of a "true" self in the first place. Unfreedom, anguish, and inequality do not arise because of something the object does to the subject, or because of something the subject does to the object, but because of the prior duality between the subject and the object itself. We are not to repress or unrepress the self, but rather undermine it; transcend it; see through it.

Now it is these three categories of psychological/political philosophy whose merger we desire (as an example, simplistic enough, of how to draw together seemingly disparate sociological theories). The point is that these theories are not, I believe, mutually contradictory, but rather complementary. Let us see:

First of all, it is not true, as the Humanist-Marxists would have us believe, that a self can exist without repression or oppression. That is, a "free self" is a formal, logical contradiction, and carries no more meaning and no more reality than a square circle. A "free self" and a "square circle" exist only in words, not in reality. Wherever there is other, there is fear; wherever there is self, there is anxiety—that is a Buddhistic and Upanishadic absolute. In politics, the Marxist argument will eventually run itself out: revolution after revolution will leave the self in anxiety, in pain, in chains—because it will leave the self, period. And while it is true that much good can (and already has) come from a fairer distribution of nature's bounty, the fundamental problems and fears remain untouched, because the structure of awareness itself remains unchanged. And likewise for humanistic psychology and psychotherapy: the momentum, too, will eventually die. After all the encountering, the primal-screaming, the gut-spilling and catharsis, the self is still self, and angst still returns.

It appears, then, that the Freudian-Conservatives have the final say, that unfreedom and inequality lie in humans themselves, not in human institutions. And they would be *half* right. For unfreedom, aggression, and anxiety are not characteristic of the *nature* of humanity, but characteristic of the *separate self* of humanity. It is not man's instincts that undo him, but his psychological appetites, and those appetites are a product of *boundary*, not of biology. The boundary between self and other causes fear, the boundary between past and future causes anxiety, the boundary between subject and object causes desire. And whereas biology cannot be destroyed, boundaries can be transcended.

It is the exclusive boundaries in and to awareness that constitute the primal unfreedom, and not any specific actions taken within or across those boundaries. As long as the soul separates itself from the All, it will feel both fear and desire, Thanatos and Eros, terror and thirst. The boundary between self and other is the terror of living; the boundary between being and non-being is the terror of dying. As long as men and women are slaves to their boundaries, they will be caught in battles, for as any military expert will testify, wherever there is a boundary there is a potential war (i.e., samsara). And the aim of the mystics is to deliver men and women from their battles by delivering them from their boundaries. Not manipulate the subject, and not manipulate the object, but transcend both in non-dual consciousness.* The discovery of the ultimate Whole is the only cure for unfreedom, and it is the only prescription offered by the mystics.

The Buddha, then—or Eckhart, or Ramana Maharshi, or Padmasambhava or Rumi or Christ or whomever one wishes to see as a mystical exemplar—is ultimately right, and we place him or her at the bottom, at the foundation, of our merger. Men and women are potentially totally free, because they can transcend the subject and the object and fall into unobstructed unity consciousness, prior to all worlds but not other to all worlds. The ultimate solution to unfreedom, then, is neither Humanistic-Marxist nor Freudian-Conservative, but Buddhistic: satori, moksha, wu, release, awakening, metanoia.

We move now to the second story of our merger. For once a boundary is constructed between subject and object, self and other, organism and environment, that self sense is then *inherently* unfree and *inherently* capable of total viciousness to itself and to others out of a sheer reactive panic to its own mortality and vulnerability. This is not *natural* to human awareness, but it is *normal,* because all normals possess a separate-self sense. And for the self sense, both repression and oppression are mandatory—not only *must* the self repress itself, screen out the apprehension of

* At the same time, the mystic does not ignore the reforms that can be made in the lower levels. The mystic transcends but *includes* the lower levels, and no true mystic would ever seek enlightenment for himself while neglecting the reforms that can and must be made on the lower levels of exchange. In fact, this is the difference between the Arhat, who neglects others in his pursuit of self-enlightenment, and the Boddhisattva, who refuses enlightenment until *all* others can be charitably ministered to and then uplifted to enlightenment. The point is rather that the Boddhisattva is not lured into the illusion that the separate self can be made ultimately comfortable through any isolated activities or reforms in the subjective *or* objective realms. The mystic solution is an ultimate one, not an intermediate one. Nonetheless, while rightly claiming absolute liberation, it would never shun the relative liberations to be effected in the interim. That, again, is the beauty of the Boddhisattva ideal. While transcending the subject and the object, it neglects neither, includes both, and finds therein a consummate unity.

vulnerability and mortality, it must as well oppress others to one degree or another in its own drive to separate self-preservation. This is where the Freudian-Conservatives enter the picture, as the second story of our merger. For if the Buddhistic solution is not taken, then the Freudian must be: the self sense (not human nature, just self-sense nature) is inherently evil and unfree, and thus repression and oppression are inevitable and even desirable to a certain extent.

But just to a certain extent, and this is where the Humanist-Marxists enter the merger. For as long as there are separate selves, repression and oppression are necessary and inevitable, but surplus repression and surplus oppression are not. The line between repression and surplus repression is, of course, an extremely fine one, and no one will ever strike upon the right formula for drawing that line. But we do have an extra bit of understanding that can make the decisions easier, for we know that men and women are not inherently or instinctually evil, but merely substitutively evil. The repression of one's Buddha Nature creates evil, and that evil must then be repressed to create "social good." Since evil is substitutive in nature, if we cannot yet usher in real transcendence for an individual, we can at least objectively choose the substitutes. If men and women were instinctually evil, then there would be no hope, whereas if they are substitutively evil, we have two choices: offer actual transcendence, or offer benign substitutes.

For, odd as it might initially sound, a fairly decent and loving society does not have to offer massive doses of Atman (that would be a utopian society or sangha), but simply has to arrange for individual Atman projects to overlap each other in something of a mutually supportive way. When this occurs, then the satisfaction of the *individual* Atman project tends also to benefit the community at large. For example, in certain typhonic hunting groups, to be a big Hero, to satisfy gloriously your Atman project, all you had to do was catch more game than anybody else —*and then give it all away*. The bigger your Atman project, the more the community benefited. In my opinion, just this arrangement is at the core of what Ruth Benedict called synergistic societies—and these were precisely the societies she found most noble, "likable," and beneficial. Benign synchronous illusions are at least not terribly deadly ones. So if we cannot yet offer Atman, let us at least look carefully at the structure of our substitutes, and ponder whether they can be more humanely and synergistically arranged.

If we now return to the three original questions we posed at the very beginning of this book, we will find that they were designed, from the start, to cover precisely these three basic categories—non-dual, subjective, and objective (Atman plus the two sides of the Atman project)—and the three basic social theories spawned by these categories—mystic, Republican, and Democratic. Question number one—"What paths to real transcendence are

available?"—refers to the mystic position, to the transcendence of subject
and object altogether (while, of course, still preserving them, but stripped
of their partiality and set-apartness). Question number two—"Failing true
transcendence, what substitute gratifications are offered?"—refers to the
Freudian-Conservative position, to all the resultant subjective desires and
terrors and hatreds that *must* arise as a result of the bounded self sense,
that are inherent in the very structure of the separate self and are *not* simply imposed by objective social institutions. Question number three—
"What price these substitutes on one's fellow men and women?"—refers to
the Humanist-Marxist position, to the fact that, even though some oppres-
sion/repression is inevitable, surplus oppression/repression is not. It
refers also to the fact that the objective cost of the Atman project can be
appalling, because when people become objects of the negative Atman
project, those people become victims: exploited, oppressed, coerced, enslaved, butchered. The study of types of exploitation is the study of the
types of negative Atman projects, and the lessening of exploitation is the
lessening or altering of the Atman projects themselves. This is at least the-
oretically possible because the Atman project is not instinctual or innate,
merely substitutive.

Both subjective unfreedom and objective exploitation are fallouts from
the Atman project, results of the search for Atman in substitute forms, the
fussing about in the world of time looking for the Timeless. Instead of
being the World, the individual tries to possess and dominate the world,
and instead of being the Self, he protects his self. But this is what Schopenhauer had to tell us as well, for the burden of his entire philosophy was to
demonstrate that each and every individual is, in fact, the entire World,
and "consequently can be satisfied with nothing less than possession of the
entire world as object, which, since everyone would have it so, is not possible to any." *There* is the ultimate cause of misery and unfreedom! Driven
by this insatiable appetite, men and women have historically walked all
over each other in the vain attempt to possess and have the All, and they
have subjected each other to untold inhumanities and cruelties, all of
which were created, ironically enough, by an unconscious God.

On the other hand, as Schopenhauer explained, by extinguishing the *individual* will to life (Eros), one could indeed fall into that prior state beyond subject and object, and thus *be* the All itself. Thus for Schopenhauer
—as for us—there was a way out of the misery of the Atman project, a way
out of the murderous compulsion "to possess the entire world as object,"
and that was to rediscover Atman itself, to resurrect a Supreme Identity
with and as the entire World Process. And that, as Schopenhauer himself
explained (using Sanskrit terms), is accomplished only by prajna, or transcendent insight into sunyata, the seamless coat of the Universe, which is
nothing other than Atman, one's own true Self, the Dharmakaya.

We would arrive at the same conclusion if we started with the whole approach of Rank, Brown, and Becker—that evil-and-anguish is the result of trying to radically deny death through fetishizing immortality symbols, that "men are truly sorry creatures because they have made death conscious," and that in trying to avoid death and mortality, they have historically brought more evil, more destruction, and more anguish upon the world than could the Devil himself incarnate. But immortality strivings are simply a subset of the Atman project, a substituting of time everlasting for timeless transcendence, and a wild and panicked lashing out at all obstacles—human or material—that seem to threaten one's immortality prospects.

But we would have to finish that halfway argument by adding that if "men are truly sorry creatures because they have made death conscious," nevertheless it is *ultimately* true that, as the Sufi Kahn put it, "there is no such thing as mortality, except the illusion, and the impression of that illusion, which man keeps before himself as fear during his lifetime." In other words, the self sense is ultimately illusory, it is a simple product of boundary, and thus ultimately death is likewise a complex illusion (the point the existentialists miss). When the self sense dies, all that dissolves is not a real entity but a simple boundary, a boundary that was never real, a boundary that was only imaginary. *But,* once individuals create that illusion of self and its boundaries, they then fear its dissolution above all else, and strive then for symbolic immortalities and cosmocentricities. Strive, that is, under sway of the Atman project, and then there follows, inevitably and relentlessly, all the horror-filled logic described by Rank and Becker and the whole existentialist movement. For these existentialists have, indeed, seen the diagnosis of mankind—sickness unto death, fear and trembling—but they have not yet pushed through to the ultimate prognosis, which in Sanskrit is none other than the above-mentioned prajna ("prognosis").

Again, there is a way out: if men and women are truly miserable creatures because they have made death conscious, they *can* go one step further and—transcending self—transcend death as well. To move from subconsciousness to self-consciousness is to make death conscious; to move from self-consciousness to superconsciousness is to make death obsolete.

All of these points are meant to be evoked by our three original questions. Does a person have access to Atman, to transcendence, to release from space, time, self, and mortality? If not, then the whole nightmare of repression and oppression swings necessarily into hellish action. The Atman project raises up its head and surveys all those obstacles that seem to prevent cosmic heroism and threaten symbolic immortality, and it will dash to pieces all those obstructions that rattle its cage of substitute gratifications. Make no mistake: every person intuits that he is God, but corrupts the intuition by applying it to his self, and he will then do whatever is necessary to confirm that distorted intuition in his own case.

Through substitute seeking (Eros) and substitute sacrifices (Thanatos), he propels himself through the ocean of other equally driven souls, and the violent friction of these overlapping Atman projects sparks that nightmare called history.

Like a finely balanced scale, the more Atman there is in one pan, the less Atman project in the other, and the final concern of a comprehensive sociology will be a study of the ways to tip that scale in favor of humanity. For men and women are unfree not primarily because of horrid appetites or oppressive institutions, but because they manufacture both of those forms of unfreedom as a substitute for transcendence. Men and women want the world because they are in truth the world, and they want immortality because they are in fact immortal. But instead of transcending their boundaries in truth, they merely attempt to break and refashion them at will, and caught in this Atman project of trying to make their earth into a substitute heaven, not only do they destroy the only earth they have, they forfeit the only heaven they might otherwise embrace.

BIBLIOGRAPHY

1. Allport, G. Pattern and growth in personality. New York: Holt, Rinehart and Winston, 1961.
2. Angyal, A. Neurosis and treatment: a holistic theory. New York: Wiley, 1965.
3. Anonymous. A course in miracles. 3 vols. New York: Foundation for Inner Peace, 1977.
4. Aquinas, T. Summa theologiae. 2 vols. Garden City, N.Y.: Doubleday, 1969.
5. Arieti, S. Interpretation of schizophrenia. New York: Brunner, 1955.
6. ———. The intrapsychic self. New York: Basic Books, 1967.
7. ———. Creativity: the magic synthesis. New York: Basic Books, 1976.
8. Arlow, J., and Brenner, C. Psychoanalytic concepts and the structural theory. New York: International Universities Press, 1964.
9. Assagioli, R. Psychosynthesis. New York: Viking, 1965.
10. Aurobindo. The life divine. Pondicherry: Centenary Library, XVIII, XIX.
11. ———. The synthesis of yoga. Pondicherry: Centenary Library, XX, XXI.

12. ———. The essential Aurobindo. McDermott, R. (ed.). New York: Schocken, 1973.
13. Ausubel, D. Ego development and the personality disorders. New York: Grune & Stratton, 1952.
14. Avalon, A. The serpent power. New York: Dover, 1974.
15. Baba Ram Dass. Be here now. San Cristobal, N.M.: Lama Foundation, 1971.
16. Bachofen, J. Das mutterrecht. 2 vols. Basel, 1948.
17. Bak. "The phallic woman: the ubiquitous fantasy in perversions." Psychoanalytic Study of the Child, 1968.
18. Bakan, D. The duality of human existence. Chicago: Rand McNally, 1966.
19. Baldwin, J. Thought and things. New York: Arno, 1975.
20. Bandura, A. Social learning theory. Englewood Cliffs, N.J.: Prentice-Hall, 1977.
21. Barfield, O. "The rediscovery of meaning." Adventures of the Mind, Saturday Evening Post, vol. 1, New York: Knopf, 1961.
22. Barringer, H., et al. (eds.). Social change on developing areas. Cambridge, Mass.: Schenkman, 1965.
23. Bateson, G. Steps to an ecology of mind. New York: Ballantine, 1972.
24. Battista, J. "The holographic model, holistic paradigm, information theory and consciousness." Re-Vision, vol. 1, no. 3/4, 1978.
25. Becker, E. The denial of death. New York: Free Press, 1973.
26. ———. Escape from evil. New York: Free Press, 1975.
27. Bell, D. The coming of post-industrial society. New York: Basic Books, 1973.
28. Benedict, R. Patterns of culture. Boston: Houghton Mifflin, 1934.
29. Benoit, H. The supreme doctrine. New York: Viking, 1955.
30. Berdyaev, N. The destiny of man. New York: Harper, 1960.
31. Berger, P. Invitation to sociology. Garden City, N.Y.: Doubleday, 1963.
32. Berger, P., and Luckmann, T. The social construction of reality. Garden City, N.Y.: Doubleday, 1972.
33. Bergson, H. Introduction to metaphysics. New York, 1949.
34. ———. Time and free will. New York: Harper, 1960.
35. Berne, E. Games people play. New York: Grove, 1967.
36. ———. What do you say after you say hello? New York: Bantam, 1974.
37. Bernstein, R. The restructuring of social and political theory. New York: Harcourt, 1976.
38. Bertalanffy, L. von. "The mind-body problem: a new view." Psychosomatic Medicine, vol. 26, no. 1, 1964.
39. Bessy, M. Magic and the supernatural. London: Spring Books, 1972.

40. Bharati, A. The tantric tradition. Garden City, N.Y.: Anchor, 1965.
41. Binswanger, L. Being-in-the-world. New York: Basic Books, 1963.
42. Bishop, C. "The beginnings of civilization in eastern Asia." Supplement to JAOS, no. 4, 1939 .
43. Blake, W. The portable Blake. Kazin, A. (ed.). New York: Viking, 1971.
44. Blakney, R. B. (trans.). Meister Eckhart. New York: Harper, 1941.
45. Blanck, G., and Blanck, R. Ego psychology: theory and practice. New York: Columbia Univ. Press, 1974.
46. Blofeld, J. Zen teaching of Huang Po. New York: Grove, 1958.
47. ———. Zen teaching of Hui Hai. London: Rider, 1969.
48. ———. The tantric mysticism of Tibet. New York: Dutton, 1970.
49. Bloom, C. Language development. Cambridge: M.I.T. Press, 1970.
50. Blos, P. "The genealogy of the ego ideal." Psychoanalytic Study of the Child, vol. 29, 1974.
51. Blum, G. Psychoanalytic theories of personality. New York: McGraw-Hill, 1953.
52. Blyth, R. Zen and zen classics. Vols. 1–5. Tokyo: Hokuseido, 1960–70.
53. Boehme, J. Six theosophic points. Ann Arbor: Univ. of Michigan Press, 1970.
54. Boss, M. Meaning and content of sexual perversions. Quoted in Becker, 25.
55. ———. Psychoanalysis and daseinanalysis. New York: Basic Books, 1963.
56. Bower, T. Development in infancy. San Francisco: Freeman, 1974.
57. Brace, C. The stages of human evolution. Englewood Cliffs, N.J.: Prentice-Hall, 1967.
58. Broughton, J. "The development of natural epistemology in adolescence and early adulthood." Unpublished doctoral dissertation, Harvard, 1975.
59. Brown, D. "A model for the levels of concentrative meditation." Int. J. Clin. Exp. Hypnosis, vol. 25, 1977.
60. Brown, G. Laws of form. New York: Julian, 1972.
61. Brown, N. O. Life against death. Middletown, Conn.: Wesleyan Univ. Press, 1959.
62. ———. Love's body. New York: Vintage, 1966.
63. Bubba (Da) Free John. The paradox of instruction. San Francisco: Dawn Horse, 1977.
64. ———. The enlightenment of the whole body. San Francisco: Dawn Horse, 1978.
65. Buber, M. I and thou. New York: Scribner's, 1958.
66. Bucke, M. Cosmic consciousness. New York: Dutton, 1923.
67. Buddhagosa. The path of purity. The Pali Text Society, 1923.

68. Burke, K. "The rhetoric of Hitler's 'battle.'" The philosophy of literary form. New York: Vintage, 1957.

Campbell, J. The masks of god. New York: Viking.

69. Vol. 1. Primitive mythology. 1959.

70. Vol. 2. Oriental mythology. 1962.

71. Vol. 3. Occidental mythology. 1964.

72. Vol. 4. Creative mythology. 1968.

73. Canetti, E. Of fear and freedom. New York: Farrar, Straus, 1950.

74. ———. Crowds and power. London: Gollancz, 1962.

75. Cassirer, E. An essay on man. New Haven: Yale Univ. Press, 1944.

76. ———. The philosophy of symbolic forms. 3 vols. New Haven: Yale Univ. Press, 1953–57.

77. ———. Individual and cosmos. New York, 1963.

78. Castaneda, C. Journey to Ixtlan. New York: Simon and Schuster, 1972.

79. Chang, G. Hundred thousand songs of Milarepa. New York: Harper, 1970.

80. ———. Practice of zen. New York: Harper, 1970.

81. ———. The Buddhist teaching of totality. Philadelphia: Univ. of Penn. Press, 1971.

82. ———. Teachings of Tibetan yoga. Secaucus, N.J.: Citadel, 1974.

83. Chaudhuri, H. Philosophy of meditation. New York: Philosophical Library, 1965.

84. ———. The evolution of integral consciousness. Wheaton, Ill.: Quest, 1977.

85. Childe, C. Social evolution. London: Watts, 1951.

86. ———. Man makes himself. New York: Mentor, 1957.

87. Chomsky, N. Syntactic structures. The Hague: Mouton, 1957.

88. ———. Language and mind. New York: Harcourt, 1972.

89. Clark, G. Archaeology and society. London: Methuen, 1957.

90. ———. The stone age hunters. London: Thames and Hudson, 1967.

91. ——— and Piggott, S. Prehistoric societies. New York: Knopf, 1965.

92. Clark, K. Civilization. New York: Harper, 1969.

93. Conze, E. Buddhist meditation. New York: Harper, 1956.

94. ———. Buddhist wisdom books. London: Allen & Unwin, 1970.

95. Cooley, C. Human nature and the social order. New York: Scribner's, 1902.

96. Coomaraswamy, A. Hinduism and Buddhism. New York: Philosophical Library, 1943.

97. ———. Time and eternity. Ascona, Switzerland: Artibus Asiae, 1947.

98. Coon, C. The origin of races. New York: Knopf, 1962.

99. Copleston, F. A history of philosophy. Vol. 7, part 1. Garden City, N.Y.: Image, 1965.

100. Curwen, E., and Hatt, G. Plough and pasture. New York: Collier, 1961.
101. Daly, M. Beyond god the father: toward a philosophy of women's liberation. Boston: Benem, 1973.
102. Dasgupta, S. An introduction to tantric buddhism. Berkeley: Shambhala, 1974.
103. Davidson, J. "The physiology of meditation and mystical states of consciousness." Perspectives Biology Medicine, Spring, 1976.
104. Dean, S. (ed.). Psychiatry and mysticism. Chicago: Nelson Hall, 1975.
105. Deutsche, E. Advaita vedanta. Honolulu: East-West Center, 1969.
106. Di Leo, J. Child development. New York: Brunner/Mazel, 1977.
107. Duncan, H. Communication and social order. New York: Bedminster, 1962.
108. ———. Symbols in society. New York: Oxford Univ. Press, 1968.
109. Durkheim, E. The division of labor in society. Glencoe, Ill.: Free Press, 1968.
110. Edgerton, F. (trans.). The Bhagavad Gita. New York: Harper, 1964.
111. Edinger, E. Ego and archetype. Baltimore: Penguin, 1972.
112. Edwards, P. The encyclopedia of philosophy. 8 vols. New York: Macmillan, 1967.
113. Ehrmann, J. (ed.). Structuralism. New York: Anchor, 1970.
114. Ekeh, P. Social exchange theory. Cambridge: Harvard Univ. Press, 1974.
115. Eliade, M. The myth of eternal return. New York: Pantheon, 1954.
116. ———. Cosmos and history. New York: Harper, 1959.
117. ———. Shamanism. New York: Pantheon, 1964.
118. Eliot, C. Hinduism and Buddhism. 3 vols. New York: Barnes and Noble, 1968.
119. Erikson, E. Gandhi's truth. New York: Norton, 1969.
120. Evans-Wentz, W. The Tibetan book of the dead. London: Oxford Univ. Press, 1968.
121. ———. The Tibetan book of the great liberation. London: Oxford Univ. Press, 1968.
122. ———. Tibetan yoga and secret doctrines. London: Oxford Univ. Press, 1971.
123. Fadiman, J., and Frager, R. Personality and personal growth. New York: Harper, 1976.
124. Fairbairn, W. An object-relations theory of the personality. New York: Basic Books, 1954.
125. Federn, P. Ego psychology and the psychoses. New York: Basic Books, 1952.

126. Fenichel, O. The psychoanalytic theory of neurosis. New York: Norton, 1945.
127. Ferenczi, S. "Stages in the development of the sense of reality." In Sex and psychoanalysis. Boston: Gorham, 1956.
128. Festinger, L. The theory of cognitive dissonance. New York: Peterson, 1957.
129. Feuerstein, G. Introduction to the Bhagavad Gita. London: Rider, 1974.
130. ———. Textbook of yoga. London: Rider, 1975.
131. Findlay, J. Hegel. London, 1958.
132. Fingarette, H. The self in transformation. New York: Basic Books, 1963.
133. Foulkes, D. A grammar of dreams. New York: Basic Books, 1978.
134. Frankfort, H. Ancient Egyptian religion. New York: Columbia Univ. Press, 1948.
135. ———. The birth of civilization in the Near East. Bloomington: Indiana Univ. Press, 1951.
136. Frazer, J. The new golden bough. New York: Criterion, 1959.
137. Freilich, M. (ed.). The meaning of culture. Lexington, Mass.: Xerox Publishing, 1972.
138. Fremantle, A. The Protestant mystics. New York: Mentor, 1965.
139. Freud, A. The ego and the mechanisms of defense. New York: International Universities Press, 1946.
Freud, S. The standard edition of the complete psychological works of Sigmund Freud. 24 vols., trans. and ed. by James Strachey. London: Hogarth Press and the Institute of Psycho-analysis, 1953–64.
140. ———. The interpretation of dreams. Standard Edition (SE), vols. 4 and 5.
141. ———. Three essays on the theory of sexuality. SE, vol. 7.
142. ———. Totem and taboo. SE, vol. 13.
143. ———. "On narcissism." SE, vol. 14.
144. ———. Beyond the pleasure principle. SE, vol. 18.
145. ———. The ego and the id. SE, vol. 19.
146. ———. Civilization and its discontents. SE, vol. 20.
147. ———. New introductory lectures. SE, vol. 22.
148. ———. An outline of psychoanalysis. SE, vol. 23.
149. ———. Moses and monotheism. New York: Knopf, 1939.
150. ———. A general introduction to psychoanalysis. New York: Pocket Books, 1971.
151. Frey-Rohn, L. From Freud to Jung. New York: Delta, 1974.
152. Fried, M. The evolution of political society. New York: Random House, 1967.

153. Frobenius, L. Monumenta Africana. Weimar, 1939. 6 vols. Extracts in Campbell, 69–71.

154. Fromm, E., Suzuki, D. T., and DeMartino, R. Zen Buddhism and psychoanalysis. New York: Harper, 1970.

155. Fung Yu-lan. A history of Chinese philosophy. Bodde, D. (trans.). 2 vols. Princeton: Princeton Univ. Press, 1952.

156. Gadamer, H. Philosophical hermeneutics. Berkeley, 1976.

157. Gardner, H. The quest for mind. New York: Vintage, 1972.

158. Gebser, J. Ursprung und gegenwart. Stuttgart: Deutsche Verlags-Anhalt, 1966.

159. ———. "Foundations of the aperspective world." Main Currents, vol. 29, no. 2, 1972.

160. Geertz, C. The interpretation of cultures. New York: Basic Books, 1973.

161. Gimbutas, M. "Culture change in Europe at the start of the second millennium B.C." Selected Papers of the Fifth International Congress of Anthropological and Ethnological Sciences. Philadelphia: Univ. of Penn. Press, 1960.

162. Globus, G., et al. (eds.). Consciousness and the brain. New York: Plenum, 1976.

163. Goffman, E. The presentation of self in everyday life. Garden City, N.Y.: Anchor, 1959.

164. Goleman, D. The varieties of the meditative experience. New York: Dutton, 1977.

165. Gopi Krishna. The dawn of a new science. New Delhi: Kundalini Research Trust, 1978.

166. ———. Yoga, a vision of its future. New Delhi: Kundalini Research Trust, 1978.

167. Govinda, L. Foundations of Tibetan mysticism. New York: Weiser, 1973.

168. Gowan, J. Trance, art, and creativity. Northridge, Calif., 1975.

169. Graves, R. The Greek myths. Baltimore: Penguin, 1955.

170. Green, E., and Green, A. Beyond biofeedback. New York: Delacorte, 1977.

171. Greenson, R. The technique and practice of psychoanalysis. New York: International Universities Press, 1976.

172. Grof, S. Realms of the human unconscious. New York: Viking, 1975.

173. Group for the Advancement of Psychiatry. Mysticism: spiritual quest or psychic disorder? New York: Group for the Advancement of Psychiatry, 1976.

174. Guenon, R. Man and his becoming according to the Vedanta. London: Luzac, 1945.

175. Guenther, H. Buddhist philosophy in theory and practice. Baltimore: Penguin, 1971.
176. ———. Philosophy and psychology in the abhidharma. Berkeley: Shambhala, 1974.
177. Habermas, J. Knowledge and human interests. Shapiro, J. (trans.). Boston: Beacon, 1971.
178. ———. Theory and practice. Viertel, J. (trans.). Boston: Beacon, 1973.
179. ———. Legitimation crisis. McCarthy, T. (trans.). Boston: Beacon, 1975.
180. Hakeda, Y. (trans.). The awakening of faith. New York: Columbia Univ. Press, 1967.
181. Hall, R. "The psycho-philosophy of history." Main Currents, vol. 29, no. 2, 1972.
182. Hallowell, A. "Bear ceremonialism in the Northern Hemisphere." American Anthropologist, 1926.
183. Hammond, N. A history of Greece to 322 B.C. Oxford: Clarendon, 1959.
184. Harrington, A. The immortalist. New York: Random House, 1969.
185. Harris, W., and Levey, J. (eds.). The new Columbia encyclopedia. New York: Columbia Univ. Press, 1975.
186. Harrison, J. Prolegomena to the study of Greek religion. London: Cambridge Univ. Press, 1922.
187. ———. Themis: a study of the social origins of Greek religion. London: Cambridge Univ. Press, 1927.
188. Hartmann, H. Ego psychology and the problem of adaptation. New York: International Universities Press, 1958.
189. Hartshorne, C. The logic of perfection. La Salle, Ill.: Open Court, 1973.
190. Haviland, W. Anthropology. New York: Holt, Rinehart, and Winston, 1974.
191. Hawkes, J. Prehistory. New York: Mentor, 1965.
192. Hegel, G. Science of logic. Johnston, W., and Struthers, L. (trans.). 2 vols. London, 1929.
193. ———. The phenomenology of mind. Baillie, J. (trans.). New York, 1949.
194. ———. Philosophy of right. Knox, T. M. (trans.). Oxford, 1952.
195. ———. Encyclopaedia of philosophy. Mueller, G. (trans.). New York, 1959.
196. Heidegger, M. Being and time. New York: Harper, 1962.
197. Herskovits, M. Economic anthropology. New York: Knopf, 1952.
198. Hixon, L. Coming home. Garden City, N.Y.: Anchor, 1978.
199. Hocart, A. The progress of man. London: Oxford Univ. Press, 1933.

200. ——. Social origins. London: Watts, 1954.
201. ——. Kingship. London: Oxford Univ. Press, 1969.
202. ——. Kings and councillors. Chicago: Univ. of Chicago Press, 1970.
203. Hook, S. Marx and the Marxists. Princeton, 1955.
204. Horkheimer, M. Critical theory. New York: Seabury, 1972.
205. —— and Adorno, T. Dialectic of enlightenment. New York, 1972.
206. Howlett, D. The Essenes and Christianity. New York: Harper, 1957.
207. Huizinga, J. Homo ludens. Boston: Beacon, 1960.
208. Hume, R. (trans.). The thirteen principal Upanishads. London: Oxford Univ. Press, 1974.
209. Husserl, E. Ideas. New York: Macmillan, 1931.
210. Huxley, A. The perennial philosophy. New York: Harper, 1970.
211. Jacobson, E. The self and object world. New York: International Universities Press, 1964.
212. James, W. The principles of psychology. 2 vols. New York: Dover, 1950.
213. ——. Varieties of religious experience. New York: Collier, 1961.
214. Jantsch, E., and Waddington, C. (eds.). Evolution and consciousness. Reading, Mass.: Addison-Wesley, 1976.
215. Jaynes, J. The origin of consciousness in the breakdown of the bicameral mind. Boston: Houghton Mifflin, 1976.
216. John of the Cross. The dark night of the soul. Garden City, N.Y.: Doubleday, 1959.
217. ——. The ascent of Mount Carmel. Garden City, N.Y.: Doubleday, 1958.
218. Johnson, F. "Radiocarbon dating." Memoirs of the Society for American Archaeology, no. 8, 1951.
219. Jonas, H. The gnostic religion. Boston: Beacon, 1963.
220. Jung, C. G. The collected works of C. G. Jung. Adler, G., Fordham, M., and Read, H. (eds.); Hull, R. F. C. (trans.). Bollingen Series XX, Princeton: Princeton Univ. Press, 1953–71.
221. ——. Symbols of transformation. CW, vol. 5.
222. ——. The structure and dynamics of the psyche. CW, vol. 8.
223. Kadloubovsky, E., and Palmer, G. (trans.). Writings from the "Philokalia" on prayer of the heart. London: Faber and Faber, 1954.
224. Kahn, H. The soul whence and whither. New York: Sufi Order, 1977.
225. Kaplan, L. Oneness and separateness. New York: Simon and Schuster, 1978.
226. Kapleau, P. The three pillars of Zen. Boston: Beacon, 1965.
227. Kenyon, K. Archaeology in the Holy Land. New York: Praeger, 1960.

228. Kerenyi, C. Gods of the Greeks. London: Thames and Hudson, 1951.
229. Kierkegaard, S. The concept of dread. Princeton: Princeton Univ. Press, 1944.
230. ———. Fear and trembling and the sickness unto death. Garden City, N.Y.: Anchor, 1954.
231. Klausner, J. The messianic idea in Israel. London: Allen & Unwin, 1956.
232. Klein, G. Psychoanalytic theory: an exploration of essentials. New York: International Universities Press, 1976.
233. Klein, M. The psychoanalysis of children. New York: Delacorte, 1975.
234. ———. New directions in psychoanalysis. London: Tavistock, 1971.
235. Kluckhohn, C., and Murray, H. Personality: in nature, society, and culture. New York: Knopf, 1965.
236. Kohlberg, L. "Development of moral character and moral ideology." In Hoffman, M., and Hoffman, L. (eds.). Review of Child Development Research, vol. 1, 1964.
237. ———. "From is to ought." In Mischel, T. (ed.). Cognitive development and epistemology. New York: Academic Press, 1971.
238. Kramer, S. Sumerian mythology. Philadelphia: American Philosophical Society, 1944.
239. Krishnamurti, J. The first and last freedom. Wheaton, Ill.: Quest, 1954.
240. ———. Commentaries on living. Series 1–3. Wheaton, Ill.: Quest, 1968.
241. Kuhn, T. The structure of scientific revolutions. Chicago: Univ. of Chicago Press, 1962.
242. La Barre, W. The human animal. Chicago: Univ. of Chicago Press, 1954.
243. Lacan, J. Language of the self. Baltimore: Johns Hopkins Univ. Press, 1968.
244. ———. "The insistence of the letter in the unconscious." In Ehrmann, 113.
245. Laing, R. The divided self. Baltimore: Penguin, 1965.
246. Lasch, C. The culture of narcissism. New York: Norton, 1979.
247. Layard, J. Stone men of Malekula. London: Chatto, 1942.
248. Lea, H. A history of the inquisition of the Middle Ages. New York: Russell and Russell, 1955.
249. Leakey, L. "New links in the chain of human evolution: three major new discoveries from the Olduvai Gorge, Tanganyika." Illustrated London News, vol. 238, no. 6344, 1961.
250. Legge, J. The texts of Taoism. New York: Julian, 1959.
251. Lenski, G. Power and privilege. New York: McGraw-Hill, 1966.

252. ———. Human societies. New York: McGraw-Hill, 1970.
253. Leonard, G. The transformation. New York: Delta, 1973.
254. Lévi-Strauss, C. Structural anthropology. New York: Basic Books, 1963.
255. ———. The savage mind. London: Weidenfeld, 1966.
256. ———. Myth and meaning. New York: Schocken, 1979.
257. Lévy-Bruhl, L. How natives think. New York, 1926.
258. Li Chi. The beginnings of Chinese civilization. Seattle: Univ. of Washington Press, 1957.
259. Lifton, R. Revolutionary immortality. New York: Vintage, 1968.
260. Lilly, J. The center of the cyclone. New York: Julian, 1972.
261. Linton, R. The study of man. New York: Appleton, 1936.
262. Loevinger, J. Ego development. San Francisco: Jossey-Bass, 1976.
263. Loewald, H. "The super-ego and the ego-ideal." International Journal of Psychoanalysis, vol. 43, 1962.
264. ———. Psychoanalysis and the history of the individual. New Haven: Yale Univ. Press, 1978.
265. Lonergan, B. Insight, a study of human understanding. New York: Philosophical Library, 1970.
266. Longchenpa. Kindly bent to ease us. Vols. 1–2. Guenther, H. (trans.). Emeryville, Calif.: Dharma Press, 1975.
267. Lorenz, K. On aggression. New York: Harcourt, 1966.
268. Lowen, A. The betrayal of the body. New York: Macmillan, 1967.
269. ———. Depression and the body. Baltimore: Penguin, 1973.
270. Luk, C. Ch'an and Zen teaching. 3 vols. London: Rider, 1960–62.
272. ———. The secrets of Chinese meditation. New York: Weiser, 1971.
273. ——— . Practical Buddhism. London: Rider, 1972.
274. Maddi, S. Personality theories. Homewood, Ill.: Dorsey Press, 1968.
275. Maezumi, H., and Glassman, B. T. (eds.). Zen writings series. Vols. 1–5. Los Angeles: Center Publications, 1976–78.
276. Mahrer, A. Experiencing. New York: Brunner/Mazel, 1978.
277. Malinowski, B. Crime and custom in savage society. London: Routledge and Kegan Paul, 1926.
278. ———. Sex and repression in savage society. London: Routledge and Kegan Paul, 1927.
279. Mallowan, M. Twenty-five years of Mesopotamian discovery. London: British School of Archaeology in Iraq, 1956.
280. Marcel, G. Philosophy of existence. New York: Philosophical Library, 1949.
281. Marcuse, H. Eros and civilization. Boston: Beacon, 1955.
282. ———. "Love mystified: a critique of Norman O. Brown." Commentary, Feb. 1967.
283. Marx, K. Selected writings on sociology and social philosophy. Bottomore, T., and Rubel, M. (eds.). London, 1956.

284. ——. Writings of the young Marx. Easton, L., and Guddat, K. (eds. and trans.). Garden City, N.Y.: Anchor, 1967.

285. Maslow, A. Toward a psychology of being. New York: Van Nostrand Reinhold, 1968.

286. ——. The farther reaches of human nature. New York: Viking, 1971.

287. Masters, R., and Houston, J. The varieties of psychedelic experience. New York: Delta, 1967.

288. Matsunaga, A. The Buddhist philosophy of assimilation. Tokyo: Sophia Univ., 1969.

289. Mauss, M. The gift. Glencoe, Ill.: Free Press, 1954.

290. May, R. Love and will. New York: Norton, 1969.

291. —— (ed.). Existential psychology. New York: Random House, 1969.

292. McCarthy, T. The critical theory of Jurgen Habermas. Cambridge: M.I.T. Press, 1978.

293. Mead, G. Mind, self, and society. Chicago: Univ. of Chicago Press, 1934.

294. Mead, G. R. Apollonius of Tyana. New Hyde Park, N.Y.: University Books, 1966.

295. Meek, T. Hebrew origins. New York: Harper, 1960.

296. Mercer, A. The pyramid texts. New York: Longmans, 1952.

297. Metzner, R. Maps of consciousness. New York: Collier, 1971.

298. Mickunas, A. "Civilization as structures of consciousness." Main Currents, vol. 29, no. 5, 1973.

299. Miel, J. "Jacques Lacan and the structure of the unconscious." In Ehrmann, 113.

300. Millett, K. Sexual politics. Garden City, N.Y.: Doubleday, 1970.

301. Mishra, R. Yoga sutras. Garden City, N.Y.: Anchor, 1973.

302. Mitchell, E. Psychic exploration. White, J. (ed.). New York: Capricorn, 1976.

303. Mosca, G. The ruling class. New York: McGraw-Hill, 1939.

304. Muktananda. The play of consciousness. Camp Meeker, Calif.: SYDA Foundation, 1974.

305. Mumford, L. The myth of the machine: technics and human development. New York: Harcourt, 1966.

306. Mure, G. An introduction to Hegel. Oxford, 1940.

307. Murti, T. The central philosophy of Buddhism. London: Allen & Unwin, 1960.

308. Muses, C., and Young, A. (eds.). Consciousness and reality. New York: Discus, 1974.

309. Naranjo, C., and Ornstein, R. On the psychology of meditation. New York: Viking, 1973.

310. Needham, J. Science and civilization in China. Vol. 2. London: Cambridge Univ. Press, 1956.
311. Neumann, E. The origins and history of consciousness. Princeton: Princeton Univ. Press, 1973.
312. Nikhilananda, S. The gospel of Sri Ramakrishna. New York: Ramkrishna Center, 1973.
313. Nishida, K. Intelligibility and the philosophy of nothingness. Honolulu: East-West Center, 1958.
314. Northrop, F. The meeting of East and West. New York: Collier, 1968.
315. Nyanaponika Thera. The heart of Buddhist meditation. London: Rider, 1972.
316. Ogilvy, J. Many dimensional man. New York: Oxford Univ. Press, 1977.
317. Oppenheim, A. Ancient Mesopotamia. Chicago: Univ. of Chicago Press, 1964.
318. Ornstein, R. The psychology of consciousness. San Francisco: Freeman, 1972.
319. Ouspensky, P. D. In search of the miraculous. New York: Harcourt, 1949.
320. ———. The fourth way. New York: Knopf, n.d.
321. Pagels, E. "The gnostic gospels' revelations." New York Review of Books, vol. 26, no. 16–19, 1979.
322. Palmer, L. Mycenaeans and Minoans. New York: Knopf, 1962.
323. Palmer, R. Hermeneutics. Evanston, Ill.: 1969.
324. Parsons, T. The social system. Glencoe, Ill.: 1951.
325. ———. Societies: evolutionary and comparative perspectives. Englewood Cliffs, N.J.: Prentice-Hall, 1966.
326. Pelletier, K. Toward a science of consciousness. New York: Delta, 1978.
327. Penfield, W. The mystery of the mind. Princeton: Princeton Univ. Press, 1978.
328. Perls, F., Hefferline, R., and Goodman, P. Gestalt therapy. New York: Delta, 1951.
329. Piaget, J. The essential Piaget. Gruber, H., and Voneche, J. (eds.). New York: Basic Books, 1977.
330. Piggott, S. Prehistoric India. Baltimore: Penguin, 1950.
331. Pope, K., and Singer, J. The stream of consciousness. New York: Plenum, 1978.
332. Price, A. F., and Wong Moul-lam (trans.). The Diamond Sutra and the Sutra of Hui-Neng. Berkeley: Shambhala, 1969.
333. Prince, R., and Savage, C. "Mystical states and the concept of regression." Psychedelic Review, vol. 8, 1966.

334. Radcliffe-Brown, A. The Andaman Islanders. London: Cambridge Univ. Press, 1933.
335. Radhakrishnan, S., and Moore, C. A source book in Indian philosophy. Princeton: Princeton Univ. Press, 1957.
336. Radin, P. The world of primitive man. New York: Grove, 1960.
337. Ramana Maharshi, Sri. Talks with Sri Ramana Maharshi. 3 vols. Tiruvannamalai: Sri Ramanasramam, 1972.
338. ——. The collected works of Sri Ramana Maharshi. Osborne, S. (ed.). London: Rider, 1959.
339. Rank, O. Beyond psychology. New York: Dover, 1958.
340. ——. Psychology and the soul. New York: Perpetua, 1961.
341. Reich, C. The greening of America. New York: Random House, 1970.
342. Reich, W. The function of the orgasm. New York: Orgone Press, 1942.
343. ——. Character analysis. New York: Farrar, Straus, 1949.
344. Restak, R. The brain: the last frontier. Garden City, N.Y.: Doubleday, 1979.
345. Rieker, H. The yoga of light. San Francisco: Dawn Horse, 1974.
346. Riesman, D. The lonely crowd. Garden City, N.Y.: Doubleday, 1954.
347. Ring, K. "A transpersonal view of consciousness." Journal of Transpersonal Psychology, vol. 6, no. 2, 1974.
348. Ritchie, W. Recent discoveries suggesting an early woodland burial cult in the northeast. Albany: New York State Museum, no. 40, 1955.
349. Roberts, T. "Beyond self-actualization." Re-Vision, vol. 1, no. 1, 1978.
350. Robinson, J. (ed.). The Nag Hammadi library. New York: Harper, 1979.
351. Robinson, P. The Freudian left. New York: Harper, 1969.
352. Roheim, G. Gates of the dream. New York, 1945.
353. ——. Magic and schizophrenia. New York, 1955.
354. ——. Psychoanalysis and Anthropology. New York: International Universities Press, 1969.
355. Rossi, I. (ed.). The unconscious in culture. New York: Dutton, 1974.
356. Roszak, T. There the wasteland ends. Garden City, N.Y.: 1972.
357. ——. Person/planet. Garden City, N.Y.: Anchor, 1978.
358. Rousseau, J. The first and second discourses. New York: St. Martin's Press, 1964.
359. Ruesch, J., and Bateson, G. Communication. New York: Norton, 1968.
360. Sagan, C. The dragons of Eden. New York: Ballantine, 1977.

361. Sahukar, M. Sai Baba: the saint of Shirdi. San Francisco: Dawn Horse, 1977.
362. Saraswati, S. Tantra of kundalini yoga. India, 1973.
363. Sartre, J. Existential psychoanalysis. Chicago: Gateway, 1966.
364. Schafer, R. A new language for psychoanalysis. New Haven: Yale Univ. Press, 1976.
365. Schaya, L. The universal meaning of the Kabalah. Baltimore: Penguin, 1973.
366. Schilder, P. The image and appearance of the human body. New York: International Universities Press, 1950.
367. Schuon, F. Logic and transcendence. New York: Harper, 1975.
368. ———. The transcendent unity of religions. New York: Harper, 1975.
369. Schutz, A. The phenomenology of the social world. Evanston, Ill.: Northwestern Univ. Press, 1967.
370. ——— and Luckmann, T. The structures of the life-world. Evanston, Ill.: Northwestern Univ. Press, 1973.
371. Sgam. Po. Pa. Jewel ornament of liberation. Guenther, H. (trans.). London: Rider, 1970.
372. Silverman, J. "When schizophrenia helps." Psychology Today, Sept. 1970.
373. Singh, K. Surat shabd yoga. Berkeley: Images Press, 1975.
374. Sivananda. Kundalini yoga. India: Divine Life Society, 1971.
375. Smith, H. Forgotten truth. New York: Harper, 1976.
376. Smith, M. "Perspectives on selfhood." American Psychologist, vol. 33, no. 12, 1978.
377. Smuts, J. Holism and evolution. New York: Macmillan, 1926.
378. Soll, I. An introduction to Hegel's metaphysics. Chicago, 1969.
379. Sorokin, P. Social and cultural dynamics. Vols. 1–3. New York: Bedminster, 1962.
380. Spengler, O. The decline of the West. New York: Knopf, 1939.
381. Stace, W. The philosophy of Hegel. New York, 1955.
382. Stiskin, N. Looking-glass god. Brookline, Mass.: Autumn Press, 1972.
383. Straus, A. (ed.). George Herbert Mead on social psychology. Chicago: Univ. of Chicago Press, 1964.
384. Sullivan, H. S. The interpersonal theory of psychiatry. New York: Norton, 1953.
385. Suzuki, D. T. Manual of Zen Buddhism. New York: Grove, 1960.
386. ———. Studies in the Lankavatara Sutra. London: Routledge and Kegan Paul, 1968.
387. ———. Essays in Zen Buddhism. Series 1–3. London: Rider, 1970.
388. Taimni, I. The science of yoga. Wheaton, Ill.: Quest, 1975.
389. Takakusu, J. The essentials of Buddhist philosophy. Honolulu: Univ. of Hawaii Press, 1956.

390. Tart, C. (ed.). Transpersonal psychologies. New York: Harper, 1975.

391. Tarthang Tulku. Sacred art of Tibet. Berkeley: Dharma Press, 1972.

392. Tattwananda, S. (trans.). The quintessence of Vedanta of Acharya Sankara. Calcutta, 1970.

393. Taylor, C. The explanation of behavior. New York: Humanities Press, 1964.

394. ———. "Interpretation and the sciences of man." The Review of Metaphysics, vol. 25, 1971.

395. Teilhard de Chardin, P. The future of man. New York: Harper, 1964.

396. ———. The phenomenon of man. New York: Harper, 1964.

397. Thompson, W. At the edge of history. New York: Harper, 1971.

398. ———. Passages about earth. New York: Harper, 1974.

399. ———. Darkness and scattered light. New York: Harper, 1978.

400. Trungpa, C. The myth of freedom. Berkeley: Shambhala, 1976.

401. Ullman, M. "Psi and psychiatry." In Mitchell, 302.

402. Vaillant, G. The Aztecs of Mexico. Baltimore: Penguin, 1950.

403. Van de Castle, R. "Anthropology and psychic research." In Mitchell, 302.

404. Van Dussen, W. The natural depth in man. New York: Harper, 1972.

405. Vann, G. The paradise tree. New York: Sheed and Ward, 1959.

406. Vaughan, F. Awakening intuition. Garden City, N.Y.: Anchor, 1979.

407. Von Hagen. The ancient sun kingdoms of the Americas. Cleveland: World, 1961.

408. Walsh, R., and Shapiro, D. (eds.). Beyond health and normality. New York: Van Nostrand Reinhold, 1978.

409. ——— and Vaughan, F. (eds.). Beyond ego psychology. Los Angeles: Tarcher, 1980.

410. Watts, A. The way of Zen. New York: Vintage, 1957.

411. ———. The supreme identity. New York: Vintage, 1972.

412. Weber, M. The theory of social and economic organization. Glencoe, Ill.: Free Press, 1947.

413. ———. Wrong, D. (ed.). Englewood Cliffs, N.J.: Prentice-Hall, 1970.

414. Welwood, J. The meeting of the ways. New York: Schocken, 1979.

415. Wendt, H. In search of Adam. Boston: Houghton Mifflin, 1956.

416. Werner, H. Comparative psychology of mental development. New York: International Universities Press, 1957.

417. Wescott, R. The divine animal. New York: Funk and Wagnalls, 1969.

418. West, J. Serpent in the sky. New York: Harper, 1979.

419. White, J. (ed.). Kundalini, evolution, and enlightenment. Garden City, N.Y.: Anchor, 1979.
420. —— and Krippner, S. (eds.). Future science. Garden City, N.Y.: Anchor, 1977.
421. White, L. The science of culture. New York: Grove, 1949.
422. Whitehead, A. Modes of thought. New York: Macmillan, 1966.
423. ——. Adventures of ideas. New York: Macmillan, 1967.
424. ——. Science and the modern world. New York: Macmillan, 1967.
425. Whorf, B. Language, thought and reality. Cambridge: M.I.T. Press, 1956.
426. Whyte, L. L. The next development in man. New York: Mentor, 1950.
427. Wilber, K. "Psychologia Perennis." Journal of Transpersonal Psychology, vol. 7, no. 2, 1975.
428. ——. "The ultimate state of consciousness." Journal of Altered States of Consciousness, vol. 2, no. 3, 1975–76.
429. ——. The spectrum of consciousness. Wheaton, Ill.: Quest, 1977.
430. ——. "Microgeny." Re-Vision, vol. 1, no. 3/4, 1978.
431. ——. "Where it was, I shall become." In Walsh, 408.
432. ——. "A developmental view of consciousness." Journal of Transpersonal Psychology, vol. 11, no. 1, 1979.
433. ——. "Eye to eye." Re-Vision, vol. 2, no. 1, 1979.
434. ——. No boundary. Los Angeles: Center Publications, 1979.
435. ——. "Physics, mysticism, and the new holographic paradigm: a critical appraisal." Re-Vision, vol. 2, no. 2, 1979.
436. ——. The Atman project. Wheaton, Ill.: Quest, 1980.
437. Wilden, A. System and structure. London: Tavistock, 1972.
438. Woolley, L. The beginnings of civilization. New York: Mentor, 1965.
439. Woods, J. The yoga system of Patanjali. Delhi, 1972.
440. Yampolsky, P. (trans.). The Zen master Hakuin. New York: Columbia Univ. Press, 1971.
441. Yogeshwarand Saraswati. Science of soul. India: Yoga Niketan, 1972.
442. Young, J. Z. Programs of the brain. Oxford: Oxford Univ. Press, 1978.
443. Zilboorg, G. "Fear of death." Psychoanalytic Quarterly, vol. 12, 1943.
444. Zimmer, H. Philosophies of India. London: Routledge and Kegan Paul, 1969.

INDEX